Literature and Society
in Imperial Russia, 1800-1914

Contributors

Robert L. Belknap · Jeffrey Brooks · Edward J. Brown
Donald Fanger · Jean Franco · Robert Louis Jackson
Hugh McLean · Victor Ripp · William Mills Todd III

Literature and Society in Imperial Russia, 1800-1914

Edited by William Mills Todd III

Stanford University Press, Stanford, California   1978

Stanford University Press
Stanford, California
© 1978 by the Board of Trustees of the
Leland Stanford Junior University
Printed in the United States of America
ISBN 0-8047-0961-0
LC 77-76153

Preface

The essays in this volume were presented to a conference on literature and society in imperial Russia that was made possible by a grant from the American Council of Learned Societies and was held at Stanford University on October 23 and 24, 1975. Convened to explore the ways in which the social and literary aspects of Russian culture have imposed themselves on each other and to suggest topics for further study, the participants fixed their attention on the components of literature as a social institution: the writer, the reader (or listener), the literary work, the codes through which the work is constituted and received.

The contributors would like to acknowledge the kind assistance of many people who helped with the conference and with the preparation of this volume. Edward J. Brown, Dorothy Atkinson, Herbert Lindenberger, and Lawrence L. Stahlberger, who chaired the four panels, and our discussants—Rufus W. Mathewson, Jr., Terence Emmons, Robert Maguire, and Hugh McLean—kept us focused on our common pursuits. Gordon Turner of the American Council of Learned Societies, who arranged for our funding, and Wayne S. Vucinich of Stanford's Center for Russian and East European Studies offered advice that was always helpful. J. G. Bell, Editor of Stanford University Press, worked with us from the beginning, providing worldly wisdom and guiding this volume into print. Susan Dolder made many excellent editorial changes that helped pull the volume together. The many kindnesses of Betty Herring, Elise Johnson, Caryl Neumark, Christine Saal, Margaret Taylor, and Anisa Zaina-sheff left us free to write, think, and talk about our papers.

We adhere to the system of transliteration used by several leading journals in Russian studies and described as System II in J. Thomas Shaw, *The Transliteration of Modern Russian for English-Language Publications* (Madison, Wis., 1967). In the text, however, we preserve the common English spellings of well-known proper names (e.g. Tolstoy, Herzen, Tatiana), and transliterate a common ending of Russian surnames as "-sky," not "-skii."

W.M.T.

Contents

Contributors

ROBERT L. BELKNAP, Professor of Slavic Languages at Columbia University, attended Princeton University, the Sorbonne, and Columbia. He has written *The Structure of the Brothers Karamazov* (1967) and is preparing a monograph on the sources of that novel.

JEFFREY BROOKS holds degrees from Antioch College and Stanford University, and is Assistant Professor of History at Cornell College, Mount Vernon, Iowa. He has written a series of papers about the rise of the mass reading public in Russia.

EDWARD J. BROWN, Professor Emeritus of Slavic Languages and Literatures at Stanford University, graduated from the University of Chicago and Columbia University. Among his publications are *The Proletarian Episode in Russian Literature, 1928–1932* (1953), *Russian Literature since the Revolution* (1963, 1969), *Stankevich and His Moscow Circle, 1830–1840* (1966), *Mayakovsky: A Poet in the Revolution* (1973), and *Brave New World, 1984 and We: An Essay on Anti-Utopia* (1976).

DONALD FANGER is Professor of Russian and Comparative Literature at Harvard University. He holds degrees from the University of California at Berkeley and from Harvard. He founded the Brown Slavic Reprint Series, wrote *Dostoevsky and Romantic Realism* (1965), and is preparing a monograph on Gogol.

JEAN FRANCO chairs the Department of Spanish and Portuguese at Stanford University, and is Professor of Spanish and Comparative Literature. Her books include *The Modern Culture of Latin America* (1967, 1970), *Introduction to Spanish American Literature* (1969), and *Spanish American Literature since Independence* (1973). She holds degrees from the universities of Manchester and London.

ROBERT LOUIS JACKSON, Chairman of the Department of Slavic Languages and Literatures at Yale University, attended Cornell University, Columbia, and the University of California at Berkeley. Among his publications are *Dostoevsky's Underground Man in Russian Literature* (1958), *Dostoevsky's Quest for Form: A Study of His Philosophy of Art* (1966), and a series of comparative essays on Russian literature.

HUGH MCLEAN, Dean of Humanities and Professor of Slavic Languages and Literatures at the University of California at Berkeley, attended Yale, Columbia, and Harvard universities. He has co-edited *The Year of Protest, 1956* (1961) and has written *Nikolai Leskov: The Man and His Art* (1977).

VICTOR RIPP is Assistant Professor of Russian Literature at Cornell University. A graduate of Cornell and Columbia, he has written essays on Nabokov and Pirandello and is preparing a book on Turgenev.

WILLIAM MILLS TODD III, Associate Professor of Russian and Comparative Literature at Stanford University, holds degrees from Dartmouth, Oxford, and Columbia, and is author of *The Familiar Letter as a Literary Genre in the Age of Pushkin* (1976).

Literature and Society
in Imperial Russia, 1800-1914

WILLIAM MILLS TODD III

Introduction

Serious lacunae in the study of Russian literature as a social institution, both in the Soviet Union and in the West, call for new research
and new approaches. Of the many ways in which literature is related
to life in society, Soviet scholarship has tended in recent decades to
ignore all save the obvious reflection of social, economic, and political conditions in the plots, settings, and characters of literary works.
As one Soviet scholar puts it, the sociology of literature, after serving
in the 1920's as a frequent pretext for nasty political squabbles, has
in more recent times limited itself to telling *what* happened in a
work, *who* said it, but not *how* it was said, thereby drawing a
rather facile distinction between the form and the content of literature.[1] The other aspects of Russian literature as a social institution
remain scarcely examined since the pioneering studies of the 1920's
and early 1930's: the composition and expectations of the reading
public; the media through which literature is transmitted to that
public (serial publication, printing, manuscript, oral recitation); the
role of criticism and censorship in mediating between writer and
reader; the ways in which the structure of a work, the choice of
genre, and the institution of literature as a whole may be related to
social conventions.

Silence has fallen over the lively debate of the 1920's between the
"vulgar sociology" that sought to imprison the writer's creativity

within the consciousness permitted by his economic class and the no less vulgar sociology that granted him the freedom to overcome his origins so that he might engineer the literary propagation of "progressive" ideas.[2] Lost, too, has been the Russian Formalists' study of "literary environment" (*literaturnyi byt*), which related the writer's literary choices (e.g., prose or poetry, genre) to the conditions of literary commerce in his time.[3] V. F. Pereverzev's unique synthesis of social psychology with the study of literary form was stamped out in the early 1930's, as Robert Louis Jackson discusses in his paper in this volume. The program by which Iurii Tynianov and Roman Jakobson sought to integrate synchronic and diachronic literary study with the study of other cultural orders was to remain for the most part unrealized.[4] In short, it could be argued that social approaches to literature suffered greater losses under Stalin than formal ones. Studies of versification and "literary language," for example, continued to appear, and Formalism has survived to inspire the work of the Soviet Structuralists; but the sociology of literature in its theoretical and empirical aspects has rarely been permitted to question the regime's appropriation of writers and their works.[5]

Only in the last decade has Soviet sociology begun to recover from these years of neglect. The Lenin Library in Moscow has initiated surveys of the reading habits of rural and town populations, taking care to distance itself ideologically from the "bourgeois" sociologists (mainly Robert Escarpit) who have provided an important stimulus for its work.[6] A second area of interest, involving literary critics, sociologists, psychologists, and aestheticians, has been literary reception in a more theoretical sense. This movement gained impetus from a conference in Leningrad in December 1968, which led eventually to the publication in 1971 of an important collection of papers, *The Reception of Art*.[7] The editor, B. S. Meilakh, promised further volumes, but as yet none has appeared. Although disappointing in its frequent lack of familiarity with Western approaches, the collection represented a positive step forward in its call for theoretical as well as empirical studies and in its attention to the forms of art. This movement in Soviet criticism has begun to stimulate analyses of particular works and writers, the most detailed being G. N. Ishchuk's monograph *The Problem of the Reader in the Creative Consciousness of L. N. Tolstoy*, which traces Tolstoy's attempts to understand his readers and their expectations and to create an ideal reader for his works.[8]

Meanwhile, the study of Russian literature in its social context has not thrived in the West. The Formalists' work has been studied, continued, and developed outside the Soviet Union—indeed, it occupies a prominent place in the Slavic departments of many American universities—but the interest the Formalists and other Soviet scholars of the 1920's took in the dissemination of literature has not been pursued. Western scholars not only have rejected the mimetic or crudely political approaches of their Soviet counterparts, but also have ignored other aspects of literature that involve social awareness, thereby granting Soviet scholarship a virtual monopoly on the study of literature and society.[9] It is indicative of Western hostility or indifference to the social functions and representative aspects of literature that a recent reviewer found it necessary to remark, "By putting his characters' ideas through the crucible of narrative and dramatic action, in which they must of necessity collide with the motives of other men and women and the constraints of the real world, Goncharov made his novels, like the great majority of nineteenth-century novels, 'social.' "[10]

This neglect is all the more regrettable in that literary scholarship has been actively developing a variety of approaches capable of addressing the lacunae in the study of Russian literature.[11] Georg Lukács, unlike most Soviet Marxist critics, has tried to relate problems of genre (not merely content) to historical conditions. His well-known distinction between epic and novel bears particular relevance for the Russian novel, as his treatment of Russian writers has suggested.[12] Another Marxist critic, Lucien Goldmann, by exploring not only the manifest content of a literary work but also its silences and the categories that structure it, has studied the homological relationships between literary, social, and intellectual structures with a subtlety of analysis that eludes more naive "reflective" theories of literature.[13]

Non-Marxist studies of literature in its social context have laid greater stress on the writer's shaping role, the force of literary tradition, and the reader's place in the literary process. During the ascendancy of the New Criticism, a number of American and English critics worked to rescue social and historical awareness from that movement's assault on "extrinsic" approaches to literature, and they demonstrated that this awareness need not mean a blindness to the power and intricacy of a literary text. Lionel Trilling's essay "The Sense of the Past" (first published in 1942 in the *Partisan Review*), René Wellek and Austin Warren's *Theory of Literature* (1949), Irving Howe's *Politics and the Novel* (1957), Wayne Booth's *Rhetoric of Fiction* (1961), and the essays of Philip Rahv and Edmund Wilson serve in various ways to reintegrate the work of literature with the historical reality from which it was created, with the values of the writer and the reader, and with literary tradition. Harry Levin's institutional approach to literature has probed the differences between literature and "life" by exploring rather than avoiding social contexts. The conventions of artistic media become the necessary difference, since Levin considers literature not a reflection but a refraction of life.[14] The relationship between writer and public that his approach suggests (but does not develop) is given a more complete sociological analysis by Ian Watt, who juxtaposes the rise of "formal realism" in the English novel with developments in empirical philosophy and in the eighteenth-century reading public.[15] Watt's investigation prompts a number of questions about nineteenth-century Russian fiction, which was produced under entirely different social conditions (largely by writers of gentry origin until well into the century), for a narrower reading public, in the face of ideologies remote from English empiricism and Protestant individualism, and in response to a well-established tradition of European prose narrative.

In recent years Rezeptionsästhetik in Germany and textual semiotics in France have brought the reader's place in the literary process to the foreground of literary criticism, challenging theories that focus on the "text itself," independent of its actualization in the reader. Drawing on communication theory and on the sociology of knowledge, two scholars from the University of Constance, Hans-Robert Jauss and Wolfgang Iser, have viewed the text as a provocation—to the reader's quest for coherence and meaning, to the reader's conventional expectations, and to prevailing social norms. In an essay suggestive for Russian literary scholarship, Jauss has studied the normative social patterns that 700 poems of the year 1857 communicated to their French readers. He based his study on the premise that

it is one of the most important although still little exploited achievements of art in helping everyday social living that it can give the power of speech to the dumb institutions of the social world, can organize lasting norms, transmit and justify those which have been handed down, but it can also raise questions about the rigidity of the institutional world, make the roles of other people comprehensible and produce agreement about norms in the process of formation and consequently combat the dangers of materialization and ideologizing.[16]

The last points take on added emphasis when one recalls that *Les*

Fleurs du mal and *Madame Bovary* joined the 700 panegyrics to hearth and motherhood among the publications of the year 1857. Jauss's project will not delight critics who subscribe to the "communicative fallacy," especially since he invades a territory (lyric poetry) usually off limits to sociological analysis; but if accounting for the social function of literature and for the power of such works as *Madame Bovary* may be included among the duties of literary criticism, then this approach deserves serious attention.

For Iser the aesthetic force of a work lies precisely in its recodification of society's norms and values, which in turn challenges the reader to find the motives underlying the work's questions and to participate thereby in the production of meaning. Thus literature, as he optimistically puts it, enables "the contemporary readers to see what they cannot normally see in the ordinary process of day-to-day living; and it enables the observers—the subsequent generations of readers—to grasp a reality that was never their own."[17] On the surface this might seem to differ little from the cognitive theories of literature familiar to students of Russian literature from reading such social critics as Chernyshevsky, Dobroliubov, and Voronsky. But the attention Iser pays to speech-act theory and the extent to which he joins such French "post-Structuralists" as Roland Barthes in insisting on a multiplicity of codes, literary and social, offer new critical opportunities for understanding the dynamic, often contradictory relationship of literature to society and prevailing thought systems. Encoding, reception, norms, and conventionality—increasingly the subjects of both sociologists and literary critics—suggest social approaches to literature that will neglect neither the dynamics of social interaction nor the forms and traditions of literature, but will see both as related aspects of culture.[18]

The papers gathered in this volume range in topic from general discussions of literary theory to empirical studies to close readings of specific literary texts. They address nearly every literary movement in nineteenth- and early-twentieth-century Russia and several major writers—Pushkin, Gogol, Turgenev, and Dostoevsky. The volume is organized, however, around four themes: theoretical problems in the relationship of literature and society, the reading public (historical and implied within the text), the rhetoric and ideologies of writers and critics, and authorial strategies for encompassing social reality in a work of literature. Of course, certain common interests cut across the boundaries of the four sections and join the papers together, for example, the myriad types of readers and reading in imperial Russia, problems of communication and encoding, and limits imposed on understanding and expression by various aspects of a social situation. A brief outline of the volume should help the reader focus on these common concerns.

The first section examines theoretical formulations, Western and Soviet, promising and moribund, for the study of literature in its social context. Jean Franco begins by analyzing the French semiologists whose work has branched off from Saussurian linguistics, Russian Formalism, Prague school poetics, and related movements in anthropology and psychology, and has produced a radically disorienting ("deconstructive"), often confused, sometimes fruitful impact on American literary criticism. Her paper outlines the movement of these critics away from an early Structuralist preoccupation with linguistic models, formal structures, and a rule-governed cosmos that excluded human agency toward a "post-Structuralist" awareness of the production and reception of texts, a deconstruction of ideologies, and a rebellion against culture's closure of the literary work. The interest of critics like Roland Barthes and Julia Kristeva in what the text cannot say (because of cultural "naturalization") opens possibilities for social and historical criticism that their own social and historical limitations have shielded from their attention: the interplay of oral and written literary traditions, the role of literature in the socialization of metropolitan and nonmetropolitan cultural groups. The problems that Franco raises are of particular importance in Russian culture, and several of the later papers, especially Jeffrey Brooks's, pursue them.

Robert Louis Jackson's paper turns to a different formulation of what the text cannot say: V. F. Pereverzev's psychosociological theory that the writer's creativity is hermetically sealed within a magic circle of images stamped on his unconscious by the conditions of his social environment. This adventurous, if not always sound, synthesis of depth psychology, literary criticism, economic determinism, and sociology is interesting for itself and for its fate: the dismantling of "Pereverzevian Marxism" in the early 1930's represents a major step in the reduction of literature and literary criticism in the Soviet Union to instruments of the state's immediate political needs. The uniqueness of Pereverzev's method (as opposed to other Soviet Marxist approaches to literature) lies in the priority it assigns to the analysis of literary form, and in its transformation of the Marxist formula "social being determines consciousness" into "social being determines the unconscious." Jackson's study treats this critical method in several contexts: nineteenth-century roots (determinism, scientism), contemporary rivals ("voluntaristic" approaches to literary production), and parallel movements (Russian Formalism, Jungian depth psychology). Ultimately, as Jackson notes, Pereverzev failed to reconcile the implacable materialism of his method with his emotional insistence on the communicative capabilities of art. His concern for literary structure lends itself well to a social analysis of literature, but the social existence of literature between reader and writer remained outside his frequently flawed "sociology."

Donald Fanger begins the section on readership by discussing the reader's place (or, rather, many places) in contemporary literary scholarship, then turns to specific problems of Gogol and his reader. Gogol—at times acutely sensitive to his readers, at times anxious and uncertain—pays considerable attention to them in both his fiction and his nonfiction. Fanger examines this awareness by asking, first of all, who those readers were: the developing public; Gogol's critics, the opinion formers whose perverse one-sidedness may have been encouraged by the Gogolian text; and finally the censor, whose reading habits were in many ways mirrored by those of the Russian intelligentsia. The paper then analyzes Gogol's understanding of his readers, as expressed in his essays, and the considerable demands his fiction places on them. The problematic in this fiction, argues Fanger, is precisely the reader's experience of the text, his search for significance, or—in *Dead Souls*—his search for something to fill that fiction's spiritual void. The important distinctions that Fanger's approach draws between Gogol's individual works and the insights that it offers into Russian culture of the 1830's and 1840's illustrate the usefulness of "the reader" as a tool of literary inquiry.

Jeffrey Brooks deals with the historical reader in the decades following Gogol—the urban and rural readers of the lower social classes, the intellectuals who sought to manipulate them, and the readers of Russian modernism. Several important problems of literary reception merit particular attention: the development of a mass reading public, without precedent in Russian culture; the canonization of the Russian classics in the early twentieth century; the "culturist" intellectuals' recuperation of Russian modernism; the cognitive and didactic reading of literature among the newly literate. In discussing readers and reading material (such as chapbooks, penny dreadfuls, and kopeck papers) that are universally ignored by academic programs in Russian literature, Brooks illustrates the persistence of traditional cognitive and didactic reading patterns into the Soviet period. His paper offers historical corroboration based on extensive research in Soviet archives and libraries for the other papers' more theoretical treatment of the ideological, didactic uses of literature.

The third part of this volume focuses on the ideology and rhetoric of specific works, writers, and readers, and views the literary process as a struggle acted out against a background of conflicting ideologies and apperceptive masses. Edward J. Brown, who examines D. I. Pisarev's treatment of *Fathers and Sons* and *Crime and Punishment*, shows how the radical critic appropriated and "rewrote" these novels, filling their interstices with details and explanations that reflected his own understanding of Russian reality. Ironically, as Brown points out, Pisarev's own behavior came to reflect the behavior of Turgenev's protagonist. Brown's account of these confrontations between critic and novel suggests that the nineteenth-century Russian novel frequently served as a provocation not only to the norms of society, but also to the ideology dominant among the radical intelligentsia.

Brown's analysis of a critic's ideology and rhetoric finds many parallels in Robert Belknap's paper, which concentrates on a writer's attempt to manipulate his reader. Belknap shows how Dostoevsky guides the reader to a rejection of the Grand Inquisitor's arguments via a potentially dangerous course of attracting the reader to those arguments, then compromising them through the use of plot, parody, reductio ad absurdum, and the subtle dissection and reworking of familiar sources (in this case, the lives and works of the radical critics). At the same time, the reader's power to ignore or misread these signals and to actualize the text according to his own ends is illustrated by D. H. Lawrence's famous interpretation of the novel, directly at odds with the reading Dostoevsky's rhetorical brilliance invites. Through modifications of communication theory Belknap re-creates the dynamic relationship between author, reader, and sources familiar to both.[19]

The fourth part of this volume addresses the relationship between fictional and social worlds as developed in novels by Pushkin and Turgenev, but the major concerns of the other parts—social and historical limitations, reading, ideology and rhetoric—remain close to the center of focus. My paper discusses Pushkin's realization of his final metaphor in *Eugene Onegin*, "life's novel." But social existence and literary creativity in Pushkin's novel function by means of conventions—the conventions that regulate the discrete areas of culture and the conventions that organize the relationship of these areas with each other. Pushkin depicts many types of conventions; his characters, including the author-narrator, observe and violate them in many ways. The catastrophes of action and expression in Pushkin's novel result not from the boundaries in which culture encloses human experience (as is usual in a social novel), but from the wealth of conventions (and hence possibilities for misunderstanding, mistiming) that the culture provides: an action by one character may be interpreted in many ways because the novel's syncretic culture offers many overlapping codes. A single part—a gesture, a phrase—can belong to many wholes.

As Victor Ripp's analysis demonstrates, Turgenev develops a different sort of social novel, one that draws on neither Pushkin's multifarious conventional possibilities nor the variety of class and occupational choices provided by Western society for such novelists as Dickens. Imperial Russia of the 1850's, argues Ripp, seemed to present two social and political possibilities: demeaning acquiescence and fruitless withdrawal. Against this choice Turgenev's novels set the gentry enclave (*Rudin*) and the family (*Fathers and Sons*). Although these parts of Russian society stand in uncertain, constantly threatened relation to the whole, the harmony they afford in Turgenev's novels shows that author seeking a resolution to the dilemma of the 1850's: how can one preserve the integrity of one's essential values, yet participate in a community of one's fellows? Turgenev's recourse to the family as a model of social harmony permits a comparison with the radical critics, who also, though differently, used the family as a narrative unit and foresaw that it might serve as a means of avoiding society's corruption. In this context Turgenev convincingly emerges not as the indecisive intellectual coward condemned by the radical critics and by Tolstoy and Dostoevsky, but as a subtle, perspicacious social novelist.

Hugh McLean's paper, originally presented to the conference as a commentary on my paper and Professor Ripp's, is included here because it synthesizes some of this study's findings and raises theoretical and historical issues that call for further thought. First of all, by applying Ripp's approach to my material and vice versa (and thereby arriving at insights that eluded both our approaches), McLean frames a part-whole problem that represents a challenge to the critical enterprise this volumes undertakes: literature, society, and ideology are in themselves areas of infinite complexity and the subjects of more than a few scholarly disciplines; their interrelations are likely to frustrate the most meticulous investigations, even collective ones.

Consequently, the work gathered here begs not only to be continued, but to be extended into fields of inquiry that this volume briefly touches—for example, the impact of various media on the reading public; the roles of literary and oral culture in determining, reinforcing, and changing social consciousness; the roles of the state, the church, and the schools in spreading literacy and influencing the reception of literature; the ways in which genres like drama and lyric poetry refract social reality.

At the same time as it points toward the need for further investigation and synthesis, McLean's paper speaks for the value and necessity of such an undertaking by returning to a topic raised in Franco's paper: recent attacks on "monumental" or "universal" understandings of a literary text. McLean rescues the "universal," "human," "existential" qualities that Western readers have found in Russian literature, but he does so precisely by describing some of the social conditions that opened the existential void before the Russian gentleman author and his gentlemen characters.

Fostering such alertness to the social context of reading and writing—despite the dangers inherent in approaching and crossing the boundaries between academic disciplines—must number among the most urgent tasks of literary criticism, especially the criticism of Russian literature.

JEAN FRANCO

History and Literature: Remapping the Boundaries

One of the problems of reading literature from the perspective of a "marginal" culture has always been that universal critical categories turn out, on inspection, to be normative and prescriptive criteria based on empirical readings of Western European texts. In the past the literatures of even Russia and Spain seemed to be ex-centric versions of a central tradition (the spatial metaphors are themselves significant), and those of Africa, Latin America, and the East usually remained beyond the recognizable limits of what constituted great literature. For this reason the questions raised by Structuralism and textual semiotics, both of which challenge evaluation and interpretation, are particularly interesting, since they appear to transcend the ethnocentricity of some American and European theories of literature as well as redraw, and even destroy, the boundaries that traditionally separated literature from other discourses. Further, in its most recent formulations, French criticism has tended to regard institutionalized literature with suspicion, as part of an ideological order, and to set itself up in radical defiance of this process of assimilation. In this paper I should like to trace some of the problems opened up by the Structuralists and by post-Structuralist critics like Roland Barthes and Julia Kristeva to see how far they can take us in remapping culture in general and writing in particular.

I

It was history that first went down before early Structuralism. The priority Structuralism gave to the synchronic system over the diachronic, suggested by analogy with linguistics, was from the first one of the movement's most scandalous aspects, and appeared to constitute an attack on history itself. Indeed, Roland Barthes confessed on one occasion, "For me the historical past is a sort of gluey matter for which I feel an inauthentic shame and from which I try to detach myself by living my present as a sort of combat or violence against this mythical time immediately behind me. When I see something that might have happened fifty years ago, for me it already has a mythical dimension."[1] Lévi-Strauss, whose writings were largely responsible for disseminating the term "structuralism," drew an analogy between myth and music, both of which he regarded as "machines for the suppression of time." On examination, however, the writings of Lévi-Strauss and Michel Foucault were less a rejection of history than a redefinition.[2] And literary history, which had according to Barthes consisted of little more than a chronicle of authors, could now be conceived as a history of literary functions.[3]

At this stage it is worthwhile to remind ourselves (at the risk of approaching the matter diachronically) of Structuralism's dialectical relationship with existentialism, which dominated philosophical, sociological, and literary criticism in the 1950's. Roland Barthes's early collection of essays *Mythologies* (1957) seems to belong quite naturally to the demystifying tradition of Sartre. Yet it was precisely Sartre's weakness as a literary critic that he emphasized the author's "project" and consciousness almost entirely, and gave little attention to the text as such or to the internal dynamics of the literary system.[4] The most thoroughgoing attempt to produce a theory that would reconcile the positive aspects of Hegelian-Marxist criticism and existentialism while taking into account the internal structure of the literary text was made by Lucien Goldmann. His "genetic structuralism," as the name implies, represented an attempt to reveal the social origins of homological intellectual, philosophic, and literary structures. In his major study of the tragic vision of Racine and Pascal, *Le Dieu caché* (1955), he traced structural homologies between this vision, on the one hand, and Jansenist religious attitudes and the closely related social situation of the *noblesse de robe*, on the other. Though theoretically rigorous, Goldmann's approach proved to be more interesting for its detailed insights than as a theoretical model.

His emphasis on coherence, his narrow definition of great literature (which alone could reflect the world view of its age), his reliance on "genius" as the catalyst of the tragic vision, his failure to take into account the internal workings of the literary system—all these prevented genetic structuralism from developing a soundly based theory and method.[5]

For the Structuralists it was a question not of discovering homologies between literary and intellectual structures, but rather of grasping the nature of different kinds of discourse. For instance, Michel Foucault's approach to the history of ideas involved the reconstruction of models of discourse prevailing at a certain time; such models were susceptible to "breaks," which resulted in a change of configuration and the formation of a new epistemology. Thus his system is marked by discontinuity: the past can be recovered only by reproducing the configurations of language that make a certain kind of knowledge possible and other kinds impossible.[6]

It is interesting that Foucault should use the terms "monument" and "document" to differentiate his "archeology of knowledge" from traditional historical study, for these are precisely the words used by René Wellek to make a crucial distinction between literature and history. But Wellek is using the terms in a very different sense. For him the significance of the monument is that its meaning must be grasped intuitively (a mode of cognition that also applies to literature).[7] For Foucault the monument must be understood scientifically, by means of intrinsic structural description. Intuition, and with it the emphasis on the intuiting subject, has no place in Structuralist thinking, which from the first was antihumanistic.

Foucault's assertion that "man is a decentered subject, a fold in knowledge" that might one day be erased "like a face drawn in sand at the edge of the sea"; Louis Althusser's declaration that history is a process without subject or goal; the priority given by Barthes to language, which "teaches us the definition of man, not the reverse"—all such statements strike at the heart of humanism.[8] The rule-governed system, not individual consciousness, conditions and informs all intellectual and social activity. This radical revision of intellectual history and the social sciences could not but appear daunting to both liberal and Marxist literary critics, who had been accustomed to assuming a common humanity that was both the subject and the goal of literature. In Leavis's "great tradition," for instance, it is this common humanity that binds together all the great works of literature. For Wellek a common humanity makes even works from societies remote in time or place (like cave paintings or Chinese landscapes) accessible to the modern critic. For Georg Lukács great literary creators like Dante and Shakespeare serve as "signposts in the ideological battle fought for the restoration of the unbroken human personality." The British Marxist Christopher Caudwell even postulated a "genotype" to account for this common human element.[9] In contrast, in place of the subject, the human actor, Structuralism posits a locus of relationships, a space traversed by "the infinite movement of discourse."[10]

II

It was Merleau-Ponty who most succinctly described the nature of the Saussurian revolution that underlay early Structuralist thinking. "What we have learned from Saussure," he declared, "is that, taken singly, signs do not signify anything, and that each one of them does not so much express a meaning as mark a divergence of meaning between itself and other signs."[11] Saussure further separated the synchronic system into *langue* (the full potential range of language) and *parole* (the individual act of enunciation), and the word itself into the signified (concept) and the signifier (acoustic image). The term "structure" in linguistics is based on the principle that though a language has only a few basic elements, these "yield a large number of combinations."[12] The original Saussurian model has since been modified or replaced by others—the glossematics of Hjelmslev, Jakobson's model based on communications theory, and models derived from the linguistics of Benveniste, Chomsky, Fonagy, and speech-act theorists. The term "semiotics," introduced to describe the study of systems of signification, has led to further confusion because it has been constantly redefined.[13]

What texts such as Lévi-Strauss's *Structural Anthropology* (1958), Barthes's *Système de la mode* (1967), and A. J. Greimas's *Sémantique structurale* (1966) have in common is, in fact, a certain kind of activity. Each writer begins with a more or less arbitrarily defined corpus, the limits of which he cannot determine in advance. The aim is to discover the smallest possible meaningful unit, by analogy with the linguist's breaking down of language into phonemes and morphemes. Thus Lévi-Strauss reduced myth to "mythemes," the smallest possible meaningful units that can be combined to form different versions of a myth. Greimas derived his semantics from a primary unit he called the "seme," and in Barthes's *Système de la mode* articles and parts of clothing become signifiers in the language of fashion. Yet another characteristic of this early Structuralism was the importance attached to binary opposition as a structuring principle, a principle that some indeed attributed to basic thought patterns.[14]

One result of applying the linguistic model to literature was an attempt to devise text grammars, for example Todorov's narrative grammar of the *Decameron*, which is based on "proper names" (characters), adjectives, and certain kinds of verbs (those modifying action and those referring to transgression and punishment).[15] There were also attempts to determine "logics" of narrative structure, for example that of Claude Brémond, which was derived from Propp's analysis of narrative functions.[16] The assumption behind such efforts was summed up by Roland Barthes in his essay "Introduction à l'analyse structurale des récits," where he declared that the narrative is "one big sentence."[17] The Structuralists' early endeavors to chart discourse, particularly literary texts, in a new way quickly brought problems similar to those that had faced the Formalists: after identifying and classifying the basic components, they had to account for the unity and organization of the text. The Russian Formalists did this by such terms as "motif" and "function." According to Tomashevsky, a literary text can be broken down into motifs that are either "dynamic" (those that change a situation) or "static," the former being constitutive. Further, these are motivated in various ways, according to whether they promote compositional, aesthetic, or realist ends.[18] Tynianov used the term "function" to describe the internal cohesion of the literary text (structural function), its relation to other works of literature (literary function), and its relation to social convention (verbal function).[19] In the work of Jakobson and the Prague school, the term "dominant function" is used to show how similar linguistic structures produce radically different kinds of verbal message. The dominant function (e.g., the aesthetic function in poetry) "rules, determines, and transforms the remaining components."[20]

For the Structuralists the problem of textual unity was aggravated by the very importance they attached to the linguistic model. A. J. Greimas, for example, simply posits the sentence as a microcosm of larger units. Then, setting out to devise a structural semantics able to account for signification in all types of discourse, he isolates semes, or elementary units of signification, which are derived from primary binary oppositions such as human/animal (*Sémantique structurale*, 1966). In *Du sens* (1970) he uses a four-term homology based on contraries (e.g., human/animal) and on contradictions (e.g., human/not human). Having elaborated a formidable taxonomy of significations, Greimas now must account for the organization of the verbal message. In *Sémantique structurale* he introduces the term "actants" to describe the universal relationships that underlie the signifying whole, whether it be a sentence, a narrative, or any other kind of signification. Basing his work in part on Propp's classification of the morphology of fairy tales, Greimas isolates six actants that must be present in the deep structures of any "semantic spectacle" in order to produce the roles and actors of the surface sentence or text. The actants are organized according to the following model:

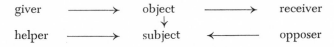

Behind Greimas's efforts is the assumption that meaning is inherent in, and accessible through, the basic structures of the text, and that literary texts are simply more elaborate edifices built on the same basic structures as the sentence. Indeed, Greimas completes *Sémantique structurale* with a distributional analysis of sememes in the novels of Georges Bernanos.

The most obvious objection to Greimas's model is that meaning in literature cannot be derived solely from linguistic features; nonlinguistic factors such as the reader's expectations (and the text's fulfillment or frustration of them) and the emotionally and culturally loaded nature of certain representation (e.g., of the family) also enter into the reading of literature and other kinds of discourse. Even if we grant that Greimas's approach can give helpful insights into the literary text, difficulties arise from his attempt to use the "micro-model" of the sentence to account for the coherence of larger units of discourse. As Emile Benveniste points out, "With the sentence a boundary is crossed and we enter a new domain."[21] It is not possible to relate the components of a paragraph or an entire text in the same way that the subject and the predicate of a sentence are related.

At this point French Structuralism had come up against two problems—the problem of what makes a text hang together and the problem of relating text to context—both of which had already faced the Formalists. Yet the movements diverged in important ways. Formalism itself and the post-Formalist theories of Roman Jakobson, the Prague school, and Soviet Structuralism were centrally concerned with the literariness of literature, and attributed the specificity of the poetic text to linguistic factors.[22] French criticism, in contrast, has tended to move away from the question of the literariness of literature, and to address itself to the problems of "textualization" in general. This is reflected in the shift from purely linguistic models to semiotics. It was the Danish linguist L. Hjelmslev who suggested that only the denotative function of language was the domain of linguistics, and that its connotative function properly belonged to the study of signs in general and hence to semiotics. As Greimas pointed out, the role of the reader now had to be brought into the description of the text. It is not my intention, however, to enumerate the different theories that have proliferated based on communications theory (Eco), on applications of speech-act theory (Todorov), or on the linguistics of Hjelmslev (Greimas).[23] Rather I want to concentrate on the more drastic implications of studies by Julia Kristeva and Roland Barthes, which involve not merely the application of this or that model but the remapping of culture itself.

III

Kristeva's *Le Texte du roman* (1970) is a semiological analysis of the fifteenth-century novel *Jehan de Saintré*. Semiology is defined as the study of "the large signifying units of discourse," for which the model can no longer be structural linguistics. Instead Kristeva applies transformational linguistics in order to separate the level of competence (genotext) from the level of performance (phenotext). The deep structure, or genotext, has three components: the actantial (following Greimas), which generates the actors; the narrative complexes, which generate the narrative situations; and "intertextuality," which relates the text to other texts. Citing M. A. K. Halliday as the authority who justifies this third category, Kristeva is somewhat nervous at straying from a purely linguistic model: "This recourse to another generator, intertextuality, does not mean that we are abandoning linguistics as a method of investigation, and still less that we do not believe linguistic science to be capable of penetrating certain subtleties decipherable by other means."[24]

Yet it is intertextuality, the category not derived from the linguistic model, that assumes the greatest importance when, having determined the actants and the operators of the narrative complexes, Kristeva comes up against the limits of this scheme of classification. She reaches these limits after classifying the narrative complexes into indicators (of time and place), connectors, and adjuncts. The adjuncts can either qualify or predicate, yet—and here is the kernel of the difficulty—the difference between qualifying and predicative adjuncts cannot always be identified on linguistic grounds. How then to explain the difference?

We must have recourse to the third generator of the novel, which we have mentioned before, to intertextuality. The role of predicate will be taken by the adjunct that in its intertextual space corresponds to the dominant features of the social discourse of which the said text is a part. It is not by chance that the role of predicative adjunct in *Jehan de Saintré* should fall to those enunciations taken from the discourse of dueling and war. These are the major signifieds of social discourse around the year 1456, when the novel was finished.[25]

Kristeva does not explain why a modern reader, to whom dueling presumably means very little, would still recognize the functionally different value of duels over clothing. In order to account for this, it would be necessary to refer to the reader's knowledge of literary and social conventions and to the kind of expectations the modern reader brings to a fifteenth-century text. And this, in turn, would involve even more drastic departures from the linguistic model.

Kristeva was very soon to move beyond an analysis based on the sentence model to a far more radical position, for she came to the conclusion that neither the structure of a work nor its status as a commodity within a market could account for its potentially subversive deconstruction of the discourse of the dominant class. She therefore increasingly turned her attention to the genotext as the locus of the unconscious drives and desires from which structure and meaning develop. Before discussing the implications of this, however, I would like to trace the distinct but similar divergence of Roland Barthes away from Structuralist analysis.

From the first Barthes's writing extended to more fields than literary criticism; he dealt with media representation in *Mythologies*, for example, and with a nonlinguistic semiotics in *Système de la mode*. But his literary analysis after the early *Writing Degree Zero* (*Le Degré zéro de l'écriture*, 1953) did develop along Structuralist lines. In his "Introduction à l'analyse structurale des récits" (1966), he used the sentence model as the basis for a Structuralist analysis. Moving away from this soon afterward, he proposed instead the study of "translinguistics" as a means of dealing with texts longer than a single sentence. And at the beginning of S/Z, which is a reading of Balzac's *Sarrasine*, he discounts earlier Structuralist endeavors altogether, likening them to the Buddhist's search for the universe in a kernel.

In *S/Z* Barthes divides Balzac's novel into lexias, or units of reading considered in their order of appearance in the text. Whereas the Structuralists had generally derived their units of analysis from binary oppositions, Barthes's lexias are arbitrary divisions. The first lexia, for instance, is the title of the story, *Sarrasine*; the second is the first phrase, "I was deep in one of those daydreams . . ."[26] Others are much longer, consisting of several sentences. This very arbitrariness constitutes a defiance of the scientific basis of Structuralist analysis.

Barthes discusses the lexias in terms of five codes (the number of which is also arbitrary). The hermeneutic code consists of those phrases and sentences that indicate a puzzle or enigma and its working out in the narrative. The semantic code consists of minimum units of signification, semes, which acquire force through repetition in the course of the text. Thus Sarrasine connotes femininity, and her appearance marks the first indication of that code, which will be reinforced by later semes. The third or symbolic code designates the structuring principle of broad antithetical relationships—inside/outside, masculine/feminine, life/death—that permit ambiguities and transformations. Fourth is the proairetic code, or code of actions, and last a cultural code that refers to the common knowledge and morality of a given period. Confusingly, Barthes also introduces subcodes, such as the code of irony, as he reads the text. He uses "connotation" to account for the text's plurality and its relationship to other systems, a usage reminiscent of Lotman's description of poetry as "multisystematic."

Barthes reads *Sarrasine* through the grid of these five codes, not with the idea of producing an interpretation of the text, but rather to demonstrate a certain kind of reading that can resist closure and reduction. A reader might invent new codes or assign the lexias differently. To give one example, Barthes assigns the sentence "Midnight had just sounded from the clock of the Elysée-Bourbon" to the semantic code connoting wealth, since Saint-Honoré, where the clock is located, is in a wealthy sector of Paris. However, one might just as easily assign it to a symbolic code, for midnight is the witching hour. Or midnight may connote fictionality, for it marks a transition between the rational world and the nonrational, between the natural and the supernatural. Midnight, like the narrator's mood of daydream, is one of the clues enabling the reader to identify the text as fictional and suggests that the proper frame of mind for reading it is a suspension of disbelief. As such, the word creates certain expectations and rules out other kinds of reading (for instance, one that would take Balzac's statements as verifiable truths). Further, any mention of time or space can be taken as a form of orientation that helps the story "to take shape."

With none of this would Barthes disagree. For the codes are not instruments of analysis, or rather not merely instruments, but are intended to show the "notation" of the text and to show how, despite the strong tendency of the hermeneutic and proairetic codes to propel the reader toward closure, the text is nevertheless best grasped as a plurality. Barthes's reading avoids one of the basic errors of Structuralism, which is to reduce the text "to its centralized organization" (S/Z, p. 7). It acknowledges that in the course of reading meanings may be forgotten. "Forgetting meanings is not a matter for excuses, an unfortunate defect in performance; it is an affirmative value, a way of asserting the irresponsibility of the text, the pluralism of systems (if I closed their list, I would inevitably reconstitute a singular, theological meaning): it is precisely because I forget that I read" (p. 11).

In order to understand more fully why both Barthes and Kristeva attempt to work against closure, it is necessary to mention Jacques Derrida's critique of the concepts of structure and the sign. In *De la grammatologie* (1967) and *L'Ecriture et la différence* (1969), Derrida removed the discussion of the sign from the realm of linguistics to the realm of philosophy. He showed that one of the foundations of Western thought is the identification of truth with the unmediated presence associated with voice. Saussure's linguistics were themselves based on an assumption of the priority of the spoken word over script. Because of this identification of truth with voice, the reading and interpretation of written texts had traditionally been regarded as a search to uncover an original meaning present in the mind of the author: writing was considered a mere supplement to speech. In contrast, Derrida argued that writing, not voice, was the fundamental vehicle of communication and, further, that its meaning need not be traced back to the original "author."

To write is to produce a mark which constitutes in its turn a kind of productive mechanism, which my absence will not, as a matter of principle, prevent from functioning and provoking reading, from yielding itself up to reading and rewriting. For writing to be a writing it must continue to "act" and be readable, even if what we call the author of the writing is provisionally absent or no longer upholds what he has written, what he appears to have signed.[27]

Writing, in Derrida's view, constitutes a set of differential relationships that can never be referred back to some "transcendental signified." Against the nostalgia for truth and origins, which he finds even in the writing of Lévi-Strauss, Derrida proposes the kind of activity which "affirms free play, which is not turned back toward an origin, and which attempts to get beyond this dream of full presence, this assurance of base and origin."[28] And he reveals a metaphysical canker in Structuralism by showing that the very concept of structure implies a center and a teleology, and that the sign as described by Saussure involves a "metaphysical complicity" in its differentiation of the signifier from the signified. This differentiation amounts to an opposition between the sensory and the intelligible that cannot be overcome unless the sign is abandoned altogether; and to abandon the sign means, paradoxically, "giving up the work of criticism which we are directing against this complicity."[29]

Derrida's writing represents an extreme example of Western philosophy's attack on its own basic concepts, and hence belongs to a debate to which Nietzsche, Husserl, and Heidegger had already contributed. This debate has undermined the "subject," since it is no longer possible to think of a consciousness outside language. In Derrida's view the subject is an "effect" or a determination of "differance"—a process of signification that is never static and can never be grasped as present. This radical break with the metaphysics of the past must now be practiced in a writing (*écriture*) that is also a radical rethinking of language.

Derrida's arguments underlie many of the attitudes held by the group of critics associated with the journal *Tel quel*, including Barthes, Kristeva, and Philippe Sollers,[30] and help to account for their increasing emphasis on écriture as a liberating practice, a revolutionary project totally different from the "linear, expressive, causal forms of writing" that dominated in the past. Sollers comments that this new theory "considers 'literature' (and the totality of the culture in which it is situated) as closed. It now exposes the envelope of that which has been thought under [literature's] name." Ecriture exposes the production of writing, which the classical texts had concealed, and breaks with the fixation of older criticism on the "work" and the "author."[31]

IV

The kind of withering exposure Sollers was talking about often seemed to reveal the literature of the past as a bag of tricks, as so many devices serving to naturalize a certain order and to disguise the arbitrariness of the relation between the signifier and the signified. The iconoclastic tendency itself was not new; it was already apparent in Sartre's writings and in Barthes's early essay *Writing Degree Zero*. But it became so intensified that Barthes, for one, developed a clear distaste for the "readerly" or classical texts, which, he declared, were "committed to the closure system of the West, produced according to the goals of the system, devoted to the law of the Signified" (S/Z, pp. 7–8). Such texts resist complete identification with the dominant ideology only because of their multiple connotations. It is hardly surprising that one characteristic focus of textual semiotics is *vraisemblance*, or verisimilitude, both in its seventeenth-century sense and as it might be textualized in more modern works. Todorov and Barthes regard verisimilitude not simply as the conventions of a certain period, but more broadly as literature's attempt to legitimize itself as the expression of the real or the natural. In criticism it accounts for the tendency to evaluate works according to the public opinion or the common morality of a given period. In modern texts it is used to make us believe that the text "conforms to reality and not to its own laws." Verisimilitude is thus a mask concealing these laws, a mask "we are supposed to take for a relation with reality."[32]

It was not only verisimilitude that came under attack, but also the charismatic role of the author and any pretense that literature could or should aspire to universality. Barthes describes the author as the "plaything" of the text. "The writer is always on the blind spot of systems, adrift; he is the joker in the pack, a *mana*, a zero degree, the dummy in the bridge game: necessary to the meaning (the battle), but himself deprived of fixed meaning."[33] Jean-Louis Baudry assails the writer of the past for considering himself "analogous to God as a 'creator,' to the priest as an instrument of the 'word,' and to the magistrate as an upholder of correct grammatical usage and the notion of linguistic admissibility." Furthermore, the claim to universality, the ideology of literature, "does not, cannot, vouchsafe the notion that historically situated 'works' rest upon a formal system which is analysable, relative, and therefore liable to be replaced by others."[34]

With this radical revisionism, certain terms—*expression, representation, reflection, origin, source*—can no longer be used unless their obsolescence is clearly emphasized, as, for instance, when Sollers groups alongside *representation* the words *exchange, identity, pic-*

ture (tableau), reflection, capitalism, idealism, and *sign.*[35] Enjoyment of classical texts needs apology and explanation, so that in *The Pleasure of the Text* Roland Barthes asks himself:

Why do some people, including myself, enjoy in certain novels, biographies, and historical works the representation of the "daily life" of an epoch, of a character? Why this curiosity about petty details: schedules, habits, means, lodging, clothing, etc.? Is it the hallucinatory relish of "reality" (the very materiality of "that once existed")? And is it not the fantasy itself which invokes the "detail," the tiny private scene, in which I can easily take my place?[36]

Under such circumstances criticism can hardly afford to set up a new canon; instead it becomes both the "reading of a writing" and the "writing of a reading." It does not tautologically repeat the text, but boldly sets out on the new path described by Edward Said in *Beginnings* when he speaks of *"making* or *producing difference,* but— and here is the great fascination in the subject—difference which is the result of combining the already-familiar with the fertile novelty of human work in language."[37] This is obviously the spirit that animates Barthes's reading of *Sarrasine,* Derrida's critique of metaphysical thinking, and Kristeva's textual "significance."

Such a criticism cannot stand apart from its object but must become a new practice, an écriture. Here its proponents become both rapturous and hermetic, since conventional language can never describe adequately what has not yet been done. Jean-Louis Baudry talks of a space with neither axis nor center:

Every utterance is effaced, burnt away by the utterance it produces, although it can persist as inscription . . . always liable to be reinvested in new utterances. In the space so defined, the signified as support for the signifier disappears, and the effect of signification derives solely from the relations which arise between the signifying elements distributed over the same surface, from their more or less apparent but in no wise innumerable combinations.[38]

What we are accustomed to describing as fiction now takes on an entirely new aspect, for it is a space "with no beginning and no end, devoid of both story and characters, thwarting any reading which seeks a finite meaning." Ecriture simply proposes a field for enunciation.

In *S/Z* Barthes attempts to describe a text he calls "writerly" (*scriptible*) in contrast to the merely "readerly" (*lisible*) text, which fosters a separation between author and reader:

Our literature is characterized by the pitiless divorce which the literary institution maintains between the producer of the text and its user, between its owner and its customer, between its author and its reader. This reader is thereby plunged into a kind of idleness—he is intransitive. . . . Instead of gaining access to the magic of the signifier, to the pleasure of writing, he is left with no more than the poor freedom to accept or reject the text. (S/Z, p. 4)

The *scriptible* text transcends criticism and makes the reader into a producer of the text: it is "ourselves writing, before the infinite play of the world (the world as function) is traversed, intersected, stopped, plasticized by some singular system (Ideology, Genus, Criticism) which reduces the plurality of entrances, the opening of networks, the infinity of languages" (p. 5). In a more recent work, *The Pleasure of the Text*, Barthes describes the hedonism of reading and separates texts into *textes de plaisir* (pleasure texts) and *textes de jouissance* (texts of bliss). The pleasure text contents and fulfills the reader and produces euphoria. It "comes from culture and does not break with it," and is "linked to a comfortable practice of reading." The text of bliss, in contrast, "discomforts . . . unsettles the reader's historical, cultural, psychological assumptions, the consistency of his tastes, values, memories, brings to a crisis his relation with language."[39]

No one has undertaken a more thorough study of this subversive process than Julia Kristeva in *La Révolution du langage poétique*, a densely argued study of over 600 pages. It is also a justification of the revolutionary breakthrough achieved in the language of Mallarmé and Lautréamont, a justification that starts by considering the very formation of the subject-in-process (as distinct from the Cartesian subject). This formidable task would have been impossible without Jacques Lacan's rereading of Freud, which involves the wholesale recasting of familiar Freudian roles. For Lacan the psyche passes through two major stages in its development. First is the Imaginary stage, when the infant, a biologically driven bundle of needs and demands, and the mother have a mirror-like relationship. This is followed by the Symbolic stage, the "symbol" being the signifier of an absence, a desire for some thing. The subject is now related to the unconscious by the signifier, the dominant signifier being the phallus. It is in this Symbolic stage that the biological becomes refracted into the social through the structures of language.[40]

Kristeva now develops an anthropological, philosophical, logical, psychological, and linguistic explanation of the differences between certain of the major signifying practices. These are narrative, which is any practice that reflects the subject-in-process (and thus is not confined to literary practice); metalanguage, which depends, as far as possible, on the suppression of negation; contemplation, which includes the signifying practice of religion and philosophy; and finally the text, the signifying practice that allows the imaginary to surface in language, for example in the avant-garde poetry of Mallarmé and Lautréamont. "Text" is not, however, coterminous with the literary text. As Kristeva explains, "Magic, shamanism, the esoteric, the carnivalesque, and (incomprehensible) poetry indicate the limits of socially useful discourse and reveal the repressed: the process that goes beyond the subject and the communicative structure."[41] Thus the avant-garde, in attacking "closed ideological systems (religions)" and also "social structures of domination (the state)," exhibits a revolutionary potential going "far beyond that of traditional socialist and communist parties."[42] Nietzsche's Dionysius returns to literary criticism by this devious route. Barthes's "text of bliss," Kristeva's "text," and the "schizoanalysis" of Gilles Deleuze and Félix Guattari[43] represent the surprising aftermath of a movement that had once sought to make literary study scientific.

v

At this point those of us who are sympathetic to the general project of deconstruction (in other words, the examination of the signifying practices which account for a text) may well part ways with critics such as Kristeva and Barthes, suspecting that their defense of an ultra-avant-garde position conceals some ideological battle of their own, a battle whose major skirmish took place in May 1968. Their polemical position contests traditional Marxism's reduction of all historical change to transformations in economic modes of production, and depends on a radical remapping of cultural history itself.

In the view of Barthes, Kristeva, and Sollers, there is a history of the sign that by no means occupies the same diachronic space as the history of the economic domination of the bourgeoisie. Kristeva's *Le Texte du roman* explores in some detail the late Middle Ages, when symbolic language, which had always referred back to the transcendental signified (God), was disrupted by the sign. The essential duality of the sign allowed the emergence of mimetic and representational art, which, it was believed, could "reproduce, copy, and re-present the real (syntactic and semantic truth)." Only in the second half of the nineteenth century did the arbitrariness of the rela-

tionship between the signifier and the signified begin to be explored,
particularly by avant-garde poets. Sollers describes this second historical break as one that

carried literature well beyond rhetoric towards a calling into question of
the fundamental categories of language, person, tense, diathesis; literary
discourse, taking charge of what "grammar" was unable to deal with, then
appears as a "remuneration" (to adopt Mallarmé's word) of the deficiencies
of language [langue]. This subversion is completed by the constitution of
a veritable space of language, put into effect by literature, no longer as a
simple discursive line at the service of the logic of the true, but as a poly-
graphism aimed at the establishment of a dialogue between writings and
logics.[44]

Kristeva's *La Révolution du langage poétique* is, in part, an attempt to document and examine this break in the writings of Mallarmé and Lautréamont, whose revolutionary language could not be
translated into a new metalanguage of oppression. Decentered,
rooted in the material of language and in the very body of the subject, "such texts do not merely respond to the anguish of an age but
reproduce its economy. That is to say, they resolve it in the bliss that
is called aesthetic pleasure, while at the same time they take apart
its structure and thus place it on the track [voie] of its own analysis."[45] Only the fact that such texts make a compromise with family
morality makes them assimilable by society.

The advantage of this new historicism for its proponents is that it
puts them at the far limits of revolutionary endeavor, a self-appointed
vanguard beyond any other kind of writing. In their view this position is simply one effect of a general reorganization of knowledge,
which involves, as Derrida explains,

the general text and what used to be thought in the guise of reality (historical, political, economic, sexual, etc.) as the simple designatable exterior
of language or of writing, whether this exterior was in the position of simple cause or of a simple accident. The effects of this upheaval, which are
simply "regional" in appearance, have thus at the same time a non-regional
opening, destroy their own limits, and tend to articulate themselves, according to new modes, without any presumption of sovereignty, with the
general scene.[46]

Derrida's language carefully avoids attributing such changes to anything but impersonal factors.

At this point we can hardly help wondering whether this revolt
against rigid systematization is not itself a peculiar need of French
culture, which is more completely the creation of the bourgeoisie

than any other culture in the world. In no other country was there such a thorough attempt to produce a homogeneous, standardized language and style of writing[47] or such a furious rebellion of the avant-garde. Indeed, the *négritude* movement originating in the French colonies focused on the language of the oppressor. From a global viewpoint, encompassing not only other European literatures but those of North America, Latin America, the East, and Africa, as well, this concern does appear to be "regional." The experience of other cultures has been notably different from that of France. For instance, orally transmitted culture is still important in Africa and other hitherto "marginalized" parts of the world, and was important until recently in Latin America. In such regions print is an instrument of the metropolitan culture in its attempt to assimilate certain sectors of a native "civilized" elite into its value system. Oral tradition, in contrast, is one of the means by which those elements considered barbaric and unproductive (and therefore rejected by the system) flourish unchecked. This oral tradition is surely as "disruptive" and "subversive" as any text of the French avant-garde.

Setting aside the charge of Gallocentrism, the greatest contribution of post-Structuralist criticism has been its delineation of the problem of reading, especially in the suggestive digressions and commentaries of Roland Barthes. The notion of grasping the text as a coherent totality has been decisively challenged. In passing, however, we might note a certain contradiction between the ideal *scriptible* text —in which thought, activity, instinct, and eros all become one—and the assertive and somewhat dogmatic tone of some post-Structuralist criticism, especially that of Kristeva.

Both Kristeva and Barthes take a position that seems to surpass traditional Marxist criticism, especially Lukács's reverent assumptions about "great literature." Yet it is only fair to point out that Marxist criticism itself has developed considerably under the influence of Lacanian psychology, as can be appreciated in Louis Althusser's rereading of Marx.[48] This rereading is a parallel endeavor to that of Kristeva and Barthes, for Althusser recasts the Marxist definition of ideology in a radical fashion that brings it closer to Barthes's description of "verisimilitude" and "naturalization." No longer is ideology an inverted reflection of the real world or a false consciousness; it now comes to cover all those forms of representation in daily life, including structures like the family, by means of which people establish imaginary relations with reality and in so doing unconsciously reproduce the dominant culture. Ideology can be recognized and transformed in two ways, either by scientific inquiry or by the work of art—which, though not itself a form of scientific knowledge, allows the reader or spectator to become aware of ideology by reproducing it and making it visible.

Althusser and his collaborator, Pierre Macherey, consider literary criticism to be a form of knowledge that takes the text as material to be transformed. The critic does this by examining the limits of the work itself, which is never a unity and must always have gaps and breaks by virtue of the very way it comes into being. The critic must make its internal distances, its "silences," speak, silences arising out of the fact that the work is not exactly what it could or should say. Thus for Althusser and Macherey, as for Lacan, "silence" or "absence" seems to be an unacknowledged way of referring to imminent causality. In such criticism some of Foucault's perceptions can be fused with a Marxist critique of literature's insertion into an ideological order that it nevertheless contests. Though these critics have not bestowed the detailed attention to the surface of the text that makes Barthes's S/Z such an exciting experience, their theory clearly distinguishes between literature and criticism, and shows that literature can never be considered a mere reproduction of ideology. The possibilities of this line of thought have not, perhaps, been fully developed, but it does offer a more manageable starting point for a socially based criticism than the more polemical positions of Kristeva and Barthes.

The remapping of culture by Structuralist and post-Structuralist critics has been a fascinating process. Beginning with a learned and rigorous attempt to classify and describe texts, the adventure has progressed through trial and error, insight and "blindness" (to use Paul de Man's term), to culminate in the daring eclecticism of Kristeva's *La Révolution du langage poétique* and Barthes's bold if idiosyncratic *aperçues*. Historically, it stands at the furthest extreme of a process whose beginnings can be detected in that separation of the historical from the poetic that Cervantes commented on in *Don Quixote*. Homer had made the epic into the fount of all knowledge. Modern literature, having been drained of the historical, the sociological, and the psychological, which formed their own logics, became an operation on language itself. For the post-Structuralists écriture now encompasses a wide range of vital endeavors once scattered over many disciplines. For the rest of us the labor of the critic is on this side of utopia.

ROBERT LOUIS JACKSON

The Sociological Method of V. F. Pereverzev:
A Rage for Structure and Determinism

> The artist is an extraordinarily complex phenomenon of
> life that calls for scientific interpretation. We must under-
> stand the artist in his causal dependency . . . as a law-
> conditioned phenomenon of life.
>
> Literature just like any elemental force must be mastered
> if we are not to be enslaved by it.
> —V. F. Pereverzev

I

On the inside page of an October 1967 issue of *Literaturnaya gazeta*
the attentive reader came across a small item reporting birthday
greetings to the 85-year-old Professor Valerian Fedorovich Pereverzev from the Secretariat of the Executive Committee of the Union
of Writers in the Russian Republic. The item read in part: "We are
sincerely grateful to you for your many years of literary work, your
talented study of the work of Dostoevsky and Gogol. These and
other works of yours occupy an important place in Soviet literary
studies."[1]

Only surviving members of a senior generation of Russian scholars
could appreciate the full significance of these friendly greetings.
The last public recognition of Pereverzev had come in the spring of
1930 in the form of a condemnatory resolution of the Presidium of
the Communist Academy. Pereverzev's critical writings were characterized, in part, as follows:

The revision of the foundations of Marxism-Leninism that is expressed
in mechanistic theory in the realm of philosophy by the neo-Kantian economic theory of Rubin and in historiography by contemporary populism
is all very closely connected with a similar mechanistic, vulgar-material-
istic revision of revolutionary Marxism in V. F. Pereverzev's system of
literary analysis—a system rooted in Menshevik ideology.[2]

The key phrase in this clutter of words is "revolutionary Marxism."
It signalized in this context the termination of a conflict that in vari-

ous forms had dominated Russian Marxist literary and cultural criticism for almost two decades. At issue was the question of the nature and function of literature and criticism: whether literature is a passive or active process; whether it should be viewed primarily as a source of knowledge, as passive cognition, or rather as a form of active consciousness, a mode of communication, a means of organizing culture, an instrument for transforming the world.

These questions, of course, had engaged pre-Marxist social critics and thinkers such as Belinsky, Dobroliubov, and Tolstoy. But the Russian Marxists, with their preoccupation with historical materialist interpretation of culture, on the one hand, and their idea of creating a revolutionary proletarian culture, on the other, brought them to a boil. The issues found some reflection in the epistemological debates between the Plekhanovites (including Lenin) and the Bogdanovites (including Gorky, Lunacharsky, and Bazarov) before the revolution. In the heat of that controversy in 1908, Gorky, opposing publication by the Znanie publishing house of Lenin's *Materialism and Emperiocriticism*, summed up what he felt to be the differences between the two camps: "The controversy flaring up between Lenin and Plekhanov, on the one side, and Bogdanov, Bazarov, and co., on the other, is very important and profound. The first two, while differing on questions of tactics, both believe and advocate historical fatalism, whereas the opposite side professes philosophical activism. For me it is clear on whose side the great truth lies." *

Twenty years later, as the New Economic Policy drew to a close and Soviet Russia entered the most ambitious, voluntaristic, and, it turned out, most violent phase of the Bolshevik Revolution, the concepts of fatalism and activism, now quite politicized and frequently vulgarized, still remained relevant in the literary-cultural debate, although the positions of philosophical activists like Bogdanov were

---

* V. I. *Lenin i A. M. Gor'kii: Pis'ma, vospominaniia, dokumenty*, 2d ed. (Moscow, 1961), p. 42. Aleksandr Bogdanov (the pseudonym of A. Malinovsky, 1873–1928) was a sociologist, philosopher, economist, literary theorist, and writer. Lenin criticized him before the revolution as a philosophical idealist. An early advocate of proletarian culture, he became one of the theoreticians of the Proletcult after the revolution. In 1911 he defined art as "both an instrument of people's intercourse and a means of gathering and systematizing their experience." Culture's essence, he believed, was "its organizing function, its shaping and strengthening of a definite social organization." *Zadachi nashego vremeni* (Moscow, 1911), pp. 14, 51. For a discussion in English of the place of Bogdanov and Bogdanovite thought in the history of Marxist literary criticism, see Daniel Lucid, "Preface to Revolution: Russian Marxist Literary Criticism, 1883–1917" (Ph.D. dissertation, Yale University, 1972), esp. pp. 266–91.

to be co-opted by Party critics. V. F. Pereverzev (1882–1968), a leading Marxist theoretician of literature in the 1920's, a disciple of Plekhanov, and a stalwart of the Marxist cultural formula "being determines consciousness," found ranged against him critics from various literary camps. "Nobody has the power to change his style," Pereverzev flatly declared in 1929, "because nobody has the power to go outside of a determined circle of images."[3] "Every artist is locked in a circle of images from which you cannot tear him out?!" cried one of Pereverzev's enraged critics. "Why, then, create the resolution of the Central Committee of the All-Union Communist Party of the Bolsheviks on questions of literature, why then carry on a tremendous but still inadequate campaign to draw the nonproletarian writers into participation in socialist reconstruction?! The theories of Pereverzev are a confession of neutralism in respect to art."[4] The pragmatic, utilitarian ethos of the new cultural revolution could not have been more bluntly stated. "According to Pereverzev," declared another critic, "the writer passively reproduces the social character of his environment. There is no place for the ideological transition of the peasant writer . . . to the positions of the proletariat."[5] "If we acted as Comrade Pereverzev advises," concluded a third critic, "we should turn ourselves into melancholics, into bored historicoliterary fatalists."[6]

The criticism of Pereverzev involved three principal charges. First, his sociological method was a passive tool of analysis: it analyzed literature as poetic "fact" but not as a "factor," not at all in terms of its function in society as a weapon for education and social change. Second, it approached the whole creative process fatalistically: it in essence denied that the artist could remake himself ideologically in his art. Third, and most important, it isolated art and the artist from ideology and politics.

The resolution of the Communist Academy repeatedly underscored the ideological and political character of the campaign against Pereverzev. It accused him of trying to "seal off literature from other forms of ideology with a Chinese wall," and of "flatly denying the active influence of the political struggle on literature and of active, conscious political intervention in the literary process." The resolution declared pointedly: "Art is a weapon in the class struggle. This obliges literary scholarship to be closely connected with the guiding criticism of the literary politics of the Party."[7]

The attack on Pereverzev reflected a developing Stalinist offensive on political, social, and economic fronts that was soon to overwhelm

Russia. Whatever its intrinsic merits or demerits as a Marxist aesthetic, his sociological method was on a collision course with Russian history. The resolution of the Communist Academy in 1930 signaled the eclipse of Pereverzev and his sociological school. He publicly acknowledged the "bankruptcy" of his "essentially antidialectical, un-Marxist formulations" at a literary discussion in 1935, and confessed to the "limited character of Pereverzevian Marxism." Ruefully he asked: "Have I found or developed what might finally be called the Marxist-Leninist scientific approach to literature? Have I mastered this approach? Of course not. . . . All is still in a process of formation and growth. Who can boast that he has found it?"[8]

The fate of many others overtook Pereverzev: he was arrested in 1938 and sent to a labor camp. After being rehabilitated in 1956, he quietly rejoined the literary community. In all, Pereverzev had spent a quarter of a century in prison and exile. Banished to Siberia in the years 1905–11, he prepared there under difficult conditions his first major study, *Dostoevsky's Writing* (*Tvorchestvo Dostoevskogo*, 1912). Much later, in the final years of his second exile, he prepared his last work, *The Literature of Ancient Russia* (*Literatura drevnei rusi*; published posthumously in 1971). He died in 1968.

Pereverzev's work may be divided roughly into three periods: the early 1900's, the 1920's, and 1930 through 1968. Pereverzev was 35 years old and already a mature scholar at the time of the Russian Revolution. By 1914 he had published major studies on Dostoevsky (1912) and Gogol (1914) and had prepared a third on Goncharov. Though the main ideas of the sociological method are put into practice in these early works, there is a complete absence of any formal Marxist theorizing; indeed they contain no reference to Marx, Engels, Plekhanov, or any other Marxist thinker. In the postrevolutionary period (1923–30), in contrast, the Marxist connection becomes very conspicuous. The quest of the scholar is supplemented by the active effort of the theoretician to promote the sociological method as the true scientific method of Marxist literary scholarship in a crowded field of competitors. These efforts culminated in 1928 with the publication by Pereverzev and his disciples of a book entitled *The Study of Literature* (*Literaturovedenie*). In the leading article in this work, as well as in a number of other articles written at this time, Pereverzev sets forth the main theoretical tenets and assumptions of the sociological literary method, its definition of literature, and its tasks. What is unique about literature—its "specificity"—is that it is "not a system of ideas, not a logical system," but always and only a "system of images." It is this fact, according to Pereverzev, that obliges us to study the image. "Whoever would undertake the study of belles lettres must put the image and the system of images at the center of attention."[9]

In his 1914 study of Gogol Pereverzev cites the French aesthetician Jean-Marie Guyau, the author of *L'Art au point de vue sociologique* (1889): "Style characterizes not only the man but also the society of a given epoch."[10] Style emerges for Pereverzev in his last theoretical writings on the sociological method as a manifestation of an all-embracing structure and determinism. In an essay on "Problems of the Marxist Study of Literature" in 1929, he summed up his idea:

Examining the work of art as an image, and the image as a projection of social character, one inevitably comes to view style as the basic category of literary scholarship. The character projected into the artistic image is always socially determined. Definite images—characters—are inevitably formed in a specific social reality, and the connection between them is objectively regulated. Hence the determinism of artistic structures. The structures born from an integral social reality form a unity that is called style. In style is revealed determinism, limitation, lack of self-will in the realm of art. Nobody has the power to change his style, because nobody has the power to go outside of a determined circle of images. Precisely because every writer moves in a charmed circle of images, a general character is typical of all the works of a writer; they all form a unified style, a unified creative work. The basis for this unity is not in the personality of the author, but in the social conditioning of the character projecting itself into images. As the projection of integral social character, the works of a writer form one integral creation, one style.[11]

Pereverzev called on the Marxist scholar to provide a pragmatic explanation of "artistic structure," which had been the direction of his scholarly efforts for almost two decades. There was nothing subversive in his appeal to focus on the image. But there was something dangerously out of step in 1928 in his insistence that "it is not the business of the historian of literature to talk about philosophy and philosophical currents or trends in the realm of journalism and social thought; it is not even his business to deliberate on criticism and the critic. All this lies outside the boundaries of the scholarly study of literature."[12]

The appearance of *The Study of Literature* coincided with the launching of a major attack on Pereverzev by his increasingly numerous critics inside and outside the Russian Association of Proletarian Writers. Literary, social, and philosophical issues were joined. A lengthy and thorough discussion ensued, which ended in 1930 with the total rout of Pereverzev and his sociological school.

II

Politics—the "active influence of the political struggle"—without question was the most immediate factor determining the fate of the sociological method. Yet major issues rooted in Marxist aesthetic and cultural philosophy were involved in the dispute between Pereverzev and his critics. One way to approach these issues is to ask whether the Marxist's concern for literature and culture is Marxist primarily because of a preoccupation with the social genesis of culture and its art forms, a preoccupation with art as a passive reflection of reality, or because of a concern for the social role of literature, for art as a form of active, transforming consciousness.[13] Marx and Engels had little direct advice to give on this question. But they provided the foundation, albeit a fractured one, for early efforts to apply Marxism to literature and society in their concept of the relation between being and consciousness, the keystone to the whole doctrine of historical materialism. "It is not the consciousness of men that determines their being," according to Marx, "but, on the contrary, their social being that determines their consciousness."[14] The mode of production, he emphasized, determines the social, political, and intellectual life process. At the same time, however, while "men are the products of circumstances and upbringing," it must not be forgotten that "circumstances are changed precisely by men and that the educator himself must be educated."[15] Engels later modified Marx's stress on economic determinism to allow for interaction between the various elements in the superstructure (political, juridical, philosophical, religious, literary, artistic, and so on) and for the action of these elements back on the base. "It is not that the economic position is the *cause and* [is] *alone active*, while everything else only has a passive effect. There is, rather, interaction on the basis of economic necessity which *ultimately* always asserts itself."[16]

Ideally, the Marxist cultural formula "being determines consciousness" posits a creative interaction between the components of determinism and freedom, between the passive and the active, or voluntaristic, elements. Man, particularly on the threshold of historical action, maximizes his freedom through his recognition of necessity. In approaching this formula, however, early Russian Marxist cultural critics tended to stress one or another component in the dialectic. An emphasis on determinism—that is, an examination of culture as a validation of basic assumptions of historical materialism—was certainly characteristic of the genetically oriented aesthetics of George V. Plekhanov (1857–1918), whereas a preoccupation with the organizing function of literature and culture, with literature as a form of active consciousness, was characteristic of the aesthetics of Aleksandr Bogdanov and, much later, of the English Marxist Christopher Caudwell.[17]

Plekhanov summed up his Marxist approach to literature in 1900:

I hold that social *consciousness* is determined by social *being*. For a person adhering to such a view, it is clear that any given *ideology*—also, therefore, *art* and so-called *belles lettres*—expresses in itself the *striving and moods of a given society*, or—if we are involved with a society divided into classes—of a *given social class*. For a person who adheres to this view, it is clear also that the literary critics who undertake to evaluate a given work of art must first of all elucidate precisely what aspect of *social (or class) consciousness* is expressed in this work.[18] (Plekhanov's italics)

As the "first act" of materialistic criticism, then, Plekhanov proposes that the Marxist cultural critic translate the idea expressed by the artist in his work from the "language of art to the language of sociology, to find what may be called the sociological equivalent of a given phenomenon." The "second act," inseparable from the first, is to make an aesthetic evaluation of the work.[19]

The writer, Plekhanov asserts, contemplates reality in imagery. The critic's task is to bring to light the objective social and ideological processes intuited by the artist and embodied in his work. The critic's stance is dispassionate. His duty—here Plekhanov employs the famous dictum of Spinoza—is "not to laugh, not to weep, but to understand."[20] He must look at literature "not from the point of view of what ought to be, but from the point of view of what was and is."[21] "Scientific aesthetics" is not prescriptive, nor does it seek to "proclaim eternal laws of art"; it is as "objective as physics."*

In his rigorously objective stance toward the work of art and in his genetically oriented literary method, Pereverzev is certainly a close disciple of Plekhanov. But whereas Plekhanov seeks to validate the Marxist thesis "being determines consciousness" in a broad cultural,

* Plekhanov, "A. L. Volynskii, 'Russkie kritiki,' " in his *Sochineniia* (Moscow, 1923–26), X, 192. This objective approach to literature and criticism was to be overwhelmed in the late 1920's by the utilitarian and prescriptive tradition of aesthetic criticism inherited from the Russian radical democrats N. A. Dobroliubov (1836–61) and N. G. Chernyshevsky (1828–89).

social, and historical context—by discussing the origins of art, the relation between art or artist and society, periods of art, and so on—Pereverzev turns directly to the text itself and to the task of disclosing the social genesis of artistic forms. He accents the special aesthetic orientation of his literary method in the introduction to his study of Gogol in 1914. "The history of literature to date," he writes, "resembles more belles lettres than science. Critics and historians of literature delight more in living in the clouds and singing hymns and elegies than in busying themselves with painstaking analysis."[22] Critics, he notes, have written "productively" and "with originality" about Gogol, but precisely "about Gogol"—about his life, his personal psychology, his relation to Western writers.[23] The weakness of modern Gogol criticism is that "it continues to babble about romanticism and realism instead of taking up a careful analysis of the peculiarities of language and contents of his works, and studying the inner logic which brings the various elements of the work together into a whole."[24] Out of what "stylistic and psychological elements," Pereverzev asks, did Gogol's work take shape? What is the growth of the "organism of Gogol's work in itself, in its inner essence"?[25] The critic, Pereverzev insists, "must get closer to the artistic work, enter into a more intimate communication with it, look deeply into its life and structure."[26]

Pereverzev's demands on the critic, first made in his study of Dostoevsky in 1912, anticipate the rigor of the early Formalists, such as Roman Jakobson, who wrote with irony of those historians of literature who in analyzing an artistic work enlist the full support of the various social sciences: "Instead of a science of literature one comes up with a conglomerate of home-grown disciplines." "If the science of literature wants to become a science," Jakobson concludes, "it must recognize the 'device' as its only 'hero.'"[27] Pereverzev, of course, is concerned with the relationship between aesthetic and social structures, a question that does not concern the early Formalists. Moreover, as he wrote in 1929, the "organic point of view conceives of art not as a device but as an image. . . . The device is only an attribute of the image."[28] Nonetheless, the strong emphasis Pereverzev gives to aesthetic analysis, as well as his preoccupation with the unity of the text, suggests certain affinities, albeit general ones, with the Formalists.*

* In this connection, the Formalist critic A. G. Tseitlin asserted in 1923 that "only where sociological synthesis is based on the solid ground of stylistic studies can one emerge with firm, reliable conclusions." He cited by way of

Pereverzev proposes to examine the work of Gogol

as a body, uniquely organized, with a uniquely organized psychology, as objective being, the expression of which is composed of the material elements of style and objectively given images. I will try to break down the style of Gogol's work into component elements, and to reveal their connections with each other and with the content of Gogol's art. . . . To disclose the intimate linkage and mutual dependence of all parts of Gogol's work, its inner logic and organic harmony—such is the fundamental goal of this work.[29]

Close textual analysis is the first and major demand of Pereverzev, a noteworthy one in the history of Marxist criticism. His second task— which he sees as integral with the first—is to "analyze the connection of Gogol's work with his social milieu," to "present his work as the product of a definite social group, as a vivid aesthetic embodiment of the life of a certain social unity," to interpret "all the special features of language and form, all the pictures, images, and characters on the basis of this social foundation."[30] Thus Pereverzev sets forth the same two acts of criticism as Plekhanov, but, significantly, he reverses their order: he gives priority to *aesthetic* analysis, to a preoccupation with the work of art as an aesthetic structure.

Two distinct impulses, then, make themselves felt in Pereverzev's major studies. First is an impulse toward a close formal analysis of the work of art, with an emphasis on establishing typologies of character-images. Involving the concept—basically romantic in its roots—of the work as an organism, this reflects the interests of an age that was already bringing forth such brilliant literary scholars and critics as Jakobson, Zhirmunsky, and Eikhenbaum. The second impulse is toward an analysis of the work as a genetically determined structure, an impulse finding expression not only in Marxist thought but also in Aleksandr Veselovsky's thesis that "in the poetic forms we inherit there is a certain objective regularity generated by the socio-psychological process."[31]

Pereverzev matured as a scholar in a world strongly dominated by the nineteenth century's quest for determinism and law in all areas of science and culture. One need only recall, for example, Dr. Claude Bernard's determinism, the "intimate connection of phenomena

example the chapters "Style," "Genre," and "Portraits" in Pereverzev's study of Gogol in 1914. "O marksistakh i formal'nom metode," *Lef*, no. 3, 1923, p. 129. Tseitlin nonetheless takes Pereverzev to task for defects in the sociological method. Pereverzev replied to this criticism in his preface to the second edition of his Gogol study, "Gogolevskaia kritika za poslednee desiatiletie," *Gogol* (Ivanovo-Voznesensk, 1925), pp. 11–17.

which permits us to foretell their appearance or provoke them, not only revealing nature to us, but making us masters of her"; Freud's "conviction amounting almost to a prejudice that all mental events are completely determined"; or Zola's idea that description in a novel must represent "the state of environment which determines and completes the man."[32] In the background of sociological literary scholarship, exercising an influence on European and Russian scholars alike, was the French critic Hippolyte Taine (1828–93), with his view of the causal dependence of literature on "race," "milieu," and "moment," his emphasis on "type" ("le personnage régnant . . . le modèle"), and his concept of criticism as "neutral" analysis.[33]

Pereverzev combined an interest in materialist aesthetics with a preoccupation, typical for his time, with the psychology of the creative process. In 1911 the Marxist literary critic V. V. Vorovsky set forth a theory on the formation of images that parallels Pereverzev's thought. He wrote:

> The creative psyche is insensitive to the endlessly small. It is receptive only to the whole, the total, the finished images from which it constructs the ideal, or the real but inevitably artistic reflection of life. Its elements are images and types that join together as though ready-made. The process thanks to which these types and images make their appearance in the brain of the artist, that is, the process of typicalization . . . , takes place outside the sphere of consciousness, and the artist has no power to influence it or to order it in another direction. That is why the artist is here a slave of life and of his psyche, which has been prepared by this same life.[34]

Pereverzev's first study of Dostoevsky in 1912 is in large part a typological study of the character-images in his novels. Sociogenetic analysis of "living images" here is supported by an intuitional theory of the artistic process. The sociological method of Pereverzev essentially represents a fusion of interests in sociology and psychology.

III

The sociogenetic emphasis of Marxist aesthetics, in Pereverzev's view, is based on the fact that "literature is a function of social life, subjected in its being and in its development to the social imperative. It is this fact that makes it possible to speak of the Marxist method in literary studies as the 'sociological method.' "* The point of de-

* Pereverzev, "Neobkhodimye predposylki marksistskogo literaturovedeniia," in V. F. Pereverzev, ed., *Literaturovedenie* (Moscow, 1928), p. 9. Pereverzev is not entirely happy with the term "sociological method." "Insofar as the Marxist method regards literature as a social phenomenon," he writes, "it must be

parture of this method is the Marxist cultural formula "being determines consciousness." Pereverzev put the matter bluntly in 1928: "In order to be a Marxist in the scholarly study of literature, one must have a materialist understanding of literature. The general formula of this understanding is well known: literature, as the object of critical study, like every fact of consciousness, is determined by being. In other words, the poetic work has its basis not in subjective contemplation but in objective reality."[35]

Seeking out the "explanation of poetic phenomena," Pereverzev sharply distinguishes between "subjective movement" and "objective being," the "movement of ideas" and the "movement of material reality," in the work of art. He is tireless as always in his critique of what might be termed extracurricular approaches to literature. The idealist seeks ideas at the basis of a work of art; he attributes huge importance to the writer's conception of his work; he is "up to his neck in the psychology of the writer, in his 'dreams and thoughts,' seeking explanations of [the writer's] creative work. He digs into letters, diaries, rough drafts, attempting to penetrate the secret of the birth of poetic fact.... But the conceptions of the poet reveal nothing of poetic fact.... Not ideas but being lies at the basis of a poetic work."[36]

How does Pereverzev understand the term "being"? In the narrowest of his formulations, it is the "socioproductive process that determines the mode of existence of a people, their consciousness and poetic work."[37] In the broadest definition being is simply "social environment" or the "life of a specific social environment." These are terms Pereverzev uses in his study of Gogol, whom he defines as "chiefly ... even exclusively, the artist of the small landowning environment and its variants."[38]

Gogol's social environment, according to Pereverzev, plays the crucial role in the formation of his art. Though his personality, the literature around him, and the historical moment are all closely re-

ranked among the sociological methods. But the fact is that the term sociological method is an extremely vague one capable of leading to methodological confusion, a term that, perhaps, should even have been dropped from our usage entirely. In essence there is no sociological method and can be none, because we have as many sociological methods as we have sociologies." Pereverzev refers to "idealistic sociologies," as well as to a "whole series of methodologies in literary criticism that rest on a sociological foundation" but nonetheless have a very distant relation to Marxism, for example, Taine's. Pereverzev believes that "the Marxist method should have been called not the sociological method but the historical-materialist method." *Ibid.*

lated to his works, in the final analysis these elements themselves are a "product of social environment, of its elemental growth, its collective work." Moreover, their influence is superficial, going no further than plot or theme. Social environment is more than the sum of these elements. "Everyday life [byt], character, language"—here we have the "very essence" of Gogol's work. Here we have elements "not created by personality, by the epoch, or by literary influences, because they existed before the epoch, before the literary influences, constituting the life of a definite social environment for which Gogol found the most appropriate aesthetic forms."[39]

Gogol's world, then, turns out to be more complex—and at the same time more vague—than the term "small landowning environment" suggests. In practice, though Pereverzev does relate the art of Gogol to economic infrastructures,* he also relates it to linguistic and social-psychological patterns, to the collective experience and personality of the group. It is this intangible, unrecorded, but all-pervasive environment, rather than the chronicle of literary or historical events, that in Pereverzev's view gave rise to Gogol's richest and most original artistic impulses. Pereverzev gives full due to Gogol's fantastic interweaving of elements of realistic milieu with literary, historical, and epic elements in the *Dikanka Tales* and "Taras Bulba"; but he finds Gogol's most authentic genius in *Dead Souls* and other works in which he draws on the absurd, disjointed, grotesque—but *realistically* grotesque—world of the small landowner. Gogol knew this world intimately. He grew up surrounded by

images of trivial empty types, paintings of absurd, ridiculous scenes, and a language as curious as the environment itself, to which he gave artistic, albeit fantastic, reality in his *Evenings*. . . . This environment influenced him directly . . . served as a source for the living impressions. Later . . . when he worked on *Dead Souls* Gogol recalled these impressions of childhood and youth that nourished and bathed his creative genius. . . . Independent of will and consciousness Gogol absorbed these impressions, took in a rich supply of persons, images, scenes, words, which were preserved in the subconscious depths of his psyche, and which in waves broke onto the field of his consciousness at moments of creative work. Images and scenes imbued with these impressions came easily to Gogol. This explains why images and moods imbued with the environment of small landowners take up the most prominent place in Gogol's work.[40]

* For example, Pereverzev explains the "mechanical structure" of Gogol's *Dead Souls* as resulting from the atomistic character of the primitive serf economy; there were few "material connections between the economic units," and therefore these units, the manorial estates, related to each other in a purely mechanical manner. *Tvorchestvo Gogolia* (Moscow, 1914), pp. 111–12.

This passage is especially noteworthy for its stress on the subconscious character of the creative process. Here there is no question of class ideology or ideas playing the central role in the artistic process, only the intuited "voice" of "class environment that formed the psychology of the poet," as Pereverzev put it in 1929, the "voice of class sounding in the individual, from which there is no escape."[41] The creative psyche is formed "independent of will and consciousness." At the time of his creative writing, Gogol's earliest subconscious impressions "broke onto the field of his consciousness." The image is an intuited, not a logically apprehended, structure. It has nothing to do with conscious ideology and, indeed, may conflict with it: the "subconscious sphere of the psyche ... authoritatively determines the creative process, often contrary to the strivings of a person."[42]

Artistic consciousness—or unconsciousness—is for Pereverzev nothing more than objective reality–become–psyche. This conversion usually takes place at an early stage in personal development, but the class or social essence of the artistic psyche remains qualitatively the same at all stages. Strictly speaking, the artistic psyche has never been "influenced" by the social environment; rather it is formed of it. In turn, then, the work of art at its deepest level—the creation of images—is the psyche's intuition of itself, that is, of the collective "being" of which it has always been organically a part.

Recalling the Marxist cultural formula, "being determines consciousness," we should have to say that its real meaning for Pereverzev is *being determines the unconscious*. What seems to have engaged his special interest from his earliest studies is the role of the unconscious in the formation and fixing of the artist's psyche, in establishing a bond between the artist and the life of the collective. "The idea of the unconscious is something scholars of art have known about for a long time," Pereverzev observed at a conference devoted to Freudianism and art in 1925. There have been other interpretations of the unconscious apart from Freud's purely sexual one, he went on, among them the Marxists' own "more profound" theory: "We consider the unconscious to be the voice of the group, the voice of the collective in the human psyche. The unconscious here is not that which specifically belongs to the individual, but that which comes from somewhere out of the biological depths, out of the mass element. That is the group, the collective which lies in the individual psyche."*

* "Vystupleniia po dokladu V. F. Friche: 'Freidizm i iskusstvo,'" *Vestnik kommunisticheskoi akademii*, 12 (1925): 260–61. Despite a clear interest in

Pereverzev, indeed, does have a theory of the unconscious, but it bears more resemblance to Jung's ideas about the creative process and the place of the collective unconscious in art than to anything in Marx. Jung's terminology differs from Pereverzev's, as does, more importantly, his philosophical idealism. But the main content of his argument is the same. Jung writes:

The essence of a work of art is not to be found in the personal idiosyncrasies that creep into it—indeed, the more there are of them, the less it is a work of art—but in its rising above the personal and speaking from the mind and heart of the artist to the mind and heart of mankind. The personal aspect of art is a limitation and even a vice. . . . The artist is not a person endowed with free will who seeks his own ends, but one who allows art to reach its purposes through him. As a human being he may have moods and a will and personal aims, but as an artist he is "man" in a higher sense—he is "collective man," a vehicle and moulder of the unconscious psychic life of mankind. . . . [The artistic] vision is the imagery of the collective unconscious. This is the matrix of consciousness and has its own inborn structure. . . . It makes no difference whether the artist knows that his work of art is generated, grows and matures within him, or whether he imagines that it is his own invention. In reality, it grows out of him as a child its mother. The creative process has a feminine quality, and the creative work arises from unconscious depths—we might truly say from the realm of the Mothers. Whenever the creative force predominates, life is ruled and shaped by the unconscious rather than by conscious will, and the ego is swept along on an underground current, becoming nothing more than a helpless observer of events.[43]

Pereverzev's interest in psychological and psychoanalytical theory cannot be doubted. His reference in 1922 to Dostoevsky's "psychoanalysis of the revolution" points to his own literary method, which, with its emphasis on the determining deep structure of the unconscious, is in certain respects a materialist adaptation of notions of Freud, Jung, and others. His "class analysis" of Dostoevsky and Gogol is neither more nor less than a social psychoanalysis of each writer's unconscious, of his world of images, of his earliest subconscious impressions. But the final referent in Pereverzev's social psychoanalysis is not the idealist world of the unconscious, not the world of the id or of universal archetypal imagery, but the objective materialist world of social being. Here Pereverzev remains the orthodox Marxist.

Freudian thought, Pereverzev regarded it as an "out-and-out idealist system." The historical-materialist process can in no way be identified with Freud's "sexual mysticism." *Ibid.*, p. 260.

IV

The most immediate Marxist source for Pereverzev's general theory of the image is Plekhanov. The philosopher, Plekhanov wrote, "comprehends truth in concepts, the artist contemplates it in the image."[44] A superabundance of "logical thought," he believed, is detrimental to the integrity of the artistic work. According to him, one weakness of populist belles lettres was the writers' emphasis on "social interests over literary interests."[45] Apropos of Gorky's novel *Mother*, Plekhanov maintained that the "role of preacher of Marxism does not suit Gorky at all." And he adds ironically that an understanding of Marxism would be of "irreplaceable benefit" to Gorky, for "it would become clear to him how little the role of preacher, that is, the man speaking principally the language of logic, suits the artist, that is, the man speaking principally the language of images."[46]

Plekhanov's distinction between the language of image and the language of logic is supported by his concept of art as akin to the game or play in primitive society.[47] The game directly reproduces utilitarian activity, but without pursuing immediate, utilitarian goals. Real utilitarian activity, for example the hunt, preceded the game. The "resolution of the question of the relation of labor to the game—or, if you wish, the game to labor—is of the greatest importance in the explanation of the genesis of art."[48]

Pereverzev picks up this view of art as a game and uses it to buttress his notion of the image as belonging to a special nonrational category of contemplation.

Art as a game and art as an image are essentially adequate formulas, because the game is realized only in the image, and because to play means to create an image. The image of a cat chasing after a mouse is a cat playing with a ball. In art the image is separated from that which is playing; it is objectified and leads an independent existence in the form of statues, pictures, plays. This objectification is the act of artistic creation.[49]

The artist, then, "plays" and in playing creates an image, reproduces conduct, psychology, social character. "A system of conduct reproduced, or, what is the same thing, [social] character reproduced: here we have an image. It is impossible to play without making an image. The image is the essence of the game."[50] This reproduction of social character or psychology takes place "outside the immediate struggle for life," just as the game is a reproduction of utilitarian activity without pursuing direct, utilitarian goals.

Clearly, this objectification of the image involves no reworking of

social character. The writer makes no conscious decision in reproducing the primary material of art. The image is always socially determined. Its content, whatever the author's view of that content, is
always first of all the psychology of social character; in art it is the
psychology of the image—its thoughts, its ideology—that is important. "The ideology of the image, together with the image itself, is
the objective essence of the artistic work." In contrast, Pereverzev
maintains, "the author's understanding of the images—the 'idea' of a
work—is not directed to its objective nature. The understanding of
the images is rather the subjective property of the understanding
subject [i.e., of the author himself]. It is just this subjective element
that is unessential to the scholar of literature."[51]

The concept of the image as the objective essence of the work of
art—the distinction between the ideology of the image and the author's understanding of it—was not novel. In Russian criticism both
Belinsky and Dobroliubov before Plekhanov had noted that the artist's poetic thought may diverge from, or even contradict, his rational
thought or intention. A writer's real thought, Dobroliubov believed,
is to be found in his living images: "In these images the poet may,
imperceptibly even to himself, grasp and express an inner meaning
long before his mind can define it. Sometimes an artist may even
completely fail to grasp the meaning of what he himself is depicting;
but the purpose of criticism is to bring out the meaning hidden in
the creations of the artist." *

The Ukrainian philologist and Slavist A. A. Potebnia (1835–91),
whose influence at the University of Kharkov was strong when Pereverzev was studying there at the beginning of the 1900's, early elaborated a theory of "inner form" (the image) not as content itself but
as the medium through which content manifests itself. "We relate,
for example, the quality and relations of figures depicted in a painting, events and characters in a novel, and the like, not to content, but
to the image, to the representation [predstavleniia] of content; we
understand the content of a picture, a novel, as a series of thoughts
evoked by the images in the viewer and reader, thoughts that served

---

* N. A. Dobroliubov, "Temnoe tsarstvo," in his *Izbrannye sochineniia*, ed. A.
Lavretskii (Moscow, 1949), p. 130. Or again, in this same article (p. 104), Dobroliubov observes: "Frequently even in abstract discussions [the artist] expresses concepts strikingly in contradiction with what he expresses in his artistic
work." Belinsky wrote earlier: "The thought expressed by a poet in his creative
work may contradict the personal conviction of the critic without ceasing to be
true and universal. . . . Man may err . . . but the poet . . . cannot err and speak a
lie." Belinskii, "Mentsel' kak kritik Gete," in his *Sobranie sochinenii v trekh
tomakh* (Moscow, 1948), I, 429–30.

as the groundwork for the images in the artist himself at the time of the creative act."[52] Potebnia, however, acknowledges that the author may understand these thoughts differently than the readers or viewers. The completed work of art, Potebnia suggests, leads an independent life:

> It continues to live not in the artist but in those who understand it. The listener may have a much better understanding than the speaker about what lies hidden in the word; and the reader may grasp the idea of a work better than the poet. The essence, the power, of such a work lies not in the author's understanding of it, but in how it works on the reader or spectator, hence in the inexhaustible potential of its content. This content, fathomed by us, that is, put into the work, is really determined [*uslovleno*] by its inner form [the image], yet may not at all have been a part of the calculations of the artist, who creates in a way that satisfies momentary, sometimes very narrow needs of his personal life. The service of the artist is not in that *minimum* of content that came to his mind at the time of creation but in a certain elasticity of image, in the capacity of the inner form to evoke the most diverse content.[53]

The image, then, is for Potebnia the living center of the work of art. He rejects the notion that it has an unchangeable or absolute content. The image may be relatively immobile, and the content derived from it quite variable (though the reverse is also possible). Potebnia does not suggest that the image is open to any and all interpretations. But the "very same artistic work and the very same image may act differently on different people, and differently on one person at different times, just as one and the same word may be understood differently by different people."[54] The author's minimum content, it follows from Potebnia's interpretation, is at best only *one* interpretation, one note in what, after Bakhtin, we should call the polyphonic orchestration of a work of art. Whether an artist admires his work or subjects it to deserved or undeserved condemnation, "he stands before it as an outsider making an evaluation; he recognizes its independent existence."

Pereverzev views the author's relation to his work in much the same way as Potebnia. He recognizes too, that the work of an author, for example Dostoevsky, may give rise to very different interpretations. But though insisting that Dostoevsky's living images are "not dolls, not toys, but life itself," Pereverzev nonetheless attributes the "babble of opinions" around him to the lack of an analytical approach —that is, a literary methodology that distinguishes between the objective content of a writer's images and authorial interpretation.[55] Like Potebnia, Pereverzev finds all crucial meaning in the image (for

Pereverzev always living, embodied images); like him he suggests that this meaning may contradict the author's understanding of the image. But unlike Potebnia, Pereverzev posits an objective, socially determined meaning in the image, and as Marxist scholar seeks to bring out that meaning. He essentially turns Potebnia's idealist aesthetic theory on its head and bases it on a materialist foundation.

The image, in Pereverzev's words, is the "basic structural element of an artistic work."[56] It is the pivotal element in his formula for the artistic reproduction of reality, which holds that "being" organizes a work of art. Being stands in relationship to the work as both subject (the writer himself) and object (the deep reality depicted by the writer). "Only by examining being as a dialectical unity of object and subject is it possible to say that it determines an artistic work." The task of the Marxist scholar, then, is to discover the laws of connection between the object and the subject, to find "in the object of poetic depiction its subject, in the depicted . . . the depictor." "Precisely at this point one approaches that being which lies at the basis of a given work, that social reality where, in the living socioproductive process, object and subject, the concrete objective world and the concrete man, are found in organic fusion."[57]

The point where the unity of subject and object is achieved—that is, the point where "objective reality becomes the thinking subject . . . where consciousness . . . enters organically into the system of reality"[58]—is the image. The image is a "system of conduct," a "character" reproduced.[59] In turn character, "social character," is the "conduct of man conditioned by his position in the productive process. . . . To explain a given character means to find that position in the productive process out of which the observed system of conduct, the observed character, of necessity emerges."[60] "The objective regularity of the system of images," Pereverzev concludes, "is determined by the objective regularity of the productive process. . . . There are no other determining factors."[61]

V

Pereverzev's critics accused him of eliminating consciousness from the artistic process, of transforming the artist into a passive, mechanical medium for the reproduction of reality. Indeed, the relation between artist and objective reality in the creation of images is as complete in Pereverzev's scheme as is the relation between the tree and nature in Tolstoy's "Three Deaths." This de facto elimination of consciousness from the creative process not only eliminates the active role of the artist, but also places the formation of the image beyond the direct influence of the class struggle and ideology in general. Pereverzev views class consciousness, at least where the creation of images is concerned, not at all as a category of conscious ideology, but as unconscious social and psychological experience embodied in social character and transmitted directly through the image.

This line of thought led Pereverzev to a unique and, from the standpoint of a great deal of Marxist thought, aberrant view of the relation between base and superstructure. In his so-called "monistic" theory all the elements of the superstructure—politics, literature, religion, law, and so on—are arranged in a series of "parallel ranks" that, like branches of a tree, exist independently of one another. Pereverzev acknowledges the complex, many-sided character of social life and the simultaneity of change in different ranks or categories of the superstructure; but he insists that the "changes in one rank are in no way explained by reference to interaction with another rank."[62] Here there is no causality. "Painting cannot create anything in the image system of literature; political life cannot create anything in the image system of painting. Here nothing is created, there are only parallel ranks. Here there is coexistence, but no causal connections."[63] Pereverzev scoffs at "contemporary pluralists" who talk of the interaction between various elements of the superstructure, and then add without fail that "ultimately everything is determined by economics."[64] "When you get to this 'ultimately' you might as well not have got to it, you might as well consider the most important influence on literature to be all these so-called interacting factors."* All that will remain to the Marxist scholar, Pereverzev concludes ironically, will be to "return peacefully into the shadow of the cultural-historical method."[65]

What for Pereverzev was a holdover from the cultural-historical method was for his critics a sense of dialectics. Pereverzev, wrote the critic Ral'tsevich, "rejects the inner connections between the differ-

---

* "Voprosy marksistskogo literaturovedeniia," *Rodnoi jazyk i literatura v trudovoi shkole*, no. 1, 1928, p. 99. Clearly, this is a criticism of the somewhat more flexible understanding of the relation of the superstructure to the base that Engels had adopted in his later years. "Marx and I," Engels wrote, "are ourselves partly to blame for the fact that younger writers sometimes lay more stress on the economic side than is due to it. We had to emphasize this main principle in opposition to our adversaries, who denied it, and we had not always the time, the place, or opportunity to allow the other elements involved in the interaction to come into their rights." Engels, letter to Joseph Bloch, Sept. 21, 1890, in Karl Marx and Frederick Engels, *Selected Works* (New York: International Publishers, n.d.), I, 383.

ent elements of the superstructure and especially their interpenetration; he rejects the internal contradictory whole formed by the different elements of the superstructure. He will not tolerate a unity of opposites and runs from contradictory unity as from the plague."[66] But Pereverzev returns again and again to his basic materialist premise: "Social determinism leads to economic necessity. Social determinism in the Marxist world view lies wholly in the process of production, and nowhere else."[67]

Pereverzev does not deny the role of the class struggle in literature, but finds it not in any authorial point of view (or, in any case, not primarily there), but deeply embedded in the author's system of images. The class struggle, in this sense, is apprehended unconsciously by the artist; it is part and parcel of the history of his perceptions of living images. "Every image is politically active," Pereverzev asserts. "The image . . . that organizes the style of a work . . . is thoroughly political. . . . The class struggle is a great and complex process, all of man is wrapped up in it. . . . In my books the class struggle is given in every image because the class struggle is to be found in the psyche of every man."[68] Pereverzev's study of Dostoevsky provides the best illustration of his point. Dostoevsky is the "poet of the city," the depictor of the socially and economically depressed class of "decadent petty bourgeoisie"—those who live "by personal labor, at one and the same time a worker and a small owner . . . independent urban workers ranging from artisans to people in the intellectual professions."[69] This group, existing precariously between the hammer of capitalism and the anvil of the oppressed classes, seeks to avoid destruction. Feverishly it casts about, now rebelling and rising to heights of cynicism and self-will, now submitting and seeking out paths of mysticism and religion. Its psychology, complex, hopelessly divided, and desperate, reflects its social position.

Over the petty bourgeoisie a curse hangs, as over the biblical fig tree: it is sociologically fruitless, incapable of a historically constructive role. The tragedy of this class lies in the fact that its revolutionary impulse neutralizes its reactionary impulse, and its reactionary impulse neutralizes its revolutionary impulse: the stormiest tensions of revolutionary energy are resolved in reaction, and the most intense reaction must be resolved in revolution.[70]

Pereverzev posits the psychological "double" as the governing, "autogenous" image in Dostoevsky's work. In his view the ambivalent psychology of the double ultimately reflects, in its complex behavior and vacillation between rebellion and submission, the ambivalent *social* position of the petty bourgeoisie. The double, as well as the variant self-willed and meek types splitting off from it, in this sense gives expression to a complex class struggle. But this struggle at root is not a reflection of the social or political point of view of the author; it is not something that a writer arbitrarily introduces into his work; it is not a product of consciousness.* The class struggle, Pereverzev affirms, is

the very same—only more complex—productive process. Indeed, the productive process is finally the struggle for life, and the class struggle is only one of the manifestations of this struggle for life: in special ways, with special means, every class carries on a struggle for life, because the basic interrelationships of classes are created at the base of specific productive forces. Just this activity of people, this living struggle, is the very productive process.[71]

Pereverzev's observations here on the nature of the class struggle and its relation to the productive process are, to say the least, extremely vague. One recognizes an effort to close the gap between the sign and the signified, between the abstract Marxist notion of the productive process and the concrete social reality or social relations covered by the term. Pereverzev's concept of environment or being, as we have noted, though always given a specific class label, nonetheless seems to involve the sum of everyday life. He speaks doggedly of the direct determinism of the productive process, yet understands by this term the "activity of people," the "struggle for life" (an echo, perhaps, of those "biological depths" from which the artist unconsciously draws his materials). It is clear, in any case, that in his Marxist theory as in his literary practice, he telescopes the superstructure and all its class relations and ideology back into the base, back into that being where the artist's first perceptions are unconsciously born and formed. "He understands causality," wrote one of Pereverzev's critics, "as involving the direct, immediate conditioning of ideologies by productive relations; these relations are viewed as the only source for the development of literature."[72]

Pereverzev thus lays the basis for his concept of the organic nature

---

* Pereverzev does not deny, of course, that Dostoevsky's personality, his views, and his general character are reflected in his living images, or that one might conclude from a study of his images that Dostoevsky was himself a double and an ideologist of the decadent petty bourgeoisie. "But all the same, the images of Dostoevsky are not Dostoevsky, and Dostoevsky is not his images. In order to study the images of Dostoevsky, one needs only his works, whereas the study of Dostoevsky himself as a living personality necessarily involves his biography, an examination of the historical milieu in which he lived." *Tvorchestvo Dostoevskogo* (Moscow, 1922), p. 228.

of the artist's relation to the social-economic deep structure, for direct artistic intuition of the image. Here in the deep structure is to be found the inescapable determinism of objective reality, the inescapable social and psychological fatality of class being that a writer inherits without choice and, so far as the formation of the substratum of his art is concerned, without the mediation of consciousness. It is this determinism of objective reality, in Pereverzev's scheme, that constitutes the dialectical counterpart of what he calls the "determinism of artistic structure." The function of class analysis is to bring to light the social causality resulting in the creation of the image, and to reveal the artist's place in that process:

> It goes without saying that when we are concerned with class analysis we are not concerned with evaluation. We engage in class analysis only in order to understand the artist scientifically, that is, to reveal him as a causally conditioned phenomenon. . . . The artist is an extraordinarily complex phenomenon of life that calls for scientific interpretation. We must understand the artist . . . in his causal dependency as a law-conditioned phenomenon of life.[73]

All the heroic and naive faith of the nineteenth century in science is expressed in these remarkable words of Pereverzev.

VI

The art historian Arnold Hauser has written of the dangers of pragmatic explanation, whether genetic or teleological, of art. "No doubt scientific explanation involves simplification, analysis of the complex into such components as occur in other complexes also. Outside the field of art this procedure does not destroy anything really in the essence of the object, but when applied to art, it eliminates the object as presented in its completeness, the only way in which it can be properly presented."[74]

The sociological method, in its sociogenetic emphasis at least, is a good example of the dangers of explanation. In their criticism of Pereverzev, however, many Soviet critics were concerned not so much with defending the integrity of the work of art, its multivalent and multidimensional life, as with using both art and the artist as instruments of social change. Broad epistemological questions and narrow political issues were often closely interwoven in their polemics. Pereverzev, it was charged, conceived of class being as something independent of the superstructure of interacting classes, whereas, one critic insists, it is precisely in terms of the whole complex class struggle that a writer, "in spite of the limits laid down by class, has

the possibility of broad artistic comprehension of social reality."*
Thus the class nature of a spiritual phenomenon is determined not
only by subjective psychological aspects, Pereverzev's critics argued,
but also by the objective comprehension of reality. The so-called
Leninist aesthetics of cognition, which gained ascendency with the
defeat of Pereverzev's "vulgar sociology," A. Voronsky's "objectivist"
literary theories, and other unorthodox interpretations of Marxism,
in theory broadened the criteria for evaluating a work of art; in fact,
however, it served to legitimize a quite pernicious, ideologically
oriented criticism.

Pereverzev's image-oriented criticism, his sharp distinction between the ideology of the image and the ideas of the author, served
to defend the integrity of the artist before political and ideological
evaluation. The writer's personal idea or confession, Pereverzev insisted, is not the affair of the scholarly Marxist student of literature.

We demand only psychological truth from the artistic image, whereas from
the artist himself we demand logical truth. The artistic image may err
logically, may have no logic at all, and yet remain profoundly truthful because it embodies in itself the psychology of real people, because it is
psychologically truthful. But when an artist makes a mistake we are not
concerned with psychological truth, but with the real existence of the individual artist. We demand that he think logically and correctly. Before
an artistic image I ask myself: is it real, is it possible? And once it appears
real to me, I take a lively interest in it, I have a desire to study and clarify
it to myself as a definite kind of human psyche.[75]

"Is it real, is it possible?" Does the image have "psychological truth"?
This is Pereverzev's first criterion for evaluating a work of art: the
criterion of "inner truth, the sincerity of a work of art." † The criterion for judgment here is basically aesthetic. The critic asks whether
the image is truthful not to some abstract standard but to a particular
life-style and psychology of real people. The writer himself may not
recognize the specific, indeed relative, truthfulness of his images. He
may, like Dostoevsky, have a broader interpretation of their truth.
Thus according to Pereverzev, Dostoevsky falsely believed that the

---

* A. Gurstein, *Voprosy marksistskogo literaturovedeniia* (Moscow, 1931), p.
22. Pereverzev's critics, of course, cited Lenin's assertion that for dialectical
materialism "there does not exist a fixed and immutable boundary between relative and absolute truth." *Materialism and Empirio-criticism* (New York, 1927),
vol. XIII of *Collected Works of V. I. Lenin*, p. 107.

† *Tvorchestvo Dostoevskogo* (Moscow, 1922), p. 229. Pereverzev's second criterion is "originality and freshness of content, the reproduction of a new, hitherto unknown corner of life"; his third is "scope and significance of the area of
life depicted." *Ibid.*

"psyche he depicted was not merely the psyche of a specific environment, but that such types of people were possible at all times and in all circumstances ... that the forms of psyche depicted in his novels spanned the whole spiritual life of mankind, that no other forms existed, that he had plumbed the depths of the universal soul."[76] These relatively truthful images do, in Pereverzev's view, arouse profound and universal emotions in the writer, and in turn, evoke a universal response in the reader. But for Pereverzev the writer and his images are nonetheless firmly fixed in a temporal, class-limited, realistic cosmos; like a scientist Pereverzev measures their objective content invariably by the criteria of the social and historical moment.

Pereverzev, however, was capable of rising above the limitations of his theories even as he formally adhered to them. His remarkable preface to the 1922 edition of his study of Dostoevsky, entitled "Dostoevsky and Revolution," clearly indicates that he recognized in Dostoevsky's petty bourgeois types a depth and significance going beyond the relative truth of class and moment. All of modern literature, he notes, "follows in Dostoevsky's footsteps":

Dostoevsky remains a contemporary writer. Our times have by no means outlived the problems he takes up in his work. For us to speak about Dostoevsky still means to speak about the most painful and rooted problems of our contemporary life. Caught up in the whirlwind of a great revolution, buffeted about amid the problems posed by it, passionately and painfully responding to all the peripeteia of the revolutionary tragedy, we find in Dostoevsky our very own selves; we find in the way he states the problems of revolution the kind of passion and fever we might expect to find in a writer who was passing through the revolutionary storm with us.[77]

Pereverzev, it is true, remains loyal in his preface to an objective class understanding of Dostoevsky's images. "Insofar as the revolution is moved by proletarian energy, it lies outside of Dostoevsky's ken," but "our great revolution has to a large extent been moved by the forces of the petty bourgeoisie."[78] The blend of reactionary and revolutionary impulses in the petty bourgeois type is relevant to the understanding of the "peripeteia of the revolutionary tragedy." But what is striking about Pereverzev's preface is his stress on the broad cognitive, indeed prophetic, character of Dostoevsky's art. Though rejecting Merezhkovsky's view of Dostoevsky as a prophet of the revolution, Pereverzev advances his own notion of him as a writer who "profoundly understood the psychological element of revolution," and clearly saw "what many in his time and even in the days of the revolution did not even guess."[79] "This great artist and student of the soul was alone with his mournful knowledge. His contemporaries had a poor understanding of him, indeed really could not understand him, because his vision was too keen, and it is difficult for a blind man to understand one who sees."[80] Had Pereverzev's own eyes been opened by the cataclysmic events of the Russian Revolution? In any case, he recommends Dostoevsky's "psychoanalysis of revolutionary Russia" as deserving of close attention,[81] especially the novel *The Devils* and its impressive message.

Dostoevsky is alien to all idealization of revolution. Revolution is cruel and immoral. . . . Revolution is the work of the insulted and injured. . . . We are accustomed to regarding the insulted and injured as pitiful and do not suspect that there is much in them that is terrible. . . . Revolution carries with it horror, terror, despotism. . . . Deprived of freedom, oppressed to the status of one among a herd of cattle, the slave rises to dizzying heights of freedom and self-will, unrestrained by any law or morality. . . . Drunk with freedom the slave becomes a despot. . . . "Without despotism there has never been freedom or equality," says Peter Verkhovensky, a hero of the revolutionary underground, expressing a favorite thought of the author. . . . Dissecting and disclosing layer by layer the soul of the revolutionary underground, Dostoevsky penetrated to its most intimate secrets. These were secrets the members of the revolutionary underground themselves did not want to see and timidly avoided. They grew angry with him because he made a public display of that ominous cacophony of the revolutionary underground to which they consciously or unconsciously turned a deaf ear.[82]

In its condemnation of Pereverzev, the Communist Academy called his preface "Dostoevsky and Revolution" an "unconcealed Menshevik view of the revolution, in which the proletariat is in complete dependence on the oscillations and caprices of the petty bourgeois element."[83] Though this is not a totally correct reading of the preface, there is no question that the so-called "oscillations and caprices" of the petty bourgeoisie served Pereverzev as a metaphor in what may be taken as a critique of the demonic element in the Russian Revolution. In this critique Dostoevsky's "mournful knowledge" casts a dark shadow over the revolutionary past.

The resolution of the Communist Academy condemning Pereverzev in 1930, however, provides ample evidence in almost every sentence that its principal concern with the sociological method was not its interpretation of the class character of the Bolshevik Revolution in 1917 and 1918 or its view of the classics but its political impact on the developing cultural revolution. The view that "nobody has the power to change his style, because nobody has the power to go outside of a determined circle of images" had explosive implications on the eve of the greatest upheaval in Russian history—the agricultural, industrial, and cultural revolution of 1929–39. Pereverzev's notion that the "Party spirit of a writer is determined not by conscious tendencies but by subconscious experiences,"[84] his view that "inspiration is the voice of class sounding throughout the whole sphere of the subconscious,"[85] offered little hope for change in an artist whose psyche was formed either in prerevolutionary society or in a chaotic postrevolutionary world lacking deep proletarian social foundations and traditions. Pereverzev's sociological method, with its scholarly objectivity and its distinction between a writer's ideas and the ideology of the image, offered clear support to the so-called "fellow travelers" (the term was first used by Trotsky), the nonproletarian writers who basically accepted the revolution but remained uncommitted in the 1920's to Marxist doctrine and proletarian ideology. "Artists in whom subconscious experiences are organically formed in conscious tendencies, with conscious Party spirit," Pereverzev wrote, "are not often met. Obviously, to erect a superstructure of conscious Party ideology over the psychological being of an artist is an exceptionally difficult business. And it is better not to have an ideological superstructure at all than to have one that is not in accord with the psychological being of the artist." On the whole, Pereverzev regarded the extremely nominal Party affiliation of the fellow travelers as a very useful "prophylactic measure against falsification and insincerity—the mortal enemies of art. The sphere of consciousness of the artist must always be permeable to the psychic waves of the unconscious. So long as that permeability exists, the sincerity indispensable to the artist is preserved. Ideology, the conscious tendency, most often violates this permeability."[86]

Pereverzev was expressing views that in one form or another had been put forth in prerevolutionary times by Plekhanov and Vorovsky and echoed in the immediate postrevolutionary period by the critic Aleksandr Voronsky, Trotsky, and others. "One cannot approach art in the way you approach politics," Trotsky declared in 1924. He spoke of the "huge role played by the subconscious processes in the artistic work" and added: "To turn himself consciously around on his own axis, even though only a matter of degrees, is a most difficult task for the artist, one not infrequently connected with a profound, sometimes fatal crisis. Yet we are confronted with the task not just of an individual or temporal upheaval but a class, a social revolution in art. This process is lengthy, very complex."[87]

Plekhanov, Vorovsky, Pereverzev, Voronsky, and Trotsky were all Marxists in the orthodox sense. They had absorbed the first lesson of Marxist materialism: being determines consciousness. But it was a lesson that Russian rulers like Ivan the Terrible, Peter the Great, and Stalin consistently ignored. Russia and its inhabitants in 1929 were about to undergo a revolution unparalleled in European history. The fate of the sociological method reflected the larger fate of a nation where the most fundamental changes have always come from the top. In the decade of 1929–39 the Marxist formula was turned on its head: consciousness—brutal and unrelenting—uprooted the being of Russian life. The history of Russian culture in the Stalinist era attests to a nearly fatal crisis. The legacy of that crisis in post-Stalinist Soviet Russia is the slow search for foundations—for being.

VII

A reevaluation of the sociological method was in order in the late 1920's, but conditions were not propitious for an objective examination. Whatever the merits of anti-Pereverzevian criticism—and at its best it represented a genuine effort to expand the horizons of Marxist scholarship beyond the limits of sociogenetic analysis—it was bent and distorted by political and cultural utilitarianism. Pereverzevian Marxism was perceived as a direct attack on the specifically Russian tradition of pragmatic utilitarianism that had its roots in the writings of Dobroliubov, Chernyshevsky, and Pisarev. The critic V. Ral'tsevich, toward the end of a two-part critique of the sociological method in 1930, denounced Pereverzev for his struggle against the "progressive aesthetic theories" of the materialists of the 1860's and for his attempt to discredit their normative, utilitarian approach as metaphysical. In words that sum up the dominant ethos of the period, Ral'tsevich wrote: "Marxists also hold to the view of the 'utilitarianism' of all human actions, concepts, and strivings, though they have an incomparably more profound understanding of this utilitarianism than did the materialists of the 1860's. The practical class-proletarian, economic-socialist, and political significance of our demands in the realm of art is the supreme principle of Marxist-Leninist aesthetics. We need only the kind of art that facilitates the class struggle of the proletariat and of socialist construction, helps the proletariat and laboring masses to understand their vitally important economic tasks, inspires them to struggle with the rot that both surrounds them and still resides within them."[88]

The rout of so-called "vulgar sociology" represented a victory for the radical tradition of utilitarian aesthetics in Russian criticism. It signaled the end of a short-lived period under Soviet power of relatively open inquiry and frank debate in the realm of Marxist literary criticism. In 1928 A. V. Lunacharsky attributed the lack of unity in Marxist criticism not only to the complexity of the tasks facing literary critics, but also to the fact that "Marxist literary scholarship is still in a very early developmental stage."[89] By the early 1930's an artificial unity had been achieved, and the foundations for an independent, many-sided development of Marxist aesthetic thought had been effectively destroyed.

There can be no sidestepping the fatal flaws of the sociological method. Out of the Marxist cultural formula, "being determines consciousness," Pereverzev forged a sociopsychological method that could hardly explain either the artist or the rich and varied forms of his art. In order to posit an absolute, binding necessity, Pereverzev eliminated freedom. All that gives art (or the living image) its capacity to contest the given at any moment in reality—that is, the generative, broadly interpretive, and ultimately imaginative force enabling the artist to transcend the limits of his immediate social environment and history—is regarded by Pereverzev as nonessential to the literary specialist. "To hazard the contradiction," Emerson wrote, "freedom is necessary. If you please to plant yourself on the side of Fate, and say, Fate is all; then we say, a part of Fate is the freedom of man. . . . So far as a man thinks, he is free. . . . Man can confront fate with fate."[90] The sociological method, of course, relegates thought to an inferior status in art. In his effort to isolate a precise social-psychological class deep structure in a work of art, Pereverzev in essence split the work into active and passive elements, and formally polarized the language of logic and imagery. The rigid distinction between the ideas of the author—the theme of a work, his conscious intentions, and so forth—and the ideology of the image narrowed to an extreme the whole question of class analysis, plunging it into the realm of a personal and collective unconscious. Such a distinction might have had some validity had Pereverzev limited himself to a purely descriptive typological analysis of a writer's system of imagery. He wished, however, not merely to affirm the unity of a writer's imagery, but to define it in terms of strict social causality. Pereverzev's bifurcation of the living image rendered difficult if not impossible an integral interpretation of the work of art.

What gives the sociological method its paradoxical character is its strange fusion of a valid psychological notion of aesthetic intuition with a narrow and implacable materialism. The general notion that the artist's aesthetic vision is closely related to his earliest experience and impressions was harnessed to a "scientific" belief in absolute social causality. Taine had claimed that if the forces of race-milieu-moment could be "measured and deciphered, one could deduce from them, as if from a formula, the characteristics of future civilization."[91] Pereverzev took the completed work of art, the writer's system of images, as a microcosmic civilization and then postulated, and attempted to pinpoint, an all-determining, measurable, specifically social environment. His efforts involved a number of mistaken assumptions about the work of art, but they were limited by something else as well: a good psychologist and a connoisseur of literature, Pereverzev was a poor sociologist. His Marxism—that is, what he thought about social and economic processes, social classes and institutions, social determinism, and the like—was not supported by detailed social research and documentation. In his perceptive and frankly critical introduction to Pereverzev's 1912 study of Dostoevsky, P. N. Sakulin, while praising Pereverzev for his general literary effort and for making the first "real sociological analysis" of Dostoevsky, nonetheless sharply criticized him for his narrow class focus. Sakulin took to task precisely the sociologist Pereverzev: "In order to be fruitful a sociological method presupposes a precise preliminary analysis of social conditions and a precise use of terms. It is very easy in this type of analysis to fall into the habit of making overly hasty sociological generalizations."[92] Sakulin undoubtedly isolates here one of the most important weaknesses in Pereverzev's method: the absence of solid sociological research. Moreover, he was the first critic of Pereverzev to suggest the limits of the sociogenetic approach to literature. "Dostoevsky, like Tolstoy," he noted, "is one of those great writers who create, of course, in definite social conditions, but who outgrow all initial limits in their development. Their art, one might say, rises upward in spiral form."[93]

Pereverzev nonetheless occupies an important place in the history of Marxist literary thought. He is the first Russian Marxist scholar to put into practice the notion that the real validation of the materialist interpretation of culture must take place not alone in general discussions of art and society, but also, and primarily, in studies analyzing the materials of art—style, structure, imagery, genre, and the like. This movement from the general to the specific, though indubitably narrowing the relatively broad horizons of Plekhanov's Marxist aesthetics, was an important step forward. In this sense Pereverzev's prerevolutionary literary work might be defined as one of the earliest examples of Marxist "chamber" scholarship.

No analysis of Pereverzev's sociological method as theory—particularly in the programmatic and dogmatic form in which it was expounded in the late 1920's—can do justice to his early studies of Dostoevsky and Gogol or to his valuable post-1930 scholarly work, which goes beyond the scope of his early theory. Ranking as a major Dostoevsky scholar, Pereverzev contributed much to the understanding of the artistic style and fictional techniques of both Dostoevsky and Gogol. He was a perceptive analyst of literary character, and his typological studies of systems of images are of general literary and psychological interest. His passionate rationalism and confidence in the scientific method establish him in his early work as something of a forerunner of contemporary Structuralist critics. Though the sociological conclusions he drew from his analyses are sometimes (but by no means always) wrong, the problems he poses are provocative. The limitations of Pereverzev, in the final analysis, are those of his quest: his self-conscious, disciplined effort to create a coherent methodology of literary analysis that would master literature both aesthetically and sociologically. At the same time, it is this singular striving for total scientific explanation of the literary text that gives his work its special interest.

Pereverzev's dry materialism was offset by a passionate emotional idealism. When he considers the function of art, he closely follows Jean-Marie Guyau (*L'Art au point de vue sociologique*, 1889) and Tolstoy (*What is Art?*, 1897) in their view of literature as a socializing phenomenon, a form of communication or emotional communion between men.* At the conclusion of his study of Dostoevsky, Pere-

---

* "Art is a human activity consisting in this," writes Tolstoy, "that one man consciously, by means of certain external signs, hands on to others feelings he has lived through, and that others are infected by these feelings and also experience them." *What Is Art? and Essays on Art*, trans. Aylmer Maude (London, 1938), p. 123. Guyau also speaks of the "infectious power of emotions and of thought." "Art is an extension, through feeling, of society to all of nature's beings, and even to those beings conceived as surpassing nature, and finally to those fictional beings created by the human imagination. Therefore the artistic

verzev stresses Dostoevsky's own deep emotional involvement with his living images. "The moment of creation for Dostoevsky was a moment of intense sympathy and hate": he rejoiced, grieved, and wept over his heroes. It is because of such "sincerity and deep sympathy," Pereverzev believes, that every great artistic work "stirs the heart." He notes the power of Dostoevsky's art to evoke a sympathetic response in the reader, to "compel him to feel more deeply all the importance of Dostoevsky's work, to compel him to appreciate more fully the significance of Dostoevsky's ideal of solidarity." Finally, Dostoevsky's picture of suffering man, alienated from society and trapped in the "social mechanism," arouses the reader to social action. "In this capacity to move the heart of living people, to awaken in them the feeling of anguish and pain for the poor and 'underground' people, to stimulate their thought and will to energetic action, I see the significance of the art of Dostoevsky. This capacity, I think, ought to be valued most highly of all in him."[94]

The significance of Dostoevsky's art, then, lies not in any ideological message or religious preachment (Pereverzev's study is directed against the message-oriented criticism of Merezhkovsky and others), but in the power of artistic emotions embodied in living images to arouse social feelings in men. Dostoevsky's work, therefore, plays a distinctly social role, but it plays that role as art. The moral truthfulness of his images is inseparable from aesthetic form and emotion. This concept of the function of art has much in common with Dostoevsky's own aesthetic outlook.[95]

Pereverzev's view of the living image as the source of the moral and social power of Dostoevsky's art coexists, somewhat uncomfortably, with his view of this same image as petty bourgeois in its objective social essence. How does one get from the relative class truth of the image, which we perceive dispassionately, to the emotionally moving absolute truth of the living image? The writer, one is forced to conclude, driven out the front door by the sociological method, returns secretly through the back to reclaim his images, to lift them out of their social circle, to invest them with his own pathos, and to give them roles in a drama that he himself actively directs.

The problems raised by Pereverzev's dual approach to literature—his view of literature as both fact and factor—cannot be resolved in

---

emotion is essentially social; its effect is to enrich the individual life by making it merge with a life that is larger and more universal. *The highest goal of art is to produce an aesthetic emotion of a social character.*" *L'Art au point de vue sociologique* (Paris, 1889), pp. 19, 21.

the context of the sociological method. Pereverzev himself, it would appear, arrived at this conclusion. In the preface to his posthumously published *Literature of Ancient Russia* (1971), he wrote:

Literature is a means for the most intimate, earnest, and heartfelt communion between man and man, between the artist and reader. The artistic image, if it be genuinely artistic, that is truthful and alive, is a revelation of the soul of the artist, his confession, an openhearted disclosure of his deeds and thoughts. The inner life of man, all the movements of his heart and mind, are revealed in literature.[96]

These lines signal Pereverzev's abandonment of the most extreme positions of his sociological method. Yet at the same time they affirm his lifelong view of the living image as the ideological and structural center of the literary work.

DONALD FANGER

Gogol and His Reader

This book has come out, therefore a reader for it must be
sitting somewhere in this world.
        —*Gogol's (entire) review of a book published in 1836*

The event of a text's life, that is, its authentic essence, always
develops on the borderline of two consciousnesses, of two
selves.
                                        —*M. M. Bakhtin*

My title might as plausibly have referred to Gogols and readers, both
the phenomena in question being elusive, enigmatic, and multiform.
Still, because there is one total Gogolian text, there must ultimately
be one textual Gogol, and any unriddling has sooner or later to address the singularity of the problem.[1]

To speak of unriddling is to follow Gogol himself, who insisted
repeatedly that his existence was textual, and that that text constituted a riddle whose key lay in the future.[2] In the year of his death,
Viazemsky explained the riddle in terms not of Gogol but of his
audience: "Everyone saw in him what he wanted to see, and not
what was really there." In good part this situation arose from the
way Gogol's work resisted approach via the usual critical categories,
as it continues to do. Too precociously modern to be accounted for
in terms of "romanticism" or "realism," it nonetheless bears the imprint of its time far too plainly to be comprehended by the kind of
vocabulary appropriate to his twentieth-century continuators (sym-
bolists, "neo-realists," surrealists, absurdists). Some of Gogol can be
caught in these nets, but the terms for an adequate understanding
need to fit *all* of his heterogeneous oeuvre, and they must be deduc-
ible from it. Lacking them, we can only echo Biely's acknowledgment (in 1909!) that the riddle persists: "We still do not know what
Gogol is."[3]

The problem, then—still vital—has by now a history of its own, and anyone who writes on Gogol while ignoring that history runs the risk of contributing directly to it rather than to its clarification or solution. The only hope of escape from this pernicious dialectic is, I think, to begin by recognizing it. That belief, in any case, explains the historical emphasis of the remarks that follow. Gogol's most brilliant texts have too often been studied apart from their relation to his total text (producing two Gogols, one to be celebrated, the other to be deplored or dismissed), just as the total text has too often been considered apart from the cultural-literary context that fed, constrained, and ultimately incorporated it. Newly construed as an exploration of the literary function in Gogol's time (and after), a historical approach can facilitate a more nuanced understanding of his achievement—and that, in its turn, can be of use in applying nonhistorical critical perspectives to his work. It can, in short, generate new questions, enhance, and on occasion invalidate. What it cannot do is limit or preclude: there is no conflict with immanent criticism as such.

The concrete purpose of this inevitably sketchy paper is to suggest how the concept of the reader—the object of increasing attention in recent years—may offer one key to comprehending Gogol. Not only does it represent a surprisingly neglected constant in his own writings (which, for all their miscellaneousness, evince a steady concern, both explicit and implicit, with the reader, both collective and individual): it is all the more promising in that it can be pragmatic as well as theoretical, and can operate on every level of the problem, from the contextual periphery to the textual center.

A few quotations may clarify the point.

1. *The Reader*

One might begin with Roland Barthes's complaint a few years ago that "the image of literature to be found in contemporary culture is tyranically centered on the author, his person, his history, his tastes, his passions." Such information, Barthes objects, is irrelevant to the experience of literature because centrifugal, the center being the work itself—"that neuter, that composite, that oblique into which every subject escapes, the trap where all identity is lost, beginning with the very identity of the body that writes." This truth may be less than universal, but the case of Gogol (whose biography is so much thinner and more fictive than his fictions) goes far to support it. Barthes's statement about Mallarmé in France easily accommodates a Gogolian substitution:

Though the Author's empire is still very powerful (recent criticism has often merely consolidated it), it is evident that for a long time now certain writers have attempted to topple it. In [Russia, Gogol] was doubtless the first to see and foresee in its full extent the necessity of substituting language for the man who hitherto was supposed to own it; for [Gogol], as for us, it is language which speaks, not the author: to write is to reach, through a preexisting impersonality—never to be confused with the . . . objectivity of the realistic novelist—that point where language alone acts, "performs," and not "oneself": [Gogol's] entire poetics consists in suppressing the author for the sake of the writing (which is, as we shall see, to restore the status of the reader).[4]

A similar emphasis on texts as experience is articulated by Borges. Deploring formalism as "a common propensity to consider . . . the arts as a sort of combinatory game," he observes: "Those who play that game forget that a book is more than a verbal structure, or a series of verbal structures; a book is the dialogue with the reader, and the peculiar accent he gives to its voice, and the changing and durable images it leaves in his memory."[5] This might seem to legitimize highly individual, not to say idiosyncratic, readings of a sort scarcely susceptible to study, and thus to exclude the normative. But, as Mandelstam reminds us, the fact is inevitable: "The distortion of a poetic work in the apprehension of the reader is an absolutely necessary social phenomenon; to struggle with it is difficult and useless: it is easier to provide Russia with electrification than to teach all its literate readers to read Pushkin as he is written and not as their emotional needs require and their mental capacities allow."[6]

The shift here from singular to plural is instructive, suggesting as it does that certain misreadings, when shared, may characterize an epoch, constituting a chapter in the kind of cultural history, Rezeptionsgeschichte, proposed in our time by Hans-Robert Jauss. The pluralized reader, then, has a pragmatic existence; but he has another, nameless and perhaps even more important, as Walter J. Ong argues in his essay "The Writer's Audience Is Always a Fiction." "It is really quite misleading," Father Ong reminds us, "to think of a writer as dealing with an 'audience.' . . . More properly, a writer addresses readers—only he does not quite 'address' them either: he writes to or for them. . . . 'Audience' is a collective noun. There is no such collective noun for readers, nor can there be. 'Readers' is a plural. Readers do not form a collectivity, acting here and now on one another and on the speaker as members of an audience do." Calling the audience a fiction in this context means two things: "First, that the writer must construct in his imagination, clearly or vaguely, an audience cast in some sort of role"; and second, that the audience "must correspondingly fictionalize itself," each reader playing "the role in which the author has cast him, which seldom coincides with his role in the rest of actual life."[7]

As we shall see, these notions take on special point in connection with Gogol, who frequently mistook his fictive (i.e., desired, potential) audience for the actual (refractory, disappointing) one. Suffice it here to recognize that both are legitimate and necessary objects for study. What form should such study take? Nikolai Rubakin, a turn-of-the-century pioneer in investigating the contemporary Russian reading public, offers a negative model: his earnest positivism allows his monographs at best a purely sociological value. Far more sophisticated and promising is the approach called for—in vain, as it turned out—by Aleksandr Beletsky in his 1922 article "On One of the Immediate Tasks of Historical-Literary Scholarship: The Study of the History of the Reader." Sensitive to the phenomenological intricacies of the literary enterprise, Beletsky persuasively develops the thesis that without a history of the Russian reader the history of Russian literature "is one-sided and will inevitably offer conclusions that are only half-articulated; whatever precision it may attain . . . , without this second half we cannot fully or properly understand any of its aspects."[8]

The central figure in this history, it is now widely recognized, must be, in Victor Lange's words, "defined and specified not merely as a sociological factor but as a function within the poetic procedure of the work itself." Of the several names that have been proposed for him—"ideal reader" (Wayne Booth), "average reader" or "archilecteur" (Michael Riffaterre), "implicit reader" (Wolfgang Iser)—Lange's may well be the most useful: "What I have in mind is neither the relationship to a given text of a sociologically definable reader, nor the role of an explicit reader figure within the narrative action, but rather the issue of a writer's purpose in building into his work a system of directions that will set the perspectives and presuppositions of the text, and that may be said to define the 'necessary' rather than the 'ideal' reader."[9] This "system of directions" has been brilliantly discussed by Liane Norman, who observes that it is "the initiation of the reader into the premises and mode of the story [that] creates the crucial linkage between one kind of reality and another."[10] Because her argument depends on more subtlety than summary allows, I will note only that the linkage of which she speaks raises in fresh perspective the whole problem of convention,[11] which is itself at once a cultural fact and a textual presence.*

What all these theoretical statements share is an insistence that the work of literature is more than a text, that a text only becomes a work of literature, as Péguy put it, through "a joint act, the joint operation of the reader and the read."[12] Some extremely suggestive implications of this have been explored recently by Stephen Gilman, who argues that "it is not we who are inside the world of the novel but rather the novel which is inside us—providing us with what Cervantes . . . explained as *nueva vida* (new life)." This, of course, is a point with which the Gogol of *Dead Souls* would agree; moreover, Gilman's fresh approach to the operations of prose fiction is one that might finally put to rest all the fruitless discussions of Gogol's "realism." The novel, he writes, is "the kind of literature which presents a fictional world *not necessarily resembling our own but in a fashion*

---

* To percipient contemporaries such as V. F. Odoevsky, it was clear that the new conventions Gogol proposed, like the novelty of his language, represented something to which "the public has not yet grown up"—a fact borne out by Senkovsky's constant mockery of Gogol's language, particularly of his having designated *Dead Souls* a *poema*. (Odoevsky on *Mirgorod*, quoted in B. Eikhenbaum, *Lermontov* [Leningrad, 1924], p. 34; for Senkovsky on Gogol's language, see V. V. Gippius, ed., *N. V. Gogol: Materialy i issledovaniia* [Moscow-Leningrad, 1936], I, 226–42, 245–46.) Two years before *Dead Souls* Lermontov addressed the same problem in his preface to *A Hero of Our Time*: "Our public is still so young and simple-minded that it doesn't understand a fable if it doesn't find a moral at the end. It does not recognize jokes, and does not feel irony. It is simply badly brought up. . . . Our public is like a provincial who, overhearing the conversation of two diplomats belonging to hostile courts, remains convinced that each of them is deceiving his own government in favor of a mutual and most tender friendship." Lermontov goes on to note how some readers took offense at seeing his "hero" presented as a model, while others construed it as a self-portrait, and still others took one or another character as a personal attack. This last tendency, as we shall see, plagued Gogol all along. In the authorial asides of *Dead Souls*, he repeatedly confronts the unreadiness of the Russian reader of his time to recognize the conventions of fiction; the implicit contract between writer and reader simply could not be taken for granted in the Russia of the 1840's. (Even near the end of the century the problem remained; Shklovsky, speaking of parallelism in Tolstoy and Maupassant, finds the former more primitive and explains the fact in terms of the French reader's greatest experience and longer tradition, which make him more sensitive to violations of a familiar canon. Viktor Shklovskii, *O teorii prozy* [Moscow-Leningrad, 1925], p. 63.)

resembling the way we experience our own—thus its natural realism less of mirrored content than of *unfolding process*. And it does this because its printed language reaches directly into our inner store of experience, draws upon it, and rearranges it imaginatively into a new spatiotemporal sequence—which is to say into Cervantes' 'new life.' "[13] Here is an insight that might yield fascinating results if applied to Chapter One of *Dead Souls* or to "The Nose." It accords strikingly with Gogol's preoccupations during the last decade of his life, specifically with the problem of producing texts that could come to independent life within the reader and, by the very complicity required of him, alter his consciousness in a lasting and beneficial way. Gogol's evolution was complex and contradictory; he envisaged different readers at different points in his career, and with varying degrees of clarity. But his lifelong effort to define for himself the position of the writer in Russia was always accompanied by an awareness of his no less problematic counterpart, bearing out Wayne Booth's axiom that the author creates "an image of himself and another image of his reader; he makes his reader, as he makes his second self, and the most successful reading is one in which the created selves, author and reader, can find complete agreement."[14]

These examples may indicate something of the range of recent theoretical interest in the reader. Not all theorists, of course, are drawn to application, and I have cited only such statements as promise new and useful results in attacking the Gogol problem. I have been interested neither to refine or to reconcile these several approaches; clearly, someone seeking to develop a unified theory would find a number of them divergent in emphasis and even mutually exclusive. For present purposes, however, the very multivalence of the concept of the reader is more an asset than a hindrance, for it permits that concept to fit a body of material that is itself complexly various, though single.

The task would be easier if the evidence had already been marshalled and interpreted under a number of key headings, among them the following.

The Russian Reading Public, 1825–1850: Quantity, Quality, Receptivity. The Russian reading public appears to have been developing rapidly just before and during Gogol's appearance on the scene.* No

---

* Surveying the subject in 1842 Shevyrev distinguished four stages: "In Lomonosov's time reading was a matter of conscious effort; under Catherine [the Great] it became one of the luxuries of the educated class; in Karamzin's

study of it could explain his genius, but one might suggest the limits within which that genius was fated to unfold—limits set by the expectations of literature then current (Gogol's own and others'), the range of acceptable literary language (particularly in prose), and the stock of generic devices then available in Russian,[15] as well as by such purely sociological factors as the number of publishing outlets available, the nature of literary journals and the number of their subscribers, the average printings of books, their prices and the conditions of access to them.

Materials for such a synthetic and interpretative study are at hand in histories of Russian publishing like Kufaev's and Muratov's; in compendious biographies like Barsukov's life of Pogodin; in memoirs (Panaev's, Annenkov's, S. T. Aksakov's, Bartenev's, Herzen's); in the contemporary critical writings of Belinsky and Shevyrev; in such histories as Zamotin's and such recent studies as those of André Meynieux.[16] Moreover, the writings and letters of key figures of the time —Gogol himself, Pushkin, Marlinsky, Bulgarin, Lermontov, Senkovsky, Samarin, Herzen, the Aksakovs—are surprisingly rich and still-untapped resources in this respect.

Even a superficial survey of these sources reveals a central development in Gogol's time, which might be summarized as follows. Through the 1820's and early 1830's, readers of current literature with any pretensions to seriousness were largely concentrated in the capitals. Many were themselves writers or would-be writers, and more often than not they knew each other socially, since both the production and consumption of literature—at this time chiefly poetry —tended to be very much a class affair.* In 1827, when this situation was drawing to a close, Pushkin could still identify almanacs— expensive, usually aperiodical miscellanies—as the main vehicles of Russian literature.[17] These could almost be regarded as the product

---

time, a requisite badge of enlightenment; with Zhukovsky and Pushkin, a social need." In the year of *Dead Souls*, he finds "literature has become a necessity of social life, and a noble eagerness for reading has awakened in virtually all parts of Russia." Quoted in N. Barsukov, *Zhizn' i trudy M. P. Pogodina* (St. Petersburg, 1888–1910), VI, 255–56.

* One of the best twentieth-century scholars of Russian literature puts it even more strongly: "The differentiation of the intelligentsia into 'writers' and 'readers' was then only beginning and those outside the close circle of 'the few,' the 'brotherhood of Parnassus,' were looked upon as 'rabble' [*chern'*]. Literature was largely a 'domestic' matter, a diversion for the leisured who were capable of combining *otium con dignitate*." P. M. Bitsilli, "Pushkin i Viazemskii (K voprosu ob istochnikakh pushkinskogo tvorchestva)," in Sofia Universitet Istoriko-filologicheski fakultet, *Godishnik*, XXXV, 15 (1938–39), p. 3.

of a few salons; they implied, by and large, a resolutely antiprofessional attitude toward the writer's calling. * As Viazemsky, himself a victim of this modish dilettantism, observed in the same year: "According to the social code of our society, authorship is not a vocation whose representatives have their rights, their voice, and their legitimate domain in the assemblage of ranks of high society. The writer in Russia, when he is without pen in hand, apart from his book, is an abstract, metaphysical being; if he wants to be a positive being, then he had better have in reserve some outside calling, and that episodic role will eclipse and outweigh the principal one."[18] Small wonder that about the same time Odoevsky could identify the bulk of Russian readers—the nucleus of the "mass" reading public that was to crystallize in the next decade—as consisting of those "who have abandoned the simplicity of earlier ways without attaining European culture [obrazovannost'], and who have stopped on some atrocious middle ground. . . . These people have not yet suspected that there are literary men in Russia; they ask who it was who wrote *Ruslan and Liudmila*, while reading *The Ladies' Journal*—the one from Frankfurt."[19] Scorned by the arbiters of literary taste, it was such people that Faddei Bulgarin had in mind when he dedicated his four-volume works (*Sochineniia*) in 1827 "To the Russian reading public, as a sign of respect and appreciation."

It was they who made Bulgarin's second-rate novel *Ivan Vyzhigin* the best-seller of 1829, overshadowing Pushkin's *Poltava*, which moved Pushkin and his friends to found their *Literary Gazette* in the following year as a challenge to those who were "morally and intellectually corrupting the reading public" by flattering and pandering to it.[20] In part because of the nonprofessionalism of its guiding lights, the *Literary Gazette* did not last long. Because of its political unreliability, neither did Kireevsky's *European*—a journal which, as Pogodin lamented, "with the names and articles of Zhukovsky, Baratynsky, Yazykov, and the like, [had] only fifty subscrib-

---

* On salons, almanacs, and the changing relation of literature to Society (and society) in Gogol's time, see M. Aronson and S. Reiser, eds., *Literaturnye kruzhki i salony* (Leningrad, 1929), esp. pp. 77–78, for Count V. A. Sollogub's account of the four aristocratic houses where the cultural elite met in the 1820's and 1830's. Aronson (p. 81) comments on the changed situation by the middle of the century: "The circle [kruzhok] and salon are . . . supplanted by the journal. In the second half of the nineteenth century, that is where writers meet each other and their reader. There is no necessity for direct contact. But in order for the journal to take over the function of the circles and salons, decades of stubborn struggle for the formation of [new] groupings of readers [chitatel'skie kadry] were required."

ers"!21 As if to underline the unequal competition, the banning of
Kireevsky's journal coincided with the bookseller Smirdin's project
for *The Housewarming*, a volume that united most of the commercially successful writers with most of the best. Here was successful
(because indiscriminate) commercialism, and it was institutionalized
the following year (1834) with the founding of the *Library for Reading*, Russia's first "thick journal," which boasted an unprecedented
five thousand subscribers, many of them in the provinces, and offered
appallingly varied contents: something for everybody. Its editor,
Senkovsky, as Gogol observed, "considered his public to be rabble
and forgot that perhaps fully half of Russia's readers already stood
higher than that language with which he addressed them."22

But Gogol himself vacillated both in his estimate of that audience
and in his own practical relation to it. And his vacillations had less
to do with an adherence to "aestheticism" or "elitism" than with his
highly conscious, evolving creation of an authorial self and of an
actual (as well as an imagined) readership. To understand this a
concrete sense of his context is essential. Figures alone hardly tell the
story, but they are suggestive: *Dead Souls*, long awaited and prompt-
ly hailed as a major event in Russian letters, was published in an
edition of 2,400 copies and reprinted only four years later. The author himself expected it to sell better "than any other book" (XII,
49): he hoped for 4,000 readers (XI, 269)!

A History of Gogol Criticism. Fame, Rilke said, is the sum of the
misunderstandings that gather round a name. Gogol's fame—his immediate and continuing *presence* in Russian literature—has always
borne an eccentric but highly indicative relation to his writing. And
it is, of course, the creation of his readers, especially of their more
aggressively articulate minority, the critics. When the critics are not
telling us useful things about Gogol's texts, they are still, inevitably,
telling us useful things about the literary situation in (and against)
which he wrote. The raw materials have been collected, published,
and republished; some exist by now in English translation.23 What
we lack in any language, however, is an *interpretative* history of
Gogol criticism in Russia, one that would seek to interrogate the
material, so much of which has been cited ad infinitum without ever
having been placed in a coherent intellectual context, let alone considered as a factor that might have influenced Gogol himself as, in
increasing isolation, he improvised a vocation and a body of work.

Gogol doggedly sought fame—and recoiled at what he took to be
the misunderstandings on which it rested. That he was often unre-

liable in identifying these; that idiosyncrasy and personal pathology color his reactions; that he seems almost willfully to have misrepresented (when he did not simply ignore) his own achievements—all this is not to the point here. What is, is the tendency of critics—who set about to mediate between the author and the broad readership he sought—to deny or promote that fame for their own reasons.

Belinsky offers a prime example, and it is positively astonishing in view of his enormous influence that there is still no independent critical tracing of his complex relation to Gogol. Canonized in Russian and Soviet thought for over a century, his name provokes weariness in the Western scholar, who is likely not to realize either the depth of the critic's early, purely literary, percipience or the extent to which he later suppressed it, failing to discuss "The Overcoat" in any detail and virtually ignoring the artistry of *Dead Souls*. In his 1835 article "On Russian Stories and the Stories of Mr. Gogol," alongside a foolish insistence on Gogol's "absolute truth to reality"—an insistence explicable in the light of his adherence to Schelling's philosophy at the time[24]—one can find a repeated emphasis on Gogol's "poetry," a defense of unconscious creation, and a penetrating definition of "the essence of his genius" as lying in "a comic animation, always in the process of being overcome by a profound feeling of melancholy and dejection." Belinsky terms Gogol's stories "lachrymose comedies," "funny when you read them and sad when you have read them."[25] But having once recognized Gogol's genius, he then proceeds to neglect its terms, seeking instead to exploit it for his own principled ends. Annenkov, who was close to both writer and critic, explains Belinsky's response to *Dead Souls* in this way:

This novel opened up to criticism the only arena in which it might undertake the analysis of societal and social [*obshchestvennye i bytovye*] phenomena, and Belinsky held fast to Gogol and his novel as to a godsend. He seems to have regarded it as his life's calling to treat the content of *Dead Souls* in such a way as to preclude the assumption that it contained anything other than an artistic picture, psychologically and ethnographically faithful, of the current position of Russian society. . . . [His] task consisted chiefly in trying to drive out of the literary arena—forever if possible—both the preposterous, wily, and self-serving detractors of Gogol's *poema* and the enraptured well-wishers who failed to descry its true purport.[26]

A picture of considerable complexity emerges, involving Gogol's defensive reaction not only against Belinsky, but against most of the other critics as well, who, regardless of party line, tended to take a

similarly instrumental attitude toward his creation. On the pragmatic level, this intensified his desire to bypass the critics and establish a direct relationship with individual readers, a desire that led to
some bizarre results. At the same time, it confirmed Gogol's sense of
aloneness in the face of the nation's cultural expectations, which
found grandiloquent expression near the end of his novel: "Russia!
What is it thou wouldst have of me? . . . Why dost thou gaze so, and
why has everything in thee turned its eyes, full of expectation, on
me?" Moreover, the eccentricity of criticism raises important questions about the nature of writing that can so easily and plausibly
support the most varied interpretations.

Finally, the role of critics as deliberate opinion-formers—"readers
who have taken up the pen," in Beletsky's phrase—suggests a related
but discrete piece in the contextual puzzle, one that might be labeled
"Reputation and Iconography." Published criticism, after all, represents only the most readily available reaction of contemporary readers. Conversations, letters, and journal entries provide more spontaneous and no less valuable evidence. Unintended for publication,
many have nonetheless been preserved in memoirs, in scattered
editions of correspondence, and in such compilations as Shenrok's
Materials Toward a Biography of N. Gogol and L. Lansky's "Gogol
in the Unpublished Correspondence of Contemporaries."[27] They too
await their interpreter, who might find a partial model in Ovsianiko-
Kulikovsky's pioneering attempt to explain why some of the most
intelligent readers of Gogol's time—Herzen, Nikitenko, S. T. Aksakov
among them—should have drawn such strange and sweeping conclusions, so little capable of textual demonstration, about Gogol's
novel, thus setting in motion that chain of one-sided interpretations
which has bedeviled Russian (and not only Russian) thinking about
Gogol's work ever since.[28]

Gogol and the Censors. No understanding of Gogol's Russian
reader can be accurate that does not take into account the ubiquitous
censor. "Among the rights of a Russian subject," Count Uvarov
wrote, "the right of written communication with the public is not
included. That is a privilege which the government can grant and
rescind as it sees fit."[29] This might suggest too simply that the government was seeking to control a natural alliance between two suspect groups, writers and readers—as was indeed at times the case.
But the censorship also reflected a common (and persisting) Russian
attitude toward literature which sees the printed word as a kind of

untested drug, from whose possible ill effects the public stands in need of protection.* In this sense the censorship sets itself in loco parentis to the young reading public, and could well represent the judgment of a significant part of that public. Such an interpretation, which still deserves to be tested, was articulated late in the nineteenth century by M. I. Sukhomlinov:

The history of the censorship is a vital and necessary support for the history of literature. The significance of the censors' activity has been undervalued in this respect. Attention is usually confined to fragmentary reports of curious and amusing cases. . . . But it is not in such exclusiveness and eccentricity that the historical interest of the censorship's actions and findings resides. Those who amassed a depressing reputation as the "geniuses of obtuseness" [only] expressed more vividly and naively what their quicker and more adroit associates and inspirers managed to confuse to such an extent that it is hard to penetrate to the real sense of their various circumlocutions and phrases. The heart of the matter lies in the fact that, thanks to the captiousness of the censorship, many features have been preserved which would have vanished without a trace, but which are valuable for the history of literature because they reflect the impression made by literary works on a [particular] society's readers. . . . In the verdicts of the censorship and in the considerations on which they were based are reflected more or less clearly the concepts and views prevailing at one or another time in the various strata of our society.[30]

Here is one concrete example. The April 1841 number of the Slavophile journal *The Muscovite* (*Moskvitianin*) included ten little anecdotes, one of which began: "A petitioner comes to an office to inquire about his case and approaches a table where a scribe is sitting engrossed in the *Northern Bee*, perhaps reading some uplifting article by Mr. Bulgarin." This led Count Uvarov to reprimand the

---

* Gogol himself came perilously close to this view by the late forties. In "An Author's Confession," after characterizing the good a properly prepared writer might do his society, he observes that a writer who had failed to school himself in Russian and universal citizenship might, conversely, exercise a harmful influence, and one in direct proportion to his artistic gifts; he cites George Sand as a case in point. He then goes on to construe his own experience with *Selected Passages* in light of the quasi-magical power of words: "If even that book, which consists of no more than reasoning, produces (as has been alleged) delusions and disseminates false ideas; if from those letters, as has been said, entire sentences and pages remain in one's head like living pictures—what would have happened if I had come forward with the living images of a narrative composition instead of those letters? I myself sense that I am stronger in that area than in reasonings. As it is, criticism can still dispute me, but in the other case it is unlikely that anyone would have had the power to refute me. My images are seductive and would have stuck so fast in [readers'] heads that criticism could not have dislodged them." VIII, 457–58.

editor for his lack of seemliness and taste; at the same time it led Count Benckendorf, the chief of the gendarmerie, to write Uvarov:

Having read [these anecdotes] with the greatest astonishment, I find that it is not so much the censor who is to blame for their publication as the publisher of the journal, for articles of this kind show his lack of respect for the educated public, along with a desire to cater to the most depraved class of people; moreover, such anecdotes evidence not only tastelessness in the publisher, but also an abuse of the trust the Government has vouchsafed him as a journalist, for to exhibit office functionaries [*chinovniki*] in such an improbable and repulsive fashion, to slander them by imputing behavior and actions that do not exist in the class of office functionaries at the present time, and to attribute disgraceful characters to them is a crime against the Government of which those functionaries are organs. [I find further] that the inclusion of such articles, which make the right-thinking [*blagonamerennyi*] reader indignant and provide pleasure only to those disloyal persons who seek occasions to have a laugh at the vocation of office functionary and so insult the Government, constitutes proof of the crudest tastelessness and intellectual depravity, of a false and harmful view of objects of state [*gosudarstvennye predmety*], and of the disloyalty [*neblagonamerennost'*] of the publisher himself. . . . These reasons, in my view, would quite suffice to prohibit Mr. Pogodin from publishing *The Muscovite*.[31]

This was going too far even for Uvarov, who tactfully registered his disagreement; at the same time, however, he put Prince Odoevsky up to warning Pogodin and company that they should never regard the censor's approval as sufficient: "On the contrary, you should protect the censor, being people more educated, more capable of exercising that flair which divines what impression even the most innocent article may produce in the reader." When going over the proofs, Odoevsky suggests, "forget for the time being that you are publishers; try to become readers."[32]

The censorial attitude thus spread well beyond the censor himself. It assumed the closest possible relationship between literature and life, regarding the printed word primarily as an influence on attitudes, and attitudes as a predisposition to action. The censor in this respect represented "the necessary reader," only too typical in his philistinism. The most frequent complaint in Gogol's published work after 1835—that is, after he began writing deliberately for the broadest possible Russian audience—is about the touchiness of whole classes to collective insult. This, as we have seen, was a matter of prime concern to the authorities, and it persisted even after Gogol's death. The censor had qualms about republishing "Nevsky Prospect" posthumously. "The description of various scenes in the life of an officer who is presented in a ridiculous light makes the whole story a dubious candidate for approval," he wrote in 1854![33]

On other occasions the censor might stand for the ideally close reader. "The content is fantastic," one of them noted of "The Nose" three years after Gogol's death, when a new edition of the collected works was being planned: "The aim of the author is obscure and capable of being interpreted in different ways, and therefore the passing of this story requires the permission of the Chief Censorship Authority."[34] The awkward position of a censor of some literary sensitivity is evident from the case of Nikitenko, who wrote Gogol a cordial letter full of discriminating praise for Dead Souls at the same time that, according to Pletnev, he was crossing out "everything" in the manuscript.[35]

As for Gogol, the actions of the censorship certainly gave point to, and may actually have fed, the emphasis in his work on emptiness and arbitrariness.* Ironically, it was the same Nikitenko who, when Gogol was just beginning his career, noted in his diary (December 30, 1830) that "the year just ending has brought little that is comforting for enlightenment in Russia. . . . Many works in prose and verse have been banned for the most insignificant reasons, one may even say without any reasons.[36] To this Gogol added his own ratification at frequent intervals—right up to the year of his death, when he observed of the censorship that "its actions are enigmatic to the point where one begins willy-nilly to suppose it to be harboring some criminal intent and plot against those very regulations and that very policy by which (judging from its words) it purports to be guided" (XIV, 240). Indeed, he speaks of having abandoned his first project for a stage comedy out of the conviction that it could never be approved (X, 262–63), and his agonies over the censorship of Dead Souls are well documented. What other effects this chronic anticipation of an unwelcome close reader may have had, we can only conjecture.

In one important respect, all the same, the censor may fairly represent the reading public at large: in his search for implication, convinced that he was reading messages out of literary texts, he was at least as likely to be reading them in. The blurring of this crucial dis-

---

*This elusive question of social-artistic analogy has been broached by at least two of Gogol's most penetrating critics in connection with The Inspector General—briefly by V. V. Gippius, Ot Pushkina do Bloka (Moscow-Leningrad, 1966), p. 113, and at length by Iu. Lotman, "Khlestakov," Uchenye Zapiski Tartuskogo gos. un-ta, 1975, vyp. 369.

tinction is an enormously significant fact of Russian cultural history, and it deserves to be studied as such rather than simply perpetuated in statements like George Steiner's that "all of Russian literature ... is essentially political" because "it is produced and published, so far as it can be, in the teeth of ubiquitous censorship."[37] This, to be sure, only echoes Vogüé's explanation of Russian literature to his fellow Frenchmen late in the nineteenth century. For a series of reasons, he writes,

philosophy, history, the eloquence of the podium and the bar—not to mention the tribune—are genres almost absent from this young literature; what one finds in other countries under these arbitrary labels goes, in Russia, into the vast framework of poetry and the novel, ... the only [forms] compatible with the demands of a censorship formerly implacable and today [1886] still highly suspicious. Ideas pass only when concealed in the flexible threads of fiction; but there they all pass; and the fiction that shelters them takes on the importance of a doctrinal treatise.[38]

The mistake here is to see the process as arising invariably from authorial intention; in fact, where serious literature is concerned, what is in question is much more the disposition of certain readers to find their preoccupations met by the writers they admired. The special function of literature—cognitive, shading into doctrinal—existed in nineteenth-century Russia, but largely for the consumers. It was not the major writers who, in other circumstances, might have occupied other social roles (by and large they already did); it was rather the major critics. Belinsky himself, as Chernyshevsky astutely observed, could well have become a tribune in a society that allowed such a function; as it was, he channeled that impulse into his writing on literature—and sought to attribute it to Gogol, among others.

The reading (or misreading) habits of the Russian intelligentsia are still an unstudied subject. What seems beyond doubt, however, is that they mirror those of the censorship (of which they were the direct result), and that they began to take form around the work of Gogol.

The value of all such contextual considerations, I repeat, lies in their direct relation to Gogol's own career and works. These works appear so often to be a creation out of nothing* that it has been easy for critics to treat them as if they arose in a vacuum. They did not:

* *Tvorchestvo iz nichego*, Shestov's phrase for Chekhov, is infinitely more applicable to Gogol. Cf. Belinsky's observation in his 1835 article "On Russian Stories and the Stories of Mr. Gogol": "Mr. Gogol is a master of making everything out of nothing."

the varieties of absence that permeate his writing and come to constitute his dominant theme represent more than creation. They represent responses to the literary-cultural situation in his time.

The sketch that follows is far from exhaustive, but it may suggest some lines of correspondence between our theory and Gogol's practice. That it is discursive should be taken as a sign of its being exploratory—and of respect for the reader's freedom to draw inferences.

11. *Gogol and His Reader*

Throughout his career Gogol's major quest was for a relationship with an audience. The first lines he published besought the public's favor on behalf of his own pseudonymous poem; his last book was meant to influence a readership which, he foresaw, would comprise "half of literate Russia." He vacillated between dreams of an ideal public and clear-sighted views of what was really available to him, sometimes confusing the two, finally pursuing the moment when his soul should unite with his reader's in a kind of transsubstantiation that would strengthen and ennoble both and lead to a new stage in the evolution of the Russian spirit. Over the years the degree of fictiveness would vary widely, increasing as Gogol became more impatient of "practical" and concrete results. Then he would confuse his biographical with his textual self, his actual with his posited reader. Each, he thought, would teach the other; each would do the work of the other. The development is uneven; the data must be sought in his practice as well as in his thought. Gogol's texts, in other words, even when they appear to be *professions de foi*, need to be seen at the same time as instrumentalities. He had designs on his reader no less than on himself, and if there is any consistency in his career, it comes from his constant efforts to discover and form both.

The first, Petersburg period of that career (1829–36) shows him, in Annenkov's words, "a completely free man, carving a way for himself with exceptional skill."[39] Two years before his arrival he had written a school friend already serving in the capital how he envied "the sweet assurance that your existence is not without significance, that you will be noticed and appreciated" (X, 80). The equation here is revealing. Indeed, it may not be too much to say that from the time of his very first writings Gogol was pursuing a relationship: seeking to fashion a publicly presentable self, he sought at the same time to discover a public that might value and so validate the presentation. As in a courtship, preoccupation with the self and the other alternated, being reciprocal.

"What strange thing is this: *Evening on a Farm near Dikanka*? What kind of evenings? And launched on the world by some bee-keeper! God save us!" Gogol's first volume of stories opens disarm-ingly with an act of double ventriloquism—the voice of a hypotheti-cal reader filtered through the voice of a fictive narrator, Rudy Panko, the garrulous old provincial beekeeper. Just two years before, *Hanz Kuechelgarten* had been offered to an "enlightened public" that was no less a figment of the author's imagination than the poem's German hero; now, rather more enlightened about that public and suitably masked, Gogol can flaunt his ironic awareness of what it means "for a rustic like me to poke his nose out of the backwoods into the great world"—and turn that awareness to creative account. The very compositors who set these stories in type chuckled at them, he reported to Pushkin, from which he concluded that "I am a writer quite to the taste of the rabble [*chern'*]" (X, 203). What he gave his readers, by and large, was entertainment of a kind then in vogue, but of unprecedented quality.[40] With one exception these stories are built around plot, which is to say that experience is offered to the reader in conventionally vicarious guise, enhanced but hardly over-shadowed by the occasionally exotic language or eccentric character of the narration itself. That strategy changes decisively after the sec-ond volume of *Evenings*.

Mirgorod, his next collection of stories and a pivotal work in his development, is Gogol's most intimately revealing book.[41] It shows him bringing to consciousness and seeking perspective on the kind of self-expression that went more directly into the earlier tales (and effusive fragments like "Woman"). Thus the importance of his new orientation toward the Russian reader, who is now invited to take the author as a *semblable*, if not as a *frère*. In "Old-World Land-owners" the title characters are recalled "from here" (*otsiuda*), a point outside and above their little world, by a narrator devoid of idiosyncrasy who explains local usages in literary Russian. In the opening pages of "Taras Bulba," the old Cossack leads his sons into a parlor "decorated in the taste of that time, of which hints have remained only in songs and in folk poems [*dumy*] that are no longer sung in the Ukraine" (II, 43–44). "Viy" is equipped with a footnote explaining (rather misleadingly, but that is not to the point here) the Ukrainian nomenclature and informing the reader: "This whole tale is a popular legend. I have not wanted to change it in any way, and tell it almost as simply as I have heard it told." Even the story of the two Ivans, published previously as another of Rudy Panko's, appears here without that attribution, and equipped with an ironic preface: "I consider it my duty to state in advance that the occurrence described in this story relates to a very distant past. Moreover, it is a complete invention. Mirgorod is now quite different. The buildings are different; the puddle in the middle of town has long since dried up; and all the dignitaries—the judge, the clerk, and the mayor—are respected and loyal people." *

These brief examples, which could be multiplied, may suffice as indications of Gogol's shift of position: *with his reader* he looks down and in on the world portrayed, its very presence colored by the framing acknowledgment of its absence. Whatever else they may be, the stories of Mirgorod are essays in evaluation; and to the extent that one may speak of problematics in them, one must speak of attitudinal problematics. This is most obvious in the keynote story, "Old-World Landowners," where Gogol presents his ambivalence so artfully that generations of readers, compelled to share both his affection and his uneasiness over it, have debated the relative human worth of these good-natured cretins—overlooking the fact that Gogol's concern is not with the value of *living* such a life, but rather with the value of a certain way of life *in the spiritual economy of an occasional visitor.*

The companion piece to "Old-World Landowners" is the last in the collection, "The Story of How Ivan Ivanovich Quarreled with Ivan Nikiforovich," and it signals further progress in Gogol's working out of his own new structural entities. The challenge these presented to the common reader of the time may be gauged from the remarks of the *Northern Bee*'s reviewer, who recognized the art in Gogol's performance but could not reconcile it with what he expected of Art:

[This story] describes the prosaic life of two neighbors in a poor provincial town, with all its uninteresting details, and describes it with astonishing fidelity and liveliness of colors. But what is the aim of these scenes, which arouse nothing in the soul of the reader except pity and disgust? They contain nothing amusing or touching or funny. Why, then, are we shown these tatters, these dirty rags—however artfully they may be presented? Why draw an unpleasant picture of the backyard of life and humanity, without any apparent aim?[42]

---

* II, 221. This preface, apparently written in pique over Gogol's earlier trials with the censorship, was itself most probably prohibited by the censor of *Mirgorod*; it survives in only one known copy of the 1835 printing, and was noticed only in this century (II, 750–53). For a summary of the facts, see F. C. Driessen, *Gogol as a Short-Story Writer* (The Hague, 1965), p. 168.

As Gogol continued to explore this vein of what we now call "Gogolian" writing, similar complaints continued to be voiced (indeed, he parodies them at the end of "The Nose"), symptomatic of the unpreparedness of readers for the new code he was fashioning. These readers looked for character and story, fidelity to the "reality" of the world they took for granted, and found only the semblance of such things. More: they expected to be touched or amused unambiguously; they expected fictions to allow some final resolution of attitude in one of these keys. In short, they expected a reinforcement of the "normal" as they conceived it—in artistic decorum and in the experience conveyed—and found it challenged instead.

Gogol himself all too soon was to move closer to such readers, conceding that he had laughed in his first works "gratuitously," without a clear aim. That was when he had already formed his talent—when, in the present interpretation, the energy that had been absorbed in fashioning an original medium was freed by the success of that effort to substitute a "why" for the "how" that had hitherto preoccupied him. The story of the two Ivans, however, is all "how"—a triumph of sustained narrative self-invention, and so a kind of tour de force. Gogol has taken the slenderest of events, the most minimally drawn of characters, as the basis (one might almost say pretext) for a narration abounding in subtleties of tone and expression, which teases the reader with abortive hints of undeveloped themes.

That teasing, an incidental and perhaps unconscious feature in the story of the two Ivans, becomes central in "The Nose." The first draft of the story had ended by explaining that "everything described here was a dream" of the hapless protagonist, Major Kovalyov (III, 399), thereby rationalizing bewilderment and illustrating Gogol's own definition of a dream as "simply incoherent excerpts, which have no sense, taken from what we have thought and then joined together to make up a kind of salad" (X, 376–77). By removing this rationale in the published version, Gogol turned his story into an experiment in absurdity—a puzzle without a key and a provocation to his readers. "An exceedingly strange story!" he exclaims at the conclusion of the first published version:

I absolutely can't understand anything in it. And what is all this for? What is its relevance? I'm sure that more than half of it is implausible. . . . I confess I can't understand how I could write this! Besides, it's generally incomprehensible to me how authors can take up that kind of subject! Where does all this tend? What is its aim? What does this story prove? . . . Even supposing that there are no rules for the fancy, and granting that many absolutely inexplicable things do really happen in the world, still, what have we here? Why Kovalyov's nose? And why Kovalyov himself? No, I don't understand, I don't understand at all. (III, 400)

Further refining his text for the collected works of 1842, Gogol subtly adjusts this closing emphasis. The authorial voice no longer articulates the reader's rational objections but plays with them, and ends by pointing not to the creative but to the ontological mystery: "And nonetheless, despite everything, although, of course, one may grant this and that and the other, may even—well, but where are there not absurdities?—All the same, when you think it over there really is something in all this. Whatever anyone may say, things like that do happen in the world—rarely, but they do happen." (III, 75.)

The censor's hesitation over this story (noted above) must thus be seen as an unwitting tribute to a characteristically Gogolian masterpiece, in which the problematic is defiantly displaced from the experience related in the work ("content") to the reader's experience of the text. Henceforth, this is the rule of Gogol's practice. Only two unfinished fictions, "Rome" and the second volume of *Dead Souls*, will depart from it, with results judged disappointing by the author and his readers alike.

The mid-1830's, to which these stories belong, also witnessed the young writer's first major exercises in the area of nonfiction—his historical-pedagogical-aesthetic potpourri *Arabesques*, and some substantial journalistic pieces. The former, often jejune and bombastic, is noteworthy nonetheless for the two essays devoted to contemporary artists. One deals with the painter Briullov's gigantic rendering *The Last Day of Pompeii*. "His works," Gogol observes, "are the first that can be understood (though differently) by the artist with the most highly developed taste and by the man who doesn't know what art is" (VIII, 113). The relation of the artist to a mass public was by this time paramount for Gogol. He had already confessed a year before, "I don't know why I thirst so for contemporary fame," and had spoken of being haunted by visions of a large, responsive audience (X, 262–63). But he repeatedly expressed repulsion for the writers who commanded one; thus his annoyance at his mother's misattribution to him of something by Senkovsky: "His filthy writings please only the lower class" (X, 314). Briullov was valuable as an example of how one might keep faith with one's art and at the same time appeal to those who were not equipped to appreciate such fidelity. Briullov's painting, "a universal creation" because "it contains everything," showed how artistic inclusiveness could find its counterpart in a broadly inclusive audience; his idea "belongs completely to the taste of our century, which in general, as if itself sensing its own terrible fragmentation, aspires to combine all phenomena into general groups and selects intense crises that can be felt as one whole mass" (VIII, 109). Gogol underlines the dangers of such vivid appeal in the hands of a false talent, and a passage in the original draft makes clearer than the published version how far literary considerations preoccupied him in writing about these matters. Strong effects, he says there, are particularly revolting in literature "when they are produced with the aim of shameless merchants [*torgashi*], and not of people who breathe art. Their consequences are noxious because the good-natured crowd will accept a glittering lie." (VIII, 645–46.)

The same preoccupations inform the essay "A Few Words About Pushkin," but they are elaborated in a different key, leading to different conclusions and serving a broader personal strategy. When Pushkin wrote romantically of the exotic Caucasus and Crimea, Gogol notes, he astonished "even those who lacked the taste and mental development to be able to understand him" (VIII, 51). Everyone quoted him; his fame spread with unprecedented and enviable rapidity. And this, Gogol insists, was legitimate because the bond between poet and reader was authentic: "A poet can even be national when he is describing a quite alien world but regarding it with the eyes of his national element, with the eyes of the whole people, when he feels and speaks in such a way that it seems to his compatriots that they themselves are doing the feeling and speaking" (VIII, 51). When Pushkin transferred his attention to the heart of Russia, however, seeking to be "a fully national poet," his broad appeal began to wane. The closer to home he turns his attention, the less able his readers are to follow him. Gogol's explanation is that though the mass of the public believes it wants a truthful rendition, in fact it will not accept one because it is not prepared to appreciate an appropriately lowered subject matter and style as being literary.

The poet's dilemma in the face of this situation constitutes the heart of the essay. So long as he confines himself to objects that justify a vivid style, the public—and its money—will be on his side. But if he chooses to be loyal to truth alone, then he must bid farewell to a readership unable to see that "a wild mountaineer in his warrior's costume" and "our [Russian] judge in his threadbare, tobacco-stained frock coat . . . are both phenomena that belong to our world [and] must both have a claim on our attention" (VIII, 53). The more ordinary the object, Gogol writes, the more one must be a poet in order to draw the unusual out of it without violating truth. But the more one is a poet in this way, the greater is his miscalculation—"not with respect to himself, but with respect to his multitudinous public." Pushkin's shorter works (*melkie sochineniia*) illustrate this (VIII, 54).

So Gogol takes his stand alongside Pushkin against the uncomprehending reading public. But when he deplores the paucity of "true judges"—"In all Petersburg there are perhaps only some five individuals who understand [literary] art deeply and truly" (X, 362)—he is engaging in more than self-congratulation or elitism. For he is deploring the state of the reading public *to* the reading public, a fact that makes this the boldest pedagogical essay in his book. The pessimism of his conclusion is thus not absolute; it underlines the challenge contained in such statements as that Pushkin's works "can only be completely understood by one whose soul contains purely Russian elements, whose motherland is Russia, whose soul is so delicately organized and developed in feeling that it can comprehend Russian songs and the Russian spirit, devoid though they be of surface brilliance" (VIII, 54). The ideal reader adumbrated here needs to be not so much an aesthete as a cultural patriot; he requires not so much rare gifts as "a taste higher than the one that can only understand excessively sharp and large-scale features" (VIII, 54). What he needs chiefly is an orientation—and Gogol, in preferring the "internal brilliance" that does not leap to the eye over "cascades of eloquence," puts all his effort into elucidating one. His essay, addressed to the reading public at large, propagandizes for a new scale of aesthetic values and a newly sensitized public taste. The hope that this bespeaks is reflected even more energetically in the journalism to which he turned soon after the publication of *Arabesques*.

Only three years before, in 1832, Gogol had dismissed journalism categorically, observing with relief that Pushkin had abandoned his plan to publish a newspaper: "To take up the discredited trade of a journalist at this time hardly speaks well even for someone who is unknown; but for a genius to engage in it means to sully the purity and chastity of his soul" (X, 247). In the meantime, however, the *Library for Reading* had appeared, had assembled the largest readership to date in Russia, and was complacently monopolizing it. Some worried about the commercialism of the enterprise—the high salaries paid to Krylov and Senkovsky as nominal and effective editor, respectively; the generous remuneration offered to contributors (and even to noncontributors, so long as they would consent to having their names listed on the cover); the willingness to buy out prospective competitors.* Gogol's concern lay elsewhere, and he voiced it at length in his brilliant article "On the Movement of Periodical Literature in 1834 and 1835," published in the first number of Pushkin's *Contemporary*. Noting evidence over the past two years of "a general need for intellectual food" as the result of a significant increase in the numbers of readers, he concentrates on the response to that demand, chiefly as offered in the *Library for Reading*, which had set up as the unique because all-inclusive organ of current Russian writing.

Unique Gogol grants it to be, but hardly all-inclusive: "With the publication of the first issue, the public saw clearly that the tone, opinions, and ideas of *one person* dominated the journal, and that the names of writers in the brilliant column filling half the title page had only been rented for the occasion to attract a greater number of subscribers" (VIII, 157). So he proceeds to consider Senkovsky's practice, discovering in him a kind of literary Nozdrev:

After reading everything he has put into this journal, following all his words, we cannot but pause in astonishment: What is all this? What has made this man write? We see a man who certainly does not take money for nothing, but works by the sweat of his brow, not only worrying about his own articles but ever reworking other people's—in short, a man who is inexhaustible. What is all this activity for? (VIII, 158–59)

Reading his criticism, it is impossible to determine what he likes and what he doesn't: "In his reviews there is *neither positive nor negative taste—there is none at all*" (VIII, 160). Yet this same man as editor announces boldly: "In the *Library for Reading* things are not managed as they are in other journals. We do not leave any story in its original form, we rework every one. Sometimes we make one out of two, sometimes out of three, and the piece is significantly improved by our revisions." (VIII, 162.)

---

* In a letter of January 10, 1836, apropos of his plan to publish a journal, Pushkin reports: "Smirdin [the publisher of the *Library for Reading*] is already offering me 15,000 to back off from my enterprise and become a contributor again to his *Library*. But although that would be profitable, I can't agree to it. Senkovsky is such a rogue, and Smirdin such a fool, that it is impossible to be connected with them." A. S. Pushkin, *Polnoe sobranie sochinenii v desiati tomakh*, 2d ed. (Moscow, 1958), X, 560. Smirdin was also ready to pay up to a thousand rubles for permission to list certain authors as having articles forthcoming; see Aleksandr V. Zapadov, ed., *Istoriia russkoi zhurnalistiki XVIII–XIX vekov*, 3d ed. (Moscow, 1973), p. 162.

One is tempted to read these last words as Gogolian invention, but his quotation is direct; all the emptiness, vulgarity, and sheer improbable mindlessness he found on the literary scene rather *fed* his artistic writing. Reflections of it are to be found in *The Inspector General* (in Khlestakov and the mayor alike); they are surely present as well in *Dead Souls* (whence his insistence on the serious national import of trivial characters and empty speech). In this article, however, Gogol's view is comparative and analytic. Surveying the ineffective competition, he finds it dwarfed by the *Library*, which stands among its rivals "like an elephant among the lesser quadrupeds" (VIII, 165):

Their battle was too uneven, and it seems they failed to take into account that the *Library for Reading* had some five thousand subscribers, that the opinions of the *Library for Reading* were spread in layers of society where people had not even heard of the existence [of other journals] . . . , that the opinions and works published in the *Library for Reading* were praised by the editors of that very *Library for Reading*, hiding under different names, and praised with enthusiasm, which always has an influence on the larger part of the public; for what is ludicrous to educated readers is believed in all their simpleheartedness by more limited readers of the kind one must assume the *Library*'s readers to be, judging by the number of subscribers—the majority of whom, moreover, were new people who had not hitherto been familiar with magazines and consequently inclined to take everything as gospel truth. (VIII, 166)

Finally, he notes, the *Library* had reinforcement in the 4,000-strong circulation of the *Northern Bee*, which occupied an analogous position among Petersburg newspapers (VIII, 166).

The attempt to break "such an unprecedented monopoly" by setting up a new rival in the *Moscow Observer* he finds misguided from the start, because that journal arose not from a consciousness of the reading public's needs, but rather from its writers' discomfort with the whimsical tyranny and thoroughgoing commercialism of the *Library*. It attacked the sellers and ignored "the poor customers."

Gogol's central concern is with these customers, particularly those in the provinces, for many of whom regular reading might be a novelty.* He seems to have wavered in his estimate of their present

---

* In his first draft he distinguishes such readers as constituting the crucial sector of the *Library*'s influence. This journal, he writes, "has spread across the immeasurable face of all Russia, through all its enormous but unequally educated provinces. In every provincial town it has found some subscribers. All those whom life in the province . . . has condemned to boredom have flocked eagerly to the new journal, which promises them constant reading for a whole year. The landowners, the civil servants in the towns—people who have hitherto

state of development; but his notion of the reader here is in any case a composite one, embracing the actual and the "implied" reader, and favoring the kind of writing that cultivates discrimination by supposing its possibility. Among the key questions he finds neglected by all the Russian journals are these three: "Why has poetry been replaced by prose compositions? What is the degree of development of the Russian public, indeed what is the Russian public? In what does the originality and distinctive nature of our writers consist?" (VIII, 172.) The article concludes with what amounts to a call for the deliberate creation of a literary culture—the marshalling of a usable past, the illuminating of present tendencies at home and abroad—by writers turned critics. Excised from the printed version of his article were passages evincing a more sustained attempt at persuasion: "An ineradicable reproach must lie on [writers of talent] if they shut their eyes completely to the opinions that are constantly being born and circulating everywhere, engaging everybody, because, say what you will, those opinions are creating and educating the majority of the reading public, and an incorrect, corrupted upbringing must weigh on the souls of great writers if they had not lifted their voices" (VIII, 536–37).

This article marks the high point of Gogol's active optimism with respect to *la chose littéraire* in his time, an optimism characterizing his *Inspector General* as well, which was even then being readied for performance. "The theater is a great school," he had written (VIII, 562); "profound is its allotted task. To a whole crowd, to a thousand people at once, it reads a vivid, useful lesson." When the crowd failed to take that lesson, Gogol fled abroad, renouncing all interest in the contemporary. The story of his reaction to the premiere of his comedy is a familiar one and need not be rehearsed here; his disappointment was commensurate with the hyperbolic hopes he evidently placed on this first confrontation with his audience. Mochul'sky has suggested, not implausibly, that he expected his audience to show signs of on-the-spot moral regeneration; Viacheslav Ivanov makes a similar case in more measured terms by identifying the play as "intrinsically and Aristophanically comic" in the way it portrays a social microcosm that is meant to mirror, entertain, and edify the

---

rarely held a book in their hands—have taken to the new, long, and varied reading in these enormous tomes. Only the capitals, whose eternal hurrying movement avoids large volumes like the plague, have greeted the appearance of the new journal with indifference." VIII, 520.

social microcosm which its spectators comprise.[43] What is clear, if only from the structure of *The Inspector General*, is that Gogol intended it to be not the representation but the agent of significant experience. The one honest character in it, he said, was laughter (V, 169). But there is no laughter *in* the play; it arises only in the spectator (or reader), uniting him with the author.

That, at any rate, was Gogol's conscious theory and aspiration from this point on. In his own retrospective accounts he explains this new intentionality as a "sacred legacy" from Pushkin, who had urged him to undertake something major and yielded to him (with whatever degree of willingness or unwillingness) the ideas for *The Inspector General* and *Dead Souls*. Both works are set in the provincial heartland of Russia, symbolic of the national essence; both make central the theme of perception; and both provoke the reader to supply a significance whose absence is artfully underlined in the texts. Gogol is now seeking to harness the gifts he has proved in his earlier writings.

"The Overcoat" offers a striking example in this context. Like "The Nose" it invites the reader to find "something in it"—and this time the something can be named. The themes of urban impersonality, bureaucracy, poverty and comfort, meekness and pride, justice, love, Christian charity, literature itself, all make their appearance in the text. Those who claim that "The Overcoat" is not "about" these things are demonstrably mistaken, though hardly more so than those who claim that it is. The serious themes of "The Overcoat" are unprecedentedly numerous—that is what marks the story as belonging to Gogol's later period—but they make their fleeting appearance in an arbitrary narration whose tendency is to move on, rather than to develop, reconcile, or resolve them. Reading the story is thus like looking through a kaleidoscope: the constituent elements of the changing patterns are limited in number; one can recognize them, wonder at the variety, while noting how the recurrence of certain patterns appears more than fortuitous, but less than primary. In this kaleidoscope's successive patterns we see images that prompt reflection; these are related, we may come to realize, to other, less arresting images. Each turn contributes to a growing familiarity with the separately enigmatic shapes, and so intensifies the search for that perpetually elusive yet constantly potential pattern which might fix them all in positions of analyzable beauty.

There is, of course, no such fixity in Gogol's story. That was the point first recognized by Eikhenbaum, who insisted on seeing "The

Overcoat" as pure performance.⁴⁴ But there is no such purity either. Gogol may not satisfy the reader's conventional expectation that a story should ultimately be comprehensible from a single point of view, but he keeps that expectation alive enough to make sport of it. Once this is recognized as an index of the story's peculiar mode of being, it becomes possible to see that there is, after all, an ultimate, stable and inclusive theme: "The Overcoat" is "about" not the questions it contains but the question they finally evoke in the bemused reader. It is about significance and nonsignificance *as such*. It embraces particular instances that look like themes but actually function, in their incompleteness, only as cues.

The radical novelty of this problematic text, then, lies in the way it provokes a quest for significance, for the sense in which humble phenomena may contain it, for the criteria by which it may be identified. This quest—the more tantalizing because it is presented with seeming randomness, like a game of blindman's buff—is enacted in the narrative, whose arbitrary shifts of level and perspective represent the obstacles in that search. Gogol's best art had always avoided unambiguous statement to pose self-regarding questions in the form of riddles. Here and in *Dead Souls* he raises the level of those riddles to accord with his new conception of the comic writer as servant of the vaguest but highest ideals—ethical, moral, religious, civic— their ideality guaranteed precisely by their vagueness. In its range both of tone and of theme, "The Overcoat" represents a giant step in the direction of his novel. A hermeneutic challenge, intrinsically elusive and endlessly evocative, it is, like that novel, Gogol's monument—not to the power of social reality in art, but to the possibilities of art in the social reality of his time (and ours).

"The Overcoat" came out in 1842, almost simultaneously with *Dead Souls*, which apparently eclipsed it. The critics noticed it only in passing; its author noticed it not at all: neither in any letter nor in the two accounts he left of his career as writer! One reason may lie in Gogol's constantly growing concern with being "properly" understood, which first appeared in the aftermath of *The Inspector General*. Immediately following the first performance he had begun to draft "After the Play" (*Teatral'nyj raz"ezd*), a dramatized survey of audience responses in which the eavesdropping author refutes, endorses, and supplements the disparate views of his public. (This work too was finished and published in 1842.) Being thus no longer disposed to present his art to the reader without comment, Gogol may well have regarded his story as an aberration, too largely a throwback to an earlier manner to merit special attention alongside his recent experiments with a poetry he now saw as "the pure confession of the soul," "the truth of the soul, [which] can therefore be equally accessible to all" (VIII, 429).

"My works differ from those of others," he wrote in mid-1842, "in that everyone can judge them, all my readers without exception, because the objects are taken from the life that circulates around each one" (XII, 82). Still, he took steps to offer guidance. To the familiar narrative voice he adds in *Dead Souls*—for the first time—another, distinctly authorial voice, whose role is that of self-justifying creator. Thus, for example, we read in the last chapter: "Had the author not looked more deeply into [Chichikov's] soul, had he not stirred at the bottom what slinks away and hides from the light, had he not revealed the most secret thoughts that one man never confides to another, but rather shown him as he appeared to the whole town, to Manilov and the other people, . . . [readers] would be happy with him and would take him for an interesting person." But then, he adds, striking the didactic note that separates the world of this work from that of *The Inspector General*, "the reader's soul would have gone undisturbed" and "on finishing his reading . . . he might [simply] turn again to the card table, the universal Russian pastime" (VI, 243).

The narrator's work is presentation; it embraces the projections and perceptions of the characters and offers them, embellished and in a new perspective, to the reader. The author, by contrast, appears as such, hinting at a larger enterprise of his own, as enigmatic as Chichikov's, which he likens to a journey. The passages where his voice dominates might together bear the title given Gogol's posthumous "Author's Confession," constituting as they do crucial passages in "the tale of [his] authorship." All are keyed to the question, Why? Thus in Chapter 3 (VI, 58): "But why be concerned so long with Korobochka? Whether it's Korobochka or Manilov, a thrifty life or unthrifty—let us leave them behind!" This author's voice is seldom ironic; rather, it sets forth the norms by which the purely narrative ironies are to be understood, thus differentiating the method of *Dead Souls* from that of "The Overcoat" and evincing a new directness in Gogol's articulation of his fundamental themes—his vision (in the double sense) of Russia and of himself as writer—which come together near the end in the famous lyrical passage beginning "Russia! Russia! I see thee; from my wondrous, beautiful, far-off place I see thee . . ." (VI, 220–21).

Such grandiloquence has few precedents in Gogol's published writing, though it appears in many letters and in such intimate fragments as "1834" and "Nights at a Villa." It is what he took to be the unmediated language of his soul, and he was to offer it increasingly to his public as the conviction strengthened in him that "the pure confession of the soul and not... art or human intention [*khoten'e*]" constituted poetry (VIII, 429). Here was a corrective to art's liability to misinterpretation, which had caused him such anguish in connection with his play; and it was all the more appealing since he looked beyond the upper-class public for his readership, confident that *Dead Souls* would sell "better than any other book" (XII, 49). The authorial interpolations (as opposed to narrative comment) in *Dead Souls*—confessions and admonishments, pleas for sympathy and defiant complaints—are an integral part of Gogol's design, but they remain conspicuously outside the world of the novel, like the fragments of an introduction the author feared his readers might pass over.

What gives *Dead Souls* its amplitude is the central theme of Russia and Russianness. It supplied a rationale for the most puzzling of Gogol's earlier tendencies as a writer: the repeated emphasis on absence and displacement, on things being not where and what they should. Identifying his book as a poetic statement about Russia ensured that every oddity, every irrelevance, every absurdity in this comedy of attribution could lend its weight to the painful because concrete sense of a symbolic absence. Moreover, as an entity at once polished and open-ended, *Dead Souls* brought together in literary form the flux of impulse, habit, and material things that constituted the raw material of a national self-consciousness constantly evoked by the narrative. Fixing that flux between the covers of a book, Gogol made it an object of contemplation.

His more-than-Cervantine intention plainly had *nueva vida* as its goal. Through a process we might today call consciousness-raising, the individual reader would be moved to new life in the moral sense; and readers in their collectivity would be moved to a new consciousness of community, which might replace in real life the social void depicted in the book. Though characteristically extreme, such intentions are not without their logic; in any case they signal what will inform all of Gogol's writing from this point on—an explicit concern with the effect of his works in and on society. Now writing about as well as for his reader, Gogol seeks a more direct relationship with him. "I know in advance," he wrote in mid-1842, "what will be printed about me in this journal and that, but the opinions of people who are deeply practical, who know life, who have much experience and much intelligence, who have turned all these things to advantage, are more precious to me than bookish theories that I already know by heart" (XII, 82). It was not only a matter of theories. The furor around *Dead Souls*, praise and condemnation alike, dismayed him. Annenkov reports that he was "horrified at the success of his novel among Westernizers."[45] He was hardly less uncomfortable at the way his friends, whether liberals or Slavophiles, fought over him, invoking Gogols of their own imagining (XII, 437). In the mid-thirties he had courted a public and suffered from a paucity of critical accounts that grasped the novelty of his efforts. A scant decade later he found himself the object of readers too impatient and critics too sympathetic for comfort. Unable to clarify the situation with the next installment of his fiction, he turned directly to his readers with a solicitation and an offering, each as astonishing as it was quixotic.

The solicitation came in the form of a preface to the second printing of *Dead Souls* (published after the original edition of 2,400 had sold out, in 1846). Entitled "To the Reader from the Writer [*sochinitel'*]," it opens: "Whoever you [*ty*] may be, my reader; in whatever place you stand; in whatever calling you may find yourself; whether you are distinguished by high rank or are a man of the simple class; if God has given you the understanding of reading and writing and my book has found its way into your hands, I ask you to help me." Help is necessary because "in this book many things are described falsely [*neverno*], not as they are and as they really happen in the land of Russia, because I could not find out about everything.... Moreover, through my own waywardness, immaturity, and haste[!], there arose all sorts of mistakes and slips, so that there is something to correct on every page: I ask you, reader, to correct me." (VI, 587.)

The partnership here envisaged even extends at one point to something like co-authorship (VI, 589). Fantastic as it may appear, it marks Gogol's aspiration to a new literature of "artless simplicity," which every reader might recognize as "a true mirror and not a caricature," something taken "from the very land, the very body, of which we are part" (XIII, 280, 263). That he proved powerless to produce it does not alter the fact that he anticipated and prepared the way for it. The literary aims he articulated in the forties—an evocation of reality that would at the same time be a communication from soul to soul, producing a shared awareness, purposeful and patriotic, sensible and Christian—were to be realized by the next generation, particularly by Tolstoy and Dostoevsky, who both shared his insistence that the transformation of Russia had to begin "directly with the self, and not with [any] general cause" (XIII, 107).

The bizarre and contradictory sides of his published writing in the 1840's cannot be blinked, but they should not be allowed to obscure the significant influence that writing exerted, or Gogol's startling if baffled prescience. A case in point is the offering that appeared almost simultaneously with his preface—his last book, *Selected Passages from Correspondence with Friends* (1846). "Half of literate Russia," he thought, would read it (VIII, 343), and he may not have been far off the mark. Certainly it enlarged the role of the writer in society, and by the reactions it provoked (e.g., Belinsky's famous "Open Letter to Gogol") did much to crystallize the Russian intelligentsia.* But it did more. The large share of attention it gives to literature and the literary scene shows Gogol responding to his own call of ten years before that writers take up criticism to educate a public and help fashion the still-shadowy institution of Russian literature.

With respect to the public, he advocates readings from the Russian poets and defends the theater as "a pulpit from which much good can be spoken to the world" (VIII, 268). The aim is didactic only in the most general sense, his immediate emphasis being on the power of art to lift audiences out of themselves. There is more than a hint

---

* One Petersburg reviewer in fact proclaimed the book "a literary auto-da-fé," and Belinsky's friend Botkin exulted in the prevalence of adverse reactions, seeing them as signs of a "direction in Russian literature from which even a talent stronger than Gogol's cannot deflect it; Russian literature took what it liked from Gogol, and it has now thrown him away like the shell of an egg that has been eaten." Botkin, letter to Annenkov, Feb. 28, 1847, quoted in N. Barsukov, *Zhizn' i trudy M. P. Pogodina* (St. Petersburg, 1888–1910), VIII, 579. This cynical remark typifies the passions aroused by *Selected Passages*, which found their most eloquent expression in Belinsky's "Open Letter," full of angry disillusionment with the man he had cast in the role of "one of [Russia's] great leaders on the path toward consciousness, development, and progress." Such a role, paradoxically, was not one to which Gogol had previously aspired; Belinsky argues that it was nonetheless inevitable, since "only literature, despite the Tartar censorship, shows signs of life and progressive movement" in expressing the developing forces of Russian society: "That is why the writer's calling enjoys such respect among us. . . . The public . . . sees in Russian writers its only leaders, defenders, and saviors." Belinskii, "Pis'mo k N. V. Gogoliu," in his *Estetika i literaturnaia kritika v dvukh tomakh* (Moscow, 1959), II, 633, 638. The confrontation is historically fateful. It marks the triumph of social concern, which was to dominate Russian literature for the remainder of the century, as well as the split between major writers and their most influential critics.

in all this of Tolstoy's notion of art as a contagion of feeling to which readers of all classes may be equally susceptible. Small wonder that the sage of Yasnaya Polyana, preparing his own treatise, should have found that Gogol "says, and says beautifully, what literature should be," adding that he, Tolstoy, was only "trying with all my strength to say what Gogol said wonderfully about this in *Selected Passages*."[46] The connection deserves to be noted as one vindication of Gogol's conscious effort to marshall and extend a central tradition in Russian letters.

To that effort he devotes the longest and most clear-sighted essay in the collection, "What Ultimately Is the Essence of Russian Poetry, and in What Its Peculiarity Consists." The subject had long preoccupied him; three times before he had attempted it, only to burn the results. Now he saw it as central, "essential to my book" (XIII, 110). Construing poetry as serious verbal art in general, he finds room in his historical tracing—perhaps the most perceptive and nuanced to date—for the prose of Pushkin (whose *Captain's Daughter* is "decidedly the best Russian narrative work") and Lermontov (whose prose he finds unequaled for "correctness, beauty, and fragrance"). The aim of the essay is to characterize the distinctive features of the most noteworthy Russian artists from the mid-eighteenth to the mid-nineteenth century, thus preparing an assessment of the relation of Russian literature to society. His appreciations are shrewd and far from tendentious, his conclusion—that a usable tradition exists, that the expressiveness of literary Russian has been progressively refined, but that it has not yet managed "either to teach society or to express it" (VIII, 403). Literature as an elite enterprise has "only gathered into a heap the innumerable shadings of our various qualities"; nowhere has it "fully expressed the Russian individual" in his ideality or in his actuality (VIII, 404). Yet that is what he sees as the order of the day. Clear-sightedly and nonprescriptively he notes that "neither Pushkin nor anyone else should stand as a model for us: different times have already come" (VIII, 407). And he closes with a prophetic vision of a new literature that will "call forth our Russia— our Russian Russia, not the one that some jingoists point to, and not the one pictured from across the sea by our transplanted citizens, but a Russia drawn out of our very selves and then presented to us in such a way that every last one of us, whatever our differences of upbringing and opinion, will exclaim with one voice, 'This is our Russia' . . ." (VIII, 409).

Beyond this the peculiarities of Gogol's temperament and talent would not permit him to go. *Selected Passages* as a whole shows him unable to avoid the kind of grotesquerie that had been the hallmark of his achievement as a comic writer. Where the logic is impeccable, his premises are often weird; where the premises are sound, the logic may be suspect; where both premises and logic seem reliable—as in the autobiographical "Four Letters . . . Concerning *Dead Souls*"— their strictly factual accuracy may be questioned. The tangle is virtually impossible to sort out. "Four Letters," with all its astonishing vagueness, hyperbole, and simultaneous confession and concealment, shows ominous tendencies toward solipsism. The presentation of his earlier works as a kind of exorcism or therapy, and the blurring of the boundaries between himself, his readers, and the abstract Russia that unites them, testify to a tragic confusion even while providing a fitful illumination of his art. That kind of confusion had earlier served as the matrix for an enigmatic art offered without a key. Gogol's attempt to provide the key—to achieve clarity and self-transcendence—proved that he could paralyze his creativity, but not his eccentricity of expression.*

The generally negative reaction to *Selected Passages* merely compounded that paralysis, involving Gogol in a series of increasingly tortured self-justifications in which he portrayed the book by turns as a provocation, a probe, a test of readers, an essay in self-awareness, a lesson to impatient admirers who kept trying to push him into premature publication. As part of that process he even undertook to tell at length the story of his career as a writer (published only after his death as "An Author's Confession"). That account is anything but complete: it ignores all but three of his works, together with all the complexities of his previous writing, views, and situation. In essence it is a plea for something like Arnoldian high seriousness in the new literature required by the new times—and a cry of anguish that he cannot provide it. Emphasizing alternately his own needs and those he imputed to the Russian reader,† Gogol observes near the end of

---

* Cf. Siniavsky, *V teni Gogolia* (London, 1975), p. 286: "Just at the time he becomes a caricature, the comic element deserts him." This captures the irony of Gogol's situation, but seems to put the cart before the horse.

† E.g., "It is necessary that the Russian reader really feel that the character presented to him has been taken precisely from that very body from which he himself has been created, that it is a living thing and his own body" (VIII, 453). The separateness of fictive and actual persons seems somewhat in peril here; and the beginning of the next sentence ("Then only will he himself merge with his hero") further complicates the question by suggesting the likelihood that reader, character, and writer may be one and the same in Gogol's unconscious mind.

this long document: "How it happens that I should be entering into explanations of all [this] with the reader is something I myself cannot understand" (VIII, 463). Could he have realized when he decided not to publish the piece that he was by now talking only to himself?

So Gogol ends with a dramatic demonstration that "the writer's audience is always a fiction" (though one, as Mandelstam pointed out shrewdly,[47] whose existence no writer can doubt without doubting his own). Gogol's impasse, his sense of unreadiness and inadequacy, grew in tandem with the specificity of his designs on the reader and hence on himself as writer. Practical intention thus closed off to him the truth of Pasternak's observation that "writers who understand clearly what they are doing must produce very little and very badly."[48] This situation needs to be explained in terms broader than those of personal psychology: it would not be hard to show how Gogol's public encouraged him to feel thrust into a role of cultural leadership he could neither refuse nor fulfill.

These remarks, however, may suffice to indicate the potential scope and pertinence of my title. Gogol's case, I think, leaves little doubt about the productiveness of the reader as a literary-historical tool and as a concept in immanent criticism. But Gogol's case is a special one, and despite Norman Holland's recent dictum that "from a medieval *why* to the *how* that underlay the three great centuries of classical science, we proceed [inevitably] to a psychoanalytic *to whom*,"[49] the broader applicability of reader theory remains an open question.

In its absolute form that question might be phrased as follows: Does the concept of the reader (psychoanalytic or not) have any unique and inevitable usefulness in the criticism of particular works? To this the answer must be that there has not yet been enough refining or testing of theory to permit serious debate. My own suspicion is that in considering literature as art, the reader as tool more often than not may resemble those absorbable surgical sutures that lose their identity as they do their job; i.e., that in many cases the concept is resolvable into more conventional categories, so that its utility, though real, is less than unique. When traditional criticism speaks of tone, pathos, absurdity, laughter, the grotesque, structure, or meaning, it always has in view (albeit implicitly) "the actualization of a text in the reader," and it is not clear how much is to be gained by dwelling explicitly on that fact.

The question Gogol's example prompts is rather a relative one:

Under what circumstances does approach via the reader promise special advantages for understanding a writer's career or works? Here the answer would appear to be, when that writer challenges existing conventions—openly, radically, and successfully, thus setting tradition on a new course. One way or another, the study of "the reader" is the study of necessary assumptions about the literary function, on a whole series of levels from the broadly social to the concretely textual. Conventions are the ratification of particular assumptions; they represent agreement on the code. In this connection Gogol is exemplary precisely because he is eccentric. The precocious modernity of much of his writing rests on a kind of displacement that was to become common only in the twentieth century. His works, like any major writer's, provide significant experience, but in a new way. Baffling empathy, minimizing "content" while maximizing the emphasis on form, Gogol withholds significance so largely from the experience *in* his best works only to require that it be sought and found in the experience *of* those works—which is to say, by the reader, on the level of his engagement with the text.

JEFFREY BROOKS

Readers and Reading at the End of the Tsarist Era

What image better conveys literature's entanglement in society than the book in the hands of the reader? The act of reading is a social act. The manuscript becomes a book and the book reaches the reader through a social process. Actual readers, reading a book or spurning it, compose the essential environment for the existence of literature. These readers may loom large or small in the writer's eye, but an awareness of the ongoing activity of reading can hardly fail to infiltrate his world. Readers draw literature into life and life into literature, and their attitudes toward books and writers, their ways of reading, form a changeable latticework of meaning and expectation around the printed word. The critic can find in this clues to literary manners, and the social historian can look to readers and their varying preferences for indications of cultural harmony or discord. These literary signs of cohesion or stress are particularly significant at the crucial point in Western historical development when mass literacy first became commonplace. At that juncture the written word dominated the articulation of social values, and the development of dis-

The author wishes to thank the International Research and Exchanges Board and the Russian and East European Center of the University of Illinois for their support and assistance. I am also grateful to the following people for their helpful comments: Terence Emmons, Alexander Vucinich, William Todd, Tom Garst, Bruce Lincoln, Charlotte Rosenthal, Diane Koenker, Norman Naimark, David Longley, James Nelson, Anna Kalnins, and Eric Kollman.

tinct literary audiences, distinguished by different reading experiences and attitudes, delineated the cultural contours of the emergent social divisions of the industrializing societies.

The breakthrough to mass literacy in Russia in the late nineteenth and early twentieth centuries produced various groupings of readers or publics separated along the lines of the main social divisions in tsarist society. Industrialization and concomitant social changes destroyed the image of a small, homogeneous reading public in the wilderness of illiterate peasant Russia, an image that had fascinated many nineteenth-century writers. Lermontov complained about his audience in the preface to A Hero of Our Time at the end of the 1830's, but it was all the same "our public." Pisarev divided readers into younger and older generations at the end of the 1860's, but they were all expected to read the same books. At the end of the 1880's Saltykov-Shchedrin bemoaned the paucity of serious readers—the "reader-friends" who valued writers with convictions—and derided the "reading masses" for their infatuation with the amusements of the "petty press"; but even this lower order of reader was not entirely excluded from the potential public for belles lettres.[1] In the last decades of the tsarist era, the effective audience for the printed word expanded at an astounding pace, and several rival publics solidified, each with its own particular reading habits and its own rather exclusive, well-defined tastes. Bridges linked these publics (most importantly the classics), but their separateness as literary subcultures was quite apparent. A reordering of values among educated Russians gave the traditional public for belles lettres new perspectives and an altered sense of community. At the same time, within this educated audience appeared a small but significant reading constituency wedded to the exclusive and exotic literature of Russian modernism. These changes paralleled the dramatic emergence of a mass reading audience in the countryside and in the cities, and for this audience developed a variegated literature that roughly articulated its hopes and fears.

During the half century following the emancipation of the serfs, the classic simplicity of the Russian social structure shattered. The image of two Russias, the Russia of the educated and the Russia of the illiterate masses, lost its verisimilitude, but the resultant cultural stratification left Russia no less divided. The reading public of what is generally considered the belles lettres of the Silver Age retained the insularity of its nineteenth-century predecessor amid the flood of new readers in city and countryside.

I

If formal schooling is the indicator, the potential educated audience at the turn of the century was a relatively small one. In 1897 there were over one million people in the Russian Empire who had attended, though not necessarily graduated from, a secondary or higher educational institution.[2] Together they constituted slightly more than 1 percent of the total population of the empire and over 5 percent of all the literate. Some 90 percent of them did not go beyond middle school. The entire group was more than half male and was concentrated in European Russia. It was also overwhelmingly urban; in fact, over 16 percent of the total lived in the two capitals. By legal class category the group consisted largely of gentry and members of the so-called urban classes. Approximately 15 percent were from the clergy, and less than 8 percent from the peasantry and other rural groups.

The attitudes of Russians with postprimary education toward books and literature were shaped by their occupational experience. They were chiefly neither gentry farmers nor a Western European bourgeoisie, but rather, as a result of Russia's particular historical development, a curious middle stratum of specialists and administrators, many of whom worked for central and local government authorities. Of the over 700,000 administrators and specialists counted in the 1897 census, only 200,000 worked in private enterprise and agriculture, and nearly 370,000 served in such governmental or non-commercial sectors as health, education, cultural activities, and communications.[3]

Conditions of life in late-nineteenth-century Russia and the experience of this middle stratum tended to reinforce attitudes toward books and literature already ingrained in Russia's cultural tradition. For the first Orthodox Russian readers, who knew no literature except their own religious texts, books were holy sources of inspiration and salvation, as Nestor admonished his readers in his Chronicle. Eighteenth-century enlighteners like Novikov and Radishchev made books a means to moral and spiritual improvement, and the great nineteenth-century Russian writers demonstrated a similar belief in the innate ethical power of the written word. The gradual development of a historical approach to Russian literature in the 1820's and 1830's, and of a publicist type of literary criticism in the periodicals of the 1830's and 1840's, eventually brought a conscious critical perspective to the didactic cultural tradition; literature was perceived not only as a moral force but as an integral part of society and the progressive historical process.[4] Vissarion Belinsky was the most passionate and effective exponent of this viewpoint.[5] In the course of the great age of nineteenth-century Russian literature, he and Chernyshevsky, Dobroliubov, Pisarev, and a host of lesser critics hammered the sensibilities of educated readers with their own versions of this basic message, which complemented the didacticism of the writers themselves. Censorship encouraged the covert use of belles lettres and literary criticism for the presentation of political and social issues, and reinforced such an attitude toward literature.

It was logical for the growing numbers of educated Russians working in such areas as health, education, and local administration to feel comfortable with this critical perspective and way of reading. The very nature of their work and experience promoted it. As they struggled with the conditions of Russian backwardness, as their attempts to improve life in the cities and the countryside or merely to live what they considered a civilized life collided with policies of the autocracy, they sought inspiration and encouragement in literature, as had generations of educated Russians before them. Not unlike Belinsky, they came to see literature as an integral part of society, and again their experience led them in this direction. The avenues of political action were blocked in the 1880's and 1890's to all but the most daring, so the rank-and-file specialists and administrators began to infuse their local efforts to improve material and cultural conditions, their "small deeds," with political and social promise. They called these activities "cultural work," and believed that action in such areas as health, education, law, and agriculture could transform Russian society. Working in apparently interrelated fields like these, they assumed the interdependence of all facets of national life. They understood culture, or kul'tura, to be the way of life of the whole people in all its "economic, social, state, intellectual, religious, and aesthetic aspects," as the liberal leader P. N. Miliukov put it in his popular Essays on the History of Russian Culture, published for the first time in the 1890's.[6]

Literature from this standpoint was a product of the existing society and was expected to reflect conditions in that society. But reflection was not enough; culture, and with it literature, was to serve the transformation of society. This concept of culture found its narrowest expression in the critical demands of the radical Westernizers. More broadly, however, the stress on the fundamental importance of spiritual culture in forming the life of society and the individual was shared by intellectuals of widely differing positions, including writers like Gogol and Dostoevsky, who had little in common with the revolutionary democrats. It was embodied in the late-nineteenth-century Russian intellectuals' understanding of their own "intelligentsia culture." This term had different meanings: to liberals like Miliukov it was Europeanization; for populists like N. K. Mikhailovsky, a link between the intelligentsia and the masses; for Marxists, the path to working-class consciousness. But in each case it was more than that. For leading intellectuals, their sympathizers, and the ordinary rank-and-file specialists, "intelligentsia culture" was a way of identifying themselves, just as it had been for Novikov a hundred years before. Their "culture" set them apart from the autocratic regime and the cruelties of Russian society. Insofar as it isolated them from their milieu, it was at the root of their maladjustment; but it was also a source of hope, and they developed a particular sense of cultural mission. Against a background of lagging social progress, this middle group of intelligentsia could not help, in the words of Iulii Martov, "feeling and recognizing itself to be the bearer of that cultural progress which broke the foundations of serfdom and led Russia into the family of civilized nations."[7] Under conditions of strict censorship, the vehicle for cultural self-consciousness was quite naturally belles lettres. As they came to expect literature to perform such a central social function, these *intelligenty*, like Saltykov's "reader-friend" sought writers with convictions.

The literary sensibility or taste of the late-nineteenth-century intelligentsia reader, then, was tied both to the didacticism of the cultural tradition and to the social experience exemplified by the "cultural workers." Since this sensibility depended on an intense consciousness of belonging to a particular culture, that of educated Russians, we may call it "culturist."[*] Perceived from this viewpoint a literary work was expected to evidence inherent moral value and

[*] The terms *Kulturträger* and *kul'turnik* both seem too narrow and value-laden to be fully descriptive. My use of the terms "culturist" and "culturism" is similar to, but in some important respects different from, the "culturism" of Edwin O. Reischauer and John K. Fairbank in *East Asia: The Great Tradition* (Boston, 1960). They explain: "By it [culturism] we mean to suggest that in the Chinese view the significant unit was really the whole civilization rather than the narrower political unit of a nation within a larger cultural whole" (p. 293). Joseph R. Levenson makes a similar distinction in *Confucian China and Its Modern Fate: A Trilogy* (Berkeley, Calif., 1968), I, 100–104. In late-nineteenth-century Russia the concept of the nation, though very much alive, was associated in the minds of the *intelligenty* with a retrograde political order counterposed to their own ideals. Whereas Chinese culturism upheld the estab-

social verisimilitude. Such an attitude was a dominant feature of the Russian literary scene at the end of the nineteenth century. It suffused the pages of the so-called "thick magazines," those ideologically inspired monthlies that cultivated the sympathetic understanding of a similarly minded audience, frequently in a comradely or didactic tone. These magazines, as one liberal remembered, "filled youth with an idealism that lasted a lifetime." In *Russkoe bogatstvo* (Russian Riches) populists like N. K. Mikhailovsky and V. P. Vorontsov ("V.V.") hailed literature as the "alarm clock" of moral and political thought, one of the "most powerful weapons of struggle."[8] The populist striving in literature for Vorontsov demanded "a scientific investigation of the popular tradition," "real content," "deep social questioning and national faith."[9] Liberals, critical of the agrarian ideals of the populists, expressed their own culturist conception of literature as a facet of national self-consciousness and a means of Europeanization. A. Pypin explained in *Vestnik Evropy* (The Herald of Europe) that literature carries the social particularity and the ideals of the nation, and in this sense "social art" is natural and proper and need not be tendentious.[10]

The thick magazines reached only a limited audience in the 1880's and 1890's; the circulation of even the most successful did not exceed 15,000. Nevertheless, the potential audience was rapidly expanding, as was demonstrated at the beginning of the century by the flashy though brief success of V. S. Miroliubov's *Zhurnal dlia vsekh* (The Magazine for Everyone), which reached a circulation of 80,000 in 1903.[11] The journal's popularity was due largely to pieces by young quasi realist writers like Maxim Gorky and Leonid Andreev, who did turn a searchlight on the depths of Russian life.

The most effective literary messengers in the provinces and among the less conscious readers were the "thin" magazines, illustrated weeklies, dispersed among a passive but educated audience that expected to be entertained and instructed from a distance in popular science, history, current events, and literature and the arts. The classic example of this kind of magazine is A. F. Marks's *Niva* (The Cornfield), which was founded in 1870 as a "family magazine" with

---

lished order, Russian culturism condemned it. For many educated Russians national identity became secondary to a cultural identity based on intelligentsia values and growing out of the experience of cultural contact between Russia and the West. Feelings of cultural superiority and of alienation from their native milieu made Russian *intelligenty* conscious of the particular role they had to play vis-à-vis the masses. In this paper culturism refers to this combined sense of values and mission.

no "fighting" position and no political purpose except the propagation of "pure, healthy family principles."[12] In the course of the 1890's,
Marks's originally modest vision of a family circle gathered at home
to read his magazine gradually gave way to a more ambitious vision
of *Niva* as a cultural force bringing the best works of literature and
art to the widest possible audience. In 1891 subscribers began to receive a monthly supplement containing works of Russian literature
past and present. The regular critic in this supplement, R. I. Sement-
kovsky, told readers in his column "What's New in Literature?" that
contemporary belles lettres "acquaints readers with life and with
those questions that demand resolution."[13] Practicing what he
preached, he answered such questions as "Do we have happy marriages?" by looking at current fiction.[14] Such an attitude led readers
to expect to find current issues in current literature and timeless ones
in the classics. The tremendous success of the magazine, which
reached a circulation of 200,000 in 1900, was due in part to the literary supplement and to a subscription policy that offered as a bonus
the collected works of various Russian and foreign authors.[15]

Not only were culturist attitudes expressed in the press, but they
were voiced more informally. In 1895 an odd compendium of comments on books appeared under the title *Opinions of Russian People
about the Best Books for Reading*. It was a grab bag of clichés, saws,
advice, warnings, and lists of books solicited from educated people
by the editor and publisher, M. M. Lederle.* Here, amid amusing
admonishments that Dostoevsky is not for nervous people, that Tolstoy's suspicion of individualism could lead straight to "nihilism" and
"deep unhappiness," that folktales could deprive children of their
sense of reality, and that stories and novels with a "strong emphasis
on relations between the sexes" should be avoided at all costs, there
was evidenced a deep and abiding concern for the effect of literature on people.[16] A pedagogue applauds reading as one of the great
"linchpins of self-education and self-upbringing" (p. 3). "At seven-
teen I found a novel that opened up a whole new world before me,"
writes another respondent (p. 42). A professor lists among the books
that produced a good childhood impression *Stories from Ancient
Mythology, Stories from Russian History*, and *The Life and Habits
of Spiders* (p. 43). The painter V. P. Vereshchagin remembers Chis-

---

* Lederle sent out 2,000 circulars in 1891 to academicians and correspondents of the Academy of Science, university professors, scholars, literati, artists,
pedagogues, and public figures; the book is based on the 86 replies he received.
See reviews in *Vestnik Evropy*, Oct. 1895, p. 831, and *Obrazovanie*, Sept. 1895,
p. 100.

tiakov's *Tales of the Tartar Oppression*, and the historian M. I. Semevsky, the first editor of the journal *Russkaia starina* (Russian Antiquities), mentions Walter Scott (pp. 46, 40). The critic A. M. Skabichevsky recommends folktales for children "for their truly healthy moral content," which left him with a faith that "good triumphs" (pp. 103–4, 59). A. F. Koni, the jurist, recalls how Turgenev and Nekrasov inspired his generation with "love, pity, and closeness" to the people, but also owns a fascination with Poe (pp. 72–74). Others, among them the populist writer Ertel, recommend religious texts for the development of an ethical sense (pp. 98–99).

The respondents almost without exception testify to the effect of books on their lives. Books were important intellectually, morally, and spiritually. They were to be taken seriously and sometimes treated with caution. Most would have agreed with the editor's conclusion that contemporary literature had a great effect on the "formation" of the spirit and the personality, and might have joined him in encouraging critics to help the reader discover the moral and social value of literary works (p. 123). Lederle gathered comments not from progressive intellectuals alone; priests and conservative professors were represented as well, and almost all of them shared this traditional way of looking at literature.

A perusal of the lists of books sent Lederle offers an insight into the reading habits of educated Russians at the end of the nineteenth century. Though the majority of respondents came from educated families, they give no evidence of a standard corpus of books for young readers. "I began to read very early," wrote one regretful respondent, "and as in the case of most people, no one paid much attention to my reading and I probably read much trash" (p. 19). In their early years children read whatever "falls into their hands," wrote Skabichevsky (pp. 19–20). A pedagogue reported reading books from a local officers' library, first the historical stories of Zagoskin, then Pushkin, Lermontov, Scott, and Cooper (pp. 24–25). On another list we find fairy tales of all countries and peoples, as well as *Robinson Crusoe* and *Captain Cook* (pp. 30–31). Still another includes Scott, Dumas, Sue, Paul de Kock, Bulgarin, *A Thousand and One Nights*, Polevoi's *History of Napoleon*, and *The Moscow Oracle with the Predictions of Bruce*, one of the oldest fortune-telling books (pp. 19–20). These comments are a good reminder that, even in the midst of such concern for the influence of literature, the concept of a classical heritage of Russian literature had not yet solidly formed in the 1890's. After all, many who then reached maturity were nearly contemporaries of the great nineteenth-century authors. For them, as well as for the generation that followed, the establishment of a pantheon of classical Russian writers demanded a certain distance, a hiatus in this tradition, which was only to occur with the advent of Russian modernism.

II

The last decade of the nineteenth century was a transitional period in Russian literature and for the educated reader. The classical period was over, though few realized it. In the late 1880's and early 1890's, the most popular authors in libraries (mostly closed to the lower classes) were Lev Tolstoy, Goncharov, and, curiously enough, Sheller-Mikhailov. Turgenev and Dostoevsky were not far behind.[17] In the late 1890's V. I. Nemirovich-Danchenko, the author of travel adventure stories and the brother of the famous director, was very popular, as was the young Maxim Gorky.[18] The size of editions of books priced over 30 kopecks, that is, those not intended for a lower class audience, generally supports this picture of the educated reader's preference for a combination of light fiction and the classics.* The most published authors in 1898 were Pushkin, with over 50,000 copies priced over 30 kopecks, and Tolstoy, with 40,000. Both Nemirovich-Danchenko and the Siberian scene painter Mamin-Sibiriak also did quite well, with over 20,000 copies each.[19] None of these writers clashed dramatically with the literary sensibilities of the educated reader; they all could be understood and appreciated.

The most serious challenge to the established sensibilities of the educated reader at the turn of the century came from the modernist movement. Early in the 1890's modernist critics like A. Volynsky (A. L. Flekser), N. Minsky (N. M. Vilenkin), and Dmitry Merezhkovsky began to attack traditional utilitarian attitudes toward literature. Merezhkovsky struck hardest in his long essay *The Reasons for the Decline of Russian Literature and the New Trends*. Why were there no successors to the great nineteenth-century writers, he asked. His answer was that educated Russians and literary critics were indifferent to the eternal questions of art and denied the independent value of art and beauty. From this standpoint the culturist readers and critics were the gravediggers of Russian literature. The reaction of established intellectuals was one of anger and outrage.[20]

The argument between the intellectuals of the old school and the

---

* Books intended for a mass lower class audience can be identified by publisher, number of printer's sheets, and appearance as well as by price.

modernist writers continued well into the twentieth century. It was a crucial one. The educated reading public of the 1890's delighted in Russian classical literature as a literature of high morality, eternal questions, and heightened consciousness that explored society at all levels. Life could be seen in the works of Turgenev, Chekhov, and Saltykov-Shchedrin, and their social influence could be considered beneficial. This was patently not true of modernism. The initial clarion call of the new movement was its amoralism ("I love myself like God," Gippius), aestheticism ("A Sonnet to Form," Briusov), and personalism. For the modernists to win general acceptance among educated Russians, a new type of reader had to appear, a reader less concerned with morality and mimesis than with the personal aesthetic enjoyment of a literary work. The kind of reading public the new literature demanded, and eventually succeeded in getting, resembled the one that developed in all the major industrialized Western societies, a depoliticized public concerned with personal appreciation and personal questions, a public with a very different attitude toward literature and culture than that of the culturist intellectuals of nineteenth-century Russia.

There is perhaps no better way to demonstrate the gradual emergence of this new public and the increasing uncertainty among the old-style intellectuals than to glance at some of the literary criticism appearing after 1905 in the influential Cadet Party paper *Rech'* (Speech). In the first years after the Revolution of 1905, the liberal Cadet Party won widespread support from the new middle stratum of technocrats and specialists. Among its leaders were Russia's foremost intellectuals. As the revolutionary wave receded and the possibility of a radical transformation of Russian society became more remote, these liberal Cadet intellectuals began to place their hopes on traditional cultural progress. They believed that even though the revolution had been temporarily defeated, Russia had entered an era of democratic reform and peaceful progress. They naturally expected literature to reflect the true conditions of Russian society by expressing the democratic ideals and the optimism of the new era, and to popularize these ideals among readers. They did, however, wish to avoid what they considered the dogmatic and rude subjection of literature to political purpose they saw on the left, especially in Lenin's recently published polemic "Party Organization and Party Literature."[21]

Though the liberals affirmed in theory the writer's right to be apolitical, when they looked at literature a narrow version of the culturist view predominated, and critics set out to investigate "how the events of life are reflected in current literature."[22] Their attempts to do this proved problematic. In the decade and a half since its inception, Russian modernism had burgeoned into the dominant literary movement. A second generation of poets, novelists, and dramatists had joined the original founders to create a new type of literature. The movement lost much of its antisocial militancy and amoralism after 1905, but it remained at odds with traditional literary conventions and expectations and continued to affront the sensibilities of educated readers. Aleksandr Blok wrote poems to a "beautiful lady" who could by no stretch of the imagination be confused with suffering peasant Russia. K. D. Bal'mont glorified and romanticized the most transitory impressions, and F. Sologub, in his great novel *The Petty Demon,* constructed a monument to the madness and despair of a provincial schoolteacher's life, the very sort of life the culturist intellectuals tended to idealize. In fact, so completely did this new literature dominate the literary imagination of the era that even politically conscious quasi realist writers like Gorky and Andreev were drawn into its orbit. As a result, readers who hankered for a bit of traditional prose were often at a loss to find it, as the critics who spoke for them complained.

During 1907 regular columnists in *Rech'* interspersed political comment with haphazard literary criticism, lambasting contemporary writers for offering "a real philosophy of nonbeing" (aimed at Andreev), for drawing not people but "corpses" (Andreev, Sologub, Gippius, Merezhkovsky), and for performing empty technical feats devoid of "passion" (Blok).[23] At the end of 1907 one of the Cadet leaders, Tyrkova-Williams, sighed with relief at finally discovering a conventional story about a horse by Kuprin: "What a healthy, spontaneous breath of life permeates these little pages."[24] What readers demanded, according to Kornei Chukovsky, the paper's only professional literary critic, was "sincerity, sacrifice, and prayers"—in short, an uplifting message from a writer with strong and obvious convictions.[25]

This attack on the modernists abated in 1908 as liberals changed their minds about the nature of the times and began to discover traditional merits in modernist writing. The effective silencing of the Duma and the continuing repression in the countryside, orchestrated by the strong man of the autocracy, P. A. Stolypin, convinced many that they had been overly optimistic. Suddenly, distraught liberals found it possible to sympathize with the gloomy themes of modernist literature, which now seemed an only too appropriate reflection of society. As one Cadet leader (Gredeskul) put it, the psychology of contemporary Russian society was "the psychology of despair."[26] During 1908 *Rech'* signaled the modernists' new respectability by publishing articles, poems, and short stories by such authors as Blok, Sologub, Gumilev, Gippius, and Merezhkovsky. The writer Aleksandr Amfiteatrov even lauded Valery Briusov as a "genuine figure of literature" despite his "cynical reconciliation with Tsarist forces, his isolation from social questions, and his curiosity only for books."[27] The poet Aleksandr Blok suggested in an interesting essay about the Austrian playwright Franz Grillparzer that political reaction engenders a particular literature, and, by implication, that the gloomy themes of Russian modernism were appropriate to contemporary political conditions.[28]

The literary attitudes that seemed so deeply implanted in the educated reading public in 1907 slowly altered. Briusov could still complain in his notebook in the winter of 1908–9 about the hostile attitude toward the "decadents," the attacks on them in the press, and the fact that "all the newspapers are closed to me," but the situation was changing.[29] There was much evidence of a new atmosphere in the remaining years before World War I. The appearance of modernist works in liberal newspapers, magazines, and miscellanies signified a softening of the cultural attitudes of many educated Russians, as well as changes in the modernist movement itself, which turned toward more social themes after the Revolution of 1905. In *Rech'* occasional appeals for an old-style culturist response to the successful tsarist reaction did not interfere with the growing acceptance of the new literature. In a sense, the ideal of cultural progress through "small deeds" was a casualty of the revolution. Both countryside and city were politicized, and ideological and class barriers appeared between intellectuals, specialists, and technocrats of the middle strata, on one side, and peasants and workers and their political supporters, on the other. Among liberals the emphasis shifted away from the old stress on literature as the packhorse for social ideals and moral values, and there began to emerge a more general expectation that all creativity would ultimately contribute to the long-term progress of Russian society.[30]

One seemingly paradoxical sign of this changing perspective was the appearance of the often-misunderstood *Vekhi* (Landmarks) symposium in 1909 and the burst of polemics that surrounded it. This somewhat confused attempt by intellectuals with widely differing convictions and purposes to turn the attention of educated Russians away from political and social questions and toward "eternal" cultural ones provoked a passionate restatement of traditional culturist ideas in the liberal and progressive press.[31] Yet among liberal politicians and journalists, for all the familiar rhetoric about the social responsibility of educated society, there was a new sense that cultural progress could be very complicated, and that even the apparently apolitical artistic creativity of the modernists could in its own way contribute, in the words of the Cadet leader and historian A. A. Kizevetter, to "the continuing Europeanization of all sides of our culture."[32]

Critics can cue a literary audience and signal how a book should be read, and if a new reader was emerging in the early twentieth century, one would expect new critical signals. There was evidence of this in the work of a generation of modernist critics who either entirely disregarded the traditional culturist concern with literature as a social indicator or radically revised it. Whether plumbing the psychological depths of Dostoevsky or investigating the metaphysical implications of Tolstoy, critics such as Viach. Ivanov, Lev Shestov, V. V. Rozanov, Merezhkovsky, and Iu. Aikhenval'd tended to present literature as a path to personal or cosmic rather than social understanding. The broadest forum for such writers, aside from occasional opportunities in the daily press, was the thick magazine *Russkaia mysl'* (Russian Thought), edited by P. B. Struve and Briusov. In 1910, according to Briusov, the magazine had "the sad reputation of a dull journal." The function of the criticism appearing there, as he put it, was not to follow the readers "but to lead them."[33]

From the standpoint of restructuring reader attitudes, the most interesting of the new critics, and also the most popular, was Iu. Aikhenval'd, who often published in *Russkaia mysl'*. A self-proclaimed renegade from the Belinsky tradition of social theorizing and an admirer of Apollon Grigor'ev and Oscar Wilde, Aikhenval'd presented his own impressionistic interpretations of individual works for the stated purpose of enriching the ordinary readers' experience. He was usually preoccupied not with the social impact of literature but with the "internal drama of writer and reader."[34] Commenting on Sologub's *Petty Demon*, he stressed the slaughter of the unpleasant antihero Peredonov "within ourselves"; on Ibsen's *Brand*, the question Ibsen is asking "us"; on Sergei Aksakov's *Family Chronicle*, "the pure and bright vestiges" of life in Orenburg province to which "every Russian reader" is linked.[35]

Aikhenval'd's imagined reader, so often apostrophized in his articles, was the heir to all of art's treasures. In reply to Pushkin's bittersweet farewell to his readers at the end of *Onegin*, Aikhenval'd wrote in a cloying monologue, "Your verses are really preserved in my memory and my heart, as you wished."[36] He felt that the "reader-descendant" of Pushkin's original reader could learn from Pushkin's life and from the beauty of his poetry "to accept the world and oneself."[37] This conception of the purely personal, aesthetic, and emotional satisfaction great literature could bring its audience was a long step away from traditional views. Here culture was no longer the many-faceted conjunction of social and intellectual life, but instead the "deepening of the internal world" of the individual, a psychic flowering that manifested art's superiority to nature (à la Wilde) in "emotion for the sake of emotion."[38] Aikhenval'd's break with the culturist tradition was far from complete, and he could on occasion sound the old chords; but doing so was not his primary concern. He could praise the moral tenacity of Korolenko or Gleb Uspensky, but he felt more comfortable with Sergei Aksakov. The "dull face of reality" was always an intrusion.[39] His message to readers was usually unambiguous: seek aesthetic satisfaction and emotional fulfillment. In a time of social strife it had special appeal to educated Russians already turning from the perils of social commitment to the calmer realm of personal and vocational achievement.

The two most popular older, more conventional critics of the early twentieth century were S. A. Vengerov and D. M. Ovsianiko-Kulikovsky, who also signaled changes in reader attitudes. For Vengerov Russian literature in its great age was a "heroic symphony," a forceful, particularly Russian instrument for the expression of the social and moral strivings of the intelligentsia. In this context Gogol became the "citizen-writer" and Belinsky "the great heart."[40] The task of the literary critic-historian was simply to write the intellectual history of Russia with special attention to the interaction of literature and society. Such a critic led his reader away from aestheticism toward a concentration on content and the writer's message. In like fashion Ovsianiko-Kulikovsky wished to help the reader discover literature's didactic content, but for him the meaning of Russian literature was to be found in the compelling psychological types, such as Onegin and Tatiana, who embodied the moral and social dilemmas of an era. The critic's function was to illuminate these characters so that the reader could comprehend the historical experience of the intelligentsia.

Critics like Vengerov and Ovsianiko-Kulikovsky and readers schooled in their social-historical criticism were likely to have difficulty with Russian modernism. Ovsianiko-Kulikovsky posed the problem succinctly in an article in *Rech'* in 1910 when he complained that, though Russian literature from the time of Pushkin had reflected the changes in the consciousness of the intelligentsia, "the thinking part of society," the new literature of writers like Kuprin, Andreev, Sologub, and Artsybashev had no such focus.[41] Later in the same year he offered a hypothesis to account for the way in which modernism had supplanted traditional Russian literature. In backward countries, where "spiritual culture" was new and unusual, he suggested, a utilitarian or ideological attitude toward culture predominated; in nineteenth-century Russia this had culminated in various strands of populism.[42] However, the ideological creativity that had been the main moving force of nineteenth-century Russian "intellectual and moral progress" was being replaced by a broader, less ideological attitude toward culture in which "spiritual goods" were valued for their own sake. Though Ovsianiko-Kulikovsky remained committed to a social understanding of literature and to a realistic style of writing that could reach the masses, he had come to terms with a literature that was not a traditional "mirror of life," and accepted the legitimacy of modernism.

S. A. Vengerov's modus vivendi with modernism was paradoxical and incomplete. The fruit of it was a great critical monument to the new movement, the three-volume *Russian Literature of the Twentieth Century*, which he edited, but readers who looked to his introductory essays for guidance on how to read the modernists were likely to be disappointed. Vengerov reiterated his belief that Russian literature was didactic and ought to be so. The proof of this, he argued, was in the readers. "For the Russian reader," he wrote, "literature has always been a holy thing; contact with it makes him purer and better, and he always relates to it with a feeling of real religiosity."[43] Therefore the reader could be moved only by a writer who had something in his soul with which he longed "to infect others."[44] How then could Russian modernism, which Vengerov himself felt to be separated from the classics and even from Chekhov by an enormous moral gulf, be offered to Russian readers?[45] In attempting to answer this question, Vengerov noted that the old "god of suffering and self-sacrifice" had not deserted Russian literature completely, since after 1905 the modernists had turned more to the social themes of their traditional precursors.[46] Beyond that he simply accepted modernism as a fait accompli. In 1910 he concluded: "You can have whatever attitude you want toward Bal'mont, Briusov, Blok, and the newest 'myth-creators,' but anyone who wishes to consider the real facts ought to recognize that the new poetry prevails."[47] In his introduction to *Russian Literature of the Twentieth Century*, he pointed out parallel literary developments in Europe. Though Vengerov never felt entirely comfortable with the new movement, his work was a long step in the direction of acceptance, not only for himself, but for many readers as well.

The growing critical acceptance of modernist writings and the publication of such works in liberal magazines and newspapers indicated the emergence of a significant group of readers who no longer judged literature primarily by culturist standards. This modernist audience was only a small portion of the educated public as a whole, however, judging by the size of book editions. Briusov's early works came out in editions of 500 copies. In 1907 and 1908 his collected verses were published in an edition of 2,000, as were his collected works in 1913. Sologub and Remizov also averaged editions of about 2,000. Biely was published in somewhat smaller editions, as were poets such as Blok and Bal'mont. Even the flamboyant Mayakovsky and the clownish Severianin did not do much better. The most widely published modernists were Gippius and Merezhkovsky, both of whom had already won reputations through their polemical writings in the liberal press. Merezhkovsky's historical novels reached editions of 10,000. Modernist miscellanies occasionally reached a much wider audience. *The Wild Rose* almanac, in which Leonid Andreev often published, had an edition of over 26,000 copies in 1908. The symbolist collection *Siren*, to which Biely, Sologub, Blok, and Remizov contributed, was published in 1913 in over 8,000 copies. In 1908 the miscellany *Life* appeared in an edition of 12,000, with works by Artsybashev, Briusov, Sologub, Kuprin, and Blok.

Briusov, in a letter to Struve in 1910, complained of the "banal reader," the "stupid reader," the "big public," the "reading ladies," all of whom found the magazine *Russkaia mysl'* too dull and wanted only works that were "loud, blatant, sharp."[48] Yet in his farewell to the readers of his first magazine *Vesy*, he concluded that the modernists had succeeded in winning their audience.[49] In the preface to his marvelous novel *The Flaming Angel*, published in the first issue of the same magazine in 1907, he had addressed his expected reader in Latin as the "reader-friend" (*amico lectori*), the gracious reader to whom he could open his heart.[50]

The modernists came from traditional positivist backgrounds, as Andrei Biely pointed out so clearly in his memoirs many years later. They considered themselves "children of the divide," the descendants of the old-fashioned liberal intelligentsia who had personified the culturist outlook. Were sympathetic readers of Russian modernism likewise offspring of this milieu? The question is difficult to answer without detailed reader surveys for modernist periodicals. However, the appearance of the modernist reader was not an isolated phenomenon. Distinct audiences were also growing for a wide variety of specialized literatures in science and technology and, to a lesser extent, in social science and the arts. Just as the reader of the new technical literatures needed a certain kind of expertise, the modernist reader needed specialized literary skills and experience. In both cases the requisite skills tended to be acquired through formal higher education. The new audiences reflected the increasing specialization in all areas of knowledge and education, as well as the proliferation of distinct employment groups due to industrialization. The modernist audience cut across these occupation-based technical audiences and could draw readers from any or all of them. Yet modernist literature appears estranged from the practical world of a developing technocracy and a professional elite, and like its European counterparts provides a hostile commentary on the values of such groups. The technical audiences sought reading matter related to their occupations; their purpose in reading was utilitarian. Though some modernist readers undoubtedly read for professional reasons, there were too few literati and would-be literati to constitute an audience by themselves. Instead one can envisage members of the educated professions turning to the personal and aesthetic themes of modernist works as an antidote to the stresses of a burgeoning urban society.

Regular readers of modernist literature constituted a distinct group within the more general educated audience, and the existence of this group is one of several indications of increasing diversity in the educated public during the last decade of the old regime. Certainly the hegemony of the culturist viewpoint faded during this period. Still, there were undoubtedly many readers who sampled modernist writing and, owing to either a culturist perspective or inerudite tastes, preferred more familiar literature. In fact, as the educated audience expanded, the number of readers holding a culturist viewpoint may have increased. In the post-1905 period readers with conservative tastes clearly dominated the high-price book market. The literature that sold most successfully used a straightforward narrative to offer the culturist reader a social and moral message and other readers a good story. Literature falling into this category ranged from the nineteenth-century classics and the works of quasi realists like Gorky and regionalists like Mamin-Sibiriak to those of such popular writers on current questions as A. Verbitskaia, and even, to a certain extent, to works delving into sexual questions.

The quasi realists and the specialists in the genres of adventure and local color were widely read and respected by the educated audience in the late nineteenth and early twentieth centuries. Both types of literature were likely to satisfy the sensibilities of culturist readers. Among the writers commonly considered realists, Andreev had the most long-lived success: his overly dramatic plays and action-packed, Poe-like stories sold in editions of 10,000, and occasionally more, from the first years of the century to World War I. Maxim Gorky achieved almost instant renown at the turn of the century with his tales of tramps and tramping. The founder of the miscellany *Znanie* (Knowledge), K. P. Piatnitsky, calculated in 1903 that over 100,000 volumes of his prose works had been sold, as well as 15,000 copies of *The Philistines* and 75,000 copies of *The Lower Depths*.[51] Though Gorky remained a glamorous figure, the commercial success of his works among the educated audience was short-lived, and after the Revolution of 1905 his books appeared only in small editions. In booksellers' trade journals there were complaints that Gorky "has died as far as the public is concerned," and that his books were "dead capital."[52] Perhaps the greatest success of the realists was tied to *Znanie*, which was priced at a ruble. In 1904 no. 2 appeared in an edition of 81,000, and even in 1908, when the novelty had worn off, the miscellany regularly came out in 20,000 copies. Some of Gorky's later work reached a large audience through this vehicle.

Writers who specialized in the genres of local color and exotic adventure, such as V. I. Nemirovich-Danchenko, Mamin-Sibiriak, and A. V. Amfiteatrov, had a large, steady readership (in the case of the first two, stretching from the 1890's to World War I). In 1898 Mamin-Sibiriak's works were published in over 20,000 copies, priced at over 30 kopecks; in 1908, in over 50,000 copies; and in 1913, in over 40,000. Nemirovich-Danchenko did just as well over the same period, and after 1905 Amfiteatrov's novels of contemporary life did even better, reaching a total of over 60,000 copies in 1908 and over 100,000 in 1913. The success of Nemirovich-Danchenko and Mamin-

Sibiriak depended on their ability to take the reader to far-off, exotic places, and Amfiteatrov's on his ability to create exciting situations. In either case there was at least an illusion that the novel brought the reader information about the world and how to live in it.

Writers who investigated sexual questions achieved a special sort of popularity. Artsybashev (*Sanin*, 1907), A. P. Kamensky (*Leda*, 1910), and E. Nagrodskaia (*The Wrath of Dionysus*, 1910), who specialized in this titillating genre, as well as others who merely dabbled in it, such as Kuprin and Sergeev-Trensky, might shock the culturist reader, but their works were likely to be stylistically intelligible. Both Artsybashev and Kamensky were quite successful, and their works were occasionally published in editions of more than 10,000. Less conventional works on similar themes, such as M. Kuzmin's *Wings*, did not do nearly so well.

The most dramatic phenomenon in the elite book market in the early twentieth century was the tremendous upsurge in editions of the classics. In 1913 alone over 100,000 copies of Gogol's works appeared, and over 200,000 of Lev Tolstoy's, priced at over 30 kopecks a volume. Such figures were characteristic of the last decade before the war. Undoubtedly Tolstoy's theatrical final years and death put him very much in the public eye, yet the source of his popularity was more complicated. Throughout the press after 1905, and not only the liberal press, there took place what can only be called the canonization of the Russian classics. It was almost as if publicists wished to fill the vacuum created in the contemporary literary scene by the narrow appeal of the modernists. Politically and emotionally the post-1905 era was a difficult one for all progressives. To deal with their sense of helplessness and despair, many turned almost unconsciously to the tradition of the intelligentsia and classical literature. For moderates, who felt trapped in an increasingly polarized situation, the glorification of the intelligentsia was a substitute for action; for the left, on the contrary, it was a spur to action. P. N. Miliukov, the Cadet Party leader, consoled his followers in 1910 by telling them to remember "you are only a link in the chain of generations carrying out that cultural mission about which Turgenev spoke."[53] "Long live the great Russian intelligentsia," wrote Vengerov in the same year, "unparalleled in its heroism and therefore holy: on its shoulders is carried Russian culture and most of all a great Russian literature."[54] Even the Bolsheviks, who had an ambivalent attitude toward the classics, occasionally joined this chorus. The dramatic death of Tolstoy in 1910 was an occasion for widespread pronouncements and demonstrations, and the first open street fighting since 1905 took place in St. Petersburg when university students attempted to honor the great writer by protesting capital punishment. It was the rare intellectual who did not publish a tribute. *Rech'* hailed Tolstoy as "the conscience of Russia." "Our country is poor and lawless," wrote Korolenko, the populist novelist, "but she gave the world Tolstoy." "Who is he?" asked Merezhkovsky; "artist, teacher, prophet? No, more; his face is the face of humanity."[55]

The canonization of the classics as timeless texts in which readers should seek the answers to pressing social and personal questions was an important phase in the molding of the last prerevolutionary generation of educated readers. It meant the fusion of an older tradition of unqualified reverence for books and writers with new literary experience. Since it took place simultaneously with a growing awareness of the classics themselves as a body of writing distinct from contemporary prose, and especially from modernism, it meant the creation of a literary ideal that was almost certain to be static. This ideal was not likely to contribute to the development of a reading public sympathetic to innovative movements such as modernism, even though some of the glory attached to being a writer did accrue to a few contemporary authors, especially the more traditional ones like Gorky, Korolenko, and Andreev.

A new popular women's fiction appeared after 1905 on the borderline between belles lettres and the kind of commercial literary product suggested by the word "kitsch." A. A. Verbitskaia, N. A. Lappo-Danilevskaia, and O. G. Bebutova were the best-selling Russian authors in early 1915, according to reports from the largest booksellers in St. Petersburg.[56] Like Elinor Glyn in England and Hedwig Courths-Mahler in Germany, they gained notoriety without literary respectability. Their popularity bears witness to the emergence of an audience willing and able to pay a ruble or more for melodramatic potboilers. Verbitskaia was the most successful of these authors. Her leap from uncelebrated mediocrity to clamorous renown began, according to her own account, with the publication of *The Spirit of the Times* (Moscow, 1907).[57] This was soon followed by the first volume of *Keys to Happiness* (Moscow, 1908–13), a gushy six-volume love story that made Verbitskaia fashionable. She listed the size of the editions of all her works at the end of each new novel; by her own count, in 1914 there were well over 500,000 copies of her books in print. The average edition for each volume of *Keys to Happiness* was 35,000 copies.

Verbitskaia's works were pretentiously sprinkled with belles let-tres and philosophy, from Shakespeare to Nietzsche. She often wrote of the progress of aspiring female artists, their romantic entangle-ments and sexual adventures. Mania, the heroine of *Keys to Happi-ness*, wins her way from a shabby Moscow apartment to the summit of the European dance world, only to be destroyed in the end by an unhappy romance. For all their hyperbole, Verbitskaia's works were among the few early-twentieth-century Russian novels in which "the reading ladies," whom Briusov so maligned, could discover a sym-pathetic heroine. Verbitskaia used the proceeds from her novels to set up her own publishing house, which issued Russian translations of French, German, and English novels about women. Her friendly biographer claimed her readers were from the people, but her works appeared almost exclusively in expensive editions. Her message to readers combined traditional moralizing with appeals for personal liberation. Though the liberal press condemned her for pandering to low tastes, she considered herself a proponent of socialism and de-mocracy, and can be seen as a vulgarizer of culturist literary ideals.

Attacks on Verbitskaia often associated her work with the trash literature that suddenly flooded the Russian book market after the Revolution of 1905. This new literature was directed exclusively at neither the educated audience nor the new mass urban audience and appears to have been read by both. Sales to educated readers can be considered a sign of a further deterioration of the strict culturist view. Among these works were rough translations and adaptations of foreign detective stories, such as the adventures of Nick Carter, Nat Pinkerton, Arsène Lupin ("the gentleman thief"), and of course Sherlock Holmes. Although the stated price of a book was not al-ways the selling price, the publication of the Holmes stories and the Lupin novels in ten- to twenty-kopeck editions of 8,000 to 10,000 and in ruble editions of 4,000 to 5,000 suggests that these books had a well-heeled audience as well as a poorer one. There were also Russian specialists in this genre, for example the infamous Count Amori, who produced such gems as *The Secrets of the Jap-anese Court* (St. Petersburg, 1908) and *The Adventures of a Peters-burg Lovelace* (St. Petersburg, 1910), along with *Return of Sanin* (St. Petersburg, 1911), after the successful novel by Artsybashev, and a fictitious conclusion to *Keys to Happiness*.

Magazines arose to cater to the new demand for an entertainment literature, such as the weekly *Sinii zhurnal* (The Blue Magazine, 1910–17), which sold for two rubles a year in 1912 (without delivery).

It featured murder mysteries—including "the first collective novel," which began with a chapter by the well-known realist writer A. I. Kuprin (1911, no. 10)—science fiction, beauty contests, disaster photographs, "the latest news of the Russian cinema," an occasional seminude pinup, and steps to the newest dances. Now and then the works of respectable popular authors like D. M. Tsenzor and Kuprin appeared, and the magazine even published some early literary sketches by Aleksandr Grin. These serious writers were often glamorized. Thus Gorky appeared in a dramatic picture on the cover of the first issue (Dec. 22, 1910) and again in 1914 in no. 24 for a piece on "writers on holiday." Kuprin was photographed, rifle in hand, for his article "On Shooting" (1913, no. 28), and again in his bathrobe, "after swimming," for a piece on a fashionable swim instructor (1913, no. 47). Though this lionizing almost seems to be a mockery of the traditional image of the writer-teacher, in fact it reflected a kind of worshipful respect.

Amid all the changes and confusion of late tsarist Russia, the old-style culturist reader remained in strength. In the fiftieth anniversary symposium of the stalwartly liberal newspaper *Russkie vedomosti* (Russian Gazette), the editors hailed their numerous "reader-friends," echoing Saltykov, who were mostly professional people over 30 with a higher education and quite traditional literary expectations.[58] Certainly many of the older generation of positivist liberal intellectuals held to their earlier views of literature and their antipathy for modernism despite the more positive social content of modernist writing after 1905. P. N. Miliukov, reacting in 1909 to what he considered an anti-Semitic outburst by P. B. Struve, the editor of *Russkaia mysl'*, connected such coarseness with the apoliticism and amoralism of the modernist movement.[59] Vl. Nabokov, the father of the now famous writer, in a review of a minor piece of realist fiction at the end of 1913, confessed his complete befuddlement with the contemporary literary scene, which, instead of giving "truth, sincerity, sensitivity to beauty, expressiveness," offered only "a million grimaces."[60]

More important than the survival among the older generation of a culturist way of reading that expected literature to be morally uplifting and to illuminate society was the transfer of these views to the last prerevolutionary generations of Russian readers, a process that took place in the universities, the secondary schools, the institutions of mass education, and the press. One can suppose that the exposure to culturist ideals had a particularly dramatic effect on the lower levels of the educated audience. Those first-generation middle-school pupils and new technocrats were certain to have an appreciation for the written word as presented in the schoolhouse, since it could be translated into upward mobility. They were unlikely to have the literary sophistication and language skills to appreciate modernism.

The culturist reader could on occasion be a very dogmatic one. The assumption that literature was linked with society could translate into a restrictive attitude toward the written word. The glorification of the writer's calling was double-edged: writers who fit the image could reap the praise of readers, but those who did not could be damned, as Belinsky had damned Gogol and the liberal press Briusov, as bad citizens rather than bad writers. Finally, the stress on the moral importance of literature and its influence on the reader led educated librarians and schoolteachers to a dogmatism of a different sort when they attempted to prevent what they considered harmful literature from falling into the hands of the masses. On occasion such private acts of censorship could be quite far-reaching, extending not only to the works of Verbitskaia but also to those of Leonid Andreev. With the appearance of a new mass reading public in the late nineteenth and early twentieth centuries, the efforts of the culturists, with all their shortcomings and virtues, did in fact bear fruit, but not entirely that which was sown.

III

The mass reading public burst suddenly on the writer's world at the turn of the century as a phenomenon without precedent in Russian cultural history. What kind of readers would the "sphinx" of the people produce? What would be their demands, their literary tastes? Lev Tolstoy asked himself these questions in the 1860's, and his conclusions, based on observations of and work with peasant children at his own school, disturbed him for much of the rest of his life.[61] He found that the people, when literate, had their own literature and a way of reading that seemed to rule out much of what was best in belles lettres. On the eve of the emancipation of the serfs, the question of a mass reading public was a speculative one; a few decades later, when an ocean of ordinary people had achieved rudimentary literacy, the question became real.

According to the 1897 census 26.5 million people, or 21 percent of the population of the empire, answered "yes" to the question "Can you read?"[62] More than two-thirds of these potential readers were peasants, at least by legal class designation. Although the cities were the centers of literacy—the urban literacy rate was more than twice the rural—the vastness of the rural population placed over 70 percent of the literate in what were designated as rural areas.[63] Not only was this nascent reading public rural, it was also young: just over 58 percent of the literate population of both the empire and European Russia were aged 10 to 29. (Correspondingly, the literacy rates in this age group as a whole were relatively high, ranging from over 60 percent in the cities to slightly below 30 percent in the countryside.) The patriarchal nature of Russian society was revealed in the predominance of male literacy: over two-thirds of all the literate in the empire were men, young men aged 10 to 29 alone constituting nearly 40 percent. The rapid rate at which literacy rose in the late nineteenth and early twentieth centuries tended to perpetuate these distinctions rather than alter them, since the expanding school system continued to cater more to boys than girls.

The great reservoir of literate people outside the major urban centers was not only an enormous potential reading public in itself, but also the source from which most of the urban literate came, a great school for Russian readers. Nearly three-fourths of the rural literate were men, 40 percent of whom were aged 10 to 29. Although the rural literacy rates for both European Russia and the empire were under 20 percent, in the developed provinces of Moscow and Petersburg the rates were 27 percent and 39 percent, respectively—high enough to indicate a definite literate presence in the villages of these areas.

The traditional literature of the Russian peasant was known as *lubochnaia literatura,* or literature based on the themes of the *lubki* (sing. *lubok*), the charming, often primitive popular engravings that had fed the religious and secular imagination of the masses as far back as the seventeenth century, and before that the imagination of the upper classes as well. The lubki were named for the *lub*, the bark of the lime or linden tree, on which they were first carved, or according to some for the hawkers' baskets made of this material, in which they were carried and sold.[64] The lubki engravings illustrated scenes from the Bible, visions of the Last Judgment, lives of the saints, folktales, rhymes, jokes about the battle of the sexes, and many other subjects serious and humorous. Since many of the earliest prints were copies of European originals, the lubki were initially called *friazhskii,* or Western European sheets.[65] They were sold at the Spasski Gate in Moscow from the late seventeenth and early eighteenth centuries, and came under official censorship for "disgraceful" pictures of Peter the Great even before his death.

The literature of the lubok was at first, like the engravings, one of religious themes and European models. During the nineteenth century it branched out into many other areas. By the late 1880's special publishers of lubok literature were issuing a million cheap pocket-sized books a year, composed of one to three printer's sheets of 32 pages each, with bright, lively pictures on the covers and exciting titles. The religious literature consisted of saints' lives—for example, *George the Conqueror, Nicholas the Miracle Worker, Holy Vasily: The Moscow Miracle Worker, Alexei the Man of God*—as well as *The Life Beyond the Grave, The End of the World and the Last Judgment*, the Gospels, the Book of Hours, the Psalters, and some Bibles.

Secular literature also came in many forms, some of it predating Peter. There were free renditions of Western European tales in the genre mocked by Cervantes, such as *The Story of Bova, the King's Son* (who was known as Buovo de Antona in Italy, Beuves d'Antone in France, and Bevis of Hampton in England) and *The Story of the Brave Knight Frantsyl Vensian and the Beautiful Princess Rensuven*, set in Spain and Turkey. Though most of these early tales, like the saints' lives, were produced in popular Russian versions by unknown writers, some had known authors, for example, *The English Milord George* by Matvei Komarov, an eighteenth-century writer whom the early Soviet critic Victor Shklovsky considered one of the founders of the Russian novel. Besides heroic epics on foreign themes there were historical subjects such as *Kuz'ma Minich, the One-Armed: The Glorious Novgorod Citizen in the Year of 1612* and *Ermak Timofeevich: The Conqueror of Siberia*, and pseudo- or semihistorical ones such as *How the Soldier Saved Peter the Great* and *The Battle Between the Russians and the Kabardintsy*. There were also domestic and foreign fairy tales like *Ivan Tsarevich and the Firebird, The Twelve Swan Brothers, The Gold of Arabia*, and *The Enchanted Castle*. By the 1880's writers of lower class origin were producing a steady stream of books. V. Volgin wrote *A Night with Satan* (Moscow, 1892), *The Foolish Heart: A Merry Story* (Moscow, 1896), and *A Corpse Without a Grave* (Moscow, 1915); Kassirov (I. S. Ivin) wrote *The Terrible Magician and the Brave and Powerful Knight Pogdai: A Story from the Time of the Holy Prince Vladimir* (Moscow, 1902) and *The Revengeful Gypsy, or a Criminal Against His*

Will (Moscow, 1915). In addition there were songbooks, books of dream interpretation, guides to letter writing, and almanacs listing the holidays of the saints, the phases of the moon, and much else that was less certain. As one lubok writer bragged in defense of this type of literature, these books offered the masses a complete literary menu for spiritual education, moral reflection, historical curiosity, flights of fancy, simple amusement, and practical advice.[66]

The literature of the lubok had its own publishers and a distribution system to get the books to the peasants in the villages. The publishers were located mainly in Moscow, and since many had their shops on Nikol'skii Street, the literature of the lubok was sometimes called "Nikol'skii Street literature." As often as not these entrepreneurs of popular culture were themselves but a few steps removed from the peasantry, and frequently knew no literature besides that of the lubok. Gubanov, one of the most prolific publishers, was a literate peasant from Tula who doctored horses and hawked books before he went into publishing. Morozov, a peasant from Tver, peddled green onions when he first came to Moscow, then engravings, and finally became a lubok publisher without ever learning to read. I. D. Sytin, who ultimately developed the largest publishing firm in Russia, began working as an assistant to a fur-trading uncle. When a promised position with a merchant in this line fell through, he found work with a lubok publisher and eventually went into business on his own.[67]

The books of the Moscow lubok publishers were brought to villages, fairs, and bazaars by wandering traders called *ofeni* (sing. *ofenia*), who traveled the whole of Russia.[68] There were rich ofeni with assistants and horse carts full of goods—not only books, but also engravings, icons, soap, combs, textiles, and much else—and poor ones, sometimes called *khodebshchiki*, walkers, or *korobeiniki*, after the baskets in which they carried their goods. Something between a fast-talking confidence man and a rural intellectual, the ofenia wandered the country taking money or products in exchange for goods and looking for good harvests. As one reported, "When the muzhik has bread and money to burn, there is where the ofenia lives."[69] Not always literate themselves, they often chose their books by cover alone or took what they could get. Many bought on credit, and expected their wares to sell for two or three times what they paid. Ignorant though they were, they were still worldly travelers to many with whom they came into contact, and it was most often the ofenia's praise of this or that book that determined the peasant's purchase. Since the ofeni praised what they had, in the 1880's and 1890's the choice of the peasants' reading material was often made by the publishers on Nikol'skii Street where the ofeni bought their books. (Subsequently, provincial distribution centers also played a role in determining what was available.) The taste of the publishers and the ofeni was generally conservative. Both tended to stick to what they knew and trusted. Sytin remembered how his first employer, the publisher P. N. Sharapov, recommended a bevy of soul-saving books to him: one to make him stalwart "for pure and brave feats," one to teach "patience, virtue, kindness, and labor," and a third to "avoid sin and know what it is."[70] For the ofeni the peasants were often a captive audience who, but for an occasional trip to the city or a visit by city folk, had almost no other means of obtaining books.

In the world of the nineteenth-century Russian peasant, the only indigenous purveyors of books besides the ofeni and an occasional priest were the teachers in the "free schools," or "domestic schools of literacy," run by the peasants themselves.[71] Perhaps the oldest type of school in Russia, these were small, informal gatherings with self-appointed teachers who often had only the qualification of rudimentary literacy. Large numbers of these schools appeared in rural Russia soon after the emancipation in response to the peasants' demand for literacy, a demand stemming from their knowledge that the literate army recruit had an easier and shorter term of service, and their belief that the reading of holy books improved one's chances for salvation. The existence of these schools was legally recognized by the state in 1882, and in the late 1880's the government began converting many of them, at least formally, into church primary schools. Owing to this reclassification, as well as to the expansion of the secular school system, the number of free schools declined. By official count there were more than 17,000 free schools in European Russia in 1903, 15,500 in 1906, and only 4,000 in 1911.[72] (Certainly these figures are understated, since the schools were informal and not always easy to identify.) The late nineteenth century was a time of great tramping, and the teachers in these schools, whether retired soldiers, people from the clergy, literate peasants, former servants, or (in Siberia) miscellaneous exiles, were often wanderers, hired and boarded by a few local villagers to teach their children how to read and "how to live by God."[73] In such schools, which were usually attended for a single winter and almost exclusively by boys, the literary culture of the lubok was usually preserved intact, and the textbooks were most often lubok editions of the Psalter or other religious books. The purpose of such learning was practical, whether in a religious or a secular sense.

It was the official state school system that first transplanted the nontraditional literary culture of the outside world to the villages of Russia. These schools were usually administered by the Ministry of Education, the church, or the provincial *zemstva* in the 34 provinces where those local representative institutions operated. The great expansion in the rural school network began in the 1890's and continued into the years of the First World War. In 1880 there were over 22,000 rural primary schools in the 60 provinces of European Russia (including the Warsaw district), with a total of over a million pupils; in 1911 there were over 80,000 schools with over 4.5 million pupils.[74] Of the more than 100,000 primary schools in the empire in 1911, almost 90 percent were classified as rural, and these were attended by over 80 percent of all primary school children. Many rural schools were church primary schools, established by the government and the church from the 1880's on in an attempt to ensure the loyalty of peasant Russia. In 1911 there were officially almost 34,000 such schools with over 1.8 million pupils, or over 30 percent of all primary school children in the empire.[75]

In church primary schools the main subject was usually "the law of God," and much class time was spent on church singing, Church Slavonic, and reading of the Psalter and the Book of Hours. The church schools did not dramatically alter the traditional cultural atmosphere of the village, but the secular schools most certainly did. Even though many of the teachers in the primary schools were peasants (30 percent in 1880, 36 percent in 1911) or members of the clergy (38 percent in 1880, 20 percent in 1911),[76] primary school education was a dramatic incursion into the world of the peasants. Among the comments of teachers in the early twentieth century can be found complaints that along with enlightenment the schools brought "disrespect for parents and old people," "short, colored shirts, shoes, lacquered boots, short jackets, breeches, wide belts, peaked caps of all colors," and dreams of far-off "rivers flowing with milk and honey."[77] Schools also brought books, not only textbooks but library books. By 1911 over 70 percent of all the primary schools in the empire had libraries for "outside school reading" by pupils.[78] Only 13 percent had libraries specifically for adults, but since many schoolchildren brought books home to read aloud, all of the libraries reached an adult audience. By 1916 the zemstva had also founded some 15,000 "people's libraries."[79] The libraries open to the peasants offered a very limited selection, often no more than a couple of hundred titles, which were heavily weighted in favor of religious and patriotic works in accord with government regulations up to 1905.[80] Nevertheless, these libraries brought a sampling, however meager, of nontraditional literature to the villages.

The primary school was the basic means by which simple literacy was spread in the villages. The school and zemstvo libraries made a small selection of books available. Beyond these were the efforts of culturist activists interested in raising the level of the masses and bringing intelligentsia culture to the villages. They engaged in a whole range of educational activities, from Sunday schools and public readings to the establishment of "people's houses of culture" and the publication of special cheap editions of books for the masses. The direct attempt to transform the peasants as readers, and to supplant the literature of the lubok with a "good literature" from educated Russia, was most clearly evident in the public readings and the publication of "people's books." In these efforts the culturist activists were heirs to a long tradition of hostility to lubok literature, a hostility stemming in part from the competition for readers between lubok writers and aristocratic writers in the late eighteenth and early nineteenth centuries. N. A. Nekrasov enshrined this feeling in his poem "Who Lives Well in Russia?" when he wrote:

> Will the time come
> When the muzhik
> Will return from the bazaar
> Not with Blucher
> And the stupid Milord
> But Belinsky and Gogol?*

The most active arena in the battle of the culturist activists against the literature of the lubok was the public reading. Begun in the 1870's by the government in an attempt to discourage the drunkenness of workers in the capitals, readings spread in the late 1880's and early 1890's to the countryside.[81] They were strictly controlled by the Ministry of Education, which authorized several committees to publish special texts for this purpose, including an occasional literary classic ("Taras Bulba," *The Captain's Daughter*), but more often works such as *Alexei the Man of God, The History of the Holy*

---

* Nekrasov, *Komu na Rusi zhit' khorosho* (Moscow, 1964), p. 53. Blucher, the Prussian general who fought Napoleon, apparently appeared in a lubok print. Milord refers to the lubok novel *The English Milord George*.

Land, The Life of the Mother of God, The Empress Catherine the Great, and *The Christian Feat of the Soldier.*[82] Not surprisingly, many of the early readings had a religious tone to them. A report from several villages in Petersburg province noted that readings began with a prayer. At one, during a "description of Eden," a peasant cried out, "Ah, how good it was in paradise!" The teacher at another reported that when the reading was over the older peasants thanked him, saying "they felt just as if they were in church."[83] Nevertheless, the tone of the readings eventually changed. After 1905 the rules were relaxed and the main subject matter became the shorter works of classical writers and realistic contemporary writers, as well as special stories written "for the people." These activities took place on a large scale: in 1910 in rural Russia there were nearly 200,000 readings in over 15,000 schools.[84]

The attempt to reach "the reader from the people" with books, pamphlets, and periodicals in the second half of the nineteenth century and the early twentieth was, of course, a variously political one. Official Russia, the radical intelligentsia, and concerned intellectuals of moderate persuasion produced a vast quantity of printed matter intended for the masses. Militant populists of the 1870's, mixing folklore and radical economics, composed a special propagandistic literature to convey their message. Though they often had to read their booklets aloud to illiterate peasants and occasionally saw the paper in them used for cigar wrappers, some of their illegally printed works—for example, S. M. Stepniak-Kravchinsky's *The Shrewd Naum* (3,000 copies published abroad in 1875) and *Story of a Kopeck* —circulated in small numbers throughout the late imperial period.[85] Successive groups of revolutionaries, including the Bolsheviks, drew on this experience, but the lack of an effective distribution network and the vigilance of the tsarist police hindered their efforts and those of the populists. As a result, until 1905 radical propaganda hardly reached the populations of the major cities, and even in 1917 such efforts were only briefly more successful.

The propagandistic activities of the government and the church were extensive. In 1887 almost three million copies of religious books were published, and in 1901 over sixteen million.[86] In 1909 the Holy Synod alone printed nearly 800,000 copies, and the Palestine Society and various monasteries printed another 600,000.[87] Religious literature, often distributed through church primary schools, was a tremendous force in peasant culture in the late nineteenth and early twentieth centuries, but its influence was not entirely the result of church efforts. Many of the successful church publications were saints' lives and traditional religious literature that traveled in the sacks of the ofeni and circulated in the villages without difficulty. Church publications unfamiliar to the peasants, such as the religious and patriotic *Sel'skii vestnik* (The Rural Herald, 1881–1917), did not fare so well. In 1893 this newspaper claimed 35,000 paid subscribers, and in 1915, before printing was expanded for dispersal among soldiers, the circulation was about the same.[88] Though it had considerable success among the peasants in the 1890's, its circulation did not keep pace with rising rural literacy.[89]

The most successful attempt to create a nontraditional printed literature for the "reader from the people" was certainly that of the progressive and moderate culturist intellectuals, and a measure of their success was the entry of a totally new type of book, the work of belles lettres, into the literary culture of the rural and urban lower classes. Once established, such books continued to circulate commercially and were republished and sold by lubok publishers themselves. Though there were attempts to produce "people's books" as early as the 1830's, such publications did not appear in large numbers until the last three decades of the nineteenth century, when various heirs to the enlightenment tradition of Novikov—private publishers motivated by philanthropic considerations, enlightened capitalists, and culturist organizations such as the zemstva and the Moscow and St. Petersburg Committees on Literacy—deluged the book market with them. By 1895 there were more works of this sort published (355 titles, 3,176,847 copies, excluding religious books) than lubok literature (109 titles, 1,578,100 copies).[90] However, it was one thing to publish a book and another to get it to the peasants. Most of the books published for the people in the 1880's and 1890's never left the publishers' city storehouses. In 1894 the St. Petersburg Committee on Literacy published nearly 500,000 copies but sold only slightly more than 150,000, and most of these went to other educated distributors who hoped to be able to disperse them.[91]

The first culturist publishing house to reach a peasant audience was the firm of Posrednik (Intermediary), a joint endeavor begun in 1884 by Lev Tolstoy, V. Chertkov, and the young lubok publisher I. D. Sytin. Sytin, who already commanded a well-developed network of ofeni and knew peasant tastes, was able to design and price the books to resemble the lubok literature that he continued to publish, to the dismay of some culturist intellectuals. Into the sacks of the ofeni went the new Posrednik books, and the firm's titles soon turned

up on the lists of books owned by peasants that interested intellectuals and others compiled.[92] The firm laid no legal claim to the books
it published, and the works were often republished. The example
of Posrednik was infectious. Other educated publishers, such as those
of the magazines *Russkaia mysl'* (Russian Thought) and *Russkoe
bogatstvo* (Russian Riches), began to put out their own books in
lubok format, and Sytin, in cooperation with Posrednik, distributed
these also. One of the Posrednik editors subsequently claimed that
in its first four years the firm published twelve million copies of its
own and distributed another eight million published by other firms
(including religious books).[93]

Posrednik and the other early culturist publishers had a well-
defined mission. Through their mediation the first modern literature
from educated Russia to reach the peasants in quantity turned out
to be a particular sort of literature, a teaching literature that sought
to be true to life. Posrednik's announced intention was "the best content at the cheapest price," and by the best content it meant "as near
as possible to the teaching of Christ."[94] "Books ought to strive to
improve morality," wrote a member of the firm in 1892.[95] "Literature
is inseparable from life," read the statement of the editors in 1894;
"each literary work is a moral or immoral act of its author, and therefore the question of what to write is identical with the question of
how to live."[96] The books published by the firm bore out this purpose. Works by Tolstoy, V. M. Garshin, V. I. Nemirovich-Danchenko,
and A. I. Ertel', works by "writers from the people" like V. I. Savi-
khin and S. T. Semenov, and snippets from foreign writers—all were
instructive and carried a Tolstoyan message to the reader. Other
publishing firms that did not share Posrednik's philosophic position
nevertheless attempted to do much the same thing. V. N. Marakuev
founded his Narodnaia Biblioteka (People's Library) in 1882 in order
to give the masses "healthy and reasoned food"; he felt that literature
should be "positive in the sense of [creating]a positive type, in the
sense of a positive Russian idea."[97] Even publishers who claimed
that the people needed no special literature, for example the St.
Petersburg Literacy Committee, expected their books to bring the
reader a certain message. "Faithful to the worldly truths of life at
the end of the nineteenth century," wrote the committee's historian,
"the publications of the society sketch before us the painful picture
of the material needs of the simple people, . . . their struggle, . . . the
conditions of their reality."[98]

The culturist perspective, so firmly established in the publication of books "for the people" in the nineteenth century, remained a major force in the twentieth, as developments sparked mass publishing efforts on an ever greater scale. The Russo-Japanese War prompted book shipments to soldiers; the St. Petersburg Literacy Committee alone sent half a million copies.[99] During the Revolution of 1905 firms like Donskaia Rech' (Don Speech) took advantage of the relaxed censorship to publish quasi-realist writers such as Andreev, Gorky, Serafimovich, and Kuprin on a mass scale, as well as works on social questions and popular science. At the same time the new political party presses created an enormous brochure literature. In 1906 alone the Cadet publishing house (Narodnoe Pravo) issued well over 700,000 booklets priced at five kopecks or less.[100] In the interrevolutionary period firms like Pol'za (Benefit) continued the tradition, issuing over a million copies of books in 1908 at an average price of twenty kopecks; Posrednik itself in the same year published over 1.5 million copies.[101] In 1909 approximately 2.25 million copies of works by classical or well-known contemporary authors appeared in "people's editions."[102] A much broader selection of books appeared in mass editions in the twentieth century than in the nineteenth, but the traditional stress on the moral, instructive value of literature remained. The culturist activists who worked in mass educational institutions, libraries, Sunday schools, "houses of culture," zemstvo bookstores, and primary schools, through which much mass literature was distributed, made the moral point quite clear, even when it was not emphasized in the works themselves.

The same impetus that led some culturist intellectuals to publish books for the people led others to study the mass reader. As a result the new readers were observed wherever they were, in the schools and libraries, in village reading rooms and factory barracks. The books in their possession were listed. Individual readers were questioned about their preferences, and their spontaneous remarks were written down by librarians, schoolteachers, and those who carried out public readings. Publishers of books for the people appealed for critical comments. Enlightenment societies gathered testimony from the countryside and the cities. Interested zemstvo activists used their networks of local employees to gather information. What did the masses read? How did they approach the book? What were their literary tastes, their cultural attitudes, their understanding of literature? In the 1880's and early 1890's, three relatively systematic attempts were made to survey those in a position to observe the new readers in different parts of the country, as well as those new readers themselves who were able to respond to such an inquiry. In 1885 a "program," or list of questions, was circulated by D. I. Shakhovskoi, in 1888 and 1891 two versions of a second program by A. S. Pruga-vin, and in 1889 the third and most successful query by N. A. Ruba-kin.[103] The surveys of Prugavin and Rubakin bore fruit; Prugavin published his conclusions in two editions of *The Demand of the People and the Duty of the Intelligentsia* (St. Petersburg, 1890, 1895), and Rubakin in his *Studies on the Russian Reading Public* (St. Petersburg, 1895). Both were able to gather much personal testimony, not only from teachers and others close to the masses, but also from peasants and workers themselves, and Rubakin continued to collect such materials up to World War I.*

The new readers were also studied by some who observed their habits on a day-to-day basis. The two most perceptive efforts of this sort were made by the wandering populist writer S. A. An-sky (Rap-poport), who lived among miners and peasant laborers and pub-lished his conclusions in two editions of *The People and the Book* (1894, 1913), and by the circle of Kharkov Sunday school teachers led by Kh. D. Alchevskaia, who tested the response of urban and rural teenagers and adults to thousands of books, and published a record of their experience in three volumes of *What to Read to the People?* (1884, 1889, 1910). These culturist activists, of course, had axes to grind. Some, like An-sky and Prugavin, were populists who believed in the need for a special mass literature that could reach the people on their own plane. Others, like Alchevskaia and her circle, wanted to prove the masses capable of reading all "good" lit-erature, including the Russian classics as well as Tolstoy and the Posrednik editions. Still others, like Rubakin, tried to take a middle position. The biases of these writers are clear, as is the impression-istic nature of much of their material, but its value stands undimin-ished. Their observations are so detailed, and they gathered such extensive personal testimony, much of which has survived in manu-script, that their work transcends these limitations. Their conclusions may be questionable and sometimes contradictory, but their labor created an incomparable record of the experiences of ordinary peo-ple with books and literature.

* Rubakin's collection, including some replies to Prugavin's program, is lo-cated in the Manuscript Section of the Lenin Library (f 358) and was used by the author. The contents of the archive are described in *Zapiski otdela rukopisei, Gosudarstvennaia Ordena Lenina Biblioteka SSSR Imeni V. I. Lenina* (Moscow, 1963), pp. 63–206.

The early populist emphasis on literature for the peasants was well placed since literacy was most often achieved where the majority of schoolchildren actually were, that is, in the villages. The reading experience of the newly literate peasant was the first step in the development of a mass reading public, not only in the countryside but in the cities as well, as rural migrants swelled the urban population. S. A. An-sky suggested quite perceptively in his *The People and the Book* (1913) that to the peasants there were three types of reading: religious or godly (*bozhestvennoe*), fairy-tale (*skazochnoe*), and worldly or pertaining to life (*zhiteiskoe*).[104] The first two were the basic categories of lubok literature; the third referred to the high or educated literature that reached the peasants through the mediation of culturist activists.

The distinction between godly-religious books and secular fairy tales was fundamental to the peasants' attitude. Testimony from the villages throughout the late nineteenth and early twentieth centuries is replete with descriptions of the peasants' preference for the religious book, which, as Rubakin put it, was "surrounded by some kind of halo" in their eyes.[105] The old read such works "because they wish salvation," writes a field-worker and shovel-maker from Kaluga province. "Godly is better, especially when they read in a church way," comments a woman in a village near St. Petersburg about a public reading. For the peasants these were books with great utility for improving life on earth and ensuring one's place in heaven. "Very curious to read how olden peoples and tsars lived," a zemstvo schoolteacher records a peasant woman commenting, "but all the same there is not great use in that for you." "Only in those books [the religious]," writes a peasant to the newspaper *Sel'skii vestnik* (Rural Herald), "do I find something useful."[106]

In fact, being able to read such books, and therefore being able "to understand the word of God," was one of the reasons the peasants gave in favor of literacy.[107] The oldest types of bookish villagers were the *chital'shchik*, who read the Psalter over the dead, and the *nachetchik*, a devotee of scripture and other religious books who answered fellow villagers' questions by consulting the lives of the saints or the Psalter.[108] "Such lovers of scripture," writes a rural schoolteacher of the nachetchiki, "exist in every village and everyone knows them."[109] Their attitude toward books was extremely moralistic. In answer to an inquiry about the works of Pushkin in *Sel'skii vestnik*, one such reader compared the poet unfavorably to his favorite saint, explaining that whereas "the deceased Pushkin met his death through the female sex," the holy Kiprian "was a terrible charmer, could speak with the dead, and did not seduce young girls."[110]

The overwhelming presence of religious books—saints' lives, the Psalter, the Book of Hours, the Gospels—was indicated in most surveys of books in the villages well into the twentieth century, but this does not mean that all the peasants who had them read them.[111] The church primary school system was a funnel for such literature, and religious books were often handed out in the secular schools as well. On lists of books owned by peasants, religious books frequently are noted as gifts rather than purchases.[112] In libraries, which almost always contained a substantial amount of such literature, religious books were rarely requested, since most of the readers were young and presumably uninterested in religion.[113] Adult peasants, however, considered these books important, and they played a significant physical role in a world in which demons and other supernatural beings had a place. A curious study of the books among peasants in Moscow province in the early 1880's concluded that the Psalter was the most widely owned book, not only because it was often used to teach children to read, but also for other reasons.[114] The peasant who had it could save his family money by reading it over the dead himself instead of paying a priest or a *chital'shchik* to do so. It was also thought that "the man who has read it from cover to cover forty times will be forgiven a certain quantity of his sins." In some locales it was used as a means of divination, and there was a method of hanging it from the ceiling in order to identify a thief.

The book, in its most primal sense, was for the peasants charged with mystery, and just as this mystery could be godly, it could also be demonic. A turn-of-the-century traveler related the following story from a contemporary Siberian village.[115] The peasants were awaiting a cholera epidemic that had already struck a neighboring village when a poor German craftsman appeared who spoke Russian badly and carried a notebook listing all the villages through which he was to pass. He met some peasants and showed them the book, asking how to get to the next village. Since none of the villages listed had been struck yet by the epidemic, the peasants became suspicious and decided that the strange man with the book was the cholera itself. In order to save themselves and their neighbors, they drowned the unfortunate German in a marsh.

The respect accorded by peasants to religious books did not extend to the secular literature of the lubok. There was a split in peasant attitudes toward these fairy tales and stories of knights. According to many witnesses such works were widely enjoyed. "They are endlessly read and reread," writes an opponent of this literature, "and always with unwavering interest."[116] Whenever the peasants read or hear a tale of strength, an informant of Rubakin's explained, "they always remember Bova Korolevich and Eruslan Lazarevich, saying 'so it was that there were such champions in olden times, and what are we today? People are like flies.'"[117] This literature was widely dispersed and unlike the religious books always purchased on the peasants' own initiative. Yet when asked for their opinion about these books, the peasants invariably replied "they are only tales," "one gets nothing from nothing," "all that is untrue," "nonsense." Such books were read "because it is a holiday, from nothing to do, to have a laugh and kill some time, and, well, because they are also curious."[118] At a reading of fairy tales a teacher noted that the grown-ups looked away "as if ashamed."[119] This kind of peasant response to the original secular literature of the villages is important because it reveals that the demand for moral teaching, so characteristic of the oldest type of village reader, was not abandoned in the face of this captivating fiction, but instead only temporarily and often superficially suppressed. Though the peasants read these books avidly and possessed them in large numbers, when questioned they clearly felt that the proper attitude toward such literature was a negative one. When the new secular literature of the culturist activists finally arrived in the villages, the peasants' attitudes toward books and reading were already well formed, and the new literature was judged according to criteria established for godly writing and fairy tales.

Most of the first books published for the people by official Russia and culturist intellectuals lent themselves easily to a traditional religious understanding. A rural reading in St. Petersburg province in 1890 of a brochure on the life and assassination of Alexander II produced such comments as "glorious book," "look, it is not godly reading, but it is no worse then godly," and "yes, he did much good"—as well as weeping when the reader reached the Tsar's death.[120] About another reading of the same booklet a Sunday school student remarked, "Tears flow against your will and one becomes pained for those villains who took such a tsar from us."[121] The reaction to literary works, usually chosen by teachers and librarians for their moral thrust, was quite similar. Thus when Turgenev's story "Biriuk," about a stern but kindhearted forester who refuses to punish a poverty-stricken peasant for stealing an oak, was read by the Kharkov teachers at a rural Sunday school in the 1880's, the young peasant audience identified the characters in terms more reminiscent of a saint's life than a lubok romance. They condemned the thief, whether he stole from poverty or not, because "he was all the same a thief," and applauded Biriuk because he was "good, sincere, and honest"; "loved to do good"; "had an honest soul and a peaceful and chaste heart"; "had a Christian, merciful, and maternal heart." [122]

Rural teachers encouraged the peasants' tendency to find moral lessons in what they read. Tolstoy's story "By What Do People Live?," in which an angel, thrown to earth to find the answer, is befriended and taken home by a good bootmaker, was a favorite among culturist activists in the 1880's and 1890's. The lesson of the story—that people live by love—was unflinchingly driven home to peasant readers by the Kharkov schoolteachers, and when they asked "By what do people live?" they usually got the answers they sought. [123] "People live by love and love is God," responded a twelve-year-old. Older pupils liked the book because "it teaches us how to live as God orders." At one reading a youngster thought he was hearing "prayers such as they read in church," but an older child explained that it was about "how people loved one another." One child thought the angel might be sent by the devil, but the teacher showed the class a picture of an angel to make certain no one missed the point. At the end of the story, when the angel returned to heaven, all the girls cried and one listener crossed himself.

When such books as Tolstoy's stories were read aloud informally among the peasants, and there was much unorganized reading aloud, the results could be quite unexpected. An-sky, who had great sympathy for Tolstoy's efforts, related his own experience in reading "By What Do People Live?" to peasants without explaining the story ahead of time. [124] The angel, who first appears lying on the ground naked, having just fallen from the sky, was taken for a drunk. There is some irony in this since many temperance books were published by the culturist activists. When the angel later smiles at the wife of Semion, the bootmaker, and the text says the wanderer had "caught her fancy," the listeners let loose a hail of gibes and jokes directed at the host and the guest, with remarks like "this Semion is a fool." Usually, An-sky explained, there was a listener who knew the story and who would keep quiet until he could stand it no longer, then cry out, "What's with you cackling idiots! The wanderer—he's an angel." The result would be a shamed and uncomfortable silence.

Peasant readers not only looked for the moral of the story, but also, especially in contemporary works, took the characters for real people and attempted to decide if they had acted justly or not. To them the purpose of a serious story was moral instruction. In the early twentieth century, one of the Kharkov schoolteachers sent a copy of Chekhov's story "Peasant Women" to a favorite pupil who had married an ordinary peasant and returned to the village some years before. The teacher instructed her to read the story aloud in the village and report back. The response of the peasants to this tale of an unhappy marriage that ends in adultery and murder was both remarkable and typical.[125] After the reading the villagers immediately set to judging the guilty couple, and a group of older peasants insisted on dictating a statement, which began:

I, the woman Paraska, and grandpa, father-in-law, mother-in-law, the woman Mar'ia, Grigory, and others—all of us accuse Mashenka. Only one old person accuses him. We all say she is guilty. She seduced him to sin. If she had not yielded to sin, this would not have happened to him. If she were a good woman, then after his stupid words she ought not to pay any attention to him, but to throw him over altogether. But if it already happened so—he is a young person and she also—they might have sinned and sinned again; but when the husband arrived they might have thrown this nonsense from their heads and confessed to him.

The woman who read apparently explained that their views of the story would be sent to the city, and the testament concluded: "We ask you to write to us, even if not right away, and tell us on what basis they decided about this book among you in the city—who was guilty? Ah yes, it is a disputable book." The other opinions expressed were quite similar, though the woman who read the story to the peasants did not judge the characters so simply.

This way of reading was something more than seeing literature as a mirror of life. It put literature in life by demanding both mimesis and didacticism simultaneously. A teacher from Moscow province explained, "Readers respect books with a content similar to fact."[126] An-sky suggested that the realism of the new worldly literature led the peasant reader to accept everything printed in a serious book as true and all the characters as real people.[127] Moreover, in reading a book or listening to one, the peasants seemed to relive their own experiences. A book set in preemancipation times sparked memories of serfdom. Turgenev's dog story "Mumu" reminded a peasant child of a lost dog.[128] During many readings the peasants wept at their own sorrows. A nineteen-year-old woman returned "By What Do People

Live?," explaining that when she read aloud at home, "the whole evening at our house is sometimes passed in sobbing."[129]

The approach to stories as tales of life similar to the lives of saints meant that readers expected books to have a proper beginning and a conclusive ending, either in death or in old age. After a reading of "By What Do People Live?" the peasants asked An-sky if the bootmaker and his wife had been canonized.[130] A Soviet culturist activist complained soon after the October Revolution, "The peasants take books from me to read and afterward they say that the books are good but they have no ending."[131] Similarly, peasants expected didacticism. "Reading a book," wrote a 22-year-old Cossack in 1913, "I demand that it enlighten the mind and also teach something—how to live."[132] Is a book useful, a Viatka peasant was asked at the turn of the century. "Very useful," he answered; "it calls forth reflection, diverts one from inaction."[133] Of course such a moralistic response was a legacy of religious reading. A peasant wrote to the Vladimir zemstvo asking for books and explained that whenever he found something to read, "I greedily throw myself into reading it, and sometimes during the reading of such stories it happens that I am sick to tears, and sometimes there is some kind of uplifting of the spirit—a shining, joyful, unwavering faith in the providence of the Almighty."[134]

The deep involvement of peasant readers in what they read, and their respect for it, did not necessarily extend to the authors of such literature. Like the lives of saints, which had characters, a story, and a message but no apparent author, the new worldly literature was accepted by the peasants without much concern for who wrote it. When questioned about the author of a story, they were not interested and replied: "Who the hell knows," "let him be cursed."[135] Asked about the author of *The Captain's Daughter*, which he had just read and apparently enjoyed, a peasant answered: "I don't know, and what is it to us to know that; we will know much and get old all the sooner."[136] In this fashion the peasant readers divorced a literary work from its author, whom they were more likely to judge by his personal life than by what he wrote. The process of creativity, according to An-sky, was assumed to be merely recording what happened. Listening to "Bezhin Meadow" a peasant remarked, "But he [Turgenev] lies there as if asleep, the sly fellow, watching; even though he's lost he's about his business."[137]

The peasants' idea of books and their way of reading resulted from a syncretic interaction of new experiences and influences with traditional customs and beliefs. As this audience developed it be-came increasingly secularized, or at least increasingly familiar with a secular literature of belles lettres and later popular science, but basic attitudes toward books changed very slowly. Yet these readers, as individuals and as generations, lived in a rapidly changing his-torical context that affected them as readers. The nineteenth-century village was a world in which even reading habits were seasonal. A church primary school teacher who went from hut to hut in a vil-lage in Tula province at the end of the century asking the peasants what they read was answered: "Batiushka! Now is not the time to read books, now whoever knows how to read books gives it up; . . . but when winter comes, there will be long evenings, then from bore-dom why not listen or read a little, but now everyone is in the field, yes, in the field."[138]

Although seasonal reading remained the rule in much of rural Russia, the expansion of the school system and of other institutions of mass education encouraged a more regular use of books. Equally important in their influence on the peasant reader were economic and social changes. The progressive transformation of the rural econ-omy and the peasant commune, the increasing demands of the fac-tories and the communication network for labor, and the flight of landless and dissatisfied peasants to new settlements all tended to shatter the insularity of village life and increase the availability of books. The spread of a money economy gave the peasants more opportunity to buy what they wanted either in cities or in local markets, and in the early twentieth century there are reports of books appearing in village shops, especially near factories. The pop-ulation of Russia was on the move, and books traveled as well. Part-time and seasonal factory workers brought books from cities and factory districts back to their villages. Peasants on the road to Siberia or elsewhere often carried some reading matter with them. Secular reading was a step in the disintegration of traditional peasant cul-ture: it eased the peasant out of the self-contained village commun-ity. As knowledge of the outside world penetrated the villages, the peasants became more desirous of worldly books, and increasing numbers of local entrepreneurs and concerned culturist activists were ready to satisfy this demand.

The social effects of war and revolution marked village reading habits in early-twentieth-century Russia as they did the whole tenor of rural life. The Russo-Japanese War of 1904–5 brought newspapers into the villages of European Russia on a hitherto-unprecedented scale. The war sparked interest in the outside world: peasants wanted to know the news, and undependable and irregular official reports from the local administration stimulated their curiosity rather than quenching it. A self-educated peasant from Tver wrote Rubakin in the spring of 1905 that "up to the war our peasants read no newspapers and considered them superfluous."[139] Another correspondent from Tula wrote: "The peasants of our village, interested in the war with Japan, subscribed to the newspaper *Russkoe slovo* [The Russian Word], and every evening a circle of several people gathered to read it."[140] There were similar reports from other provinces. According to one from Moscow province, the peasants "gather in circles to read the news of the Far East"; and a *volost* administration in Nizhegorod province was besieged by peasants with requests "to provide a newspaper to read or if the newspaper is taken, to tell the news about the course of the war."[141] There is some evidence that newspapers continued to appear in the villages during 1905, and one of Rubakin's correspondents from Ekaterinoslav claimed that during the 1905 telegraph strike, when there were no newspapers to be had, the peasants read revolutionary leaflets instead.[142] Some of the booklets published during the revolution certainly did circulate in the villages and, according to some accounts, continued to appear even after they were banned.[143] The First World War had much the same effect as the Russo-Japanese War on the village readers who remained at home. Then too peasants eagerly sought newspapers, and those serving as soldiers had increased contact with periodicals.

As rural literacy became more common and non-lubok books filtered down into the villages, new types of readers appeared. Dedicated culturist activists expected these "peasant intelligenty" to bring traditional respect for religious books to the new books of educated society, belles lettres and popular science. For Rubakin these readers were the heirs of the old scripture buffs, but unlike their predecessors commanded book knowledge applicable to the everyday world. In his 1895 study of the reading public, he focused on those rural readers who tended to confirm his image of "the intelligentsia from the people": inquisitive, open-minded, and respectful toward educated Russia and its learning. As examples he offered such peasant writers as S. T. Semenov, a Posrednik author and friend of Tolstoy, and K. I. Tesikov, a rural self-taught astronomer, both of whom lived in the countryside, looked with some suspicion on the city, and had excellent relations with culturist intellectuals.

There were indeed rural intelligenty as Rubakin envisioned, for example, the peasant from Viatka province who sent his autobiography to *Krestianskaia gazeta* (The Peasant Newspaper) in the 1920's.[144] His family was illiterate. He finished school in 1889 at the age of twelve and began working in the fields with his father, but he felt restless and at sixteen left home to become a carpenter. He joined an artel or guild of woodworkers and wandered the countryside, living in a society "such as Gorky described in 'The Lower Depths,'" but maintaining ties with his family and the land. "Soon after leaving school," he related, "there appeared in me from somewhere an attraction and love for books," but he had nothing but the copy of the Gospels he had received at graduation. After reading that over and over again, his search for books began: "Whether I understood or not, it was all the same: the only thing was to read." His list included Bova Korolevich and the lives of saints, Tolstoy, Knut Hamsun, Feuerbach, and much else. As he wandered he read to others, but "my listeners," he complained, "were interested in merry stories," and after their laughs they would return to their earlier conversations about daily affairs "with a somewhat guilty look." In 1912, missing the land but unable to find a place in his own village, he emigrated to Siberia and settled on the Chylm River in the province of Tomsk, where he was in fact a messenger of books and culture, and where in 1917 the revolution found him.

The model rural *intelligent* of the culturist intellectuals was probably the exception rather than the rule. Education itself did not necessarily mean respect for educated Russia. The lubok writers, such as Kassirov (I. S. Ivin), were intelligenty from the people who were quite willing to criticize the culturist intellectuals and their books.[145] Many of those rural inhabitants who managed to gain some education had no love for village life at all. For example, an invalid soldier who became literate in the army wrote in desperation to the provincial zemstvo: "My talent is perishing in the village, and I want to serve the people and the state."[146] Such individuals, even when they stayed in the village, did not always act as centers of culture. A peasant librarian in Viatka province wrote to the zemstvo: "A few people came to have a look [at the library], but they threw the books down, spat, and went home." He concluded, "I tell you that no one reads."[147] The isolation of these budding intelligenty in their villages was not atypical. Many took advantage of what opportunities there were to abandon the countryside, or if they stayed escaped from the peasantry by becoming schoolteachers or employees of the local administration. Those who remained often did come to revere books and literature as the nineteenth-century culturist activists had hoped, but as readers they tended to have more in common with the lowest level of the educated public than with the ordinary literate villager, since their new positions gave them access to a broader literature.

IV

The development of rural literacy and the diffusion of books among the peasants, both from lubok publishers and from culturist activists, represented the first stage in the formation of a mass reading public in Russia. The second was the appearance of a body of worker readers, intermediaries between rural Russia and the cities who constituted the essential mass base for a lower class urban public.[148] Workers tended to be more literate than the peasants. In 1897 literacy among male and female workers in transport, industry, and trade was more than twice as high as rural literacy in European Russia.[149] Workers were more likely to come into contact with the educational institutions of the culturist activists. Workers' children, especially when they were in the cities, were more likely to be in school, and workers themselves could attend such novel urban enlightenment institutions as "people's universities," "houses of culture," and various technical and factory programs. Their attitudes could, therefore, be expected to show the influence of such efforts. The culturist activists in contact with the workers were often socialists, but they were no less dedicated to a highly moral understanding of books and literature than their less radical fellows. Among the workers were organizations of self-education and self-help, inside and outside the trade unions, and these also tended to display the traditional reverence for the written word.

Contemporary observers of worker and peasant readers found significant differences between the two. The most obvious was the workers' preference for secular rather than religious literature. The miners and tramps to whom An-sky read never asked for godly books, but instead were "heavily burdened by such reading and found it uninteresting."[150] Reports of free libraries for workers support this conclusion: for example, 22 percent of the holdings of the Pushkin Reading Room in Petersburg were religious, but in 1888 only 2 percent of the books taken out came from this category.[151] Noting the same trend, Rubakin suggested that it was a result of the workers' experience with man-made machines and the peasants' dependence on whimsical nature.[152] An-sky, who perceptively noted the workers' deep respect for religious books, blamed their unwillingness to listen to them on the contrast between "the sinfulness of their lives and the holiness of the religious books."[153] Respect for religious literature was as much a part of the workers' cultural heritage as it was of the peasants'; and even when their experience led them away from such literature, a sense of its value remained. Many workers began their reading with religious books. A student at one of the Russian Technical Society schools at the turn of the century recalls an early passion for fantastic stories, saints' lives, and tales of witches.[154] In 1909 the budding writer A. S. Novikov-Priboi, who grew up in a village in Tambov province and then served in the Baltic fleet, remembers how as a youth "from time to time I read books, but they were all soul-saving."[155]

The daily lives of the workers were clearly such that the moral homilies in traditional religious literature, as well as its mystical element, were likely to seem implausible. The experience of the Kharkov Sunday school teachers with several saints' lives published by Posrednik was perhaps typical. At a reading of *The Life of the Holy Filaret Milostivyi* (Moscow, 1886), the ten- to twelve-year-old children "listen with full interest and reverence," but do not accept the lessons of the story. When questioned on the scriptural passage about the birds of the air and the lilies of the field, the students gave such replies as "The birds fly and don't do any harm and the Lord feeds them, but people can't do it and they ought to work"; and "A bird is what?—she pinches something and flies off, but they catch a person and slap him in jail." Similarly, during another such reading, despite "tremendous interest and attention," the students showed neither "enthusiasm, delight, nor a thirst for feats."[156]

Worker attitudes toward belles lettres and other secular literature were also different from those of the peasants. The workers were avid readers of adventure stories—translations before the Revolution of 1905 and after it Russian originals as well. According to An-sky they liked to lose themselves in a book: they "listen to reading greedily, rapturously, with a kind of morbid delight."[157] Among workers there was no indication of the peasants' guilty ambivalence toward the fabulistic tale. For Rubakin such escapist reading was a step toward the classics: for An-sky it was a manifestation of the workers' need to flee into "a completely different world."

Yet worker readers shared some traits with peasant readers. They read more widely, their judgments were more independent, but they too sought a moral applicable to life and felt deep personal ties with fictional characters. At the Tiflis Women's Sunday School in 1890 a new student, dissatisfied with the reading, asked for "something godly, useful," and an older one replied that "the comedy of Ostrovsky was not written for laughter, but for its usefulness."[158] A Moscow Sunday school student at the turn of the century later recalled: "Leaving the school after finishing the course, I passionately occupied myself with useful books, informing myself about life." These, he explained, perhaps in reference to Dostoevsky, were most of all "preaching novels about the life of unhappy families and insulted people."[159] An-sky suggested that workers disliked blatant moral teaching but did want to find "truth" in what they read.[160] A good example of this is the critical written comments of workers at the Kharkov Men's Sunday School about Chekhov's "Muzhiki."[161] It makes one think about "why the Russian muzhiki live in poverty and are drunks and brawlers," wrote a 35-year-old metalworker. A 27-year-old typesetter found the content "good" but complained that "everything is poverty, poverty and ignorance": the "hope I feel ought to be in every person is completely absent." Another typesetter went further, blaming Chekhov for creating a story that "does not say anything about the good side of the muzhik," and that might mislead "the reader unfamiliar with the muzhik"; he wanted to know "why there isn't one example" of good people. The belief, so clearly exhibited here, that serious reading ought to instruct and uplift the reader represents a commingling of the experience and traditions of rural Russia with the injunctions of culturist educators.

Though their reading habits were in some respects similar to the peasants', the workers, concentrated in the cities with a high rate of literacy, formed the core of a new lower class reading public for whom the written word was increasingly the dominant means of articulating social values and developing class consciousness. Unlike the countryside the city was an environment filled with printed words. In the streets, in the shops, and in places of work, announcements, signs, newspapers, and books beckoned those who were able to read. Workers had more money to spend than peasants and, small though their expenditures on "culture" were, they were still significant. The workers were consumers who bought almost everything they needed to live, in contrast to the peasants, who continued to meet most of their needs through their own agriculture. The workers had the opportunity to purchase a wide variety of books and periodicals, and also had access to newspapers and magazines through beer halls and taverns. Libraries existed, though they were not always heavily patronized. Often workers would seek books elsewhere, either because the libraries did not have what they wanted or because they were afraid to ask.[162] Some highly conscious workers undoubtedly resented the patronizing tone in many educational institutions. A trade union paper complained after the Revolution of 1905: "In the 1890's the enlightenment of the workers took place; now the movement goes under the flag of worker self-education; in the absence of workers' control, schools and other teaching outside of the schools constitute a powerful weapon in the hands of the rulers of life."[163] The book or newspaper the worker could not get in the library was often an example of the new popular literature that developed in the cities primarily after 1905.

The worker readers had a significance out of proportion to their numbers for the same reason they were so politically important: their concentration in the major cities. It was the formation of a large urban audience that provided the final impetus for the appearance of a commercial mass literature aimed primarily at the lower classes. The most obvious indicator of this new urban audience was literacy. In 1897 there were over 7.5 million literate people in the cities of the empire, nearly 6 million of whom resided in the cities of European Russia. Over 60 percent of the literate urban population of both the empire and European Russia were men, and of these over 57 percent were aged 10 to 29, as were most of the literate women.[164] The urban book and periodical market was dominated by the two capitals, Moscow and St. Petersburg, with a combined literate population in 1897 of over 1.25 million.[165] The literate in the capitals were also predominantly young and male. The great majority of the inhabitants of the two capitals were not natives, but were instead migrants from the relatively poor countryside, who arrived in increasing numbers in the first decade of the twentieth century. In 1900 among the nonnative inhabitants of St. Petersburg, who constituted almost 70 percent of the city's population, the literacy rate was over 60 percent. By 1910 the number of new arrivals had passed 1.25 million, and 70 percent of them were literate.[166] The situation in Moscow was similar: the new arrivals constituted just over 70 percent of the city's population, and the literacy rate among them ranged from just under 60 percent in 1902 to over 66 percent in 1912.[167] Since the great majority of these migrants were already past primary school age when they arrived in the city, the literate among them had learned to read and had first come into contact with books in the countryside, most likely at a rural primary school. In fact, in 1910 the literacy rate among migrants to St. Petersburg from 1906 to 1909 who were twelve years of age or older when they arrived was more than 86 percent for men and nearly 60 percent for women.[168] Most of the literate among these new arrivals had learned to read before they reached the city. In the process the majority, who were peasants, had acquired the rudiments of traditional peasant attitudes toward books and literature. Their experience in the city, if they became workers, probably modified their attitudes in the ways described above.

Most of the urban literate were uneducated. In all the cities of the Russian Empire there were only a million people in 1897 who had attended a secondary or higher educational institution, however briefly—less than a seventh of all the urban literate.[169] In Moscow the educated constituted a similar proportion of those who could read, and in St. Petersburg slightly more than a sixth.[170] The concentration of such a large, predominantly lower class, potential literary market eventually ensured the emergence of a commercial mass literature. An urban subliterature existed in the late nineteenth century, but it was primarily a literature for merchants, the petty bourgeoisie, and the service people with whom they had contact—waiters, coachmen, servants, and the like. Such was the clientele of N. I. Pastukhov's *Moskovskii listok* (Moscow Sheet, 1881–1917), a glib, reactionary, anti-Semitic, scandal-mongering paper that covered the family affairs of prominent merchants, advertised pianos and tools, and convinced its readers to pay seven and a half rubles a year (without delivery in the 1890's) on the strength of its regular serial novels, potboilers with titles like *The Bloody Sin* and *The Dawn of a New Life*. The master of this fiction, A. M. Pazukhin, wrote scores of novels, with subjects ranging from an innocent in the clutches of city sharpers (*The Moscow Vultures*, Moscow, 1896) to the affairs of merchants like "Sveshnikov and Sons" (*After the Disaster*, Moscow, 1898) to the Revolution of 1905 (*On the Barricades*, Moscow, 1906) and the world war (*The War Storm*, Moscow, 1915). Yet for all his versatility, his novels, like *Moskovskii listok* and the rest of this nineteenth-century subliterature, failed to become firmly established among the lower classes, though such things were read on an irregular basis by workers and doormen and shopkeepers.*

---

* *Bibliografiia periodicheskikh izdanii Rossii 1901–16*, II (Leningrad, 1959), 358, gives the circulation of *Moskovskii listok* as 45,000 in 1910. The circulation of the Moscow *Gazeta kopeika* reached 60,000 in 1909, its first year of publication, according to the same source, I (Leningrad, 1958), 369.

Only after the Revolution of 1905 did an urban mass literature emerge, which was primarily a literature of the city poor in all their myriad guises. For the first time the literary preferences of the urban masses were translated into effective demand, which, within the limits imposed by censorship and the varying intentions and purposes of publishers, resulted in the appearance on the market of a whole range of new publications. At the outset this literature showed characteristics of both the old lubok publications and the late-nineteenth-century serial novel, and it did not entirely distinguish itself from either. Characteristic was the detective adventure craze that swept the cities after 1905. Though most of these stories were referred to as "Nick Carters," "Sherlock Holmeses," or "Nat Pinkertons," or were billed as the adventures of Lord Lister, Antonio Mussolino, or Arno Kraft ("the German Goliath"), they were not all foreign translations. Pinkerton himself disclaimed all responsibility for the Russian "Pinkertons," which he called "fairy tales," and accused Russian hack writers of "speculating in my name."[171] It was certainly native literati who concocted such gems as *The Daughter of Pinkerton and The Cruel Mother* (by Tekstorm, Moscow, 1910?), *Evno Azef (The Anarchist Detective): The Unusual Escapade of the Great Agent Provocateur* (St. Petersburg, 1909), and *The Detective Murderers: The Duel Between Sherlock Holmes and Nat Pinkerton* (Izd. Sazonov, Moscow, 1909), the last with an advertisement for the lubok classic *Pan Tvardovsky* on the back flap. Many of these books, even when priced at over a ruble, sold for much less; for example, *Jack, the Terrible Murderer of Women* (obviously Jack the Ripper) was published at a ruble and a half (Izd. Sazonov, Moscow, 1909?), but was advertised by the Moscow bookstore of F. A. Aparin for 50 kopecks. This advertisement appeared on the back of the lubok classic *Gromoboi* (Moscow, 1913), together with such titles as *The Terrible Ataman Cartouche* (50 kopecks), *The Doctor Bandit* (1 ruble 50, 1,359 pages), *The Gallery of Genius Detectives Known to All the World* (35 kopecks), *The Triumph of Labor* (1 ruble 20), and *Garibaldi, the People's Hero of Italy* (50 kopecks). Many such books appeared both in "whole" editions and serially, as did *The Adventures of Cartouche: The Bravest Bandit Ataman of All Times*, which was published in three-kopeck sections in editions of 20,000 in 1907.[172] The detective craze peaked in the first decade of the new century, sinking from a high of twelve million copies in 1908 to nine million in 1909 and eight million in 1910, at which time the average edition of such books was nearly 17,000 copies and the price approximately five kopecks.[173]

The clearest indication that the mass urban audience had attained the cohesiveness of a separate reading public was the appearance of the "kopeck" newspapers in both capitals and a number of provincial cities soon after the Revolution of 1905. The viability of these papers depended on a concentration of literate lower class readers with a little ready money and uninterrupted access to distribution points, a situation found only in the largest cities of Russia. The newspapers were named for their price, a single kopeck until World War I raised the price of paper and thus of the newspapers (to two kopecks). The first such paper (*Gazeta kopeika*) appeared in Petersburg on June 19, 1908, and on April 20, 1909, a Moscow edition (*Moskovskaia gazeta kopeika*) was issued by the same editor-publishers, M. Gorodetsky and V. Anzimirov, with an announcement that though independent, it was closely related to the Petersburg edition. The kopeck papers were an instant success. Within ten months the Petersburg edition had a circulation of 150,000, equal to that attained by Sytin's *Russkoe slovo* (Russian Word) in the course of a decade of steady expansion.[174] By July 1909 the kopeck papers of the capitals claimed a total circulation of 300,000, with an additional 350,000 for their weekly magazine supplement.[175] The daily circulation of the Petersburg *Gazeta kopeika* exceeded one million in 1917.[176]

Who were the kopeck readers? According to the journal of the Moscow city council in 1912, "a majority of the adult working population" of the capital read nothing but *Kopeika*, "which they receive in beer halls," and perhaps lubok editions of detective stories. Lenin had no illusions on this subject: in the same year he called on the workers of St. Petersburg to spend their "workers' kopecks on a workers' newspaper." The poet Demian Bednyi fumed against the kopeck papers in two poems in *Pravda*. L. M. Kleinbort, one of the most perceptive contemporary observers of the proletarian cultural scene, guessed the papers' secret to be their appeal to "the lower categories of labor," and he was forced to agree with a worker who said that "in the mornings you arrive at the shop and you see the workers are busy reading the newspaper *Kopeika*."[177]

The kopeck papers did well for a number of reasons. They provided lively and detailed coverage of the world of the urban poor at a low price. In the Petersburg *Kopeika* in 1909 there were stories about workers' enlightenment institutions (no. 171), "the tramps' stock exchange" (no. 339), "the pirates of the Neva" (no. 344), the hypnotist "heroes of the dark kingdom" (no. 369), and street musicians (no. 328). In the same year the Moscow paper ran stories captioned "The Society of Joiners, Turners, and Carpenters" (no. 75), "Among the Bakers and Pastry Makers" (no. 117), and "Beastly Murder" (no. 8). It also carried selections on health and science, and in 1911 collected significant amounts of money from workers in many factories for famine relief. As well as presenting readers with information about city life, the papers aspired to a cultural role. Far from being the trash publications that many intellectual observers mistook them for, they echoed, perhaps in a distorted way but nevertheless recognizably, not only the elemental literary tastes of the mass reader, urban and rural, but also the dreams and admonishments of the culturist activists. In the Petersburg paper in 1909 Shevshchenko is hailed as "the poet of serfdom" (no. 219), Gogol as "the awakener of social conscience" (no. 237), and Chekhov for his great knowledge of and love for the "simple people" (no. 536). In June 1910 the Petersburg *Kopeika* summed up its first two years of existence by claiming that it "tried to awaken the reader's interest in society," to prompt "civic feelings," and to encourage in the reader "a striving to develop, to search for bright and pure ideals" (no. 686). Similarly, on April 26, 1909, in the first week of its existence, the Moscow *Kopeika* dedicated its entire issue to Gogol, with appropriate quotations from Belinsky, Chernyshevsky, and others. In its first few months the Moscow paper offered regular subscribers a choice of ten books from a list of a hundred that included the works of Gogol, Pushkin, Lermontov, Kol'tsov, and Zhukovsky, as well as Heine, Goethe, Flaubert, and Zola (no. 191). In addition, all subscribers were to receive large color portraits of Chekhov and the populist writer N. N. Zlatovratsky. In 1912 the editor, Anzimirov, hailed books as "a source of wisdom, as a friendly adviser, as something holy."

The greatest drawing card of the kopeck papers was undoubtedly their serialized novels, and no issue of the papers was complete without one. These escapist adventure stories were similar to American dime novels in their larger-than-life heroes and fast-moving plots, but they also were very much tailored to the familiar demands of worker and peasant readers—for empathetic characters and situations, for information about far-off and exotic places, and for half-scientific, half-romantic excursions into the world of the occult. Among the heroes and heroines of the Moscow edition were such characters as the revolutionary schoolteacher Silin, who lost his post at a rural primary school in "the days of freedom" (1909, no. 109);

Nikolai Zharov, a proletarian artist who returns to factory life after a three-year bout with tuberculosis (1912, no. 251/817); the poor but pretty Lila, who sells herself to a rich man for an easy life (*Trudovaia kopeika*,* 1909, no. 1); and Zhenia, a lower middle class girl who comes to the city and is lured into a bawdy house (*Trudovaia kopeika*, 1912, no. 33/190). In the Petersburg edition Masanov, a circus strongman of impoverished gentry origins, prefers prizefighting and breaking chains to university study (1909, no. 455); and the regular super-hero of that edition, the reforming bandit Anton Krechet, a latter-day Milord George, wanders all over Russia and to France, Germany, and Japan attempting to find a new life with his true love. In these novels, often republished at 20 or 30 kopecks right up to 1917, sometimes in editions as large as 40,000 (*Anton Krechet*, St. Petersburg, 1909, 20 kopecks) but more frequently 10,000, the lower class reader could find a model hero or heroine, often one whose life was an attempt to do good.

In the last few years of the empire there appeared another dramatic indication of the presence of a mass public, though not necessarily an urban one. This was the tremendous upsurge in the publication of works by those who had come to be understood as the classical writers. In 1908, 500,000 copies of works by Tolstoy priced at less than 30 kopecks, nearly 140,000 copies of Pushkin, and about 40,000 each of Gogol and Turgenev were published.[178] In 1913 Tolstoy fell to 400,000, but there were over 500,000 copies of Pushkin, over 400,000 copies of Gogol, and over 150,000 copies of Turgenev, all priced at less than 30 kopecks. These books reached peasants as well as workers. No contemporary authors approached such figures in the cheap book market. When Verbitskaia was at the height of her fame in 1913, a 32-page illustrated edition of *Keys to Happiness* was issued in 50,000 copies. Some of the authors published by Posrednik had large editions. Perhaps the most widely read of the contemporary authors were the same conventional scene painters and adventure writers who were so successful with the educated public, writers like Mamin-Sibiriak, who had 80,000 copies published in 1913, and V. I. Nemirovich-Danchenko, with almost 40,000 in the same year. Among the familiar realist writers only Leonid Andreev was published on this scale. The books of these authors, along with the works of classical writers, were all a literature in which, with a bit of prompting, the new readers could find "life" and a moral comment on it.

---

* *Trudovaia kopeika* was the Monday edition of the Moscow newspaper.

A wide selection of inexpensive reading matter was available to lower class inhabitants of Moscow and St. Petersburg on the eve of the revolution, ranging from works of belles lettres and popular science to detective stories, kopeck serials, and *lubochnaia literatura*. Exposure to such variety may have softened traditional attitudes toward books, but the content of the kopeck novels suggests that earlier cultural ideals had not lost their force. The diversified popular literature of the capitals, which was perhaps distributed or reproduced in other large cities, did not effectively extend its influence to the countryside. Peasant readers remained in 1917 half-way between the thriving indigenous literature of the lubok and the type of educated literature the dedicated culturist activists channeled in their direction.

v

The range of readers and reading at the end of the old regime showed several characteristics of the cultural world of a modern industrial society. The urban poor formed a cohesive mass reading public with a special literature, the boulevard novels of the kopeck press. At the other end of the literary spectrum, an elite public read its own particular belles lettres in the form of modernism, a literature that, despite prophetic flashes of social consciousness, remained exclusive, exotic, and closed to the lower classes by the difficulty of its language and its often personalized subject matter. Between the two publics was a sizable group of educated and semieducated readers who liked narrative fiction with a clear plot and empathetic characters.

Transcending these similarities with Western literary culture were certain peculiarities of literate Russia. As the end of the old regime approached, the entire Russian audience was in flux. Peasants continued to attain literacy in ever greater numbers, slowly altering the cultural climate of rural Russia and swelling the urban mass public through migration. A politically conscious, self-educated intelligentsia from the people did develop and, in accord with the expectations of the culturist activists, entered the cultural worlds of the intelligentsia and came to appreciate it, but such readers were a tiny minority. The educated audience itself had separated into an elite public of modernist readers and a larger audience whose tastes were more in line with traditional culturist assumptions. The vast majority of lower class readers in the countryside and in the cities, despite their social condition, shared many of the attitudes of traditionally minded educated readers; but they remained estranged, in their cultural sensibilities and in their daily lives, from the milieu of the intelligentsia and the intellectual world of modernist creativity.

The lower class audience, a product of Russia's cultural heritage and of almost 40 years of work by the culturist activists, exhibited traits of both. These were readers who, for all the melodrama they might consume, had a highly idealistic and purposive understanding of what they read. They demanded a didactic literature in conventional style and had little tolerance for Russian modernism and the tastes of the modernist reader. They adopted the strictures of the culturist intellectuals about the moral and social purpose of literature, blending them with already deeply rooted cultural assumptions that the written word must be true both to life and to a higher moral ideal. Most of the intelligentsia from the people shared these views and expressed them with a special passion. The literary tastes of many educated readers coincided roughly with those of the masses and the intelligentsia from the people, but their perspectives were wider and their break with the traditions of rural Russia more complete. The traditional sensibility of the masses and the dreams and efforts of the culturist intellectuals conjoined in a demand, shared by a majority of readers from the educated and the mass audience alike, that literature both fulfill its holy mission and be true to life. This demand, satisfied in part by the variegated literature of the late imperial era, entered the cultural dowry of prerevolutionary Russia.

EDWARD J. BROWN

Pisarev and the Transformation of
Two Russian Novels

I. *The Problem of Life and Art*

I want to discuss Dmitry Pisarev's critical transformation of two
Russian novels that deal with the problem of the nihilists, Turgenev's
Fathers and Sons and Dostoevsky's *Crime and Punishment*, and in
so doing to explore not only his techniques as a sociological critic
but the social context of his own work. It seems appropriate to begin such an investigation with the remarks of a critic who resides at
a galactic distance from Pisarev, a decadent and an aesthete, Oscar
Wilde. Both Wilde and Pisarev were concerned with the relationship
of life and fiction, but Wilde maintained that life is either inferior
to art or else its slavish imitation. Let me remind you of that delight-
ful collection of paradoxes whose final effect in our time has been to
reduce the formula "life imitates art" almost to the level of cliché.
Vivian, the author of the article on the decay of lying, says of the
origin and fate of art:

Art begins with abstract decoration, with purely imaginative and pleasur-
able work dealing with what is unreal and nonexistent. This is the first
stage. Then life becomes fascinated with this new wonder, and asks to be
admitted into the charmed circle. Art takes life as part of her rough material, recreates it, and refashions it in fresh forms, is absolutely indifferent to fact, invents, imagines, dreams, and keeps between herself and
reality the impenetrable barrier of beautiful style, of decorative or ideal
treatment. The third stage is when life gets the upper hand, and drives
art out into the wilderness. This is the true decadence, and it is from this
that we are now suffering.[1]

Let me give a few examples of Wilde's brilliant formulation of the matter in terms of particular works. He says of Wordsworth, who went to nature for inspiration, "he found in stones sermons he'd already hidden there." And as for Shakespeare's Hamlet and the passage about holding the mirror up to nature: "They will call upon Shakespeare—they always do—and will quote that hackneyed passage about art holding the mirror up to nature, forgetting that this unfortunate aphorism is deliberately said by Hamlet in order to convince the bystanders of his absolute insanity in all art matters." "The Greeks thought that realism in art makes people ugly," says Wilde, "and they were right." "Schopenhauer has analysed the pessimism that characterizes modern thought, but Hamlet invented it." "The nineteenth century, as we know it, is largely the invention of Balzac." "Robespierre came out of the pages of Rousseau." "Literature always anticipates Life. It does not copy it, but molds it to its purpose." And he says of Russian literature, which brings us back to my topic, "The nihilist, that strange martyr who has no faith, who goes to the stake without enthusiasm, and dies for what he does not believe in, is a purely literary product. He was invented by Turgenev and completed by Dostoevsky." That there is some justice in that final paradox I think I can demonstrate.

Let us now traverse the galactic distance that separates Wilde from the Russian radical critics of the mid-nineteenth century, those decadents who drove art out into the wilderness. The Russian critic Chernyshevsky, whose aesthetics Pisarev accepted, maintained that all art is subordinate to life, that it is dependent on the external world for both its content and its form.[2] The critics of the mid-century firmly established in the Russian literary world what Wilde regarded as a decadent idea, the idea that art, however imperfectly, does reflect life. This is the basic, unargued assumption of Pisarev's mature critical work. Moreover, Russian novelists themselves seem to have accepted this notion without reflection. Gogol, who knew very little about Russia, believed that he was holding a mirror up to her, and that if the image seemed cracked or distorted, the fault was with the subject. Turgenev felt obliged to justify his behavior as a writer of novels by insisting on their importance as a kind of historical record. As he put it in the much-quoted foreword to the 1880 edition of his works:

The author of *Rudin*, written in 1855, and of *Virgin Soil*, written in 1876, is one and the same man. In the course of all that time, I tried, within the limits of my powers and ability, conscientiously and impartially to describe and incarnate in appropriate types both what Shakespeare calls "the body and pressure of time" and the quickly changing countenance of educated Russians.

And yet critics of the twentieth century tend to consider Turgenev as an artist involved primarily with the craft of writing and to question the relevance, even the sincerity, of this statement, written long after the novels had become themselves historical facts, their social significance well established in Russian sociological criticism.[3] Eikhenbaum has argued that Turgenev created an illusion of reality by the use of the frame technique; Grossman identifies the "miniature" as particularly characteristic of Turgenev and suggests that his forte is the creation of brief portraits, bits of dialogue, and independent scenes; Vasily Gippius in his brief comments has illuminated the structure of a Turgenev novel both "static" and "dynamic"; Richard Freeborn's attention is given principally to characteristics of style and portraiture; and Virginia Burns's recent study of *Fathers and Sons* attempts to establish that plot, in the sense of *siuzhet*, is an important feature of Turgenev's best novel.[4] Ralph Matlaw has argued very convincingly that Turgenev was more concerned with aesthetic matters than with the historical or social content of his novels. Such, in the main, is the view of Turgenev from the twentieth century; and yet the novelist himself repeatedly explained his novels to himself, to his correspondents, and to his Russian readers, and each explanation emphasizes their derivation from and reference to the social reality of contemporary Russia.[5]

A somewhat analogous pattern emerges when we compare the critical view of Dostoevsky's work that obtained in nineteenth-century Russia with modern critical analysis. Nineteenth-century critics, including Pisarev, never doubted that Dosoevsky's intention in his novels was to advance a particular view of men and of the real world. Dostoevsky also knew perfectly well, or thought he knew, what he was doing; his correspondence and his journalistic writing leave no doubt about that. But the twentieth century, on the whole, has appropriated him for its own purposes. Consider the work of Bakhtin, who finds that the novels are "polyphonic," that each viewpoint is given for its own sake, that each voice in the sharply discordant argument has equal validity—that, as a matter of fact, Dostoevsky, for all his fluency and power, wasn't really saying anything.[6] The dialogues he constructed, according to this interpretation, present ideas in a state of dialectic tension; the important thing, then, is the artistic structure that Dostoevsky made out of a philosophic medley. A more recent critic, Jan Meijer, who does not fully agree with Bakhtin, still cautions us against looking in the novels for "messages." These, he maintains, "are much easier to draw from the *Diary of a Writer*, or in general from his articles and letters, than from the novels."[7]

In the case both of Turgenev and of Dostoevsky, modern criticism heeds the admonition of William Wimsatt about the "intentional fallacy" and does not presume to know what those novelists "intended," or what relation their work had to the historical context. I emphasize this because we will see that, paradoxically, the nineteenth-century critic Pisarev had his own version of the "intentional fallacy," and this made it possible for him, like the moderns, to discover in those novels, not what their authors intended, but what the critic is able to find or possibly create himself.

As for the historical context, the reality represented in the "realistic" novel was, as I have said, the prime concern of mid-nineteenth-century Russian writing and criticism, and that tradition continues in the Soviet Union today, not only in the debased and dishonest form of official criticism, but most notably in the literary performances of Solzhenitsyn. Powerful and moving evidence of the persistence of this old tradition is found in his recent *The Calf Butts the Oak* where he gives a record of his thoughts as he prepared his Nobel lecture. He says that in the lecture he had intended to speak only about social and intellectual life both East and West, but that when he read the lectures of previous recipients he realized such a talk would be a violent breach of tradition:

It would never have entered the head of a writer from the free world to talk about such things. For that they have other platforms, places, and occasions; Western writers, when they gave their lectures, spoke of the nature of art, of beauty, of the nature of literature. . . . And apparently I was expected to talk about the same things. But to discuss the nature of literature or its possibilities would be for me a difficult and boring treatment of what is of secondary importance: what I'm able to do, that I'll do and show; what I can't do, I won't attempt to discuss. And if I gave such a lecture, just how would former prisoners react to it? Why was he given a voice and a platform? Was he afraid? . . . Has he betrayed the dead?[8]

For Solzhenitsyn literature is necessarily involved with social and political reality. A Russian writer who turned his face away from that reality and concerned himself with purely aesthetic matters might seem to him guilty of cowardice or betrayal. Literature ought to be real and earnest. Solzhenitsyn himself might be astonished to hear it, but his words echo closely Pisarev's thoughts on the place of literature in Russian life, which he expressed with clarity and force throughout his brief literary career. In an article he wrote in 1861 early in his career as a critic, Pisarev compared the situation of literature in Russia with that in the West:

[Russian realistic novels] have for us not only an aesthetic but also a social interest. The English have Dickens, Thackeray, and Eliot, but they also have John Stuart Mill; the French have journalists and socialists as well as novelists. But in Russia the whole sum of ideas about society, about the human personality, about social and family relations, is concentrated in belles lettres and in the criticism of belles lettres; we do not have an independent moral philosophy, we do not have a social science, and so we must look for all of this in literary works. . . . Many of our writers have become writers only because they could not become social figures or political writers; and as for those who are genuine artists by vocation, they too have been obliged to become journalists in some aspect of their writing activity.[9]

And in that same article he goes on to say that Russians cannot honor lyric poets such as Fet, Polonsky, and other "microscopic poetasters." To such writers, who have no more title to be called artist than a hairdresser who has invented a new coiffure, the younger generation will put the following questions: "What have you done for us? How have you enriched our minds? . . . How have you instilled in us the spark of hatred for the filthy and barbarous aspects of our life?" Pisarev spoke with aversion of Turgenev's wonderful story "First Love," where there are neither ideas about nor commentary on Russian problems; such stories seemed to him a betrayal of hungry and miserable, poor and stupid Russia. The central problem of Russian life was the problem of poverty. "We are poor because we are stupid and we are stupid because we are poor," he wrote in the essay "The Realists" (III, 9), and it seemed to follow from this that the central concern of literature ought to be "the poor and the naked." In order to break out of the vicious circle of poverty and ignorance, Pisarev called for an "economy of intellectual forces," their concentration on the central problem. The program for literature left no room for the purely aesthetic experience; the well-known nihilism of his article "The Destruction of Aesthetics" can be understood only in relation to this general program. The products of art— poetry, painting, architecture—waste intellectual capital to satisfy the taste for luxury of the upper classes. Any activity directed toward aesthetic enjoyment alone is a social waste. "The right to pass final judgment on literary works belongs not to the aesthete, who can only judge form, but to the 'thinking man' who judges content, that is to say the facts [*yavleniya*] of life" (III, 435).

11. *Pisarev and Bazarov*

I will not in the short space of this paper be able to say much about Pisarev's biography, nor can I do more than sketch his materialist philosophy, which came to him, in the main, from Vogt, Moleschott, and Büchner. It would be an interesting project in psychohistory to investigate his early life as a bright and obedient child, a great joy to his mother; his early interest in philological and literary studies, which he demonstratively abandoned in favor of journalistic writing and the propagation of the natural sciences; his long struggle with a manic-depressive psychosis and his confinement in a mental hospital; his strange relationship with his mother, who was frantically possessive and jealous of his independence; his incarceration for four years in the Peter and Paul Fortress for having written an article regarded as seditious, where he experienced a period of peace and calm—broken, his correspondence tells us, by his release (his mother too was quite happy during that period; at least she knew where he was)—and where his most important essays were written. Nor will I have anything to say about his death at the age of 26 from drowning, an accident that may have had a heavy ingredient of suicide, but that in any case fulfilled a lifelong fear and expectation of death by drowning, a fate he narrowly escaped on two occasions before the final event. Let me just say that Pisarev was, from his own experience, probably as great an expert on abnormal mental states as Dostoevsky.

I would like to turn my attention now to Pisarev's treatment of *Fathers and Sons*. That novel when it appeared provoked a confusion of criticism, both from the right and from the left, from old and young alike.[10] What, everyone asked, is Turgenev trying to tell us in this confrontation of a radical young materialist—blunt, crude, and angular—with several members of the liberal landowning aristocracy? Are we to admire him? Sympathize with him? Imitate him? In the contemporary debate over the novel a certain pattern emerges: conservatives saw in Bazarov a sympathetic portrayal of the young radicals and were unhappy with Turgenev; the young radicals regarded Bazarov as a negative character and a slander upon themselves, and they wrote scornfully of the novel and of Turgenev. A brilliant exception on the left was Pisarev, who embraced Bazarov as the representative of his own generation and his own style of thought, and accepted the novel as a great work of art.*

In his transformation of the novel Pisarev is not without critical subtlety. He points out that Turgenev is an artist and that as an artist he produced "not a dissertation but a deeply felt and accurately drawn picture of contemporary life" (II, 28). He opens with a general statement on the "strange charm" one finds in reading a novel that is not rich in incident, whose basic idea is not especially sound, that has neither a beginning, a middle, nor an end, nor any carefully worked out plot. Pisarev was probably the first to utter the judgment that later critics from Henry James to Richard Freeborn (and even Turgenev himself) have made of Turgenev as a writer of fiction, namely that his novel is constructed out of "types and characters, scenes and pictures." Turgenev does not understand the younger generation, said Pisarev, or else he understands them in his own way; yet the mirror he holds up to them, though it alters the natural color of things, nonetheless reflects them faithfully. "It is interesting to trace," he says, "the effect on a man like Turgenev of the ideas and urges that are now stirring in our younger generation and that, like everything that is alive, manifest themselves in the most various forms, seldom attractive, often very original, and sometimes ugly" (II, 7).

Pisarev reveals almost in spite of himself a sensitivity to art and an appreciation of the role it plays, though it is not clear that he ever satisfactorily defined the nature of art. In the article "Turgenev, Pisemsky, and Goncharov," written a few months earlier than "Bazarov," Pisarev asks the question "What is an artist?" and offers an answer that emphasizes the necessary connection, in his mind, of literary art and social reality.

You will notice that we all may observe a case of street violence, but not all of us will be deeply affected by it; it will not move all of us with the same force. What thoughts would visit a sensitive person who witnesses, let's say, such a deed as the beating of a cabman on the street? That event will appear to him as only one episode in a lengthy drama . . . played out every day without witnesses in various poor lodgings, on the streets . . . wherever the poor and the weak endure their bitter lot at the hands of the rich and the strong. The imagination of such a sensitive person would work in the missing details; a natural human feeling, nurtured by a many-

* Pisarev first analyzed the novel in the article "Bazarov," which appeared in *Russkoe slovo*, no. 3, 1862. The text used here is in *Sochineniia* (Moscow, 1955–56), II, 7–50.

sided education, would give warmth to the whole picture, and thus, out of a coarse street scene, there would arise a work of art, one that would have an effect on the reader, stir him deeply and oblige him to take thought. One who is sensitive by his nature and his education, and who has acquired the skill to communicate his experience to others in such a way that they will experience what he experienced, feel what he felt, such a man is an artist. (I, 193–94)

And in that passage (which, incidentally, is strongly reminiscent of Tolstoy's view of the artist), Pisarev emphasizes that an artist who uses words, a writer, cannot escape the need to express both thought and feeling, cannot avoid taking a stand. Pisarev assumes that Turgenev could not have invented the Russian nihilist, even though he could not have known any young radicals closely. As an artist he must have observed them, and his sensitive imagination filled out the picture and produced in the character Bazarov a fictional generalization faithful to the realities of Russian life.

Pisarev here is very close to Henry James's idea of what the art of fiction involves. In his essay "The Art of Fiction," James engaged in a subtle and civilized polemic with a long-forgotten critic, Mr. Walter Besant, who had many regrettable ideas about the writing of novels. Among these was the notion that the novelist must write from direct experience, that his "characters must be real and such as might be met with in actual life," that "a young lady brought up in a quiet country village should avoid descriptions of garrison life." James answers that the experience from which a writer writes is a more complex matter than Besant supposes:

Experience is never limited and it is never complete; it is an immense sensibility, a kind of huge spider web of the finest silken threads suspended in the chamber of consciousness, and catching every airborne particle in its tissue. It is the very atmosphere of the mind; and when the mind is imaginative—much more when it happens to be that of a man of genius—it takes to itself the faintest hints of life, it converts the very pulses of the air into revelations. The young lady living in a village has only to be the damsel upon whom nothing is lost to make it quite unfair (as it seems to me) to declare to her that she shall have nothing to say about the military. Greater miracles have happened than that, imagination assisting, she should speak the truth about some of these gentlemen. I remember an English novelist, a woman of genius, telling me that she was much commended for the impression she had managed to give in one of her tales of the nature and way of life of the French Protestant youth. She had been asked where she had learned so much about this recondite being, she had been congratulated on her peculiar opportunities. These opportunities consisted in her having once, in Paris, as she ascended a staircase, passed an open door where, in the household of a *pasteur* some of the young Protestants were seated at a table around a finished meal. The glimpse made a picture; it lasted only a moment, but that moment was experience.[11]

James concluded by saying that Besant's charge to write only from experience would be a "tantalizing monition" if the writer failed to heed James's own advice to "try to be one of the people upon whom nothing is lost."

For Pisarev as for James the artist is a source of "truth," but he need not write from experience only. Turgenev, though he had read the publications of the young Russian radicals, had little direct experience of them; according to his own account he had only brief accidental encounters with two young doctors whose attitudes and opinions both fascinated and repelled him. But since he was one of those people "upon whom nothing is lost," the fleeting glimpse was enough. The novel *Fathers and Sons*, according to Pisarev, not only possesses "artistic beauty" but also "stirs the mind," forces the reader to "reflect" (II, 8). The feeling with which it is permeated is "sincere." Moreover, the idea that the novel took form *in spite of* what Turgenev intended is, as I have said, Pisarev's basic critical assumption, which he states explicitly in many ways:

When he created Bazarov, Turgenev intended to smash the character to bits, but instead of doing that he gave Bazarov a full measure of honest admiration. He intended to say that our younger generation had taken a false turn, but he said: in our younger generation is our only hope. Turgenev is not a dialectician or a sophist; he could not, in the images of his novel, try to demonstrate some preconceived thesis, no matter how true in the abstract or useful in practice this thesis might seem to him. He is first of all an artist, a man who is unconsciously, even in spite of himself, sincere. . . . It would be impossible for him to manipulate [his characters] according to his own whim, and thus turn a true picture of life into an allegory with a moral tendency and a virtuous conclusion. The pure and honest nature of the artist wins the day . . . and through his sure instinct makes up for everything else: for the mistaken ideas, the one-sided development of the story, and the obsolete notions. (II, 48)

Only an artist, that special kind of being, could have produced *Fathers and Sons*. And Pisarev speculates, quite correctly, that if an author belonging to the "new generation" had written the book, it might have been very different. Bazarov would not have been an angular seminarian (*bursak*) who dominates the other characters by the power of his own mind; he might instead have been transformed into an incarnation of those ideas that are the essence of the character type:

He would have been a clear representation of the author's own ideas and attitudes, but the character would hardly have been the equal of Bazarov in truthfulness to life and vividness of portrayal. . . . To us, the members of the younger generation, it would of course have been much pleasanter if Turgenev had concealed and camouflaged his graceless angularity; but I do not believe that in thus playing up to our arbitrary needs the artist would have involved himself as deeply in the manifestations of real life. (II, 29)

Pisarev anticipates that many critics of his own persuasion will find fault with Turgenev because he did not present a "positive character" in Bazarov, a model human being, a shining knight of thought, "fearless and irreproachable," but he scornfully rejects the value of such positive characters (II, 25): "We must not, in the name of realism, idealize either ourselves or our movement. . . . We are surrounded by barbarism and ignorance, and as a matter of fact we ourselves are, God knows, not all purity and light." Later in the article he returns to this point. He anticipates that critics will berate Turgenev for that phony and pathetic "liberated woman" Kukshina, and ask him why he did not portray a Russian woman emancipated in the finest sense of the word (II, 35): "But that would have been a pleasant lie, and a lie in the highest degree unconvincing. I might ask, where would Turgenev have found the colors for the representation of such things as do not exist in Russia and for which Russian life offers neither the proper soil nor enough room?"

Pisarev's firm rejection of the notion of the "positive hero," of characters intended for imitation, and of purposeful, didactic literature naturally raises the somewhat vexed question of his attitude toward the novel *What Is to Be Done?*, which appeared just one year after his article on *Fathers and Sons*, as well as toward other didactic novels of the radical left. His rejection of that genre, and by implication of *What Is to Be Done?*, was modified somewhat by his favorable comment on Chernyshevsky's novel in the article "Mysliashchii proletariat" (IV, 7–50), but a close inspection of his remarks shows, I think, that he placed the work in a different category entirely from *Fathers and Sons*. At no point does Pisarev ever bestow on Chernyshevsky the honored title of artist. Rather he treats the novel as a valid and important essay, with concrete fictional illustration, on several themes: the rational organization of human relations, the establishment of a just social order, the liberation of women, and the magnificent future that will surely result from the application of sound good sense to all human affairs. Pisarev identifies, it seems to me, an ingredient in the novel that does save it from fatuity: the author's unashamed belief in the future and his enthusiasm for the human enterprise. "All of the author's sympathies are unquestionably on the side of the future; those sympathies are given without stint to those beginnings [*zadatki*] of the future that can be discovered in the present" (IV, 9). Pisarev emphasizes that the novel *What Is to Be Done?* is not about the present but about the future, and not only in Vera Pavlovna's fourth dream. The "new people" are elements in a kind of experiment: if human beings can learn to act as *they* act, then what might our life be like? And again: "The author implements [*provodit*] in his novel all his theories and convictions, and thus produces a work in the highest degree original and quite remarkable." But, as I say, Pisarev would never confuse a work of that sort with a work of art, Turgenev's *Fathers and Sons*. Rufus Mathewson, in his *The Positive Hero in Russian Literature*, contrasts the artists with the radicals, pointing out that "For the great Russian novelists ideas and doctrine were not excluded, but were contained in character, and made a function of the whole man. . . . The radicals, on the other hand, were interested in ideological man. In their view of literary truth . . . character was a function of doctrine."[12] Pisarev would not have disagreed with our contemporary critic's formulation of the matter, though he assigned considerably greater weight to Chernyshevsky's fictional experiment.

Having identified the novel *Fathers and Sons* as a true statement about contemporary Russian life, Pisarev then proceeds to analyze its scenes and characters in considerable detail. Here it develops that as well as a critic and a social thinker, Pisarev is an artist manqué, one who uses the material of the novel not only as evidence, but also to produce a new creation of his own. He explains what happens in the novel, expands and expatiates, makes clear what is problematic, continually fills in missing details of the picture, and speculates on the motivation of the characters. The phrase "he must have felt" or "he must have thought," followed by an informal exploration of the character's mental processes, occurs at least a dozen times in the two essays "Bazarov" and "The Realists." Turgenev in *Fathers and Sons* introduces Bazarov without supplying the reader with any background information: he seems to say, here he is, this is what he looks like, this is how he talks and acts. It is a totally objective characterization; the reader is given no entry into Bazarov's thought processes, nor are we able to account for his nihilism in terms of his life. The inward life of Bazarov, however, is supplied for us by Pisarev, especially the psychological details of his relationship to his parents and the curious, unspoken history of his unhappy love affair with Odintsova. In so doing Pisarev gives us information that does not fit Turgenev's artistic plan, but that we would want to have if the story of *Fathers and Sons* were a true case history. Pisarev relies on his own fertile imagination for this information, and at one point he says, "The reader may perhaps think I have invented Bazarov and Odintsova" (III, 51). Indeed the reader might very well think so, and with justice, but Pisarev insists that everything he says is based on the "factual" material in the novel, and he elaborates: "I must demonstrate that I am not inventing and that everything I say is based simply on a correct understanding of those materials which Turgenev provides, and which, it seems to me, Turgenev himself does not always view from the proper perspective, although the factual details are always astonishingly accurate in his novels" (III, 51).

We have here an interesting assumption about the relationship of art and truth, and the relationship of writer and critic. The artist works under a compulsion to reveal the truth about life, though he may not quite understand what he is doing. The critic then steps in and explains to him and to his readers the full significance of the events he has recorded in his novel. Explains to him, for instance, that Bazarov had experienced the hard lot of a poor student at the university and comes by his radicalism naturally (the material for this conclusion is contained in the laconic observation of the elder Bazarov that "he never asked for a penny"). Explains that Bazarov, in his references to his parents, is not really a harsh, unfeeling son, but one deeply saddened by his inevitable alienation from them (III, 23). Explains that Arkady, for whom some readers, and perhaps Turgenev, felt a certain sympathy, is really a useless appendage to Bazarov and will probably develop into a social parasite in the fullness of his days. He explicates at length features of Bazarov's love affair that Turgenev, an artist, only shows us (II, 39). And the critic as historian places Bazarov in diachronic relationship to the Onegins, Pechorins, Rudins, and Beltovs, who also embodied, he believed, social tendencies (III, 141).

The second article in which Pisarev deals with *Fathers and Sons*, "The Realists," is a programmatic statement in which he tries to give a complete and coherent account of his materialistic views, not in abstract, philosophical terms, however, but by delineating the features of a social and intellectual movement then developing in Russia. Hard evidence for the existence of such a movement Pisarev draws from literature, chiefly from *Fathers and Sons*. The fictional character Bazarov has now become his model and his ideal, and he enters a vigorous defense of that ideal against the crude attacks of the radical left, especially the critic of the *Contemporary*, Antonovich.[13] Antonovich's review of *Fathers and Sons*, entitled "An Asmodeus of Our Time," can only be described as obtusely partisan, to the point even of distorting the material in the novel. This critic tells us that Bazarov is a cardsharp and a rake, a glutton, almost a drunkard, cruel to his parents, coarse and without ideals; such are the sons as Turgenev presents them, according to Antonovich. But the fathers, he says, "are just the opposite of their sons, they are moral people, modestly and silently they do good deeds.... Even such an empty fop as Pavel Petrovich is raised on stilts and presented as a fine human being."[14]

Pisarev has no difficulty annihilating Antonovich. It would seem that when Turgenev's novel held the mirror up to them, let them see themselves in all their "angularity," the radicals roared with indignation at the image and even exaggerated its faults. They recognized many of their own features in Bazarov, but missed the much more important fact that Bazarov's ideas were their own, and that both in the novel and in life, he and they were tragically isolated in the Russian environment.

Not only does Pisarev find in the novel the truth of Russian life; he now finds, as I said, his own ideal in the character of Bazarov. I doubt very much that Oscar Wilde had heard of Pisarev when he wrote that Turgenev had "invented the Russian nihilist." Others have suggested, however, that Pisarev and his friends were a prime example of life imitating art. But the relationship of life and art is immensely more complex than Wilde's effete theoretician imagined. In his essay "Bazarov Once Again" Aleksandr Herzen dealt with this complex process, pointing out that "Pisarev recognized himself and others in Bazarov, and supplied what was lacking in the book."[15] Herzen goes on:

This mutual interaction of people and books is a strange thing. A book takes its whole shape from the society that spawns it, then generalizes the material, renders it clearer and sharper, and then is outstripped by reality. The originals make caricatures of their own sharply drawn portraits and real people take on the character of their literary shadows. At the end of the last century all German men were a little like Werther, all German women like Charlotte; at the beginning of this century the university Werthers began to turn into "Robbers" à la Schiller, not real ones. Young Russians were almost all out of *What Is to Be Done?* after 1862, with the addition of a few of Bazarov's traits.[16]

Herzen here touches the nerve of the question, and of course the inspiration of his comment was the behavior of Pisarev himself vis-à-vis Turgenev's novel. In his first discussion of the novel in the article "Bazarov," Pisarev made the point that the artist, in spite of his intentions, reveals a particular reality to us; then he proceeded to fill in what was missing in Turgenev's picture. Having transformed the novel into a document favorable to the nihilist cause, Pisarev went one step further in his second discussion of it, written two years later in the fortress prison, and transformed Bazarov into a "model," almost a "positive hero," for a part of the younger generation.

Pisarev's effort to fashion *himself* as an image of Bazarov is a striking episode in the long love-hate relationship between life and art. Like Bazarov, Pisarev as an individualist stands apart from the radicals of his time; for him the central concern of revolution must be the individual human personality. Like Bazarov, Pisarev is indifferent to the organization of a mass revolutionary movement. Bazarov, we remember, answers Arkady's pious thought on the need to organize things so that even the most insignificant peasant might live in a nice, white, painted cottage: "But I've grown to hate your most insignificant peasant, your Philipp or Sidor, for whose welfare I'm supposed to wear myself out and who won't even say 'thank you' to me . . . yes and I don't even need his thank you. All right, so he'll live in a nice white cottage and I'll be pushing up daisies. So what?"[17] Pisarev explicitly excludes the lower orders from the ranks of the realists: they are simply machines, but machines susceptible to hunger and fatigue. His program involves not organizing the masses but training leaders (III, 67–68).

Bazarov gives all his energy to the discovery of new facts in the natural sciences. Pisarev too rejects other forms of learning in favor of the natural sciences, and he points to Bazarov dissecting frogs (II, 392): "There you have it," he wrote; "in the frog you will find the rescue and renewal of the Russian people." Bazarov wastes no time on idle pleasures or the breathless worship of nature, and Pisarev locates as the most important quality of the young realists that they "economize intellectual forces." Once again he turns to Bazarov, who provides him with a motto (III, 11): "Nature is not a temple but a workshop, and man is a workman in it."

Pisarev's views on art as he finally set them down, and as nearly all the secondary sources represent them, seemingly involved a violent adjustment of his own nature to fit the demands of his model, Bazarov, but here the matter becomes especially complex. Bazarov's rejection of art was ignorant and absolute; we recall his many unhappy aphorisms on the subject: "Why should a grown man read Pushkin?" "Why is art necessary when you have your own experience of life?" "A decent chemist is twenty times more useful than any poet." Such views were organic and natural to Bazarov, and to many others among the new men; they were not organic and natural to Pisarev but had to be learned—and he never learned them well. His articles on literature, especially some of his earliest studies, betray sophistication and taste, and place him in a quite different category from other radical critics of the sixties. (He later apologized for those articles as the "mistakes of an immature mind"; III, 139.) All of the books tell us that he dismissed Pushkin as a "colossal relic," but the sense of that remark, and of his polemic with both Belinsky and Chernyshevsky about the worth of Pushkin, has not been adequately illuminated. Pisarev knew and appreciated Pushkin and other poets, and he never attempted to "cast overboard" the greatest world poets. The article on Pushkin's lyric in fact pays special devotion to Shakespeare, Goethe, and Schiller as poets who have added something to the sum of human thought and experience, who are not, in other words, "*just* artists." His point is that Pushkin—our "little" Pushkin, "whose artistic virtuosity is a device for initiating the reader into the sad secrets of his innermost vacuity"—has no place with the world's great poets. His was a feud with the "artist as such," with the "seer" whose hands no broom or other useful implement has ever violated (III, 375, 376).

Armand Coquart in his excellent study of Pisarev makes the point that the critic's rejection of art was not the result of any lack of feeling for art, but rather of a desire and a need not to understand. I would suggest that the need arose in part from his close identification with his "favorite literary hero," who, as we remember, thought Pushkin "must have been a military man." Pisarev was not, as Bazarov was, insensitive to art and ignorant of literature, but once having transformed a fictional character into an argument for his own cause, he tended to adopt and even exaggerate the character's views. And thus it happened that Turgenev's *Fathers and Sons*, a work of art, contributed under Pisarev's ministrations to the anti-aesthetic movement of the sixties.

Turgenev himself was by no means unhappy with Pisarev's articles on *Fathers and Sons*, repelled though he was by the critic's views on art and by his contempt for the older generation.[18] Turgenev's interest in Pisarev and his respect for him as a critic are understandable; in spite of filling out the novel and using it for his own purposes, Pisarev has given us the best critical analysis of *Fathers and Sons* written by a contemporary, a piece of criticism that, despite the heavy imprint of the Russian nineteenth century, bears serious comparison with the best analyses of the twentieth century. The critic's work of transformation, as I have called it, is a labor of love. Pisarev does not speak of such things as structure, but he has located three important features of the novel's composition: the central position of Bazarov and his total isolation from all the other characters; the function of Bazarov in revealing the other characters while remaining himself an enigma to the end; and Bazarov's fate in the novel as a wanderer, never at home anywhere, not even in his own home, and doomed to die early in Russia because there was nothing else for him to do there. The pages in Pisarev's articles that illuminate Bazarov's homeless state, the lines that describe his death and justify it in artistic terms, the sensitive account of Odintsova and Bazarov, all of this is evidence of Pisarev's sympathetic identification with the central character, but it also reveals that in spite of himself he was still sensitive to the presence of art.

III. *Pisarev and Raskolnikov*

Pisarev performed a characteristic critical operation on Dostoevsky's *Crime and Punishment*, another novel that, as he understood it, described him and his friends the nihilists. Not only does he answer Dostoevsky's notions on the morality of the young radicals; once again he thoroughly transforms the novel, and uses the material in it as evidence for his own social, political, and ethical views. It would be easy and obvious to assert that Pisarev ignores or misunderstands the philosophical content of the novel, or that he seems unaware of its existence as a work of art. Such a judgment would be justified only in part and would leave out of account Pisarev's subtlety of purpose and skillful performance in the essay "The Struggle for Life."

Pasternak once said that it is not Raskolnikov or his crime that fascinates us, but the presence of art in the novel; Pisarev was acutely susceptible to the presence of art even in a novel written by an ideological enemy. Of that there can be no question. In his article as it appeared in the journal *Delo* in 1867, he said of Dostoevsky:

Readers of Dostoevsky's novel have been deeply shaken by the close psychological analysis that characterizes the works of this writer. I sharply disagree with his ideas, but I cannot help recognizing in him a powerful talent, one capable of transmitting the most subtle and elusive features of normal human life and its inward processes. He is an especially keen observer of morbid mental states, which he subjects to very careful analysis and evaluation, and which he seems to experience in his own person.[19]

Most readers of Pisarev have never seen that appreciation of Dostoevsky because it appeared only in the journal article in 1867 and was omitted from the first edition of Pisarev's collected works, published between 1866 and 1869.[20] Subsequent editions all omit the paragraph, though several refer to it in a footnote. There has been some speculation on the reasons for the omission, but the probable explanation arises from the fact that the essay "The Struggle for Life" appeared in the journal in two separate installments under different titles. The paragraph in question was an introduction to the second installment, and when the two were consolidated in the collected works, this introduction was not needed and the laudatory paragraph was omitted.

However, the introductory statement to the article as a whole is also quite clear in distinguishing between Dostoevsky as an artist and as a thinker. That paragraph repays a very close reading since every phrase has its effect. Pisarev professes no interest in those ideas that Dostoevsky *quite possibly* was promoting in *Crime and Punishment,* and that *might very well* seem to Pisarev indefensible; he professes no interest in Dostoevsky's partisan position in the ideological debates of the time, or in the vested interests that Dostoevsky *might* wish to support with his pen; he is not concerned with the methods Dostoevsky considers acceptable in his struggle with his literary and other adversaries. Having thus thrown a heavy cloud of doubt on Dostoevsky's ideas, purposes, and methods in his polemic with the radicals, Pisarev then sharply separates all such questions from the artistic question as he understands it, and, as in the case of Turgenev, implies that Dostoevsky, in spite of his ideological orientation, has provided valid images of the real world:

I pay attention only to those evidences of social life that are depicted in the novel: if in the novel life has been faithfully observed, if the raw facts that enter into the novel's fabric have complete verisimilitude; if the novel contains no slander on life, no false ornamentation, or any inner inconsistency; in a word, if genuine people act and suffer in the novel, struggle and fall into error, love and hate one another, and if they display evidence of real social conditions, then I approach the novel as I would a credible account of events that really occurred. (IV, 316)

The critic proceeds to examine the evidence of the novel from a sociologist's viewpoint and to analyze the motivation of Raskolnikov in the light of what we know of his life. And here, as in the article on *Fathers and Sons*, Pisarev fills out the picture with many vivid details of the poverty and humiliation that "must have been" endured by Raskolnikov and that ultimately drove him to commit the crime. Poverty and all the misery that accompanies it is the cause of the crime; at times the essay, if not Dostoevsky's novel, sounds a bit like *Les Miserables*. And in fact Raskolnikov's crime is no different from that of some poor, ignorant, and hopeless drifter of the lower class, though it has greater psychological interest because Raskolnikov is an intellectual. The inert, apathetic misery of the usual criminal Raskolnikov articulates for us.

As the second step in his argument Pisarev disposes of the idea that Raskolnikov was a free agent and therefore responsible for his actions. Not that he was mad—far from it. The evidence in the novel shows conclusively that he was sane (IV, 322–23). And yet the question remains, was he responsible for his crime?

We can accept the fact that Raskolnikov was not mad, and at the same time demonstrate that the measure of freedom he enjoyed was quite insignificant. . . . Weigh and evaluate all those petty and tormenting collisions with the coarseness and mindlessness of the people surrounding him, all those encounters that directed the stream of his thought toward one end—and then ask yourself whether Raskolnikov still had freedom of choice, and whether it was in his power to undertake or not to undertake the barbarous absurdity that terminated his lonely and solitary struggle. (IV, 325)

Here we have the most astonishing example of Pisarev's method in his transformation of the novel. With a perfectly straight face he deftly turns the argument of *Crime and Punishment* on its head. Instead of an investigation of human freedom and responsibility, the novel has become a case study in the generation of crime by the environment of the criminal.

The third step in Pisarev's argument is to dispose of the idea that Raskolnikov's "theory" had anything to do with causing the crime. Raskolnikov's sick idea that "extraordinary people" have the right to overstep and "ordinary people" are simply building material to be used by them, Pisarev argues, is a hallucination, a symptom rather than the disease itself. The theory was artificially constructed by Raskolnikov "simply to rationalize in his own eyes his plan for a quick and easy profit." In no sense was the crime a consequence of the theory; instead both the theory and the crime were the product of environment, of agonizing and unendurable poverty. Again Dostoevsky's argument is made to stand on its head. Pisarev devoted much space to a cogent refutation of Raskolnikov's "theory," and we may well ask why he found it necessary to spend so much time demolishing a notion that is expressed in the novel only fragmentarily, and that is so obviously flawed. The reason was that the dispute involved, not Raskolnikov's stated and explicit idea about "extraordinary people," but the unstated argument of the novel that the radicalism of the nihilists, carried to its logical extreme, leads to the rejection of morality and to senseless, violent actions—to the idea that all is indeed permitted to the "extraordinary" ones.

In refuting Raskolnikov Pisarev offers powerful arguments against those revolutionaries who might indeed, considering themselves "extraordinary," resort to assassination or other acts of violence. We must bear in mind that Karakozov's attempt on the Tsar took place in April 1866, shortly after the appearance of the first two parts of *Crime and Punishment*, and that Pisarev began his article on the novel not long after the attempted assassination, in an atmosphere of official terror and repression against all "dissidents."[21] The essay on *Crime and Punishment* offered him an opportunity to dissociate himself and the "realists" of his persuasion from Karakozov and the extremists. The sharpness of the schism on the left and the polemical force of Pisarev's essay can be measured by his use of the term "hallucination" to describe Raskolnikov's theory, and by implication Karakozov's deed, and his lengthy castigation of the notion that isolated individual acts of violence have an effect on the course of history. The course of history is not determined by a few extraordinary people, but by the natural course of historical events: if there had been obstacles to the discoveries of a Kepler or a Newton, these men would have had no right to forcibly remove "one or two or even a hundred people," and in any case their removal would have had no effect on the conditions generating the "obstacles." Those conditions could be changed only by means of a determined and tireless propaganda of scientific truth (IV, 349): "Because of their devotion to that truth, extraordinary people such as Newton or Kepler have sometimes become *martyrs*, but they could never turn into *torturers* for an idea, for the simple reason that torture never persuades anyone and therefore never in any way benefits the idea in whose name it is carried out."

That is a noble statement, and no doubt it applies to Keplers and Newtons, though torture in the name of an idea is not an uncommon thing in the history of religions and other ideological movements. The danger was real, and certain passages in Pisarev's essay pointedly deal with it. The following may be taken as a direct reference to Karakozov:

Humanity, according to the best and most recent thinkers, develops and perfects itself as a consequence of deep and indestructible qualities of its own nature . . . and not by any means as a consequence of the thoughts that arise in the heads of a few select geniuses. . . . Not one of these persons, no matter how great a genius he may be, can have any rational basis for permitting himself in the name of the future, or in the name of his own genius, to undertake such actions as harm other people and because of this are considered forbidden to ordinary human beings. (IV, 350)

Truly extraordinary people try to prevent bloodshed and never seek it. The "best and most recent thinkers" condemn such things. And Pisarev asks himself where in heaven's name Raskolnikov, who had been a student at the university, could have got such weird and strange ideas. The thinkers who dominate the minds of today's youth have no such ideas. We have no such ideas, Pisarev says plainly. We did not know Raskolnikov—or Karakozov. We never met him. Had he come to us and discussed his sick idea, we would have knocked it out of his head. We would have given him good books to read, Büchner, Vogt, Moleschott, Buckle (and, he might have added, Marx), books that dispel romantic nonsense about the special role in history of individual geniuses. But Raskolnikov, locked away in his little attic coffin, had no discourse with his radical contemporaries and so went tragically astray. At this point, of course, the novel is totally transformed.

"The Struggle for Life" is a powerful though veiled defense of nihilist morality, and one of Pisarev's most important ethical statements. The essay's style and structure, its poised and cool objectivity, its subtle circumlocution and careful understatement were no doubt partly conditioned by the censorship. Because Pisarev could not openly plead his case in terms of his own choosing, he was obliged to produce a piece of literary criticism that deals directly with the most vital problem of the day: the implication of nihilist doctrine for moral behavior. "The Struggle for Life" is a defense of nihilist social doctrine and morality based on the reliable "evidence" contained in the novel of a "true artist," Dostoevsky.

IV. *Afterthoughts*

I would like to look somewhat more closely at Pisarev's critical method in translating these two novels into his own terms, in referring them, in other words, to a reality that is, or would seem to be, different from the reality of the artistic works themselves. And I would suggest that Pisarev's method is simply an extreme and highly conscious example of the critical activity that takes place in any reader of those novels, but on an unconscious level. Mukarovsky makes the point in a famous essay that

the question about whether the story about the student, Raskolnikov, actually happened is . . . outside the pale of the reader's interests. Nevertheless the reader feels the strong relationship of the novel to reality, and not only to that reality which is described in the novel—to events set in Russia in a certain year of the nineteenth century—but to the reality which the reader himself is familiar with, to situations which he has experienced, or, given the circumstances in which he lives, he might experience. . . . About the novel which has absorbed the reader there have accumulated not one but many realities. . . . Thus the work of art acquires the ability to refer to a reality which is totally different from the one which it depicts, and to systems of values other than the one from which it arose and on which it is founded.[22]

Obviously the reality to which Pisarev relates the novels is neither religious, nor aesthetic, nor psychological, but social. The social reality of contemporary Russia forms the apperceptive mass against which Pisarev reads the novel. Modern readers possess a differently constituted apperceptive mass, have a totally different set of realities with which they live on intimate terms; they are less likely than Pisarev to know the smelly misery of the poor quarters of St. Petersburg in summer, or to know as a matter of experience that narrow attic room. Modern readers of the novel experience in it a different kind of reality: the religious dilemma and the mental state of the protagonist, for instance, are matters they know very well. In Pisarev's own hierarchy of values the existence of poverty and crime and the connection between them are dominant, and though we may wonder at this relative neglect of the novel as art, I would still submit that Pisarev's filling out of the picture, his reduction of the language of art to the language of sociology, has a certain validity, that it directs attention to problems Dostoevsky did not choose to treat, and provides a healthy embellishment of the great novel.

Pisarev's operation on Turgenev and Dostoevsky, however, points to fundamental problems in literary theory. Oscar Wilde, in his fastidious withdrawal from "the true and the real" in favor of invention and artifice, was presenting in a sharpened paradox the distinction offered by the Russian Formalists, and before them by Quintilian and many others, between literary and "ordinary" language. Iurii Lotman later develops, in a semiotic idiom, that same Formalist distinction when he speaks of art as a special kind of structure, one that is itself not just a carrier of information but a source of it. Modern critics as a whole agree that the specific information transmitted by art is contained in its own structure, and that when a critic or a translator attempts to retell a story in his own words, he destroys what makes it art. Such was the operation Pisarev performed on Pushkin's *Eugene Onegin*, parts of which he reduced to ordinary expository prose, then discovered that the information it contained was trivial and boring. Nabokov performed a similar operation in his translation of *Eugene Onegin* when he sacrificed everything, as he himself put it, to literal meaning.

But Pisarev's treatment of Turgenev and Dostoevsky is a special case of translation, or paraphrase, or transformation, as I have called it. Here he appropriates two verbal objects that he acknowledges as art and transforms each into non-art, into social meanings. In Kenneth Burke's phrase, he transforms a complexity into a simplicity. Obviously he could perform such an operation *only* on a work of art. He wrote at length of Chernyshevsky's *What Is to Be Done?*, but there no such transformation was necessary since the messages of that book are direct and clear, and no artistic structure offers specific information of its own. For his purposes as a critic he required a genuine work of art because only a work of art could embody the social reality undistorted by direct intention. Only the social reality interested him, however, and though he was highly sensitive to the presence of art, he preferred not to speak of it. And thus in his struggle with "hunger and nakedness," Pisarev liberated the information he needed from the complex and subtle structures of art. His concern with Russia's social needs was so overriding that it left him deliberately deaf to poetry and as a rule indifferent, in his published work, to the mysteries of art.

ROBERT L. BELKNAP

The Rhetoric of an Ideological Novel

I

This paper treats the ways in which Dostoevsky's social and ideological intentions interacted with certain of his sources in the genesis
of Ivan Karamazov and Ivan's Grand Inquisitor. These intentions
have eluded some of the best literary minds that have written about
Dostoevsky—at least these minds differ so sharply that they cannot
all be right. Let me quote two statements bearing on Dostoevsky's
intention. The first is from D. H. Lawrence's introduction to a separate edition of the Grand Inquisitor chapter, translated by S. S. Koteliansky:

> If there is any question: who is the Grand Inquisitor? surely we must
> say it is Ivan himself. And Ivan is the thinking mind of the human be-
> ing in rebellion, thinking the whole thing out to the bitter end. As such
> he is, of course, identical with the Russian Revolutionary of the thinking
> type. He is also, of course, Dostoevsky himself in his thoughtful as apart
> from his passional and inspirational self. Dostoevsky half-hated Ivan. Yet
> after all, Ivan is the greatest of the three brothers, pivotal. The passionate
> Dmitri and the inspired Alyosha are, at last, only offsets to Ivan.
> And we cannot doubt that the Grand Inquisitor speaks Dostoevsky's
> own final opinion about Jesus. The opinion is baldly, this: Jesus, you are
> inadequate. Men must correct you. And Jesus gives the kiss of acquies-
> cence to the Inquisitor, as Alyosha does to Ivan.[1]

Lawrence had not read Bakhtin's remarks about the polyphonic
novel, but he knew better than to assume that a character is a spokes-

man for the author. He offered three reasons for identifying Ivan
and the Grand Inquisitor with Dostoevsky: Ivan's greatness, his
pivotal position in the novel, and the kiss of acquiescence the Inquisitor receives. Ivan's greatness generates a rhetorical and a genetic argument. First, one may ask why an author would select such an
attractive mouthpiece for ideas he hopes to crush. Second, one can
deny the possibility of creating a truly great character without real
sympathy at some level. Lawrence argues this explicitly with respect
to Tolstoy.[2]

These are persuasive arguments, but many readers take the dia-
metrically opposite view of Dostoevsky's intent, though they may
agree that Ivan is identical with the Russian revolutionary of the
thinking type. The most concise and authoritative statement of their
position comes from Dostoevsky's own letter to his editor Liubimov
on May 10, 1879.

[Ivan's] convictions are precisely what I accept as the *synthesis* of Russian anarchism in our day, the denial not of God, but of the meaning of
his creation. All socialism had its origins and beginnings in the denial of
the meaning of historical actuality [*deistvitel'nosti*], and progressed to a
program of destruction and anarchism. The original anarchists were in
many cases men of sincere convictions. My hero takes up a topic I consider irrefutable [*neotrazimuiu*]—the senselessness of the suffering of
children—and deduces from that the absurdness [*absurd*, not *nelepost'*]
of all historical actuality. I don't know whether I managed it well, but I
know that the figure of my character is in the highest degree real [*real'-
noe*]. (In *The Possessed* there were a multitude of figures whom I was
attacked for as fantastic, and then, can you believe it, they all were justified by actuality, so they must have been imagined correctly.)

All that is said by my character in the text I sent you is based on
actuality. All the stories about children happened, were printed in the
papers, and I can show where; nothing was invented by me. . . . As for
my character's blasphemy, it will be triumphantly confuted [*oprovergnu-
to*] in the next [June] issue, on which I am working now with fear and
trembling and veneration, considering my task (the crushing of anarchism)
a patriotic exploit. Wish me success, my dear Nikolai Alekseevich.[3]

Although Dostoevsky's statement carries more authority than Lawrence's, the mere existence of Lawrence's presents a curious disjunction. Either Lawrence's article is correct, and Dostoevsky was consciously or unconsciously lying, or Dostoevsky's letter is correct, and
Dostoevsky was a rhetorical incompetent. If rhetoric is language that
makes the reader feel, judge, or act in accord with the author's intent, its success can be measured like that of the most primitive communication system, in which the sender, whether a telegrapher or

an author, encodes a message into a form that can be transmitted through a channel, anything from a telegraph wire to a line of letters folded into a book. The receiver decodes the message, and the measure of success is the degree to which the reconstituted message coincides with the sender's. Lawrence's letter is a fair example of one major line in Dostoevsky criticism. In fact, an enormous number of readers have sided with the Grand Inquisitor, and many, like V. V. Rozanov, who do not side with him have stated that Dostoevsky did.[4]

To accept Lawrence's arguments, however, one must reject the testimony of Dostoevsky's letter. The letter, of course, is a good example of a somewhat suspect literary form, one that has been studied little, although cultivated by many masters of European prose—the letter requesting the extension of a deadline. Anti-anarchism would have appealed to Liubimov and his chief, Katkov, whose journal, *The Russian Messenger*, was well to the right of center. Still, Dostoevsky's letter summarizes a position he had taken often in his journalism, and it cannot be summarily dismissed. Instead it may provide additional insights on close inspection.

Except for one rather puzzling sentence about the sincerity of the anarchists, the passage quoted falls into three parts, only the last of which promises to confute Ivan's argument. The first part traces Ivan's anarchism to the senselessness of the suffering of children, by way of the concept of the absurd that was to become so fashionable three generations later. Between this statement about the text's ideology and the statement of his intention to refute it, Dostoevsky claims absolute fidelity to his sources. Thus, where Lawrence moves directly from the author's text to his intention, Dostoevsky disconcertingly moves from the text through the sources on his way to the opposite intention.

In calling Ivan's convictions the "synthesis" of contemporary anarchism, Dostoevsky is already preparing his reader for the middle part of the passage, where the phrases "all socialism had its origins" and "the original anarchists were in many cases" actually imply that Ivan is the highest artistic achievement under the realist aesthetic of his day—a literary type, an accurate representation of an identifiable segment of society. The ambitiousness of this claim explains the modest beginning of a following sentence, "I don't know whether I managed it well," which at first glance conflicts with Dostoevsky's fear that he had done Ivan too well. Of course, the word "well" means two different things here. I use it to mean "persuasively," "appealingly," "powerfully," as Lawrence would, whereas Dostoevsky is using it to mean "typically." He offers two different kinds of evidence to support his claim to typicality. The reference to *The Possessed* expresses pride in the subsequent confirmation of a reality that did not exist at the time he wrote, whereas the sentences around it claim that every detail about Ivan is based on prior reality. The implicit paradox is real and important, but for all his love of paradox, Dostoevsky did not invent it. He merely voiced the standard doctrine of the prosaists of his day, that artists were artists precisely because they could perceive reality more sharply and subtly than other men, and could select and assemble details whose firm basis in reality explained their crystallization into accurate types, even if the author himself did not realize their implication. This paradoxical dependence of special, even prophetic, insight on photographic fidelity to reality rests on a metonymic faith in the capacity of the parts of a reality to generate a representation of the whole.

Dostoevsky's claim that his fidelity to reality has produced an accurate ideological type justifies Ivan's attractiveness and also draws attention to Ivan's sources. Ivan, as Dostoevsky and Lawrence agree, has his origins in the reality of Russian radicalism. Belinsky's letters to Botkin and Gogol, and Herzen's *From the Other Shore* provided Dostoevsky with much of Ivan's language and ideology. Indeed, these sources offer a simple answer to Lawrence's question about producing a great character without personal sympathy. A writer like Lawrence tends to equate greatness with eloquence, and others have already shown that a substantial part of Ivan's eloquence is borrowed from these authors.[5] More important, however, Dostoevsky had adored Belinsky, had participated in the Petrashevsky circle, and had talked with Herzen and possibly Bakunin enough to feel their magnetism, sometimes simultaneously with his doubts about their doctrines. At the Petrashevsky interrogations Dostoevsky said that he read Belinsky's letter to Gogol for its language, not its ideas.[6] He was desperate for excuses, of course, but Maikov's memories suggest that his testimony might by coincidence have been true.[7] For Dostoevsky in the seventies, Herzen and Belinsky might be wrong, but they were noble in their eloquence, in their willingness to sacrifice their happiness, and in that sincerity of conviction whose relevance seemed puzzling at first in the letter to Liubimov. Dostoevsky's fidelity to this aspect of his sources could have made Ivan Karamazov more attractive in his desperate love than seems fitting or strategic if Dostoevsky's letter expressed his real intent.

This conservation of rhetorical power and moral persuasiveness alters the model of the primitive communication system in a novel of this sort. Dostoevsky is in part the sender, but he also is a channel through which the qualities of his sources are transmitted intact. Jakobson, Lotman, and many others have discussed the limitations and complications of this sender-channel-receiver model. We realize, for example, along with the fact that the sender does not generate the message ex nihilo, that the codes of the sender and the receiver may not coincide, and that data outside the text may enter the interpretation. Dostoevsky's letter to Liubimov introduces the crucial question for this paper, the interdependence of the sender and the channel. Whether we think of the input into the system as a body of information Dostoevsky had gathered from his reading, his conversation, and his other experiences, or as a body of intentions generated out of these experiences, we must consider the central element in his experience in 1879—*The Brothers Karamazov.* We do not have the traditional, straightforward communication diagram of sender ⟶ message in channel ⟶ receiver, but rather this:

Sources \
⟶ Dostoevsky   *The Brothers Karamazov* ⟶ us \
Sources ⟶

As it comes into being, the message in the channel is a constant source of feedback to the sender, just as the sound of one's own voice crucially affects the way one speaks. The letter to Liubimov begins with a description of Dostoevsky's fidelity to his prior experience and ends with his reaction to *The Brothers Karamazov* as it was emerging—fear and trembling, or negative feedback. Here the sources, the intention, and the emerging text shape each other. Physicists are hard put to it to solve a three-body problem where the bodies are mathematical points and the only influence is gravitational. I do not aspire to such a solution here, but to an indication of the kind of interaction among these three entities in Dostoevsky's mind.

II

This formulation of our task suggests an obvious way to test the authenticity of Dostoevsky's fear and trembling. If Ivan's greatness is an accidental side effect of Dostoevsky's fidelity to his sources, we should find in the text a series of efforts to destroy one of the most eloquent and convincing arguments in all literature, an argument whose starting point Dostoevsky himself had called irrefutable. Indeed, it has been said that Ivan's fate in the novel is designed to show what happens to an atheist and a socialist. He is desperately unhappy; he is rejected in love; and he becomes diseased in the part of him on which he depends excessively, the brain. His suffering and his incapacity at the end of the novel are taken as Dostoevsky's vision of the just punishment of unbelief.

A more sophisticated way of refuting Ivan's position involves not what happens to him but what he does and is. Valentina Vetlovskaia has catalogued enough unpleasant actions and features of Ivan's to make a convincing case that Dostoevsky intended to discredit Ivan's argument by discrediting its spokesman.[8] Her study underlines the problem this novel presents. She shows Dostoevsky using one of the classical rhetorical techniques, the *argumentum ad hominem,* and leaves us with the evidence of Lawrence and scores of other able readers that the technique did not work. I should like to look at one of Vetlovskaia's points more closely, Dostoevsky's effort to discredit Ivan by associating him with devils.

As long as men have talked about sin, they have acknowledged its attractiveness, but in the Middle Ages evil, unlike sin, was presented as unattractive, and its embodiment, devils, tended to be represented as repulsive, filthy, stinking, vicious, and subhuman. Dostoevsky needed such devils if he intended to discredit Ivan by association with them, but the literature of his day offered a very different figure; as early as Milton, but insistently since Blake, Byron, and Baudelaire, various elements of the diabolic had had a good press. The Grand Inquisitor's devil is not a stupid and disgusting torturer, but a dire and fearsome spirit whose very name is taboo. This romantic fascination with the diabolic had weakened a literary resource Dostoevsky needed, the old devil who could provoke instant hostility. Indeed, within a few years of the creation of the Grand Inquisitor, Swinburne, Strindberg, Raspisardi, and Lautréamont had written major glorifications of the diabolic in four different languages.[9]

To counteract this loss of prefabricated repulsiveness, Dostoevsky has to train his readers to associate scorn or revulsion with the word "devil." Except for the biblical demons in *The Possessed,* devils play little part in Dostoevsky's works. Demonic figures like Murin in "The Landlady" are not connected with any particular supernatural being. But in *The Brothers Karamazov* a multitude of devils appear. Old Fyodor Karamazov introduces these creatures early in the novel, setting the stamp of his own savage weirdness on them:

You see, it's impossible, I think, that the devils should forget to drag me down with hooks when I die. Well, then I think: Hooks? And where do they get them? Made of what? Iron? Forged where? Is there a factory of some sort they've got there? Now, over there in the monastery, the monks probably believe that in hell, for example, there's a ceiling; but I'm willing to believe in hell, only without a ceiling. It works out sort of neater, more enlightened, more Lutheran, that is. . . . Well, if there's no ceiling, therefore there can't be any hooks, and if there's no hooks and all that's cast aside, that means—implausibly again—who'll drag me in with hooks, because if they don't drag me, then what will happen, where's there any justice in the world?[10]

With or without hooks these devils could not be made grand or attractive. Even where a larger spirit is involved, Fyodor's presence makes him the mocker of mankind (IX, 171):

"Does God exist or not? For the last time."
"And for the last time, no."
"Then who is laughing at mankind, Ivan?"
"The Devil, probably," grinned Ivan.
"And the Devil exists?"
"No, the Devil too doesn't."

Such talk of the Devil as a mocker and of devils as torturers shapes our response to the devil who is the Grand Inquisitor's mentor. Sometimes the torture is explicit and the devils implicit, as in the story of the Virgin's descent into hell; sometimes the reverse, as with the devils Ferapont encounters. And sometimes both the torture and the devils are explicit, as with the devils Ferapont, Lize, and even Alyosha vanquish with a cross. Ferapont and Lize share the devils' love of pain. Ferapont sees one hiding

behind the door from me, a full-sized one, too, a yard and a half or more tall; its tail was thick and brown and long, and the tip of the tail had slipped into the crack of the door; and I'm nobody's fool, so I suddenly slammed the door to, and caught its tail. And it got to squealing and started thrashing around; I took and put the sign of the cross on it, three times I crossed it. And then it died, like a spider that had been crushed. (IX, 212)

Ferapont savors the agonized extinction of this devil just as he takes physical delight in the idea of heroic fasting, and the nastiness of his twisted sensuality becomes linked with that of his imagined victim. Ivan picks up this vision of the demonic and reinforces it, in the most moving linkage of the Devil with evil that we find, his adaptation of Voltaire's remark, in response to his own catalogue of the sufferings of children: "If the Devil does not exist, and man in fact created him, then he created him in his own image and likeness" (IX, 299). Dostoevsky drew these various devils in large part from his readings in old Russian literature, and their antiquity reduces their rhetorical usefulness. Their association with the devil the Grand Inquisitor quotes remains largely verbal.

The most elaborate picture of an unlovely devil has different sources, and a far more intimate relation to Ivan. This is the devil who appears in Ivan's nightmare at the moment of Smerdyakov's suicide. Consider the following passage:

Ivan felt that he was unwell, but from some dread of telling himself quite clearly that he was sick, he turned from the light and tried to go to sleep. His sleep was heavy and fitful; he was incessantly waking up, tossing restlessly on the bed, and again dozing off for a minute.

Waking up one time, Ivan thought he would not get to sleep any more. He wanted to get up. His head was leaden; in his arms and legs there was some sort of dull pain. With an effort, he sat up on the bed leaning with his back on the corner of the room. He sat sometimes with no thought at all, sometimes there awakened in his head a turbulent and hazy consciousness that he felt bad. He would sit, would say "I feel bad," and again would senselessly focus his eyes on the opposite corner of the room. Suddenly it seemed to him as if something was stirring there. He gazed there. Just so, something was effortfully crawling out of the corner crack, shifted clumsily, and began to grow. It was some sort of likeness of a human. . . . Ivan rubbed his eyes, and then opened them again; there was no monster there any longer.[11]

This apparition of a very personal demon to a sick man comes from a novel called *Likho* (The Evil Spirit) by Dmitry Vasilievich Averkiev (1836–1905), who had been a writer for Dostoevsky's journals in the 1860's. This passage appeared in issue no. 5 of the weekly *Ogonek* five months before Dostoevsky published Ivan's scene with the devil. Dostoevsky tended to read as many journals as he could, and had made a note to himself to look at that issue.

Ivan Karamazov's devil appears in much the same way. The passage that follows contains extensive ellipses, but no change of order.

Ivan [Karamazov] was sitting on the couch and feeling his head spinning. He felt that he was sick and feeble. He was about to doze off, but got up restlessly and paced the room to keep off the sleep. At moments he imagined that he must be delirious. But it wasn't his sickness that preoccupied him most: when he sat down again, he began to glance around occasionally, as if he was looking for something. It happened several times. Finally, his gaze was fixed on one point. . . . He sat a long time in his place, firmly supporting his head on both hands and still glancing obliquely at the same point as before, at the couch by the opposite wall. Evidently something was disturbing him, some object, distracting, bothering. . . .

He knew that he was unwell, but detested being sick at that time with revulsion. . . . So he was sitting now, almost conscious of being delirious . . . and fixedly staring at some object by the other wall on the couch. Suddenly, someone was sitting there . . . (IX, 159–60)

Both passages begin with a presentation of sickness and go on to describe restless sleep, weakness and pain, and then a confusion of mind to which Dostoevsky gives the label delirium. Finally, both Ivans fix their gaze more and more firmly on a single spot, where an apparition occurs. Averkiev's Ivan expresses his incredulity with a gesture, and the creature disappears. Ivan Karamazov's hallucination remains for the entire chapter, and so does Ivan's incredulity. Dostoevsky's passage is longer, but except for the fear to admit sickness, the parallel elements appear in the same order, as if the Averkiev passage served as a framework. Dostoevsky, however, has elaborated a very different hallucination: he has retained none of the medieval qualities that Averkiev's creature shares with the devils Fyodor, Lize, Ferapont, and Grushenka describe. Dostoevsky no longer needs the little, subhuman medieval devils, but instead a being close enough to Ivan to debase Ivan's arguments, his rhetoric, and, most of all, that "dire and fearsome spirit of self-annihilation and nonbeing" with whom the Grand Inquisitor had so romantically associated himself. Indeed, as Ivan says repeatedly in this chapter, this devil *is* Ivan.

This ideological need works together with the interplay of sources to explain why Dostoevsky preserves so much of Averkiev's apparition scene but so little of his apparition. Averkiev was writing a historical novel and, like Dostoevsky, had plainly been reading folklore and nineteenth-century editions of the Russian saints' lives, which contain many demonic creatures. He would certainly have been brought up on Faust and E. T. A. Hoffman, and very probably would have encountered the Nordic tradition of the personal fetish that normally appeared just before one's own death. He had apparently learned what Freud learned from reading Hoffman, that the sense of the uncanny comes from the reintrusion of long-abandoned beliefs. But Averkiev's background and his technique plainly mark another, more important source for his apparition scene. He had learned from his old associate Dostoevsky, most specifically from the appearance of a hideous arthropod to the dying radical Ippolit in

The Idiot and the first appearance of Svidrigailov in the room of the delirious Raskolnikov in *Crime and Punishment*. Svidrigailov not only is mistaken for a hallucination; he has hallucinations—of the three victims of his unpunishable murders, his servant, his wife, and the little girl he raped. Averkiev's apparition scene combines rhetorically appealing elements shared by four of Dostoevsky's favorite sources, the lives of the saints, Goethe, Hoffman, and Dostoevsky himself. When Ivan Karamazov, like Svidrigailov, blunders feverishly and beneficently through a storm on his way to his final hallucination, Dostoevsky is returning in his last great novel to the pattern of his first one to describe the ultimate collision between the rational intellect and the moral imperative. Like Svidrigailov and Raskolnikov, Ivan is conscious of blood guilt which the law cannot touch without his confession; his dreams, like theirs, reflect his victim, in this case his father, that shrewd, insolent, sophistical, insinuating, provincial mocker and hanger-on who resembles Ivan's devil and, to Ivan's distress, Ivan himself. In short, Ivan Karamazov's embodiment of evil diverges from Averkiev's because Averkiev's sources fitted Dostoevsky's literary taste and ideological purpose better than Averkiev's text.

In fact, the interesting question is not why Dostoevsky abandoned Averkiev's hallucination as a source, but why he adhered so faithfully to the order of details in a second-rate novel when he had a multitude of sources in better literature. Here, Dostoevsky was really using the same technique he used when he presented the despicable devils of antiquity: the desophistication of a figure whose current identity offered ideological complications. This technique was certainly not Dostoevsky's invention; it seems to come from the same source as the devil's tawdry gentility. Likhachev has pointed out that medieval devils can be cruel and dirty, but that this *poshlost'* can appear only in an age of social mobility and collapsing structures. Mephistopheles has this quality at times, with Martha, for example; but here, as in Averkiev, the richness of *déjà lu* goes deeper, to a source that Goethe and Dostoevsky both quoted extensively in their texts, the Book of Job. Many scholars believe the Book of Job was written at the high point of Hebrew culture, very likely in the reign of David, when the urban sophisticates toyed like pastoral poets with the figure from their folklore of a God whose sons presented themselves subserviently before him. One of those sons was a hanger-on who spoke to God when spoken to, but a tempter at the same time, challenging goodness with cynicism—"Doth Job fear God for naught?"—and prompting the most spectacular display of innocent suffering in literature before Ivan's catalogue of tortured children.

The letter to Liubimov explains why Dostoevsky would want to use the Book of Job as a source for the most notable character traits of Ivan's devil, as well as for the technique of desophistication, which led him to such other sources as the Russian saints' lives and Averkiev's historical novel. Ivan's argument rests on the senselessness of the world, according to that letter, and the task of the novel is to confute Ivan's argument: to justify the ways of God to man. The Book of Job is the oldest and the greatest theodicy Dostoevsky knew. It begins with the argument Dostoevsky considered unanswerable, the meaninglessness of innocent suffering. Job's children are destroyed, and the full authority of the biblical narrator declares Job innocent before his suffering begins. Bildad the Shuhite and his friends have the scholarly clear-sightedness that Ivan has, and like Ivan they enunciate the tempter's argument with the most insistent eloquence the rhetoric of their time afforded. In the Book of Job as it stands (some scholars think its sources ended differently), these massively elaborated arguments are destroyed by a theophany. In Dostoevsky's most immediate source for the encounter between Christ and the Inquisitor, *Le Christ au Vatican* by Cabantous, Christ is launched like a rocket into the empyrean before the eyes of an evil, astonished pope.[12] But Dostoevsky's ideology excluded miracles or theophanies to justify or prove God. As Lia Mikhailovna Rozenblium has so clearly shown, Dostoevsky had very little of the mystic about him.[13] In his notebooks he specifically rejected mysticism as a trait for Alyosha.[14] Dostoevsky could draw his tawdry, subservient devil from the Book of Job, but in an antimystical age, with a non-mystical mind, he could not invoke the voice of God out of the whirlwind to refute the position argued by the devil and those associated with him.

III

Perhaps because some of his sources were too eloquent and others conflicted with his ideology on miracles, Dostoevsky resorted to a series of rhetorical maneuvers to carry out the confutation he had promised Liubimov. One such maneuver deflates the Grand Inquisitor with a simplicity so transparent as to be invisible.

Ivan Karamazov says at the start of the legend that it belongs to a literary genre in which the Son of God can visit earth. The Grand Inquisitor sees Him resurrect a little girl, asks Him, "Is this Thou,

Thou?" and then adds that he does not want an answer (IX, 314). Ivan comments that it would not matter for the account if the Grand Inquisitor was mistaken or delirious, so long as he spoke out. In any case, the Inquisitor addresses Christ as a being who has the power to save or doom mankind, to defy gravity, to turn stones into bread, to rule the kingdoms of the earth or else provide for the salvation of an elect. He also says that men are too feeble to obey the commandments of Christ, that in their disobedience they will suffer pangs of guilt, as well as practical misfortunes on earth, and will inevitably earn misfortunes in the hereafter (IX, 322): "Your great prophet in his vision and his allegory says he saw all the members of the first resurrection, and that there were twelve thousand of them from each of the Twelve Tribes. . . . But remember that there were only a few thousand of them in all—and gods at that—but the remainder? And what are the remaining feeble people to blame for, that they could not endure what the mighty could?"

By resort to miracle, mystery, and authority, the Inquisitor's church has imposed certain of Christ's laws on mankind and has concealed those laws demanding a moral heroism of which mankind is incapable. The Inquisitor says that disobedience to laws suppressed by the church cannot earn damnation for these unknowing sinners:

We shall tell them that every sin shall be redeemed if it has been committed with our permission. . . . There will be thousands of millions of happy children and a hundred thousand sufferers who have taken upon themselves the curse of the knowledge of good and evil. Quietly they will die, quietly will expire in Thy name, and beyond the grave will find only death. But we will preserve the secret, and for their own happiness we will entice them with a heavenly and eternal reward. For if there were something in the other world, it is surely not for such as they. They say and prophesy that Thou wilt come and triumph anew, wilt come with Thy elect, with Thy proud and mighty, but we shall say that those have only saved themselves, while we saved all. . . . And we who have taken their sins upon us for their happiness, we shall stand before Thee and shall say, "Judge us if Thou canst and darest." (IX, 326)

This intercession between man and Christ resembles Christ's intercession between man and God more than it resembles the Virgin's intercession between man and Christ in the medieval story Ivan tells about the Virgin's visit to hell. The Grand Inquisitor feels he is substituting his own punishment for that which divine justice would otherwise certainly inflict on mankind. Certainly he has incurred great sin—not only the suppression of Christ's truth, but the taking of all the lives in the autos da fé. The Grand Inquisitor believes he is doing great good on earth, preventing war and famine and despair, but his supreme exploit is more romantic than anything in Herzen: he has sacrificed the happiness of his immortal soul to save mankind from damnation.

Dostoevsky deflates this magnificent gesture with a very simple one. Christ says nothing, but kisses the Grand Inquisitor. The kiss is obviously a blessing; it burns in the Inquisitor's heart as holy things do in this novel. And if Christ can bless the Grand Inquisitor, who has imprisoned Him, concealed His word, and killed hundreds of His followers, then obviously none of the lesser sinners are cut off from Christ's salvation. The Grand Inquisitor is unable to sacrifice his immortal soul, because Christ still can pardon him, and he has no reason to do so, because mankind need not be damned. In a later chapter, indeed, Zosima reduces damnation to eternal regret at having failed to love actively during the one life that a soul is given in all eternity. Here, in a single kiss, the most absolute and most appealing part of the Grand Inquisitor's exploit becomes an empty, unnecessary gesture. He has simply miscalculated the dimensions of God's mercy. He believes that he believes in God and Christ, but actually he believes in a more Euclidean, less merciful being.

Only one commentator on this passage has asked, "What are these sins of people taken on oneself? . . . It's really just godlessness; that's the whole secret. Your Inquisitor doesn't believe in God; that's his whole secret!" (IX, 328.) Alyosha Karamazov says this before he hears about the kiss, and Ivan's answer raises several of the same questions as the kiss: "Even though it were! You've guessed at last. And really it is so, the whole secret is just in this, but really isn't this suffering?" Ivan accepts Alyosha's deflation of the Grand Inquisitor before offering his own. From Dostoevsky's point of view this willingness to see a magnificent construct vitiated makes sense, if the Liubimov letter expresses his real intention. From Ivan's point of view the Grand Inquisitor might seem to deserve better. But the legend is not offered as a simple exposition of Ivan's belief. Ivan has said, "You're my kid brother; you're not the one I want to debauch and shift from your position; I'd maybe like to heal myself through you" (IX, 296). Ivan's ambivalence makes his destruction of his own argument psychologically reasonable; but this affectionate, hesitant candor helps to make him so attractive that among all the commentators on this passage, only Alyosha with his own kiss caught the ideological irony embodied in the kiss of Christ. The rhetorical failure is almost absolute.

Dostoevsky continues this argument in the teachings of Father Zosima, and there gives an answer to the problem of evil as telling in its way as Job's theophany. Zosima doubts the reality of hell as Fyodor envisions it, with or without hooks. He agrees with the Grand Inquisitor that the teachings of Christ will fill men with guilt at their failure to live up to them, but he sings a virtual hymn of rejoicing at this guilt. Indeed, he takes one of the central doctrines of the materialists whom Dostoevsky claimed to be opposing, and turns this doctrine to his account. I mean the doctrine of universal causal connections, the belief that all things in the world are interconnected, that no event occurs without its causes in this world, that if we knew enough we would see the world as a seamless web of causes and effects. As Zosima puts it, "The world is like an ocean, and if you push at one place, it gives at the opposite end of the world" (IX, 400). In Zosima's doctrine of evil this universal causal linkage is central. He holds that every one of us at some time in his life has acted out of spite or failed to act with full goodness. If this is true, and if the world is really one, then every one of us is implicated in every sparrow's fall. Ivan had asked, "Why does God permit innocent suffering?" Instead of answering that question, Zosima turns it on the questioner and asks, "Why do you cause innocent suffering?" In a totally determined world each of us has had a part in every evil thing that happens. In this sense, Zosima proclaims, all men are guilty of all things; but unlike those who try to escape guilt, he rejoices in it as his bond with the whole of being.

In short, Zosima offers a rhetorical answer to the problem of children's suffering, which Dostoevsky in his letter had considered unanswerable. Zosima does not justify such suffering; he simply calls on the reader to share the blame. But even this did not seem to satisfy Dostoevsky. He had still another resource for the destruction of Ivan, the reductio ad absurdum, the carrying of Ivan's nature and doctrines to the logical conclusion that would discredit them. This involves the introduction into the novel of a body of characters whose analogy to Ivan is made distinct, and whose ridiculousness is made more distinct.

IV

Several characters in *The Brothers Karamazov* have closely marked doctrinal, personal, and even verbal ties with Ivan Karamazov. In another study I showed how such characters could be seen as repositories for elements in a character's sources which were not needed for that character, but which some conscious or unconscious fidelity to his sources led Dostoevsky to preserve in the novel.[15] In this section and the next, I will try to show how this collection of genetically related characters evolved into an instrument of Dostoevsky's polemic with the righteousness of Schiller, Herzen, and Belinsky as manifested in the attractive traits of Ivan and the Grand Inquisitor.

Rakitin, the seminarian on the make, is probably the most repulsive character in *The Brothers Karamazov*, though his full loathsomeness does not emerge until the chapters after the legend of the Grand Inquisitor. In his first appearance only his eyes and his exaggerated humility hint at something distasteful: "A young fellow, apparently about twenty-two, in a layman's frock coat, a seminarian and future theologian, for some reason the protégé of the monastery and its members. He was rather tall, with a fresh face, broad cheekbones, and shrewd, alert, narrow brown eyes. His face expressed utter respectfulness, decent but without any evident fawning." (IX, 51.) The narrator hints that Rakitin has some thoughts of a different sort, but a Russian reader would only begin to recognize Rakitin when he speaks:

"You're hurrying to the father superior's. I know; he has a spread. Since that time he received the archpriest and General Pakhatov, remember it, there hasn't been a spread like that. I'll not be there, but go ahead, serve the sauces. But tell me one thing, Aleksei: What means this dream? That's what I wanted to ask you."

"What dream?"

"Why prostrating himself before your brother Dmitry. And he gave his forehead a real bump, too."

"You mean about Father Zosima?"

"Yes, about Father Zosima."

"His forehead?"

"Oh, I expressed myself disrespectfully! Well, all right, it was disrespectful. So what's the meaning of this dream?"

"I don't know what it means, Misha."

"Just as I expected—he wouldn't explain it to you. There's nothing mysterious in this, of course; I guess it's just the usual 'benignorance' [*blagogluposti*]. But the trick was done on purpose. And now all the dévots in town will get talking and spread it through the district: 'What can be the meaning of this dream?' I think the old boy really is sharp-eyed: he sniffed crime. Your house stinks with it."

"What crime?"

Rakitin plainly wanted to express something.

"It's going to happen in your fine family, this crime. It'll be between your dear brothers and your Daddy with his bit of a fortune. So Father Zosima banged his forehead just in case. Later, if anything happens, '—oh, the holy elder foretold and prophesied it,' though what's prophetic about banging his forehead on the floor?" (IX, 101–2)

From this first speech any of Dostoevsky's original readers would have recognized Rakitin as a type, a certain kind of theological student, the quick, shrewd, observant son of a Russian priest, whose lively language and cynical insight into the establishment led to power, position, and sometimes wealth in the world centered about the radical journals of the time. The invented word *blagogluposti* ("benigorance") has been connected with Shchedrin,[16] but Dostoevsky certainly intended it to suggest a far more plebeian type like Dobroliubov. The quick, facile logic, the materialistic or social explanation of the religious, the special awareness of monetary and sexual concerns, the expectation of the criminal, the use of diminutives and words like "stinks," "sniffed," and "dévots," and the short, hard sentences all call to mind the articles in *The Contemporary* and, after it closed, the *Fatherland Notes* and other journals of the Russian radicals. In short, the style of this first dialogue has already implied a tie between Rakitin and Ivan that later would be made explicit. Both were setting out on careers in journalism, but Ivan was starting with the simplicity, sincerity, and intelligence of Belinsky, whereas Rakitin's style already reflected the nasty polemics of the writers in the sixties, whom Dostoevsky looked on as living parodies of Belinsky.

Though in the early part of the novel Rakitin is nothing worse than an ill-natured and somewhat sophomoric gossip, in the pages following the legend of the Grand Inquisitor, he is quickly established as a vicious parody of Ivan. Finding Alyosha crushed by the unjust mockery of Zosima's stinking corpse, he adopts the double role of tormentor and tempter as Ivan, the Grand Inquisitor, and the Devil had done, but instead of being tortured himself, he is complacent:

"Can you really [be in this state] simply because your old boy made a stench? Can you really have seriously believed he'd start throwing miracles? . . . Why, what the hell, why nowadays a thirteen-year-old schoolboy doesn't believe that. Still, what the hell—so it's your God you're mad at now, you've mutinied; they passed him by for a promotion, and didn't give him a medal on honors day. Oh, you people." . . .
"I'm not mutinying against my God; I simply 'don't accept His world!' "
(IX, 425)

Alyosha's quotation from Ivan's "mutiny" makes explicit the parallel. Rakitin has replaced Ivan as the tormentor and tempter of Alyosha.

Ivan tormented Alyosha with stories of cruelty, and tempted him to the "absurdity" of advocating vengeance. The Inquisitor tortured Christ with the woes of humanity and dared Christ to destroy him; and the Devil, the chief torturer, tempted Christ in the wilderness. All these tortures are vicarious, and the temptations are toward altruism. Rakitin offers a debased version of these trials: he exacerbates Alyosha's personal hurt, and he tempts him with food and drink and sex, the cheap materialist's equivalent for the earthly bread offered by the Grand Inquisitor, the Devil, and the Russian radicals.

Having established the parallel with Ivan, Dostoevsky proceeds to destroy Rakitin. He uses Rakitin's own denials to suggest the things denied. In two sentences he indicates not only what two people think of Rakitin, but also the petty vengefulness of his reactions: "Your dear brother Ivan once upon a time proclaimed me a 'talentless liberal bumpkin.' And you too one fine time couldn't stand it and gave me to understand that I was 'dishonorable.' All right! Now, I'll have a look at your talent and honor." (IX, 426.) In the next chapter Rakitin's destruction continues, as we learn that he brought Alyosha to Grushenka not on a whim, but because she had offered him 25 pieces of silver to do so. The reference to Judas is made explicit, and we are able to say initially that Dostoevsky's invention took the form of a systematic distortion of the Judas story in a simple direction. Alyosha and Rakitin eat together, not a religious feast, but a snack that breaks the dietary rules of the monastery. Like Christ Alyosha realizes his tempter's intent, and tells him to carry it out, but a seduction not a crucifixion is involved, and this fails instead of succeeding. The reduction of the sum from 30 to 25 pieces of silver is thus consistent with Dostoevsky's lightening of all the other elements in his fictionalized version.

Elsewhere in the novel the same depreciation of currency takes place when Smerdyakov kills his father and then hangs himself after returning the 30 pieces of paper—hundred-ruble notes—for which he has committed the crime. Another piece of nonfiction probably enters the picture here. Dostoevsky had received a letter asking for "30 rubles in silver," a normal phrase in a period when a silver ruble would purchase far more than the inflated paper ruble. The letter came from a relative he disliked, and is dated five months before the appearance of the book "Alyosha" in *The Russian Messenger*. I would suggest the following chain of associations. The 30 silver rubles for the disliked relatives suggested the 30 pieces of silver for Judas. This essentially literary association aroused a feeling of distaste in Dostoevsky, the same feeling he had for the radical journalists of his day. That complex of radicals, relatives, revulsion, and Judas—an ideological, a personal, an emotional, and a literary stimulus—suggested a rhetorical device to Dostoevsky, the use of the familiar Judas figure as a means of stimulating in the reader a prefabricated revulsion for Rakitin. This use of the name of Judas was a commonplace, of course. In Russian literature Dostoevsky could have found it from Avvakum in the seventeenth century to his contemporary Saltykov-Shchedrin, whose most famous villain is nicknamed little Judas. But the letter is the most plausible core about which this particular complex of biblical, political, and rhetorical sources crystallized.

The connection with Ivan's promising career in journalism leads to more elaborate patterns of association for Rakitin, who plans to marry a rich idiot, grow richer as a radical journalist, and build himself a stone house on the Liteinii avenue in St. Petersburg. When he takes the witness stand at Dmitry's trial, he is asked: "Are you that same Mr. Rakitin whose brochure published by the episcopal authorities I recently read with such pleasure, *The Life of the Elder Father Zosima, who rests in the bosom of the Lord*, full of profound and religious thoughts, with a superb and devout dedication to his Eminence? . . . With the sponsorship of his Eminence, your invaluable brochure has circulated and done considerable good." (X, 202.) Rakitin is embarrassed and claims that he never expected publication, obviously afraid that such a background will affect his reputation in radical circles. That is all. The subject is dropped.

It has been pointed out that Dostoevsky's readers would consider this passage realistic not only because the Russian radicals tended to emerge from the theological seminaries—one of the few places they could obtain a free education, places by their nature conducive to revolt—but because one of them, Grigory Zakharevich Eliseev, had indeed enriched himself as a radical journalist and owned a large stone house on the Liteinii avenue.[17] Eliseev's first book was called *The Biography of the Saintly Grigorii, Herman, and Varsonofii of Kazan and Sviiazhsk*. The dedication read as follows:

Your exaltedly eminent Lordship, benevolent Father and Archpastor! From your archpastoral benediction I started upon these labors, with your unceasing attention continued them, and to you I now offer this small item of my making. Your exaltedly eminent Lordship! Accept with your habitual condescension my meager offering, and with your condescension the unworthiness of the laborer will take heart for the great work. Your exalted Eminence, benevolent Father and Archpastor's humblest servant, student in the Kazan Theological Academy, Grigory Eliseev.[18]

Since a major Russian author, Leskov, had called attention to this passage eight years before *The Brothers Karamazov* in a major work called *An Enigmatic Man* (chapter 38), Dostoevsky could count on most of his readers to catch the reference, but he was plainly not using the example of Eliseev's sycophancy merely to discredit Rakitin. A direct transcription of his source would have been much more damning than the sharply abbreviated version he does offer. Rather he seems to be using Eliseev's life simply as source material, to provide the kind of data that will anchor his fiction in reality and give it that treasured capacity to fit even subsequently revealed fact which Dostoevsky claimed in the Liubimov letter. The episode is in *The Brothers Karamazov* because it happened and because Rakitin's character demanded it. It is brief because the trial was already threatening to overbalance the novel, and because the mere discomfiture was enough. In this case what started as a source became a resource, a literary reference that would identify Rakitin as a caricature of a radical, in contrast to Ivan, the apotheosis of the radical.

A similar discovery of a real-life caricature of a Russian radical led Dostoevsky to build into Rakitin parodies of one of the greatest parodists of his time, Dmitry Minaev.[19] Here the polemic cuts both ways. The reference to Minaev's parodies would have been clear to contemporary readers, and Dostoevsky was essentially using this recognition to say both that Rakitin was a Minaev, and that Minaev was a Rakitin. Since he had already linked Rakitin with Ivan, he was creating a careerist parody for the independence and ambition with which Ivan was arranging his career. Eliseev and Minaev, in Dostoevsky's mind, were to Belinsky and Herzen as Rakitin was to Ivan.

Like any respectable Russian radical of his day, including Ivan, who had written a work on the geological revolution, Rakitin was much involved with the natural sciences, especially with the materialist claim that science could explain everything. Mitya Karamazov reports on Rakitin's beliefs:

You see, there in the nerves, in the head, that is, there in the brain these nerves—to hell with them!—there are these little tails; those nerves have little tails, now as soon as they wiggle there, that is, you see, I look at something with my eyes, like this, and they wiggle, these little tails, and as they wiggle there appears an image and it doesn't appear immediately but a certain instant passes, a second, and something like a moment, that is, not a moment, damn the moment, but an image, that is, an object, or an event, now then, damn it, that's why I observe, and then I think—because of the tails . . . (X, 102)

With the care he frequently displays, Dostoevsky footnoted this passage with references to Claude Bernard, the French neurologist, materialist, and proponent of the scientific method of discovery who had been made a literary symbol in a book Dostoevsky had parodied fifteen years earlier, Chernyshevsky's *What Is to Be Done*. Dostoevsky had apparently mocked Chernyshevsky so viciously in his "Crocodile" (1865) that Dostoevsky later denied the allusion. Here I would suggest that the articles on physiology and neurology in many contemporary journals provide more than adequate sources for Rakitin's teachings as Mitya recounts them. One element, however, is missing. The articles in the journals were sometimes pedantic, sometimes superficial, often arrogant, but they were not stupid. Dostoevsky's ideological enemies were his intellectual equals, and he knew it.

Can we find a source for the sarcastic scorn Mitya heaps on Rakitin in this passage? Dostoevsky's correspondence may provide a clue, for he received letters from readers of every persuasion and every level of intelligence. Let me cite a letter that can serve as an example of a genre. It came late in December 1876 from a Kharkhov businessman named Ballin, whose letterhead proclaims that he was a dealer in sewing machines, materials, aids, incidentals for writing, educational games, scales, and disinfectant substances. S. V. Belov, who is probably the greatest storehouse of Dostoevskiana alive, informs me that these dealerships were the cover for an illegal printing press. Dostoevsky would have had no way of knowing the level of his correspondent's commitment to radical causes, but he would have felt some evidence of it in his passionate and fuzzy materialism. Ballin begins with praise for Dostoevsky's short story "The Gentle Creature," and goes on to admit that he has not read the second half, adding "Oh well, you don't get everything read." Of all Dostoevsky's works "The Gentle Creature" depends most on the climactic realization presented on the very last page. Without that it is a totally different work of art. Dostoevsky could only have responded to this opening with annoyance. The letter goes on to elucidate certain of Ballin's theories about consciousness:

Concerning spiritualism, I am fully convinced of the realness of ideas. Thought and feeling I cannot conceive otherwise than as an aggregate of organized molecules appearing in our brain as a result of external influences, and these external influences I consider to be the external expression of the life around us. I cannot conceive an individual otherwise than humanly, and therefore accept as individuals also such beings as the earthly sphere and the sun. By consciousness I mean a complicated interaction of the parts of the individualized substance in various places and at various times. Understanding consciousness in this way, it appears incontrovertible to me that consciousness develops proportionally with the cooperation of the mass. Hence I deduce a vicious conclusion—that the consciousness of the sun, for example, must exceed human consciousness by a million times, the more so because the individual psychic activity is in specific relation to the size of the surface of the individual and the surface of the sun is also very great. It's plain that in saying the consciousness of the sun, I have in mind something altogether uncomprehended by me, and not a human consciousness made great.[20]

This portentous and disconnected fabric of fashionable phrases would have become linked in Dostoevsky's mind with the materialism that underlies it, and with the self-satisfaction at the beginning of the letter, to form a real-life parody of the radical style and doctrine.

For Dostoevsky, Rakitin is related to Ivan in much the same way as the Eliseevs and Minaevs and Ballins are related to Herzen and Belinsky. The greedy, vicious, foolish epigones become the sources for Rakitin, just as the great figures become the sources for Ivan.

v

The finest parody of Ivan and his Inquisitor is Kolya Krasotkin, the thirteen-year-old schoolboy who can strike terror into the hearts of his mother, his teachers, and his classmates. Like Ivan, Kolya is very intelligent, is incessantly tortured by self-consciousness, quotes Voltaire, and has a breadth of reading that astonishes those around him. But his intelligence is a schoolboy's smartness, amusing to watch, and his self-doubt and self-consciousness involve his appearance and his wits, not his moral position. He quotes Voltaire but does not understand him, and his reading is in trivial school compendiums.

When Ivan meets Alyosha, he says he wants to see him very much: "I want to get acquainted with you once and for all, and to get you to know me.... I've finally learned to respect you; it's plain this man stands firm.... I love these firm ones, whatever they may stand on, even if they're little galoots like you." (IX, 287.) The intensity of the affection overrides the patronizing words, and Alyosha responds in kind: "You're just the same sort of young man as all the other 23-year-olds, the same young, youthful, fresh, and wondrous boy, a weanling, and to sum it up, a boy. Tell me, did I hurt your feelings badly?" When Kolya summons Alyosha, he also "very, very much wanted to get acquainted" (X, 39). Later he says, "I'm glad to know you, Karamazov. I've wanted to know you for a long time.... I learned long ago to respect you as a rare being.... I have heard that you are a mystic and were in the monastery. I know you are a mystic, but—that didn't stop me. Contact with reality will cure you." (X, 57.) Kolya here constitutes the realization of Ivan's metaphors. He is a real, not a figurative, boy, and at the simplest level he believes the patronizing words he is using. At the same time, his respect and affection for Alyosha emerge in close parallel to Ivan's.

One puzzling moment in the novel is Kolya's long account of the goose, a lame story of a piece of boyish cruelty (X, 51–52). He had asked a stupid peasant whether a cartwheel would decapitate a goose that was pecking under it. Watching from the side where the goose was pecking, Kolya winked at the right moment, and the peasant made the cart move, cutting the goose's neck in two. "You did that on purpose," people cry. "No, not on purpose," Kolya answers; but the stupid peasant says, "It wasn't me, that's the one who got me to do it." Kolya's answer has the hauteur of his intellectual superiority: "I hadn't taught him at all; I had simply expressed the basic idea and only spoke hypothetically." This guiltily rationalized account seems overly expanded in the novel, until it takes its place with Ivan's struggle to avoid admitting that his basic idea has seduced Smerdyakov into killing, and with Smerdyakov's teaching of little Ilyusha to torture dogs by feeding them bread with pins in it. The vicarious assaults on the animals remind readers of Ivan's place in the murder, and rob him of much of the sympathy that might attach to him as a misunderstood manipulator.

Kolya's behavior trivializes the ideas of the Grand Inquisitor and the Devil, as well as those Ivan expresses himself. Kolya trains the dog Zhuchka to play dead and resurrect itself, and then stages the reappearance of the dog as a miracle for Ilyusha. He exploits the mysterious secret about the founding of Troy, and crushes the boy who divulges it. He performs an exploit that is the modern child's equivalent of Christ's second temptation in the wilderness, casting himself between the tracks of an oncoming train. And he uses authority, deception, and force for the good of the little group of schoolboys, whom he treats as the Grand Inquisitor treats all humanity. The Inquisitor said:

Oh we shall finally persuade them not to be proud; . . . we shall show them that though they are feeble, though they are only pitiable children, childish happiness is the sweetest of all. They will grow timid and will start to look up to us and press against us in fear, like fledglings to their mother. They will feel wonder and terror at us. . . . Yes, we will make them work, but in the hours free from work, we will arrange their life like children's play . . . and they will worship us as their benefactors. (IX, 325)

Kolya realizes some of these metaphors. He actually arranges child-ish games and commands the obedience of the boys "like a god." He even says:

And, generally, I love the small fry. I have two fledglings on my hands at home right now; even today they delayed me. So [the boys] stopped beating Ilyusha, and I took him under my protection. I can see that he's a proud boy. I tell you that: he's proud, but in the end he has entrusted himself to me like a slave, fulfills my slightest commands, obeys me like a god, and tries to imitate me. . . . So now you too, Karamazov, have gotten together with all these fledglings? (X, 32)

Everything here echoes Ivan and cheapens Ivan. The pride of sin-ful humanity becomes the stubbornness of a pathetic child. The chil-dren or fledglings shrink, from the whole of humanity whom the Inquisitor loves and serves, to a couple of groups of children who reinforce Kolya's ego. The Inquisitor's godlike dominion becomes a child's bossiness. And Kolya's resurrection of the dog becomes a com-ment on Ivan's dreams of resurrecting the dead and all the talk of miracles, because we can see the effect of this miracle: "If the unsus-pecting Krasotkin had understood how torturingly and murderously such a moment could influence the health of the sick boy, he would not have thought of playing a trick like the one he played" (X, 46). The word "murderously" here removes Kolya from the world of real mockery and makes him an involuntary killer in his blind superiority.

Radicalism in Dostoevsky's day was almost a club, and member-ship required certain attitudes. Various novels and journalistic pieces, friendly, hostile, and ambivalent, ranging from Turgenev's *Fathers and Sons* to Chernyshevsky's *What Is to Be Done?*, had canonized the list: materialism, scientism, positivism, atheism, socialism, inter-nationalism, realism, feminism, and in the 1870's populism, all cou-pled with hostility to sentiment, tradition, prejudice, manners, the aesthetic, the establishment, and the government. Except for fem-inism and internationalism Kolya manages to take every pose de-manded of a radical. In the chapter "A Schoolboy," he begins: "They're scum . . . doctors and the whole medical filth, speaking in general and, of course, in detail. I reject medicine. It's a useless es-tablishment." (X, 22.) This remark might not seem scientistic, but in the tradition of Russia radicalism the deliverers of medical care re-ceived none of the honor accorded to the investigators of medical truth.

Kolya goes on to attack Alyosha and the boys for sentimentalizing in their visits to Ilyusha, and later, after an "impressive silence," he makes an excursion into scientism and utopian political positivism (X, 23):

"I love to observe realism, Smurov. Have you observed how dogs meet and sniff each other. They obey some common law of nature there."

"Yes, it's sort of funny."

"No, it's not funny. You're wrong about that. In nature there's nothing funny, however, it might seem to a man with his prejudices. . . . That's a thought of Rakitin's, a remarkable thought. I'm a socialist, Smurov."

"And what's a socialist?" . . .

"That's if all are equal and own common property, and there are no marriages, and religion and all the laws are the way each person wants, and, well, and so on. You're still young for that; it's early for you. It's chilly, though." . . .

"Have you noticed, Smurov, the way in the middle of winter, if it's fifteen or even eighteen degrees, it doesn't seem so cold as now, for example, at the beginning of winter. . . . With people everything's a matter of habit, even in governmental and political relationships."

Kolya then pauses to tease a benign peasant he passes, concluding, "I love to talk with the people, and am always prepared to give it its due. . . . With the people, you have to know how to talk." (X, 24.)

The picture of the young radical pontificating to a devotedly receptive follower had become ironic at least as early as *Fathers and Sons* and savage in Leskov's *An Enigmatic Man*. The catalogue of shibboleths recurs two chapters later in another setting, also as old as Turgenev, with the young man patronizingly enlightening the older about radical doctrine. The indoctrination of Alyosha also starts with the statement that medicine is villainy. After an interruption by concerns involving Ilyusha, Kolya expounds on his schoolboy cynicism toward history, which parodies Ivan's sense of the meaninglessness of history as described by Dostoevsky to Liubimov. Kolya says:

I don't ascribe much importance to all those old wives' tales, and in general haven't too much respect for world history. . . . It's the study of the series of human stupidities, and that's all. I respect only mathematics and natural science. . . . Again, these classical languages . . . classical languages, if you want my opinion about them, are a police measure. . . . They're introduced because they're tiresome and because they dull our capacities. . . . It was pointless, so how could it be made more pointless? And that's when they thought up the classical languages. (X, 54)

At this point, one boy in the group shouts out, "And he's the top student in Latin." In enunciating one of the standard doctrines of the practical and scientistic radicals, Kolya displays his disinterestedness. This rejection of what he labels "baseness" (*podlost'*) offers a child's equivalent of the nobility with which the Grand Inquisitor rejects the salvation he has the ability to earn, or with which Ivan returns his ticket. The gesture is the same, and the love for the oppressed is the same, but the schoolboy's showing off infects the reader's recollection of the Inquisitor's magnificent self-sacrifice.

Dostoevsky's central quarrel with the radicals may well have involved their attitude toward religion. Kolya follows his splendid thirteen-year-old statement that contact with reality would cure Alyosha's mysticism with this definition of mysticism: "Well, God and all." He elaborates his ideas about God, which turn out to be a travesty of Ivan's ambivalent abstention from denial.

"I don't have anything against God. Of course, God is only a hypothesis —but—I admit that He is necessary for order—for the order of the world and so on—and if He did not exist, it would be necessary to invent Him," added Kolya, starting to blush. . . . "Even without believing in God, it's possible to love mankind. . . . I've read *Candide*, in Russian translation. . . . I'm a socialist, Karamazov, an incorrigible socialist. . . . The Christian faith has served only the rich and noble, to hold the lower class in slavery, isn't that true? . . . I am not against Christ. That was a really humane person, and if He had lived in our time, He would have joined the revolutionists right away and maybe played a prominent role—that's certain, even." (X, 57)

The talk about hypotheses, the order of things, the necessity for God, and the possibility of love without God all plainly reminds the reader of Ivan. The talk about socialism, the sins of Christianity, and Christ's need to join the revolutionists recalls the Grand Inquisitor. Ivan has observed, "Everything that in Europe is a hypothesis is immediately an axiom for the Russian boy." His frequent use of the word "boy" (*mal'chik*) prepares the reader for the repetition of these doctrines by a real boy, culminating in the word-for-word repetition of Voltaire's aphorism about the invention of God. But this aphorism is the highest reach of Kolya's sophistication, whereas for Ivan it is the starting point for two passionate statements about a single vision of humanity. We have already noted the first: "I think that if the Devil does not exist, and man in fact created him, then he created him in his own image and likeness" (IX, 299). The second is so powerful that it needed Kolya's parody:

And indeed, man did invent God. It would be nothing strange and nothing wondrous for God to really exist, but the wondrous thing is that such a thought, the thought of the necessity of God, could creep into the head of such a savage and evil animal as man; it is so holy, so touching, so wise, and does such honor to man. (IX, 294)

Through this entire catalogue of shibboleths, Ivan's doctrines become associated with the conceit and embarrassed self-consciousness that are Kolya's most visible traits. The rhetorical function of Kolya's conceit is curiously related to the best-known source for Kolya. George Chulkov has shown that many of Kolya's doctrines coincide closely with statements made by Belinsky. And we know that in the early seventies Dostoevsky found conceit to be a central feature of Belinsky's character. Arkady Dolinin has summed up Dostoevsky's attitude toward Belinsky at that time by using a series of quotations from Dostoevsky's letters:

"Belinsky, that most rotten, dull, and shameful phenomenon of Russian life." "A stinkbug, Belinsky was just an impotent and feeble little talent." "Belinsky cursed Russia and knowingly brought upon her so much woe." "In Belinsky there was so much petty conceit, viciousness, impatience, exacerbation, baseness, but most of all conceit. It never occurred to him that he himself was disgusting. He was pleased with himself in the highest degree, and that was already a stinking, shameful, personal stupidity." "He related to Gogol's characters superficially to the point of meaninglessness. . . . He scolded Pushkin when Pushkin casts off his false pose. . . . He rejected the end of *Eugene Onegin*. . . ." "He didn't even understand his own people. He didn't even understand Turgenev."[21]

Perhaps here, in this vision of Belinsky, is a source for some of the conceit in Kolya, for some of the littleness and incomprehension. Of course, the nastiness that is such a conspicuous part of these letters has disappeared. Kolya can be cruel, arrogant, conceited, but there is no stinking, shameful talentlessness in him. These qualities seem to survive in two places. One is Kolya's vision of himself: "Tell me, Karamazov," he asks, "do you despise me terribly?" And the other repository for these unpleasant qualities is Rakitin, who embodies them superbly.

Dolinin argues, however, that Dostoevsky's view of Belinsky and his political attitude as a whole underwent a revolution in 1876, and that by the time *The Brothers Karamazov* began to emerge, he was expressing some of the old ardor he had felt for the Belinsky who had honored and befriended him in 1846. He refers to him as "the most honorable and noble Belinsky," and echoes Apollon Grigor'ev's claim that "if he had lived longer, Belinsky would necessarily have joined the Slavophiles." The chronological lines may not be so neat as Dolinin makes them, but the ambivalence is certainly there. If the vile and nasty traits Dostoevsky saw in Belinsky went to make Rakitin, we should look in a novel of the 1870's for some expression of the magnificent eloquence and true self-sacrifice Dostoevsky also attributed to him. Here the most obvious repository is Ivan himself. Indeed, an excellent critic of Dostoevsky, Alfred Rammelmeyer, considers Belinsky a chief source for the Grand Inquisitor, documenting his case primarily with Belinsky's letters to Botkin, which Pypin had published not long before the writing of *The Brothers Karamazov*.

If Kolya and Ivan both derive from Belinsky, one from the noble vision and one from the little, conceited vision, with Rakitin as the repository for all the vilest traits, at first glance it might seem that Chulkov had oversimplified the pattern, and that Kolya resembles Belinsky because Ivan does and Kolya is a parody of Ivan. On the basis of the notebooks for *The Brothers Karamazov*, I would suggest another pattern of development. For years Dostoevsky had been working on two projects, the life of a great sinner and a book about children. Earlier he had planned two other great novels, "Atheism" and the Russian Candide. The great sinner, whose life was to be traced from childhood, was to fall into radicalism and eventually to be saved. This career coincides not with Ivan's, not with Alyosha's, both of which have been connected with the plan, but with Kolya's. If this formulation is right, in the mid-1870's the plans for the Russian Candide, for "Atheism," for the life of the great sinner, and for the novel about children all became focused on the figure of little Kolya Krasotkin. The earliest surviving notes we have for *The Brothers Karamazov* relate to him. The figure of Ivan the radical emerges only later. Ivan then, like Rakitin, would have come into existence as a repository for traits Dostoevsky could not incorporate into a child when he merged the heroes of these four unwritten novels into a single youthful figure.

Once the character of Ivan had been spun off, it assumed the residual loveliness of Belinsky and of Aleksandr Herzen. Indeed, it might perhaps be argued that the ideological revolution in Dostoevsky's thinking which Dolinin dates to the mid-1870's was the result and not the cause of the emergence of Ivan from the mass of materials that were to become the novel. About the figure of Ivan would gather the noble doubts, the mighty pity, the love of life, of humanity, of family that were later to make him so dangerous to the ideological intentions Dostoevsky described in his letter to Liubimov. In this case, I would suggest that the child is father of the man.

VI

We no longer need Dostoevsky's letter to Liubimov or any other statement as evidence in our evaluation of Lawrence's argument that

Dostoevsky agreed with Ivan and the Grand Inquisitor. We have been looking at what Dostoevsky did, not what he said. We have ascribed his eloquence not to his sincerity but to his borrowings. We have ascribed the kiss of Christ not to acquiescence but to ideological irony. We have ascribed the pivotal position of Ivan in part to the parodic figures clustering around him. And we have offered the rhetorical energy Dostoevsky expended on the deprecation of Ivan as evidence of his good faith in promising to confute Ivan's doctrines.

In this final section we must return to the disjunction we started with and ask why Dostoevsky's rhetoric failed to convince Lawrence and many others. Lawrence, of course, was writing an introduction to a dubious enterprise, a separate edition to the legend of the Grand Inquisitor. The isolation of the passage could explain Lawrence's misreading, but not the widespread prevalence of his view. One could say that many readers read badly or read with preestablished conclusions because certain early errors have been immortalized. But major writers should have a rhetoric that will preclude such errors about the central issues of a work. The final explanation for the failure of Dostoevsky's rhetoric to communicate his intent may involve a technical truth he had mastered early in his career.

There are a number of connections between *The Brothers Karamazov* and *Crime and Punishment*. Let us consider the passage in *Crime and Punishment* where Raskolnikov has just committed the double murder and stands poised for his getaway. He opens the door and listens at the head of the stairs. Someone goes out of the building. He is about to leave when he hears someone entering the building, and he grows convinced that the person is coming to visit his victims. At the last minute he slips back and silently bolts the door, then listens, holding his breath, while this visitor and another discuss how to get in. And at some point in these three pages, the reader suddenly realizes that he too is holding his breath. The descriptions of Raskolnikov have been contagious, and without willing it or even knowing it at first, the reader has concentrated his entire poised attentiveness and desire on the escape of this murderer. In short, Dostoevsky manipulates the reader into the experience of having just committed a murder.

He uses this device many times in *Crime and Punishment*. It is not original with him, for it is a common trick in the picaresque to involve the reader's attention in the escape of a first person narrator he deplores. Stanley Fish suggests, for example, that in *Paradise Lost*, Milton inspires sympathy with Satan as a way of letting the reader experience Adam's fall, then destroys this sympathy step by step, until all the fallen angels turn to snakes; according to this interpretation, Blake's belief that Milton favored Satan rests on the beginning not the whole work.[22] Dostoevsky abandons this technique in the novels after *Crime and Punishment*; he never again shows us the mind of a murderer from the inside. But in *The Brothers Karamazov* he does take us inside the mind of a vicarious criminal, Ivan, whose "all is lawful" stimulates or liberates Smerdyakov's murderous proclivities.

By carrying his reader through a genuine experience of what it means to be a Russian radical—a compassionate, noble, generous, tortured, loving one—Dostoevsky implicates the reader in the feelings of guilt, self-consciousness, stupidity, and even savagery to which he makes radicalism lead Ivan, Kolya, Rakitin, and several other characters. The epigraph of the novel comes from the Gospel according to St. John: "Except a corn of wheat fall upon the ground and die, it abideth alone, but if it die, it bringeth forth much fruit." The seed here is the grace of God, which John says will bear fruit only if it dies. By this reckoning the Grand Inquisitor's effort to isolate mankind from evil is actually making grace sterile by not letting it die. Dostoevsky prefers to tempt his readers, as Rakitin and Ivan tempted Alyosha and as the Devil tempted Christ. He tries to carry his readers through a death of grace as dangerous as Zosima's in his youth, or Alyosha's when his faith is shaken, hoping he can bring them out beyond as fertile disseminators of grace. Dostoevsky thus is engaging not in communication but in manipulation. Instead of the semiotic model we struggled with, we need a cybernetic one.

This use of the novel for the propagation of active grace entails the danger that the process may stop at the first step, and the less grave but more likely danger that readers may interpret the author's intention as stopping at the first step. Dostoevsky took this risk, and a substantial, but I think decreasing, number of his readers have justified his fear and trembling.

WILLIAM MILLS TODD III

Eugene Onegin: "Life's Novel"

> We regard the roles that we adopt as means of imposing ourselves on society. It is only gradually that we come to realize the extent to which the role can impose itself upon the "self" which plays it.
>
> —*Elizabeth Burns*

Few periods in Russian literature so invite social commentary as the one spanned by Pushkin's writing career, 1814 to 1837. Previously a patronage system had dominated the literary milieu, but this period witnessed a rapid transition from the salons, which sheltered gentleman amateurs, to a nascent literary profession protected by copyright laws, financed by journals and booksellers, consumed by an ever-increasing readership, and practiced by writers of both gentle and not-so-gentle birth.[1] But the rapidly revolving stage offered the writer these definitions of his role—protégé, gentleman amateur, professional—more or less simultaneously, just as it simultaneously confronted him with a wealth of genres and historically distinct international styles, including classicism, sentimentalism, and romanticism. A writer bold enough to question the prejudices of his social group and literary predecessors could exercise considerable choice in this chaotic situation, and Pushkin did precisely that with genres and styles, following the flight of his imagination across the map of literary history.

Pushkin faced the social problems of this era of changing authorial roles no less boldly. Although his older contemporaries had already taken Russian poetry from the frequently venal panegyrists of the

I am most grateful to M. Ehre, L. Ginzburg, J. Gordin, M. Katz, S. Knapp, H. Lindenberger, H. McLean, and G. Schmidgall for their valuable comments on earlier drafts of this paper.

late eighteenth century and made it a refined form of entertainment for the salons, Pushkin was still vitally concerned with this process when he began writing *Eugene Onegin* in the 1820's, and he still felt it necessary to declare his independence as a writer from the patronage of the wealthy upper aristocracy and from subservience to the government.[2] One of his strongest statements appears in a letter to A. A. Bestuzhev:

> Among us, writers are taken from the highest class of society—in them aristocratic pride merges with authorial self-esteem. We do not want to be protected by our equals. This is what that scoundred Vorontsov [Pushkin's superior in the civil service] does not understand. He imagines that a Russian poet will appear in his antechamber with a dedication to him or an ode, but the poet appears with a demand for respect, as a member of the gentry with 600 years' standing. (May–June 1825; XIII, 179)

The conventions of the familiar letter of Pushkin's time encouraged such assertions of noble dignity, but Pushkin hardly issued them automatically. Behind his assertion stood the bitter reality of exile, police surveillance, debt, and an insignificant rank in the civil service. Independence and dignity had to be won, and his membership in the gentry alone was not enough to satisfy his need for them. A writing profession could help make him independent of humiliating government service and give him peace and leisure to write, but that conflicted with the prejudices of the class to which, as we have just seen, he was proud to belong.

Nevertheless, during the mid-1820's Pushkin declared his independence from the salon concept of literature as the sentimental recreation of amateurs (XIII, 95) and boldly took up his new "trade," as he called it (XIII, 59, 88, 93). But the problem of reconciling his professional aspirations, his class identity, and his authorial freedom continued to trouble him. As his financial successes of the 1820's gave way to nearly hopeless attempts to establish himself in journalism, bitter literary quarrels with opponents of nongentry origin, and the vicious social intrigues that finally killed him, his early optimism faded. The short story "Egyptian Nights," written in 1835, raises the problem of literature in a social milieu and arrives at no happy resolution of the conflict between social position, literary commerce, and inspiration. The two principal characters are poets—Charsky (a gentleman amateur) and an Italian *improvisatore*. Both preserve the miracle of talent and inspiration amid the silly clamor of their uncomprehending public, but at considerable cost to themselves as social beings. The seedy improvisor must play a buffoon's role in society; Charsky maintains his social status by cutting himself off from literary ties. The narrator calls no less attention to Charsky's dandy outfit than to the improvisor's gaudy costume; each testifies to the incompatibility of literary and social life, to the distinct roles that society makes their representatives play. Pushkin did not finish the story, but his review of Voltaire's correspondence (1836) suggests a possible conclusion. Reflecting on Voltaire's humiliating life at the court of Frederick the Great, he resolves: "The writer's real place is in his study and, ultimately, independence and self-esteem alone can lift us above the trifles of life and the storms of fate" (XII, 81). Yet even this conclusion—itself ironic within the review—is not bleak enough for the story: Charsky's social role so overwhelms him that he purges the books from his library, lest his social acquaintances think him too much a writer.

The historical awareness and keen sense of class antagonism that characterize some of Pushkin's final works and final thoughts on the writer's social position do little, however, to illuminate *Eugene Onegin*, the subject of this essay. The subtitle of the novel ("a novel in verse") and its dedicatory piece proclaim the author's intention to fuse the widely disparate resources at his command. As a free and audacious blending, reworking, and violation of literary conventions, the form of the novel is analogous to Pushkin's desired fusion of the various social images of the writer that his historical situation offered to him: the Russian gentleman amateur, the professional European man of letters, and the inspired and autonomous poet of the romantic movement. In its discussion of *Eugene Onegin*, this essay will ask whether a similar attitude toward convention, choice, and autonomy informs the ontological levels of the novel—the level on which the characters act and the level on which the self-conscious author-narrator makes them act. To this end I will define these levels, examine the range of possibilities for human action that the novel presents, and analyze the choices that Pushkin's characters make within this range.

1. *Two Realities or One?*

Pushkin's "Journey to Arzrum During the Campaign of 1829," written in 1829–35, offers an excellent point of departure for discussing his treatment of autonomy in life and art. At the outset of his journey, after denying his personal reliance on the patronage of the authorities, Pushkin underscores his independence by making his first visit to General Ermolov, who had fallen under suspicion for his ties to the Decembrist uprising. Pushkin immediately touches on another sort of dependence, art's reliance on convention, when he describes Ermolov:

At first glance, I found not the slightest resemblance of his portraits, which were usually drawn in profile. A round face, fiery gray eyes, gray hair standing on end. The head of a tiger on a Herculean torso. His smile is unpleasant because it is unnatural. But when he grows thoughtful and frowns, he becomes handsome and strikingly reminiscent of the poetic portrait drawn by Dawe. (VIII, 445)

Pushkin's first impression makes the hardly novel point that art and reality differ; the convention of drawing portraits in profile merely increases the distance between them. But as Pushkin looks more closely at Ermolov, he turns his irony on the delusion that we can communicate our perceptions without recourse to conventions, not merely linguistic ones, but those of our culture as a whole—art, literature, social behavior. To place Ermolov before the reader, the narrator finds he must become more conventional, not less. His figures become as hoary as his subject's head: an animal metaphor as venerable as mythology itself, a reminiscence from classical mythology, a facial expression (fiery eyes) from the lexicon of romantic demonism that Pushkin had so often parodied. The last two sentences of the passage strike a similar balance, this time adding the problem of the beautiful to that of the real. One conventionally significant social gesture (a smile) is rejected because it is forced and unnatural, but another (the thoughtful frown), no less conventional, pleases the narrator. As the perceived object (Ermolov) assumes his final pose, the narrator suggests that life, art, nature, and beauty *can* coincide, if only the participants in the creative act have sufficient command of the conventions their culture provides. The oxymoron "poetic portrait" combines two different types of artifice to underscore this possibility. Conventions—the necessary tools of art and perception—can imprison the artist (portraits in profile), serve as probes for investigating reality (the narrator), or join beauty and truth (Dawe). As Pushkin's travel account progresses, he continues to use and test the conventions of his culture. His freedom from domination by any one of them, the genre of the romantic travelogue, for example, is analogous to his asserted freedom on the social plane to accept or decline the patronage of the powerful. And yet he remains within the purview of conventions, just as he will never escape the borders of the Russian Empire on his journey.[3]

From its generically provocative subtitle to its concluding meta-phor ("life's novel"), *Eugene Onegin* raises similar problems: the relationship between art and life, the limits imposed on social action and artistic expression by a culture's grammar of conventions. Life and literature intersect at every turn; they are not merely analogous to each other. The author-narrator disconcertingly steps into the created world of his fiction to befriend Eugene. The narrator's muse shades into the novel's heroine, Tatiana. She, Eugene, and Lensky (a poet of sorts) try to act out the patterns of the literature they read in their daily lives: they become what they read, to alter Feuerbach's formula, no merely what they eat. Both Eugene, a dandy, and Tati-ana, the hostess of a salon, play roles that unite the social and the aesthetic. And, as the reader tries to focus on this created world, the narrator discusses his own craft so frequently that he generates what Leon Stilman has called the "second reality" of *Eugene Onegin*, the "reality of the creative process."[4]

Pushkin's oscillation between these two realities has created for his critics a problem similar to the problem of ambiguity in the psy-chology of visual perception. It has been posited that we cannot simultaneously hold two interpretations of an ambiguous picture, for example, an interpretation conscious of the artist's formal materi-als (shapes, colors, and the like) and one accepting his illusion of reality.[5] Such has certainly been the case with critical studies of *Eugene Onegin*, which tend either to concentrate on the represented world of the characters as a reflection of Pushkin's social milieu[6] or else to focus on the novel's constructive (formal) aspects.[7] Taken to extremes each reading, the mimetic and the formalistic, seriously underestimates the range of Pushkin's genius—his artful manipula-tion of styles and devices, on the one hand, and, on the other, his ability to lend striking verisimilitude to characters and their situa-tions in a few swift lines, creating individuals who became literary stereotypes for the rest of his century. Meanwhile Pushkin, twirling his two realities in a kaleidoscope of narrative viewpoints, parodies, literary reminiscences, and generic fragments, has made sure that any monistic reading will sooner or later run aground on the ontological complexity of his novel.[8]

This complexity should encourage rather than dismay the critic, for it suggests that even more readings are possible—and necessary —than the useful ones Pushkin scholarship has already given us. Especially necessary are approaches that attempt to relate the novel's

formal and socially mimetic structures, its creative and created realities, granting each its brilliance and regarding neither as a mere
pretext for the other. Pushkin's perception of Ermolov suggests one
basis for such a reading—the idea of culture, with its related social,
intellectual, and aesthetic aspects. The constituent elements of culture—literature (written and oral, of the gentry and of the folk) and
social customs (urban, rural, gentry, folk)—present the characters of
Eugene Onegin, including the author-narrator, with a set of precedents for their actions, social or literary. Sometimes the patterns can
be reconciled; sometimes they clash. At times a pattern may be successfully transferred from one area of culture (e.g. fiction) to another
(social activity); at other times the attempt is foolish. How the characters command these conventions of their culture defines them and
establishes the contrasts that shape Pushkin's novel.

II. *The Range of Culture in 'Eugene Onegin'*

> The body of intellectual and imaginative work which each
> generation receives as its traditional culture is always, and
> necessarily, something more than the product of a single
> class. . . . A culture can never be reduced to its artifacts
> while it is being lived. . . . A culture is not only a body of
> intellectual and imaginative work; it is also and necessarily
> a whole way of life.
> —*Raymond Williams*[9]

For Pushkin's most prominent twentieth-century social critics,
Blagoi and Gukovsky, an individual's possibilities within a culture
are narrowly determined by his class and historical position. *Eugene
Onegin*, however, invites the reader to consider whether an individual can assimilate the achievements of more than one social class
or historical period and can view them, not as the artifacts of a by-
gone age or a remote social class, but as models with some relationship to his own life. The possibilities of one historical period or class
situation will of course differ from those of other periods and social
classes, but the range of conventions, codes, and social patterns within a European culture is likely to be a broad one. Georg Lukács
speculates that Pushkin can depict the events of his novel with light-
ness and deftness because they arise from the structure of society and the socially determined; individual pathology, by contrast,
would require detailed analysis.[10] Yet Pushkin does analyze Eugene's
approach to the duel and Tatiana's infatuation with Eugene in some
detail, although neither character is "pathological." Pushkin's analysis
is necessary because his culture presents the author-narrator and his

characters with many possible definitions of a situation, definitions arising from a variety of class and national sources.

Such hypotheses about culture come easily—perhaps too easily—to a member of the academic community, who is likely to compress entire historical periods and national cultures into a day's reading and lecturing. It remains to be shown, before discussing Pushkin's novel in terms of its characters' choices within their broad cultural framework, that such a framework is established in the novel and that it circumscribes the lives of the characters.

The extent to which Pushkin's characters are creatures of culture, not nature, is readily ascertained by briefly comparing them with the characters of other authors Pushkin mentions in *Eugene Onegin*. Because many readers, prompted by Pushkin's use of nature imagery (moons and deer, à la Chateaubriand), associate Tatiana with the state of nature, she provides an excellent starting point.[11] She may love "artlessly" (3:24)* with her whole being, not from the flirtatious calculations of high society, but the inspiration for that love is provided by a combination of social (the gossip of neighbors), literary (the influence of epistolary novels), and socially significant natural elements ("The time had come, she fell in love," 3:7). In thus combining natural urges, susceptibility to literary models, and social being, Tatiana unites the areas of human existence that Byron assigns, broadly speaking, to three separate women in *Don Juan*: Haidee, the child of nature; Aurora Raby, "who looked more on books than faces";[12] and (as Tatiana's social hypostasis matures) Lady Adeline, the perfect hostess.

A second comparison invited by *Eugene Onegin*, Pushkin's Tatiana with Rousseau's Julie (*Julie, ou la nouvelle Héloise*), suggests that Pushkin has done considerably more to place his heroine in a persistently cultural setting. Tatiana is altogether more of a reader than Julie; indeed her French love letter to Eugene is the result of exposure to Rousseau's very novel.† And she is much more a partici-

---

* I use this notation to indicate chapter and stanza in *Eugene Onegin*.

† That Pushkin's characters relate their thoughts and actions to their reading has been discussed by a number of scholars and, of course, by the narrator of *Eugene Onegin* himself (3:10). What to make of this remains a critical problem, however, as can be seen from the differing emphasis put on it by Stanley Mitchell, "Tatiana's Reading," *Forum for Modern Language Studies*, 6, no. 1 (Jan. 1968); Leon Stilman, "Problemy literaturnykh zhanrov i traditsii v 'Evgenii Onegine' Pushkina," in *American Contributions to the Fourth International Congress of Slavists, Moscow, September 1958* (The Hague, 1958); George Gibian, "Love by the Book: Pushkin, Stendhal, Flaubert," *Comparative Literature*, 3,

pant, if not always willingly, in society. The Switzerland of the Wolmars approximates the state of nature—lakes, mountains, Julie's wild garden. Tatiana's Russian "nature" is a cultivated estate; the winter she loves is closely associated with the rituals and tales of the folk; her solitary walks (book in hand!) take her toward new social encounters and literary awareness. When she contemplates nature, it is from her balcony or through the windows of her family home, with its customs, books, and social obligations, at times inspiring, at times constricting.

It is even easier to use such comparisons to show the extent to which Pushkin inserts cultural mediation between his other characters and nature. The hapless poet Lensky only has eyes for the inevitable graveyards of elegaic verse; he learned no Naturphilosophie during his stay in Germany. Likewise Eugene lacks even the occasional feeling for nature of Childe Harold, to whom the narrator suggestively, parodistically, compares him. Childe Harold, satiated by social pleasures, can turn to a direct experience of nature:

> Where rose the mountains, there to him were friends;
> Where roll'd the ocean, thereon was his home;
> Where a blue sky, and glowing clime, extends,
> He had the passion and the power to roam;
> The desert, forest, cavern, breaker's foam,
> Were unto him companionship; they spake
> A mutual language, clearer than the tome
> Of his land's tongue, which he would oft forsake
> For Nature's pages glass'd by sunbeams on the lake.[13]

But books and language in Pushkin's created world are man-made. When Eugene leaves society and ventures into nature, he has a literary precedent:

no. 2 (Spring 1956): 97–109; and V. V. Sipovskii, *Pushkin: zhizn' i tvorchestvo* (St. Petersburg, 1907). Two new studies have called important attention to the role of literary references in structuring the reader's understanding of the novel. Riccardo Picchio accounts for the function of the novel's epigraphs in "Dante and J. Malfilâtre as Literary Sources of Tat'jana's Erotic Dream (Notes on the Third Chapter of Puškin's *Evgenij Onegin*)," in Andrej Kodjak and Kiril Taranovsky, eds., *Alexander Puškin: A Symposium on the 175th Anniversary of His Birth* (New York, 1976). Iu. M. Lotman, *Roman v stikhakh Pushkina "Evgenii Onegin"* (Tartu, 1975), p. 79, finds that literary references arouse expectations in the reader that are systematically frustrated by Pushkin. My own procedure, as shall become clear later in this essay, is to take Pushkin seriously when he mentions what his characters are reading, as if he were putting quotation marks around their thoughts and actions. In the process of rewriting the novel, Pushkin tended to shorten his characters' reading lists and to focus his attention on the entries that remained.

Eugene lived in a hermit's heaven:
In summer he arose at seven
And lightly sauntered to a rill
That washed the bottom of the hill;
In tribute to Gülnare's singer
He swam his Hellespontus too . . .

(4:37)[14]

Winter comes, but Onegin dutifully follows his Byronic script:

Childe Harold–like, Eugene subsided
Into a state of pensive sloth.

(4:44)

By reducing the vast dimensions of Byron's romantic settings, meanwhile, to those of a country estate, Pushkin places further emphasis on the culturally circumscribed life of his hero.

The narrator's powers of perception and expression by far surpass those of the other characters in *Eugene Onegin*, and he comes closer than they do to achieving a direct experience of nature—in the famous stanza on the coming of winter, for example (4:40). But even here, in one of his most starkly "objective" and unconventionally "prosaic" passages, he will not escape the pressures of his culture. Through metaphor he remains part of the human world, with its aesthetic and social patterns: "But our Northern summer is a *caricature* of Southern winters"; "a clamorous *caravan* of geese" (my italics). Pushkin's natural setting is ultimately inseparable from human work (farmers, herdsmen, a maiden at her spinning wheel) and, at the same time, from the creative work a poet must perform in communicating perceptions to an audience with definite aesthetic and social expectations. Thus the poet faces a conflict of rhyme and decorum in describing the girl: *deva* ("maiden," a poetic form) fits the demands of his rhyme, but *devka* ("wench") would lend it greater social verisimilitude. The poet chooses the former and records in a footnote the displeasure of his critics (VI, 193).

Reminded by his critics that he not only creates worlds but lives in a world which views the created one as an analogue of its own, the narrator resumes his description. His dual awareness, of both the natural setting and the cultural position of his readers, choreographs an intricate pas de deux with his audience (stanza 42) that involves the social nature of perception and communication. In the first four lines he repays his readers for their objections to his diction by pointing out the dreary predictability of their expectations: winter's frosts (*morozy*) inevitably evoke roses (*rozy*) for the dead metaphor "rosy-cheeked."

> At last a crackling frost enfolded
> Fields silvered o'er with early snows:
> (All right—who am I to withhold it,
> The rhyme you knew was coming—rose)
> (4:42)*

At the same time the irony also falls on the narrator; in making fun of the reader's expectations, he has not, after all, surpassed him in originality. But in the next two lines the poet's dual awareness serves to render the winter scene in all of its brilliance:

> The ice-clad river's polished luster
> No stylish ballroom floor can muster; . . .

Instead of attempting a plain description, the poet has drawn on the reader's experience of a cultural setting, one that unites social patterns and the arts of dance and music, to communicate his perception of nature's beauty. The gaiety of the ballroom provides a point of comparison and departure for the remaining lines of the stanza, where the sound of skates cutting the ice replaces the music, and the whirling snow, playing boys, and a clumsy goose the dancers.

> A joyous swarm of urchins grates
> The frozen sheet with ringing skates.
> A cumbrous goose on ruddy paddies
> Comes waddling down the bank to swim,
> Steps gingerly across the rim,
> Slithers and falls; in swirling eddies
> Descends the virgin snow and pranks
> And showers stars upon the banks.

Again the poet has violated decorum, and another footnote records a critic's apparent objection to the combination of a subliterary subject (skating urchins) and a periphrastic, literary style (*mal'chishek radostnyi narod*). Pushkin has creatively conveyed the merry confusion of the scene with an unconventional blend of literary and social conventions. But even for this sort of scene, which some of his contemporaries found most original,[15] Pushkin will eventually indicate

---

* In the original Russian the "you" here is more specific, namely *chitatel'* ("reader"). Pushkin may be having some fun at the expense of his friend Viazemsky, who uses the "frosts"/"roses" association in his well-known poem "First Snow" ("Pervyi sneg," 1819); but Pushkin would himself turn to the rhyme in his greatest narrative poem, "The Bronze Horseman" (1833), in order to conjure up the delight of a winter day.

a cultural precedent: "the motley rubbish of the Flemish School" (VI, 201). In short, he cannot divorce a natural setting from the humans who work and play there. In the creative process of conveying his perceptions, the author-narrator finds that nature is best rendered by confronting, not avoiding, the culturally conditioned aspects of perception—social hierarchy, aesthetic codes, life and literary experience. Byron showed us Childe Harold reading the pages of nature; Pushkin ironically shows himself, a poet in need of an audience, reading his own pages to nature (4:35).

As his novel develops, Pushkin places all his characters—urban and rural, gentry and folk—within a cultural framework that includes both social and artistic patterns. Literature, music, dance, and play are as inseparable from the lives of serfs as from the lives of gentry. Pushkin's servant girls are inevitably singing (3:39–40, 4:41). Although no sensible critic will mistake Pushkin for Harriet Beecher Stowe, he does not conceal the harshness of social inequality. The berry-picking girls are forced to sing so that they will not be able to consume the fruit. But the conditions of their work do not restrain the frolic charm of their "private song," which the narrator allows to be theirs, not their masters'. Its unashamedly playful attitude toward the battle of the sexes stands in refreshing contrast to the other culturally conditioned attitudes that frame it—Tatiana's abstract and lachrymose sentimentality, the stultifying cynicism of Eugene and the narrator, the nurse's quiet resignation.* As so often in Pushkin, culture's playful facets humanize the harshness of social and economic patterns, making them bearable or even transforming them, as we shall see in Tatiana's case.[16]

If culture is not the property of any single class in Pushkin's novel, neither is it the creation of any single class or national group. Pushkin presents culture as a sum of patterns of various times and places, superimposed one upon the other in the lives of his characters. This is clear enough for his cosmopolitan gentry, less so for the few serfs

---

* It is surprising that Pushkin's Soviet commentators have not annotated the nurse's account of her marriage (at age thirteen to an even younger boy) with the passage "Edrovo" from Radishchev's *Journey from Petersburg to Moscow*, in which a young peasant girl refuses to marry a ten-year-old boy because his father sleeps with his young daughters-in-law until his sons grow up. Pushkin's vague hint at this less than charming custom (*snokhachestvo*) of the folk suggests he is hardly the unalloyed venerator of the national folk culture that his more chauvinistic critics have made him. One notes, in passing, that the "Edrovo" passage is excised from the standard school edition of Radishchev's famous radical tract (Moscow: Detskaia literature, 1966).

who appear in the novel. But their very names testify to the "foreign" component in their culture. As Pushkin reminds us in a footnote, "the most euphonious Greek names . . . are used among us only by the simple people" (VI, 192). By giving his heroine Tatiana a name that was more popular among the folk than the gentry, yet was taken from the Greek calendar of saints' days, Pushkin simultaneously tapped a source of beauty outside the narrow limits of sentimentalist diction, underscored the folk component in her cultural background, and suggested the breadth and inclusiveness of even the most "primitive" representatives of Russian culture, the peasantry.*

This syncretic culture, manifest even in the circumscribed lives of the serfs, overarches *Eugene Onegin*, from the dedicatory piece, which promises chapters both "plain-folk and ideal" (*ideaľnyi*, a foreign loan word), to the final parts, in which Pushkin allows his heroine both the aristocratic manner of the Europeanized gentry and an enduring fascination with folklore. Seeming to argue against this syncretism however, is the emphasis the narrator places on the upbringing of his hero and his heroine: Eugene is educated by "Madame" and "Monsieur l'Abbé" (1:3); Tatiana voraciously absorbs the horror stories and superstitions of her peasant nurse (2:27, 5:5–10). This has, predictably enough, led the novel's socially aware critics to view Eugene and Tatiana as representatives, respectively, of the capital's deracinated aristocracy and the countryside's backward, traditional gentry. This is true in relative terms only. For dissolved in the innermost being of each, as it is expressed in dreams and in the most intense emotional outpourings, are other elements of the novel's syncretic cultural matrix. Tatiana's soul may be "Russian" (5:4), but she expresses its longings to Eugene in French, to the narrator's mock dismay (3:26). Her actions, not merely at the beginning, but throughout the novel, are guided by literary models.

Tatiana's dream shows most completely the range of her cultural resources, and, as a result, it has been the subject of some controversy among Pushkin's commentators. A few argue that the dream is entirely folkloric in origin, or at least mostly so.[17] Others have looked to Murillo (Pushkin had a copy of that painter's *Temptation of St.*

---

*The past borrowings of Russian culture frequently served as a polemical weapon against cultural nationalism in Pushkin's time. Essayists of the early 1800's used similar reminders of the foreign elements (Greek, Mongolian) in medieval and folk culture to undermine the position of the linguistic purists, led by Admiral Shishkov, whom Pushkin laughingly evokes in *Eugene Onegin* (8:14). For examples see N. I. Mordovchenko, *Russkaia kritika pervoi chetverti XIX veka* (Moscow-Leningrad, 1959), pp. 77–97.

Anthony at his Mikhailovskoe estate), Nodier's Jean Sbogar, Mme. de Staël's plot summaries, comic operas, chapbooks, the playful rituals of the Arzamas Society, Khemnitser's fables, Zhukovsky's ballad "Svetlana," and Griboedov's verse comedy *Woe from Wit*.[18] Dazzling as these displays of erudition are, it may be more critically fruitful to disregard for a moment the creative reality of the author-narrator and look to his created world and the cultural influences that weigh on Tatiana herself—her foreign epistolary novels and her nurse's horror stories and songs. The narrator himself encourages us to do this throughout the dream (5:11–21) by refraining from his usual comments on literature as a creative process, and by merging his voice as closely as the intricate *Onegin* stanza permits with the voice of Tatiana's subconscious mind.

In this chaotic dream world Tatiana blends the images and patterns of her sentimental readings, her folk heritage, and her social situation as Pushkin has established them earlier in the novel. For example, Tatiana's dream features a folkloric bear, but her mind's eye views that bear through the mediation of her gentry background and dresses it as a "shaggy footman" hierarchy is thus established, and the dread object is momentarily transformed by a mollifying periphrastic construction, typical of the sentimentalist manner. The dream itself—as a repository for fears, forbidden desires, punishment fantasies, and premonitions—was an integral part both of the epistolary novel and of some Russian wedding songs. Tatiana's dream, with its dangerous journey to a terrifying house, echoes the plot of the ritual laments a Russian bride delivers as part of her preparation for the wedding ceremony.[19] But when Tatiana's imagination places Eugene in that folkloric house, it does so with help from her epistolary novels.

The narrator has already described the process by which the literary patterns have overwhelmed her:

> With what unwonted fascination
> She now devours *romans d'amour*,
> With what a rapturous elation
> Yields to their treacherous allure!
> Creative fancy's vivid creatures
> Lend their imaginary features—
> He who adored Julie Wolmar,
> Malek-Adhel and de Linar,
> Young Werther, by his passion rended,
> and Grandison, the demigod
> Who causes you and me to nod—

> Our tender dreamer saw them blended
> Into a single essence warm,
> Embodied in Onegin's form.
>
> Her fancy-fed imagination
> Casts her in turn as heroine
> Of every favorite creation,
> Julie, Clarissa, or Delphine.
>
> (3:9–10)

Indeed, her reading of Rousseau's *Julie* has dictated her letter to Eugene. But readers who share the fashionable contempt for epistolary novels that Pushkin records in the famous line "Moral' na nas navodit son" ("Moralizing puts us to sleep," 3:11) will miss the pun on *son*, which can mean "dream" as well as "sleep."[20] The didactic patterns of the epistolary novel not only offer sleep to insomniacs, but can also inspire dreams and nightmares, and this is what happens to Tatiana two chapters later. In its images of violence, strife, and degradation, Tatiana's dream bears a remarkable similarity to one of Clarissa's:

Methought my brother, my Uncle Antony, and Mr. Solmes had formed a plot to destroy Mr. Lovelace; who discovering it, and believing I had a hand in it, turned all his rage against me. I thought he made them all fly into foreign parts upon it; and afterwards seizing upon me, carried me into a churchyard; there, notwithstanding all my prayers and tears, and protestations of innocence, stabbed me to the heart, and then tumbled me into a deep grave ready dug, among two or three half-dissolved carcasses; throwing in the dirt and earth upon me with his hands, and trampling it down with his feet. I awoke in a cold sweat, trembling, and in agonies; and still the frightful images raised by it remain in my memory.[21]

And it is not surprising that at this moment Tatiana's dream of imagination finds less in common with a peasant bride than with a young woman who, like herself, seeks refuge from an unhappy family situation by placing herself at the mercy of a potential seducer, a man she regards with a mixture of emotions, including fear and curiosity (5:18). Each heroine, preparing to violate taboos, is warned by her subconscious, which blends images of death and vileness with the desires that her waking mind does not so boldly admit.

But just as the folk pattern that guides the first part of the dream fades into the background, so does Clarissa's terrifying precedent fade, affecting and didactically effective as it may be. For Tatiana's position does not precisely coincide with Clarissa's. Clarissa is caught between Lovelace, the dangerous outsider, and Solmes, the repulsive "monster" whom her family has chosen for her.[22] Tatiana's family, however, has welcomed Onegin as a suitor. Thus Tatiana breaks with custom not in choosing the wrong object for her infatuation and defying her parents, but in choosing an unconventional way of approaching him. Another important difference is that Clarissa's feelings toward Lovelace are hopelessly complex, but Tatiana is unashamedly in love with Eugene. And so it is appropriate that the final developments of Tatiana's dream transform the patterns of Clarissa's. Onegin takes Tatiana away from the monsters, he is not one of them. His murderous wrath, as if fulfilling her unvoiced wish, turns not toward Tatiana but toward those who interrupt her tender scenes with him, the very people whose company Tatiana shuns in her waking life. As Eugene lays Tatiana down on his bench, her dream vision remakes him in the mold of the passionate Werther, who has dreamed of Charlotte in a similarly erotic position:

In vain do I reach out my arms toward her in the morning, when I awake from troubled dreams; vainly do I seek her at night in my bed, when a happy, innocent dream has deceived me, as if I had been sitting beside her in the meadow and had held her hand and had covered it with a thousand kisses. Ah! Then when I grope about for her in the half delirium of sleep and awaken, a flood of tears breaks from my oppressed heart, and I weep disconsolately over my gloomy future.[23]

But this moment in the dream cannot last, sustained as it must be by the murder and illicit desire that Tatiana's imagination borrows from Clarissa's dream. As Eugene murders Lensky the folkloric house in the forest reels and disappears, together with its novelistic hero and the representatives of Tatiana's depressing family and neighbors. The English epistolary novel (2:29), the book for interpreting dreams (5:23), and the mirror for folkloric fortune-telling (5:10) that crowd Tatiana's bed give no ready answer to her fears and desires. They are, rather, emblematic of the cultural elements from which, as she matures, she will assemble and make sense of her life.

In this Tatiana is not unique among the novel's cast of characters. Eugene too must structure his life with a mixture of literary, folkloric, and social materials, and we see at the end of the novel, when his dream imagination boils a brew similar to Tatiana's:

> To what end? While letters tumbled
> Across his sight beyond control,
> Desires, dreams, regrets were jumbled
> In dense profusion in his soul.
> Between the lines of printing hidden,
> To his mind's eye there rise unbidden
> Quite other lines, and it is these

That in his trance alone he sees.
They were dear tales and drole convictions
Alive among us as of old,
Weird, disconnected dreams untold,
And threats and axioms and predictions,
A spun-out fable's whimsy purl,
Or letters from a fresh young girl.

And while a drowsy stupor muffles
All thought and feeling unawares,
Imagination deals and shuffles
Its rapid motley solitaires.
He sees on melting snow-sheet dozing
A lad, quite still, as if reposing
Asleep upon a hostel bed,
And someone says: "That's that—he's dead . . ."
He see old enemies forgotten,
Detractors two-faced and afraid,
A swarm of beauties who betrayed,
A circle of companions rotten,
A rustic house—and who would be
Framed in the window? . . . Who but She!
                              (8:36–37)

The printed page, a girl's letter, folklore, love, friendship—balanced by guilt, unfulfilled desire, foreboding, obsession, violence, deception, and socially sanctioned murder. This is the stuff of culture in *Eugene Onegin*. Pushkin allows his characters no lasting refuge from it in the favorite retreats of the romantic imagination: nature, dream, and primitive society. Creativity, beauty, intelligence, truth, and emotional authenticity—all that is valued in this novel—must be won within the broadly defined limits of culture.

III. *Creative Conventionality*

One can be capable and moral
With manicure upon one's mind:
Why vainly chide one's age and quarrel?
Custom is lord of all mankind.
              —*Eugene Onegin*, 1:25*

In cataloguing the multifarious elements of culture in Pushkin's novel, we have been treating the individual's relationship to that culture as a passive one. But this is largely because we have been viewing the characters in their least controlled moments—in love, in

---

* Arndt's "capable and moral" renders the Russian *del'nyi*, which might more precisely be translated "serious," "effective," or simply "capable." V. V. Vinogradov, ed., *Slovar' iazyka Pushkina*, 4 vols. (Moscow, 1956–61). Pushkin is, as he tells us in a footnote, taking aim at Rousseau's *Confessions*.

delirium, in dreams—when elements of their national past, social situation, and cosmopolitan literary experience that they have ignored in their conscious lives assert themselves. The cultural framework Pushkin's novel constructs is the tool of a determinism, to be sure, but a very special one. By establishing its limits and suggesting determinisms that Pushkin does not engage, we will at the same time realize the possibilities for autonomy within the novel.

The deterministic power of Pushkin's world of culture is perhaps best discussed by reexamining *Eugene Onegin* as a historical novel, a genre Pushkin himself perfected in prose in the elegant symmetries of *The Captain's Daughter* (1836).* In *Eugene Onegin* the shaping force of history manifests itself in the characters' lives not in the guise of a rapacious Cossack horde, seeking vengeance for generations of social, economic, and cultural oppression, but as change in cultural possibilities and, most importantly, as "fashion." Fashion raises Eugene (1:23), seems to exhaust his lexicon (7:24), builds Tatiana's Petersburg home (8:46), and curls her hair, literally and figuratively (7:46). Lensky professes to hate the fashionable world, yet his poetry is nothing more than fashionable, with all the negative connotations of superficiaility and automation that the word bears. The narrator himself, the most conscious character in the novel, flees the fashionable world into, momentarily, Eugene's fashionable Byronism. Yet for all its ability to pervade the corners of human life, the "whirlwind of fashion" (4:21) does lack the finality of a Cossack noose or the long-accumulating pressure of social and economic oppression. Tatiana can ignore fashion and later dictate it. The narrator can boldly reject it or, better still, lend it a profundity it lacks in common currency: the word "ideal," which is merely fashionable in Lensky's verse (6:23), becomes infused with significance in the nar-

---

* Pushkin toyed with the idea of making *Onegin* a historical novel in the usual sense by inserting his hero in the Decembrist uprising, but he never realized it, except in the fantasies of certain Soviet critics. The speculation about how Pushkin might have "finished" the novel has reached such extremes among Pushkinisty that one of them, B. S. Meilakh, has finally objected to contrived reconstructions of the text; "Evgenii Onegin," in B. P. Gorodetskii et al., eds., *Pushkin: itogi i problemy izucheniia* (Moscow-Leningrad, 1966), p. 436. A more plausible approach to the historicity of the novel has been suggested by two Soviet scholars who develop the idea that although the characters of the novel are seen only until 1825, the author-narrator continued writing after the Decembrist uprising: G. P. Makogonenko, *"Evgenii Onegin": A. S. Pushkina*, 2d ed. (Moscow, 1971), p. 131; I. M. Semenko, "O roli obraza 'avtora' v. 'Evgenii Onegine,'" *Trudy leningradskogo bibliotechnogo instituta imeni N. K. Krupskoi*, II (1957), 139. Semenko finds that the chapters written after the uprising project a less ironic, more tragic authorial image.

rator's farewells (8:50–51). It is not surprising, because of his power over fashion, that the narrator inevitably colors the word with a certain contempt.

Pushkin treats the concept of historical distance—antiquity, olden times (*starina*)—with similar freedom. If "fashion" can be overcome, so can the "olden times" of literature and social custom be preserved. Indeed the noun and the adjective derived from it are inevitably used for the past that survives—in folklore (3:17), social customs (3:35), architecture (2:2), Eugene's subconscious mind (8: 36), and the poet's conversations with his muse (8.1). What fashion abandons, the imagination can recover for its own purposes. Richardson's novels were once so popular that Tatiana's mother did not have to read them to feel their influence; now Tatiana must pore over them, but they still retain their power to impose their patterns on behavior.* And disparate historical periods impinge not only on the creative mind; the narrator insists that Eugene's boredom overwhelms him amid both fashionable and ancient halls (2:2).

The ability of the novel's characters to assimilate the cultural achievements of historically distinct situations stands in marked contrast to the limitations of the characters in Pushkin's conventionally historical works. These pieces, unlike *Eugene Onegin*, are based on unresolvable clashes: Counter-Reformation Poland vs. medieval, Orthodox Muscovy (*Boris Godunov*); the westward-looking supporters of Peter the Great vs. the old nobility (*The Moor of Peter the Great*); the Westernized gentry vs. the Cossacks, with their folk culture that the gentry cannot comprehend (*The Captain's Daughter*).

There is one sense, however, in which *Eugene Onegin* shares in the generic features of historical fiction: in Pushkin's use of historical figures (himself and, in brief appearances, two friends). In dealing with a historical figure, the author bears a special responsibility to public knowledge in addition to his responsibility to expectations involving genre, decorum, verisimilitude, and other aspects of his literary performance: he must coordinate his depiction with the

---

* Stanley Mitchell calls our attention to the line of demarcation the French Revolution drew between the ages of sensibility and romanticism in Western Europe; "Tatiana's Reading," *Forum for Modern Language Studies*, 6 (1968): 2–3. But Pushkin himself, in recording this change in literary styles (3:11–12), presents it as a matter of changing taste and attaches no profound historical significance to it. By the end of the novel Eugene will be reading Rousseau (8:35), and Tatiana will have come to grips with Eugene's novels about "contemporary man" (7:22). It is interesting in this regard to note that Pushkin at times uses Richardson's Lovelace as a recurring type, not a mere museum piece of literary history that has lost its "relevance" (XIII, 71; XIV, 33, 49).

reader's "factual" knowledge of that figure's historical existence.[24] To give a rather obvious example of this sort of responsibility, in *The Captain's Daughter* Pushkin could make Pugachev an eloquent folk poet and could let him shape the destinies of the fictional characters, but it is doubtful that he would have wanted or dared to let his fictional Pugachev succeed in overthrowing the Empress.

And so Pushkin, as the primary historical figure in his own novel, establishes himself with biographical details familiar to his readers. Few of these involve the historical, political, and economic causality of realistic fiction. The poet hints at his exile (1:2) and, it is generally thought, at the fate of his exiled and executed Decembrist friends (8:51). The position of these biographical elements in the second and final stanzas of the novel gives them special emphasis, but they are balanced, even at these points, by the poet's sense of himself as a maker—of the effervescent *Ruslan and Liudmila* (1:2) and of the "free novel" *Eugene Onegin* (8:50). Between these bookends the author-narrator (the persona of a living, contemporary poet) can exercise considerable freedom in making his life, and at the same time meet his historical responsibility, for the importance of that life to his audience resides precisely in its creativity, which history has not yet ended. Indeed, Pushkin uses his historicity to delimit for his characters a period in which sweeping events, such as the Napoleonic wars or the Decembrist uprising, do not intervene to prevent him from treating society in terms of conventions, rituals, and festivals. And the class from which Pushkin takes his main characters, the gentry, is precisely the one which had the greatest access to the generous resources of Russian culture, with its folk and European heritage. This class situation, like the historical period, is more an invitation to relatively autonomous action than a deterministic barrier. Georg Lukács has very aptly conceded in this regard that "Pushkin knew it was no longer possible . . . to characterize a figure or integrate him into the plot simply by stating his position in society or his class."[25]

Although the narrator presents himself as even less oppressed by the regime of Alexander I than by literary fashions, he seldom forgets that writing is a social act—reviewed by critics, interrogated by the censor, and presented to an audience with its social patterns and its expectations about the decorum that should accompany life into literary form. The urbane, cosmopolitan audience Pushkin envisions for his work (e.g. 1:2, 3:22) causes him little anxiety, and he treats it with the familiarity of a correspondent. But its presence provides, together with conventional codes, a necessary component of any social act, and Pushkin incorporates it into both the creative (author's) and created (characters') realities of his novel. The characters, like the poet, must reckon with their audience and reach that audience through, and only through, the conventions of their culture. As determining factors these conventions are considerably more elusive than the historical, political, and economic constraints of literary realism or the laws of the organism in which literary naturalism sought to enclose human existence. But in the few social situations depicted by Pushkin's novel (the duel, the love quests of Tatiana and Eugene), conventions provide such tension, such problems of timing and understanding, that we may with little hesitation speak of *Eugene Onegin* as a social novel.

Conventions assume many guises in *Eugene Onegin*: norms and rules; fashions, which bear arbitrary temporal limits of applicability; and customs, which have greater permanence. Basically conventions are repeated actions that enable members of a culture, by a process of decoding and anticipation (with or without having to think about it), to define situations, to predict the results of their actions, and to understand the actions of others. Conventions allow Eugene, with his fashionable haircut, perfect French, and unforced manner—scant information indeed—to be accepted by high society as "intelligent and very nice" (1:4). When, however, he refuses to meet with his rural neighbors, use the particles of their polite speech, and kiss their wives' hands, his behavior corresponds to none of their conventions, and in their anxiety they imagine him an ignoramus, a madman, or a "Farmazon" (an illiterate rendering of Freemason, 2:5), since only these types would so ignore the conventions that hold society together. Then, merely by appearing at the home of an unmarried girl, he reintegrates himself into their conventional expectations and can be assigned, inaccurately it turns out, the role of a suitor. Meanwhile Tatiana, who also ignores social conventions but who is overcome by literary ones, views this silent newcomer as the honorable, sentimental hero of her novels and acts on this assumption.

Pushkin's novel presents no simple attitude toward conventions because there are so many ways of observing and not observing them, and because different ones (literary and social, for example) may have relevance to the same situation. One may observe conventions in a blindly childish fashion (Lensky, Tatiana initially), with tired resignation (the narrator giving us an expected rhyme), or with creative energy. Indeed, many of the most elegant passages in the novel, those expressing the poet's longing for Venice (1:48–49) and his love of pastoral pleasures (1:55), for example, echo familiar traditions of Western literature.[26] Disrespect for conventions in *Eugene Onegin* covers a similarly broad range of possibilities, from the creative mixing of genres (a novel in verse) to the socially acceptable eccentricity of Eugene (a talented dandy) to insultingly casual disregard (Eugene's use of his valet as his second in the duel) to potentially dangerous violation (Tatiana's letter to Eugene).

Clearly these attitudes toward conventionality can be translated into understanding or action with varying degrees of success, depending on the knowledge and intelligence of the characters who use them. "The first sign of an intelligent man," Pushkin wrote in a letter, "is to know at first glance with whom he is dealing" (XIII, 138)—and, this novel suggests, in terms of which cultural code, fashionable or traditional, literary or social. Lest this seem trivial or easy, Pushkin shows the process by which society tries to define the Eugene who returns to Petersburg after a long absence. What is the significance of Eugene's mysterious silence (8:7–8)? Which "mask" is he sporting? Is it literary (Melmoth, Childe Harold, Byron's spleen and arrogance), or social (a bigot, an eccentric, a good fellow), or one drawn from the wardrobe of sectarian fashion (a cosmopolitan, a patriot, a Quaker)? The narrator's "Do you know him?—Yes and no" provides little help. The next stanza (8:9), in which we might expect some elucidation of that remark, instead distances Eugene further by introducing romantic traits that may be even less applicable to him—a "fiery soul" and a "mind which loves room." The narrator's subsequent accusation of mistaken judgment simultaneously addresses the reader and the people at the social assembly. Yet the narrator himself, behind his blustering rhetoric, comes no closer to an understanding. Indeed, the roles of the narrator, the created characters, and Pushkin's imagined reader merge as they measure Eugene with their culture's many conventional definitions. For here, as elsewhere in *Eugene Onegin*, Pushkin conveys an illusion of a person's reality not directly, with Tolstoyan analysis, but indirectly, by emphasizing the elusiveness of character and our conflicting, inadequate methods of defining it.

Perhaps the conventions most persistently examined by Pushkin's novel are those that relate the literary and social facets of culture. And here we encounter one of the central aesthetic problems of Pushkin's time—of any time—the nature and responsibility of literature. Should the language of literature be *referential*, the representation of reality according to some standard of verisimilitude? Or *emotive*, the expression of the poet's attitudes toward his work? Or *conative*, supplicating and exhorting the reader, issuing moral imperatives?[27] Among Pushkin's contemporaries one finds reproaches on all of these grounds: *Eugene Onegin* has represented reality in an improper or insufficient manner; *Eugene Onegin* has too much borrowed material, the tone is Byron's not Pushkin's; *Eugene Onegin* lacks moral seriousness. Or, finally, can literature be language in its aesthetic function, language that calls attention to itself as an aesthetic object divorced from instrumental functions? Perhaps the tersest expression of this formalistic attitude in Western literature was issued by Pushkin himself in a polemical note to Zhukovsky: "The goal of poetry is poetry" (April 1825; XIII, 167).

These four conventional attitudes toward the relationship of literature and reality were of course represented in various admixtures in the literary movements of Pushkin's time, and by embodying them in his characters he was able to play not only with the literary devices of these movements, but with their critical orientations as well. His own comment to Zhukovsky is no less an object of the novel's irony than the other attitudes. The only unalloyed formal view of literature is provided by Tatiana's father, who neither knows nor cares anything about it:

> Her honest father, though old-fashioned,
> Last century's child, grew not impassioned
> About the harm that books might breed;
> He, who was never known to read,
> Regarded them as empty thrillers
> And never thought to bring to light
> Which secret volume dreamt at night
> Beneath his little daughter's pillows.
> (2:29)*

Meanwhile, his daughter is about to mistake the didactic imperatives of her moralizing novels by offering herself—in epistolary form, naturally—to Eugene, whom she mistakes for the virtuous heroes of Richardson and Rousseau:

> With rapturous delight she savored
> Rousseau's and Richardson's deceits.
> (2:29)

* In the original Russian the "thrillers" are even more condescendingly titled —"toy" (*igrushka*).

The irony of this is that the imperatives a reader extracts from a work need not be the ones the author intended to project—a particularly apt point in connection with these two authors, whose imagination lent more fascination to vice than to their rather dreary pictures of virtue. Pushkin emphasizes this by making the didactic epistolary novels more seductive than the lurid Gothic thrillers that replaced them on fashion's reading table.

The plot of the novel follows Tatiana's maturation in terms of her use of literature. Here, at the first stage in her development, she unconsciously takes literature to be the direct representation of reality, a direct command to act, and the direct expression of her self. Childishly, inappropriately, she locates its stereotypes in her life, acting and speaking through them. In her dreams, as we have discussed, the darker side of the epistolary novel manifests itself as a nightmare. Tatiana's total immersion in her culture makes the world a forest of symbols to her:

> And any object could impress her
> With some occult significance.
> (5:5)[28]

But, unconscious of herself as a cultural being and trapped with a limited number of conventions, she lacks the key to decode these symbols.

Gradually, however, she learns to distinguish a variety of conventional relationships between literature and reality. The patterns of her reading might suggest ways of understanding the world and even controlling it. The narrator now speculates that had she known of Eugene's impending duel with Lensky, she would have stopped it (5:18). Why? It was a convention of the epistolary novel (*Clarissa, Sir Charles Grandison, Julie*) for the heroine to oppose dueling. In this case the moral imperative of the epistolary novel would not have been a "deceit" (3:9, 29) but a sure guide to action.

The culmination of this development comes when Tatiana visits Eugene's study and reads not only his books, but his reading of them, as indicated by pages bearing the impressions of his fingernails and by words, crosses, and question marks penciled in the margins. She finds her own attitudes toward literature (a guide to action, a representation of reality, an expression of the self) in Eugene, and is supported in this by comparing his reading with his behavior toward her. The questions passing through her mind are suggested by his

reading of Byron and the two or three novels he has exempted from
his general disinterest in literature,* novels that depict "rather accurately the age and contemporary man":

> And step by step my Tanya, learning
> His mind, at least begins to see
> The man for whom she has been yearning
> By willful destiny's decree
> More clearly than in face and feature:
> A strangely bleak and restless creature,
> Issue of Heaven or Hell,
> Proud demon, angel—who can tell?
> Perhaps he is all imitation,
> An idle phantom or, poor joke,
> A Muscovite in Harold's cloak,
> An alien whim's interpretation,
> Compound of every faddish pose . . . ?
> A parody, perhaps . . . who knows?
>
> (7:24)

Here Tatiana understands from observing Eugene that life can be a
reflection of literary stereotypes, something she could not understand
when she was unconsciously following them herself. Her new approach to the relationship of literature and life is a mature one, for
she is now aware that such imitation is not a matter of mere reproduction, but can be distorted by parody or inappropriate in its context ("poor joke, a Muscovite in Harold's cloak").

The final step in Tatiana's cultural maturation occurs when she
becomes the hostess of a Petersburg salon and, as a "legislatrix"
(8:28) and "goddess" (8:27), imposes what her age considered an
aesthetic order on reality.[29] This role, it should be remembered, was
the highest form of creativity open to a woman at this time; it gave

---

*The only one of the "two or three novels" that Pushkin identified was
Constant's Adolphe. He did this in an anonymous announcement of Viazemsky's
translation of the novel, an announcement that cited the last eight lines of
Chapter 7, stanza 22, of Onegin (IX, 87). Shortly after this announcement was
published in January 1830, the first separate edition of Chapter 7 of Onegin
appeared; between that time and the publication of Chapter 8 (January 1832),
Russian readers were presented with two translations of Adolphe (by Viazemsky
and N. Polevoi) and numerous reviews of them. Given this situation, it was
hardly necessary for Pushkin to name the title of Constant's novel, as he had
done in his drafts. Pushkin regarded Adolphe as one of the ancestors of Byron's
Childe Harold. Harold replaced Adolphe in Pushkin's drafts, but not as a model
for Eugene's speech and behavior toward Tatiana, as I shall discuss below.
Readers would be all the more likely to catch Pushkin's use of Adolphe in
Onegin because Viazemsky dedicated his translation, which Pushkin had helped
edit, to Pushkin and called Adolphe "our favorite novel."

her the chance to unite, if not "magic sounds, feelings, thoughts" (as
Pushkin defines his poetic aspirations, 1:59), then thoughts, feelings,
and good conversation:

> The party talk is soon enlivened
> By the crude salt of worldly spite;
> But, with this hostess, it is light,
> Gay nonsense, free of priggish preening,
> Or, grave at times, is never brought
> To fatuous themes or hallowed thought,
> But brims with undidactic meaning;
> And its high spirits and good sense
> Are powerless to give offense.
>
> (8:23)

Lest we underestimate this achievement, almost equal in its emotional range to the novel as a whole, the narrator catalogues the
materials from which Tatiana has crafted her harmonious assembly:
fools, malicious-looking ladies, a faintly ludicrous old wit, a nasty
epigrammatist, a caricatured social climber, and overstarched traveler (8:24–26). She has taken the less than inspiring materials of her
social situation and shaped them in brilliant fashion into one of the
conventional forms of her culture. It is a creation at once aesthetically pleasing and, in its civility, morally effective. The author-narrator
underscores the parallels between her creation and his by applying
similar epithets to them—"unforced" and "free." And just as Pushkin
realizes his freedom to play with literary conventions within one of
the most intricate stanza forms in Russian poetry, Tatiana achieves
her greatest level of creativity within the sphere of high society, with
all of its norms, patterns, and potentially corrupting fashions.*

The versatility with which both Pushkin and his "ideal," Tatiana,
are able to select, discard, and order the materials of their culture
also draws them together. Tatiana of course cannot command the
narrator's entire range of emotional shadings, especially irony, and
her freedom is ultimately more a freedom of awareness than a freedom of action; but she, like her creator, can both participate in her
creation and distance herself from it, calling attention to its artificial-

---

* It is instructive to study the drafts of these stanzas, which show two other
approaches to the salon; the first is more laudatory, the second more satiric,
than the final version, which places greater emphasis on Tatiana's role. The
excellence of Tatiana's salon now depends more on her talent than on the inherent qualities of this conventional social-literary form. For a meticulous texto-
logical examination of these drafts, see N. Ia. Solovei, "Evoliutsiia temy bol'-
shogo sveta v VIII glave 'Evgeniia Onegina' (k voprosu o printsipakh publikatsii
rukopisnykh materialov)," in *Pushkinskii sbornik* (Pskov, 1968), pp. 29–39.

ity. She dismisses the social success she has fabricated as readily as
Pushkin takes leave of his novel in the final stanzas. At first it seems
that she has firmly entered her social role and has adopted the constricting ways of her rank (8:28), yet her awareness of conventions,
her other interests, her other human capabilities (such as love, memory) give her the perspective necessary for wholeness, freedom, and
creativity:

> "To me, Onegin, this vain clamor,
> This tinsel realm appears inane,
> My triumphs here, the modish glamour
> In which I dwell and entertain,
> All void . . . I would be happy trading
> All this pretentious masquerading,
> This whirl of vapor, noise, and glaze,
> For my few books, my garden maze,
> For our country dwelling lowly,
> For those dear places that I knew
> When first, Onegin, I met you,
> And now, for that enclosure holy
> Where cross and swaying branches grace
> Poor Nanny's final resting place."
>
> (8:46)

In these and in the lines where she dismisses Eugene, all of Tatiana's cultural heritage and all of the ways in which she relates to
that heritage merge. The books in which she sought to live join with
the artifacts of pastoral retreat (garden, humble dwelling); her memories unite the graveyard of a sentimentalist poem with the nurse
who taught her folklore. But literature is more than a consoling, en-
tertaining object to her; it becomes the expression of her soul and
values. Meanwhile, in Eugene's letter and behavior, to which we
shall presently turn, she has read the destructive, confused desires of
an Adolphe or a Lovelace. Having used literature to know Eugene,
she turns to it again as a moral imperative:

> I love you still (yes—why deceive you?).
> But I was pledged another's wife,
> And will be faithful all my life.
>
> (8:47)

These lines, it has been established, are adapted from a song found
among the folk, thought in Pushkin's time to have been written by
Peter I, and translated into French by Pushkin's uncle ("littérateur
russe très-distingué," as the *Mercure de France* charitably put it).
Tatiana could have read the song in M. D. Chulkov's collection of

various songs, in A. S. Shishkov's collected works (1824), or in an old issue of the *Mercure de France* (1803), or else she could have heard it from her nurse.[30] It is at once representative of the wealth and syncretic nature of Russian culture and of Tatiana's ability to draw on that culture to create and understand her life.*

Tatiana in her movement toward mastering the conventions of her culture finds no equal in Eugene or Lensky, both of whom also try to impose aesthetic patterns on social reality. Lensky begins where Tatiana begins—naively viewing literary stereotypes as the equivalent of reality (2:6–10)—and he ends there. Tatiana at least has the sense to fantasize according to the conventions of a genre, the novel, that claims the everyday as its field of representation; Lensky ineptly tries to stage various romantic *tableaux vivants* in the Russian countryside: the medieval knight playing chess with his beloved (4:26), the poet fleeing the fashionable world (3:2), the German student filled with rebellious dreams (2:6), the poet surrounded by sworn friends (2:8), the poet's beloved visiting his premature grave. But the created reality of *Eugene Onegin* will not respond to inept authorship, and everything Lensky's imagination touches becomes the stuff of parody: his friend prefers the viciousness of society to the delights of friendship and kills him in a fashionable duel; his beloved, despite the moralizing novels he has bowdlerized for her (4:26), marries the first officer to come along; a shepherd unlike any in his elegaic verse plaits a bast shoe by the poet's grave, which is soon forgotten by his beloved anyway. In all of this there is no convention—of social behavior, of literature, or of the social appropriation of literature—that Lensky uses or can use with any wit or intelligence.

Between Tatiana, whose creative use of conventions comes closest to the author's, and Lensky, whom the author-narrator will not allow to escape from the literary technique of parody, stands Onegin, whose potentially multifaceted, yet ultimately elusive presence lends him as much reality as is possible within the novel. The problems which the Pushkinian character faces in creating his life—timing, the pressure of fashion, conflicting conventions—weigh most heavily on Eugene because unlike Lensky he has sufficient intelligence and maturity to face them, yet unlike Tatiana he lacks the ability to solve them creatively.

---

*This suggests that the strength of Pushkin's heroine does not flow merely from her roots in the folk culture, as Lukács, *Writer and Critic and Other Essays* (New York, 1971), p. 251, and various Soviet critics have suggested, but from her understanding of her culture as a whole and from the intersection of its literary and social patterns, its popular and European heritage.

Eugene begins, like the others, by shaping his life according to a literary pattern, that of the dandy—cold, scornful, amorally destructive (as the novel's master epigraph suggests).[31] Although his education has prepared him for this role, he plays it with a pedantic perfection that is his own, eating the right foods, wearing the right clothes, being seen in the right places. His life is, on the social plane, analogous to a work of art understood as an end in itself, an object of aesthetic contemplation. The dandy glorifies form and, in Baudelaire's famous definition, dictates it. In this he is the male counterpart of the hostess of a salon, the role Tatiana assumes in the final chapter. But whereas Tatiana's creation, the salon, issues a moral imperative (civility) to those who join it, Eugene's creation, himself, unites the members of high society into adulterous triangles, held together by Ovid's science of love, an aristocratic fear of ridicule, and Eugene's mastery of at least thirty conventional disguises (1:10–12).*

The addition of outfits cut from literary patterns to Eugene's wardrobe (Byronic spleen, boredom) rescues him from his social activities only to enclose him within a narrower circle: himself. Unlike Byron and the author-narrator, he cannot find alternatives to social boredom in writing or nature (1:43, 56). And he becomes the "contemporary man" of the few novels that he reads:

> Where shown upon the current stage,
> Man moves with truth and animation:
> Unprincipled, perversely bent
> Upon himself, his powers spent
> In reverie and speculation,
> With his exacerbated mind
> In idle seething self-confined.
>
> (7:22)

Eugene's Byronic version of dandyism, which makes his life an aesthetic object, finds no audience in the countryside prepared to appreciate it or even accept it, except for Tatiana and Lensky, who try to fit Eugene into their own aesthetic patterns. They in turn chal-

---

* Among the tools of Eugene's artistry: hypocrisy, the concealment of hope, jealousy, a gloomy appearance, dejection, pride, obedience, attentiveness, indifference, silence, fiery eloquence, casualness, self-obliviousness, a quick and tender gaze, shyness, daring tearfulness, novelty, joking, frightening, the mind, the heart, imploring, demanding, lessons in discretion, the pursuit of love, disturbing, maligning. Underscoring the range of Eugene's talents is the far more modest list of the poet's resources in the dedicatory piece.

lenge Eugene with the two tests to which nearly all nineteenth-century Russian fiction after Pushkin was to subject its protagonists: love and the duel. Tatiana, as silly as she may have been to declare her love for somebody she had seen only once, touched Eugene to the quick. She fit none of his conventional categories, just as he was a mystery to her. So, as she had done in similar circumstances, he tries to understand her and predict their relationship through his reading. He answers her "artless" love, expressed in the words of Rousseau's Julie, with an "artless" reply, drawn (as we learn in Chapter 7) from one of the few novels he has read, *Adolphe*. The prayers and charity for the afflicted in Tatiana's letter, scenes she drew from Rousseau's novel, could have reminded him of similar activities by Constant's heroine, Ellenore. Identifying himself with Constant's bored, restless, vain hero, Eugene envisions their relationship in terms of that novel—boredom, torment, tears, rage (4:14)—and he coldly cuts it off before it can go further. This is the best understanding and the most moral action Eugene can summon from his limited literary and social existence.

The duel with Lensky presents problems of a different sort, but Eugene is still unable to deal with the conventions of his culture, and he remains "convention's playball," as the narrator aptly puts it (6:10). Upset because Lensky brings him to a large gathering of people whom spleen has led him to avoid, Eugene punishes Lensky by carrying out a conventional flirtation with his fiancée. Lensky has no choice but to call Eugene out, as Nabokov has observed.[32] Eugene has previously discussed "good and evil" with Lensky (2:16), and he knows that he is wrong to accept the challenge (6:10). But he lacks the independence to place conventional friendship, one of the most salient values of his time,* above the more compelling conventions and to seek a reconciliation. His aesthetic constructions, the amoral dandy and the Byronic rebel, turn out to have a conative, audience-directed function: the dandy implores admiration, the rebel outrage. Eugene in either costume would evoke mere mockery by refusing the duel—"whispers, the laughter of fools . . ." (6:11)—as he is well aware. Still, even if fashion forbade a sentimental reconciliation, it offered two courses of action: shoot to kill or fire into the air (as Pushkin seems to have done in a duel with his friend Ryleev). Eu-

---

* Writing in 1822, Pushkin could offer no better example of his period's periphrastic prose style than "friendship, that sacred feeling, whose noble flame . . ." (XI, 18).

gene chooses to defy convention in a petty manner; he offends Lensky by bringing a valet as his second. At the same time he ignores the convention (firing in the air) that might have eased his conscience, spared his friend's life, and earned him society's admiration.*

The author-narrator contrasts Eugene's helplessness with his own creative use of conventions. Eugene knows only one way to finish Lensky, and it haunts him in the ensuing chapters; the poet knows two ways (6:37–39) to destroy Lensky as a literary character: a literary parody (the premature death of the poet) and a social travesty (the gouty, cuckolded landowner). Eugene's nonchalant rebellion—bringing a valet as his second—runs parallel to the author-narrator's evocation of the muse in the last stanza of Chapter 7. But whereas Eugene stands trapped by a convention (the duel), the narrator makes creative, meaningful use of conventions: he goes beyond the standard postponed evocation of mock-epic to begin Chapter 8 with an evocation of the muse that is at the same time his own stylized biography.

Eugene's development reverses Tatiana's. As she matures in her ability to relate literature and life in a variety of ways, he loses control over the materials of his culture. Nowhere is this more obvious than when the two characters again face each other at the novel's close. Eugene may have become a good fellow, as several commentators have suggested, and as such he may now be able to love and appreciate Tatiana.† In his delirium he does, in fact, see her as a country girl, not as a grand lady who would make a worthy specimen

* There remains the possibility that Eugene shot to kill in self-defense. After all, he might reasonably have assumed that Lensky, the aggrieved party, would be firing in earnest. This is a mitigating circumstance, but it does not entirely excuse Eugene's choice of the more deadly alternative; had he fired first and into the air, it is not at all certain that Lensky, by then reconciled with Olga, would have shot to kill. (Anyway Eugene's only obligation as a gentleman was to face his opponent's fire bravely, not to kill him.) Pushkin presents Eugene's actions during the duel as coldly, automatically correct, which implies that Eugene was following a convention, not worrying about his own life. Eugene certainly does not use self-defense as an excuse in his subsequent thoughts, letters, or dreams about the duel. One recalls that Tolstoy's Vronsky resolved to fire into the air if the aggrieved Karenin called him out.

† Stanley Mitchell, "Tatiana's Reading," Forum for Modern Language Studies, 6 (1968): 15; G. A. Gukovskii, Pushkin i problemy realisticheskogo stilia (Moscow, 1957), pp. 266–67. The source of this understanding of Onegin's transformation, Gukovsky tells us, is Belinsky, who adduces as evidence of Eugene's sincerity precisely the part of his letter to Tatiana that is plagiarized, consciously or unconsciously, from chap. 3 of Adolphe. Tatiana, better educated than Belinsky and better attuned to the ways in which literature shapes life, cannot share the pioneering social critic's unqualified idealization of Eugene.

for his amatory science (8:37). But Eugene must, in Pushkin's novel, express this through the codes of his culture, and he has only his experiences in "love" and a few novels, such as *Adolphe*, to help him. Tatiana's firm rejection of him is her only possible response, now that she has read *Adolphe* and can see that it dictates almost all of Eugene's actions—his barrage of letters, his desire to kneel at her feet, his difficulty in controlling himself yet unwillingness to dissemble, his vague threat of suicide.[33] No doubt these phrases are as old as love itself, but their similarity to what Tatiana had read in Eugene's book suggests further correspondences with *Adolphe* to her —that Eugene desires not love but satisfied vanity, the triumph of conquering and shaming the wealthy, noble mate of a distinguished man (8:44). Eugene's silence, which clearly parallels Tatiana's earlier response to his rejection of her and the narrator's inability to write while loving (1:58), suggests that he may indeed love her; but he fails to communicate it in the only possible way, through the appropriate conventions of his culture.

I shall turn, in conclusion, to the subtitle of this essay, "life's novel," which has been taken from the last stanza of *Eugene Onegin*.* I doubt that the quotation marks will have protected the metaphor from critical commentary. One can, after all, revise a novel, but not arrest or turn back the flow of time and biological maturation. One can correct a novel's galley proofs; life gives few such second

* Since presenting this paper to the conference, I have obtained two excellent new works that also comment on the metaphor "life's novel." From different angles of approach both S. G. Bocharov and Iu. M. Lotman see *Eugene Onegin* as a process of overcoming novelistic tradition. In Bocharov's subtle stylistic analysis this is, roughly speaking, a matter of translating literature into life and making *Eugene Onegin* reproduce the open-endedness of life; *Poetika Pushkina: ocherki* (Moscow, 1974), p. 103. Lotman, *Roman v stikhakh Pushkina "Evgenii Onegin"* (Tartu, 1975), boldly speculates that Pushkin's motive force in writing *Eugene Onegin* was to create a work that would be perceived as a nonliterary reality (p. 80), as life itself (p. 65). Lotman's argument works splendidly for what I have been calling the creative (the narrator's and the reader's) level of the novel, where he shows that Pushkin created the illusion of a lack of literary structure by multiplying structural connections. Instead of carrying this awareness into his description of the interaction between characters, however, Lotman draws what seems to be an un-Pushkinian distinction between literature and life when he says that by the end of the novel Tatiana and Eugene are "completely" freed from "the fetters of literary associations" and have entered a "genuine, that is, simple and tragic, world of real life" (p. 79). "Real life" in *Eugene Onegin* is tragic precisely because it is not simple, because it offers many conventional behavioral models and hence possibilities for tragically wrong decisions.

chances. And, most important, the novel as a genre shows us actions much more completely—their causes, consequences, and the thinking of their agents—than "real life" does.

The proper reply to these objections lies in the particular conception of social existence that structures *Eugene Onegin*. There life and the novel are somehow equivalent because Pushkin's characters make them so, bridging the space between the literary and social areas of culture with conventional definitions of literature: literature as representation of reality, as self-expression, as moral guide, and as entertainment or consolation.

While the characters are constructing their lives along literary lines, the author-narrator meets them halfway by deconstructing the complete picture of life the traditional novel purports to give. He never finishes the old-fashioned novel with its happy ending that he promised us in Chapter 3 (3:13–14) because he arbitrarily and unexpectedly marries his heroine off to someone we hardly know. Pushkin severs the coincidental ties that lace conventional fiction together: Tatiana, for all of her good intentions and her reading of epistolary novels, cannot stop the duel if nobody tells her that it is going to take place (6:18). Convention permits novelists to exercise considerable license in probing the minds and describing the authentic selves of their characters, but Pushkin's author-narrator chooses to offer conflicting evaluations of his hero, as he (like the other characters) tries to interpret Eugene's silence with the codes of their common culture.

Circumstances and the independence of others can impede even the most brilliant of creators in Pushkin's novel. The narrator dominates the novel because he creates and dismisses the other characters, and because he most successfully threads his way through the culture he shares with them, separating the wheat from the chaff of that culture and engaging more powerful human resources—intelligence, heart, delight, knowledge—than any one of his creatures. Yet Pushkin makes his narrator, in the roles of both character and author, party to the risks, failures, and limitations of life. As a character the narrator cannot travel with his hero (1:51) or write and love at the same time (1:58). As author he cannot integrate Onegin's journey into the novel or satisfy the critics whom he mentions in his footnotes (1:60).

Finally, life and the novel merge in *Eugene Onegin* because each is a process of creation that allows no recourse to the fantastic or improbable except in dreams and reported legends. Each is a process that uses conventions to organize the materials of everyday life. Because there are many areas within a culture and many conventions relating these areas to each other, the possibilities for creativity are often immeasurable, but so are the chances for entrapment, confusion, and failure of coordination. The richness of a culture's conventions at a given moment can inspire a novel as original and intricate as *Eugene Onegin*, or it can permit human disaster as surely as the crushing events and processes of history.

VICTOR RIPP

Turgenev as a Social Novelist:
The Problem of the Part and the Whole

I

In the early 1850's, shortly before the publication of the first collected edition of *Notes of a Huntsman*, Turgenev began to express dissatisfaction with his literary achievements. This was a recurrent phenomenon in his career, since he believed, notoriously, that life had set him tasks beyond his capacity as a writer, not to say as a human being. As many contemporaries perceived, Turgenev's modest pose was often only a form of self-dramatization; but in this case it had concrete consequences. Specifically, the dissatisfaction with his "old manner," as he called it, moved Turgenev to contemplate writing a novel. Indeed, one preliminary definition of a Turgenev novel is that it is something different from the works he wrote in the 1840's and early 1850's, qualitatively so rather than just in length. "A novel," he said in a letter from this period, "is not merely a long story [*povest'*] stretched out, as some people think."[1]

But what a novel actually is proved a more elusive idea. Turgenev's letters contain suggestive phrases—"something big, grand," with "clear, simple lines"—but there is nothing in them that can be called an explanation. His famous commentary on the state of the Russian novel at mid-century, given in the course of a review (1852) of Evgeniia Tur's *The Niece*, is similarly unsystematic despite its greater scope. It is clear enough from the review that Turgenev makes some connection between literary genre (rather than merely literary content) and historical circumstance, but beyond this basic point there is considerable ambiguity. Here is part of the review's central passage; Turgenev has just dismissed the historical novel as "anachronistic":

There remain two other types of novels, more similar to each other than they might appear at first glance, novels we will call by the names of their chief representatives: Sand and Dickens novels. These novels are possible in Russia and, it seems, will take hold; but at the moment it may be asked, have the elements of our social life manifested themselves to the degree where a four-volume novel seeking to depict them would be in demand? The recent success of various notes and sketches proves, it seems, the opposite. For the time being we hear in Russia separate sounds, to which literature responds with similarly brief echoes.[2]

This passage is often cited in Turgenev scholarship, invariably to note that Turgenev's reference to Dickens and Sand anticipated his own movement toward the writing of novels about contemporary society. This is doubtless true, but not without qualification. Merely to glance at Turgenev's novels, especially those up through *Fathers and Sons*, is to realize that only an oblique resemblance obtains between them and the works of the great European authors. Turgenev does indeed write about contemporary society, but if his topic is the same, his approach is not, and Dickens is an especially unlikely model in one crucial respect. Dickens's works are crowded with the paraphernalia of the legitimized social structure; the actions of judges and policemen and lawyers drive his plots along, and wills and testaments, neat symbols of the pervasive influence of established law, often serve as the instruments of his narrative climaxes. Turgenev's novels conspicuously lack these features. To the extent that political or economic factors are indicated at all, they are put at the periphery of the action, as insidious rather than overt influences —for example, the peasant unrest that simmers off-stage throughout *Fathers and Sons*. And the law governing events in a Turgenev novel is not that of the statute books, but rather the ethical codes and personal decisions of a small group of individuals gathered on their isolated estates.

Turgenev seems simply to have lacked the audacity that permitted Dickens (and Sand) to venture forth into the fullness of social reality, to confront the beast of social inequity in its lair; and this would make his reference to these writers seem like wishful thinking, the fatuous invocation of an ideal beyond his capacities. In fact, Turgenev's novelistic procedure has a purposefulness of its own, which becomes apparent when it is considered in the context of the particular conditions prevailing in mid-nineteenth-century Russia. What initially appears as a deplorable fastidiousness or a failure of nerve is actually an imaginative strategy. For the most pressing task that faced thinking Russians of this period was not to denounce the evil men did to one another, or even to unmask the corruption inherent in the overarching political system—two obvious hallmarks of contemporary European realism—but rather something logically prior to such acts.*

A brief comparison of the political landscapes of Russia and Western European nations begins to indicate the nature of Turgenev's problem. Russia had no striving middle class, no tradition of a landed aristocracy, no contentious commercial interests, no influential church or judiciary, even very few private associations that could propagate eccentric beliefs. In a word, the political landscape was not only inhospitable to new ideas, as is usually the case in an established society, but remarkably bare of any entity from which new ideas might begin to grow. Of course, European authors did not unswervingly endorse the aims of the various classes, interests, and groups present in the societies they depicted, but the mere existence of such entities broke up the homogeneity of the established order, suggesting a range of competing values to be scrutinized and shaped dramatically. In Russia, with its stunted civil society, a novelist intent on questioning the ways of the world had in effect to invent a coherent alternative to the status quo, which was persuasively promoted by a powerful central government. A few disparate and isolated voices, members of that loose grouping known as *obshchestvo*, did express dissent.† But this tended to turn into empty despair (or, in more elegant guise, ironic detachment), which is to be expected from men lacking the sustaining sense of a world with real choices.

* Contemporaries were aware of this state of affairs. Even the more radical thinkers, such as Dobroliubov, consistently criticized so-called "accusatory literature" (*oblichitel'naia literatura*). See, for example, N. A. Dobroliubov, "Blagonamerenost' i deyatel'nost'," in his *Sobranie sochinenii* (Moscow-Leningrad, 1961), VI, 190–210.

† *Obshchestvo* literally means "society," but to translate it would rob it of its contemporary meaning. Society as such belonged to the government. Obshchestvo was a loose grouping of individuals who sought to oppose the prevailing forms of society. Indeed, obshchestvo was composed of such disparate elements —from Slavophiles to Westerners, from liberals to radicals—that only its shared suspicion of the government held it together. For a good account of various outstanding members of obshchestvo, see Anthony Netting, "Russian Liberalism: Years of Promise" (Ph.D. diss., Columbia University, 1970).

The forging of a meaningful counterbalance to the government was peculiarly a task for the literary imagination, for the obstacles were psychological as well as institutional. Though members of ob-shchestvo regarded themselves as foes of the status quo, it is also true that many of them, including Turgenev himself from time to time, looked to the government as the best agent of reform. Indeed many progressives, again including Turgenev, either served in the government at some time or worked in positions the government sponsored, and did not in consequence feel they were compromising their principles. These facts may at first appear to temper the view of the government as an oppressive force, but in actuality they tend rather to confirm it, by stressing how fully the government blocked the development of any other area of political activity. Even the press, much vaunted in the period after the Crimean War as a ve-hicle of independent opinion, occasionally passed under government influence.[3] The government finally appeared as not only powerful but pervasive as well, to a degree that there often appeared to be no reality except the one it sanctioned. In this situation, whether the government did evil (as it preponderantly did) or good hardly mat-tered; the overriding point is that the way it functioned prevented men from believing they could work out their own destinies. To map out a relatively autonomous realm, which is what Turgenev's novels seek to do, was thus a significant political act.

This task entails a literary procedure so different from the one Turgenev employed in *Notes of a Huntsman* that it begins to explain his unease with the earlier work. Certainly some fuller explanation than his own off-hand comments about this unease is necessary, for on the face of it, and in the opinion of many contemporaries, *Notes of a Huntsman* is a consummate achievement—both in the grace of its composition and style and in its capacity to satisfy obshchestvo's demand that literature discuss prevailing social issues. *Notes of a Huntsman* focuses on the most troublesome of these issues, serfdom, but to the extent that Turgenev confronted this evil, he also of neces-sity had to acknowledge the insidious nature of the system that sus-tained it. And indeed, the effect of his work is to show not only the power of the established order, but the pernicious influence of its values as well. Oppression is absorbed into daily life; more than a problem it becomes an enduring fact, such that even the oppressed insist on living by its code: peasant exploits peasant even as both are exploited by the landowner. And the cause of this behavior is not so much malice or greed or any other flaw in the peasant mentality as it is something more basic and more difficult to combat—the inability to imagine any social forms other than the ones that dominate Russian life.

The definitive character in this respect may well be the peasant nicknamed Fog, who appears in the sketch "Raspberry Spring." Fog is about 70 years old and a liberated serf, presumably having acquired his freedom in return for faithful service. As the major domo on a vast estate, Fog took great pains to provide the maximum pleasure and luxury for his rich master. Even now, years afterward, he will still at the slightest excuse relate the manner of life his master the count enjoyed, itemizing with something approaching love all the appurtenances that gave the estate its proper dash and color: the numerous hunting dogs, the serfs decked out in red caftans with gold braid, "the embroidered long coats, wigs, canes, perfumes, *lade-cologne* of the finest sort, snuffboxes, all those big paintings." To sum up his recollections Fog says, "When he'd set out to give a banquet —O Lord! Sovereign of my life!—the fireworks would begin, and so would the pleasure jaunts." That parenthetical exclamation is very revealing, for in such an expression of spontaneous enthusiasm and undistanced enjoyment, Fog shows how much the pleasures of the count have become his pleasures as well. The brutal truth that he was only a serf has vanished, blotted out by the general luxury. Fog has so thoroughly introjected the prevailing values that he can no longer pass judgment on the reality of his own situation or conceive of an alternative.

Even the narrator (presumably Turgenev himself), with his greater intellectual sensitivity, suffers from a comparable constraint on the imagination. He totally fails to express moral outrage, though moral outrage is everywhere called for. To be sure, this omission lets the details of serfdom come forth directly, in all their plain horror, and many critics have praised the effectiveness of the device. But since these sketches are presented as the narrator's perceptions and reactions, his failure to make a moral judgment reveals a disturbing powerlessness in the face of evil, not simply a preference for an objective mode of organization. We are, finally, forced to consider the essential ambiguity of *Notes of a Huntsman* (though it is one, I believe, that enhances rather than diminishes the work): namely, that the author of what was read as an attack on serfdom was himself of the serf-owning class. Turgenev was in fact exceedingly fair to the serfs who came under his control on his mother's death, setting them advantageous economic terms and providing health and educational facilities. But such gestures tend only to emphasize the main point, that Russians of good conscience were entangled in a system that made it appear economically and socially reasonable to own other men. Given this complicity, it is not surprising that sustaining true moral outrage proved no easy task.

Turgenev thus found himself in a dilemma. In moving to show the depravity of Russian public life, he invited consideration of his own public role, itself in part depraved. Significantly, though we are told little about the narrator of *Notes of a Huntsman*, what we do learn confirms his public orientation, his enforced participation in the world as it exists. Almost every sketch begins with him setting forth from his residence, but it is a residence totally without substance: no dimensions of the house are given, no furniture within itemized, no surrounding land described. It is only a starting point for a renewed examination of the world, seemingly no different from any other. The values of Russia's public life seem to absorb all, and in consequence the critical impulse continually risks slipping into moral ambiguity.

In striking contrast to *Notes of a Huntsman*, Turgenev's first four novels all project a stable center of values, a sense of a real home, a refuge distinct from the rest of the world. This entity often releases Turgenev's greatest eloquence, and occasionally, as in the description of the hero's return home in *The Nest of the Dvorianstvo*, he seems to be insisting on a very specialized mode of life indeed, with normal perceptions altered and man and nature moving toward harmony:

> [Lavretsky] sat near the window, not moving and literally listening to the current of the tranquil life which surrounded him, the occasional sounds of rural isolation. Over there, somewhere behind the nettles, someone is singing in a thin, thin voice; a mosquito echoes him precisely. Now the singing has stopped, but the mosquito squeaks on. . . . It is as if I were at the bottom of a river, Lavertsky resumed thinking. And always, at all times, life here is tranquil and unhurried. He thought, "He who enters this circle needs restraint: here there is no need to worry and rush about."[4]

Turgenev did not always make clear what this "circle" represented in his novels, and the titles evoke a range of possibilities: the better elements of the provincial *dvorianstvo* (as in *The Nest of the Dvorianstvo*),* the family (*On the Eve* was in manuscript entitled "A

---

* The closest English terms for *dvorianstvo* are gentry and nobility, but both distort the meaning of the Russian in various ways. I shall continue to use dvorianstvo in this essay.

Moscow Family"), or, more generally, the "educated class" of two generations (*Fathers and Sons*). In fact, Turgenev's uncertainty reflects the prevailing confusion about just where to locate opposition to the government. But whatever the precise referent of the "circle," it is something clearly distinct from the world at large, and the values it exhibits are emphatically its own.

The Turgenev novel may thus be said to function within a part-whole framework, for not only does it proceed within a circumscribed setting, it also asserts the wisdom of avoiding the fullness of Russian reality. This was a purposeful and, given the historical circumstances, a defensible political strategy; but there were risks also, and in the Tur review cited above Turgenev alludes to one danger. In remarking on the insufficiency of certain types of literature that existed "when social [*obshchestvennaia*] life was still undeveloped," Turgenev says that "for the time being we hear in Russia separate sounds, to which literature responds with similarly brief echoes." He acknowledges, in other words, that in limiting himself to a small compass, an author may deny himself any general comprehension of the national life; the depicted part must be distinct from the whole, but it must not be completely detached.* In his novels Turgenev guards against such detachment in various ways, the most obvious being the device of having his hero arrive at the "circle" *from somewhere* at the beginning of the work and depart *to somewhere* at the end. The aim is to suggest a world that although segmented is still articulated in its parts. Nevertheless, it is clear that this kind of litterary strategy can easily result in a work concerned only with private emotions and affairs, a work cut off entirely from the political life of the country, and it should be said that not all readers have felt Turgenev always circumvented this danger.

Ideally, however, Turgenev's novels position themselves at an exquisitely defined distance between extremes; they express a resistance to cultural imperatives that were equally fruitless and demeaning: acquiescence in the prevailing order or despairing withdrawal. To

---

* Turgenev is here most likely referring to the popular genre of the physiological sketch. As its name implies, the physiological sketch rendered with almost scientific detail the predicament of various social types. Since these were usually from the lower classes, the physiological sketch was in effect critical of prevailing conditions; but, almost by definition, it failed to fit this criticism into a coherent overview. It is worth noting that the passage in the Tur review ends with a reference to the epic, for that genre did purport to picture national life in all its fullness. But Turgenev dismisses the epic as well, and given its conservative implications, this is not surprising. Turgenev wants a genre that will be both critical and encompassing in its meanings.

most contemporaries these two responses seemed to exhaust the possibilities, and it was Turgenev's ability to project a third way that
gave him his particular power as a novelist. It is the same characteristic, it may be added, that best defines his novels as novels, for in
purely formal terms they seem hardly to qualify.

II

Regarding his first novel, *Rudin*, Turgenev himself vacillated in his
designation of its genre, sometimes referring to it as a long *povest'*.*
From a formal point of view it is easy to see why he was in doubt.
Rudin is quite short, only 135 pages in the collected works, and many
secondary characters are only sketched in. Also the plot is fairly simple and can be summarized briefly. Dmitry Rudin, a passionate exponent of German idealistic philosophy, unexpectedly arrives at the
gentry estate of Daria Mikhailovna and proceeds to astonish the
assembled company with his enthusiastic, if abstract, declamations
about the need for social change. Especially impressed is Daria Mikhailovna's daughter Natalia; and when, in the following days, Rudin
chooses to display his intellectual passion more directly to her, she
responds with the proposal that the two of them elope. But Rudin
hesitates, citing the need to observe proprieties. This fatal inability
to give action to his words—for so the hesitation is portrayed—has
as much as been predicted by Rudin's old university acquaintance
Lezhnev, who has insisted throughout that Rudin is incapable of real
commitment.

But all this is given a specifically novelistic resonance by the setting Turgenev has fashioned. The action of *Rudin* takes place within
a realm set apart from the world, a realm not merely distinct but
purposefully removed from a larger sphere of activity that is only
adumbrated. Turgenev makes us feel this configuration at once. The
opening scene depicts the charitable visit of Lipina, Lezhnev's future
wife, to the hut of a dying peasant woman. Turgenev here seems
intent on rendering, as he did so effectively in *Notes of a Huntsman*,
the pathos of peasant life, the sense of lives of deprivation and sto-
icism in the face of death. Surprisingly, however, these themes are
raised only to be dropped, and the drama of the dying peasant
woman is abruptly cut off. Lipina, her charitable gesture made, re-

---

* When *Rudin* appeared in *The Contemporary* in January 1856, it bore the
designation *povest'* (a long story), even though in his letters of the period Turgenev most often referred to it as a novel. When putting together his collected
works in 1880, he grouped *Rudin* with the works he considered his novels.

treats to the dvorianstvo enclave, and Turgenev directs our attention after her; in the course of the novel we hear not one word more about the peasantry. The effect of the opening is not to arouse our sympathies over the human condition in Russia, but to instruct us about the heterogeneity of the social terrain where this condition develops. Indeed, Turgenev almost immediately defines another broad area of the social milieu by remarking offhandedly that Daria Mikhailovna's influence did not extend to Petersburg, the capital and center of power, but only to Moscow, and there tenuously. By such signals we learn that the setting of *Rudin* involves more than the casual placing of dvorianstvo characters on dvorianstvo estates: the estates are isolated, but the fullness of Russian reality threatens continually to intrude.

The trappings of a distinct realm are everywhere, neatly insinuated when not made explicit; but Turgenev's purpose is less to delineate the material forms of the dvorianstvo enclave than to consider its moral implications. There is a scene early in the novel that is interesting in this respect. Lezhnev has held himself aloof from Daria Mikhailovna's parties and gatherings, scorning her intellectual pretensions and social attitudes, and he consents to visit her only to resolve a dispute about the boundary of their abutting lands. When he arrives, however, Daria Mikhailovna immediately turns to the topic of her parties, scolding him for his unsociability. By way of clinching her argument, she announces "Vous êtes des nôtres," and indeed she is inarguably right, up to a point. Lezhnev's manner during this encounter, his sense of decorum and his polite ironies, not to mention his easy understanding of the French phrase itself, confirms Daria Mikhailovna's judgment. The very purpose of the visit establishes a commonality of basic values, since landowning in Russia was limited to distinct categories of individuals. Significantly, however, these values are shown to be amenable to considerable refinement, and individuals equally owing allegiance to them may derive quite dissimilar ways of living their lives. This scene, which projects all sorts of similarities between Lezhnev and Daria Mikhailovna, at the same time fixes beyond doubt his moral superiority over her.

Such a calibration of moral distinctions is just what was missing in the opening scene, where the meaning of Lipina's effort to perform a charitable act was studiously ignored. But the more telling point of contrast is in the epilogue, which also takes the action outside the "circle" formed by the estates of Daria Mikhailovna and Lezhnev, for here the cause of moral obtuseness is made more precise. When Lezhnev and Rudin meet in a provincial town several years after the main events of the plot, Lezhnev is on his way to fulfill an obligation to administer an army recruitment, and Rudin is traveling to an enforced confinement at his home, the consequence of his allegedly subversive activity while a teacher. Both men, that is, are immediately subject to bureaucratic restraints, and we are forcefully reminded of the government's absolute sway in the world at large. We are further reminded that this sway is not only powerful but insidious, effecting compliance by seductive as well as punitive means, so that finally no alternative seems possible. As the two men sit and talk over their wine, they comport themselves as perfect equals. The fact that Rudin has rebelled against the prevailing order and Lezhnev has acquiesced in it influences their attitudes not an iota. Lezhnev does not apologize for his behavior, and Rudin does not brag of his; by the same token Lezhnev does not praise Rudin, and Rudin does not blame Lezhnev. Their recent histories, apparently so different, are collapsed into an equivalency, the moral distinctions flattened out by a world that makes all action vacuous.

It may appear perverse to belabor the question of *Rudin*'s imaginative topography when it is obvious that the visible concerns of the book lie elsewhere: *Rudin* is, after all, concerned almost exclusively with the nature of authentic action, so much so that the hero is little more than a compendium of qualities and gestures bearing on this issue. Practically the first words describing Rudin foretell a dislocation of personality—"His strong voice," we read, "did not match his slight chest"—and his very eloquence, his most impressive trait, raises the possibility of an unrealizable extravagance of the spirit. When Rudin fails the test to which Natalia puts him by suggesting elopement, our worst suspicions are confirmed. But if Rudin stands condemned, and he clearly does, the terms of the charge against him are by no means straightforward. Rudin is no simple poseur; indeed, of all the characters in the book, he is the most sensitive to the dangers of insincerity, and he is also the one who most energetically pursues the ideal of integrating values and action. Thus his ultimate failure, while it undoubtedly proves his personal insufficiency, also calls into question the concept of authenticity itself.

Put another way, the point of the novel is less to expose Rudin's flaws than to ask how such a well-intentioned and talented man can, despite himself, fall into a state of inauthenticity. The book offers only one explicit answer: Rudin's education, which proceeded under the auspices of German romanticism, clearly was a sort that could foster excess and move men to make striking gestures difficult to live up to. But in itself this is not a sufficient explanation. Turgenev also shows that such an education does not invariably lead to inauthenticity; the most idealized character in the book belongs to the same university circle as Rudin. And we know that in real life Turgenev was by no means willing to dismiss all those men of his generation who had been influenced by German philosophy—quite the reverse.

It is the imaginative topography of *Rudin*, its reliance on a part-whole framework, that dissolves much of the imprecision surrounding the meaning of authentic action. Indeed, in what is perhaps the most striking image in the book, Rudin suggests this very connection between theme and structure. The image occurs in the epilogue, after he has related the failure of his various efforts since he and Lezhnev last met. He says, "I never knew how to build. And it is quite a task, my friend, to build when you have no ground under you, when it is necessary to build with yourself as your own foundation." Rudin has just told how he has, in turn, served as the manager of a large estate, introducing new principles of agronomy (which in the context of the times implies a tampering with serfdom); attempted to construct a navigational canal; and taught at a provincial *gymnazium*, instilling hopes of a university education in students usually resigned to much less. The list of Rudin's occupations is impressive by any standard; when compared to the lives of the other characters, it assumes a Herculean dimension. But Lezhnev nonetheless dismisses all Rudin's efforts as irrelevant, and Rudin acquiesces in this judgment. Proper action apparently entails more than energy and diligence, which is to be expected in a world where all activity is assimilated into the designs of the prevailing order. As Rudin's evocative image begins to make clear, if action is to have purposeful consequences, if it is to be authentic, it must proceed from a surer ground than an individual immediately commands. Men must find a foundation, some source of alternative values, from which to propel themselves against a recalcitrant world. This also makes clear the real deficiency of Rudin's education, which was not its substance but rather the fact that it drew him abroad. Following German philosophy to its fount, Rudin denied himself the chance to find a sustaining "circle" in Russia.

In effect, *Rudin* projects a topographical rationale for efficacious action. Though it is a book about deadlock and despair, it is not totally pessimistic, for in mapping out the reasons for failure so precisely, it implies a path to success as well. Even the conclusion of the novel, which depicts the utter futility of Rudin's participation in the 1848 Paris uprising, manages to convey that measure of hope which understanding fosters. In the very last lines, as Rudin is dying, his uncomprehending comrades-in-arms refer to him as "le Polonais." In having his hero lose his life in that abortive rebellion, Turgenev reasserts the need to avoid direct confrontation with overwhelming political evil; and in having his hero also lose his name and even his nationality, Turgenev neatly indicates that the consequent failure may entail a profound loss of self, as the world moves to obliterate meaningful distinctions. Successful political action must counteract an antagonist possessed not merely of brute force but of a cunning that empties action of purpose, even as the action begins to take shape.

III

This understanding of the nature of political conflict sets *Rudin* apart from Turgenev's earlier literary works and also fixes its historical contemporaneity. *Rudin* may be set in the 1840's, but its meanings apply much more directly to the time in which it was written—when the defeats suffered by the imperial army in the Crimean campaign signaled an unexpected weakness in the autocracy and thus made an explanation of purposeful political action appear most urgent. Though the actual position of obshchestvo had probably not been much changed by the military events, the feeling had intensified that now was the time to chart political and social possibilities. *Rudin* is clearly part of a general effort to forge a new cultural ideal, one that would replace the "superfluous man," for whom the very idea of action was inconceivable. *Rudin*, however, also performs some rather specialized tasks in this area that were impossible for other cultural instruments.

To get some idea of this, it is worth referring to an essay that appeared in the same year as Turgenev's novel, "The Questions of Life" by the noted pedagogue and physician N. I. Pirogov. Because the essay managed to sum up the outstanding issues of the day in a short space, it became very popular. Its epigraph, which neatly distills these issues even further, came to be especially widely quoted:

"For what are you preparing your son?" someone asked me.
"To be a man," I answered.
"Don't you know," replied my interlocutor, "that men as such do not

exist in the world; that is merely an abstraction completely unnecessary for our society. We require businessmen, soldiers, mechanics, sailors, doctors, and jurists, not men."

Is this true or not?[5]

Pirogov's answer, in the body of the essay, is negative. The listing of occupations is elaborated to show that practical action must be approached with suspicion, for whatever the changes Russia was now embarking on, it was obvious that the old values still dominated. If action was necessary, and Pirogov granted that it was, it would have to occur in the presence of an adversary still very powerful; if the educated classes had to diversify their interests to meet changing economic and social conditions, and Pirogov granted that they did, they should still retain a commitment to humanitarian ideals. "Man as such" must act, he must go forth to remake a world now seemingly susceptible to change, but he must bring his own values with him. His actions must be the overflow of who he is, the visible reflex of an essential self, for only in this way will he be able to avoid the world's distorting conventions.

All of this is similar to the ethic projected by *Rudin*, and indeed much like the ideas of many other writers of the period. What gives *Rudin* its privileged position is Turgenev's ability to provide an explanatory topography for the concept of "man as such," to elaborate a psychological construct into one that fit on the map of social reality. The dramatic logic of *Rudin* shows that "man as such" must have some foundation from which to begin his efforts; he must command a part of the world separate from the corrupt and corrupting whole.

This is not *Rudin*'s only claim to cultural significance, however, and it is only now that I feel I am coming to Turgenev's distinguishing qualities as a man and as a writer. As a man he was irresolute, but as a writer he often managed to turn this quality into a perceptive skepticism. And thus in *Rudin*, though Turgenev seems to endorse a part-whole strategy, he also holds it up to critical scrutiny. He shows, perhaps despite himself, that the concept of "man as such," which is an integral part of this strategy, is at bottom paradoxical.

For making the criterion of value what man *is*, rather than what he *does*, may radically distort the ways in which men establish mutual contact. Without the pressure of external evidence, there is little impetus to adjust one's view of others, and none to alter one's view of oneself: men may become like random atoms, pursuing their own aims and making only fortuitous connections with each other. Turgenev's Westernizer orientation had always inclined him to some form of individualism, but it is in *Rudin*, with its reliance on the idea of the "man as such," that it assumes this extreme version. Life on the estates of Daria Mikhailovna and Lezhnev is continually marked by barbed and brittle encounters, and social gatherings suggest not real community but only a precarious equilibrium of diverse tendencies. Most of the characters, especially Daria Mikhailovna and her followers, are shown as merely rubbing up against each other, occasionally flaring up from the friction and then retreating unchanged into themselves. Even a union that is putatively successful, that of Lezhnev and Lipina, suffers from a similar constraint: the marriage is not a real engagement of passions, but a declared willingness to abide the other person for what he or she is, an agreement to perpetuate indefinitely the affectionate sparring that marked their courtship. In general, *Rudin* makes it hard to imagine how "man as such" might engender a community of "men as such."

And it is not so much a matter of personal insufficiency as of the concept itself, so that even the best individuals cannot escape its implications. In *Rudin*, as in several other of Turgenev's works, the character that most fully represents the ideal of the "man as such" is—despite the transformation of gender involved—the heroine. This made considerable sense historically, for of all Russians of the period, women were most free of the pressure to conform to the established categories of the world; it was women who could most naturally work out their destinies in the context of private arrangements and groupings.* It is worth noting in this regard that Turgenev ascribes to Natalia (as he does to his heroines in other works) a specifically domestic upbringing, one free of cramping supervision; in consequence Natalia is somewhat naive, but she is also strikingly self-sufficient, and when she does act it is not on the basis of social conventions or demands, but as the spontaneous overflow of who she is.

If Natalia has the virtues of the "man as such," however, she also has the shortcomings, and nowhere are these more apparent than at the critical turning point of the book, the rendezvous with Rudin by Avdiukhin Pond. To be sure, Rudin is much to blame for what passes

* Of course, this freedom entailed disadvantages as well. If Russian women were freer than Russian men of the need to have their existence certified by society, they also lacked the status that such certification endowed. A good introduction to the question of the role of women, which was much discussed in this period, is Richard Stites, "The Problem of Women's Emancipation in Nineteenth-Century Russia" (Ph.D. diss., Harvard University, 1967).

here; his lack of will and his invidious ability to absorb all events into a bewildering system of personal interpretations make disaster almost a foregone conclusion. But to attribute the failure entirely to his inherent "weaknesses" is to fall into the same mode of judgment employed to such unsatisfying ends by the characters in the book. In fact, the actual dramatic situation, the words and gestures we perceive as we read, makes clear that the failure of the rendezvous results in part from an ongoing dynamic between two people. More precisely, though Natalia comes to Avdiukhin Pond set on proclaiming her readiness to unite her future with Rudin's—indeed she passionately offers herself to him—her actions during the episode work to narrow drastically the acceptable basis of cooperation. Throughout the first part of the rendezvous, Natalia remains remarkably noncommittal, drily reporting the awful news that her mother has learned of their love. Natalia is testing Rudin, and the test is explicitly two-fold: will he unequivocally reassert his love in the face of difficulty, and does he understand that she would welcome such a declaration despite the trying circumstances? In other words, will Rudin instantaneously reveal who he is and recognize who she is? Rudin fails on both counts. As Natalia says, "Yes, you did not expect this, you did not know me." And as a result they must part, at once and forever. Since Natalia has invoked standards that measure people according to what they are in their essence, there is no discussion of any mitigating circumstances in the past, and no contemplation of any adjustments for the future.

Rudin is a phrasemonger, an enthusiast without sustaining drive or will, and Natalia rightly scorns him for this. But the fact remains that she has manipulated their confrontation, making it a revelation of fixed character rather than a real discussion in which the parties modify their meanings and propensities as they proceed. Stated simply, not only has Natalia used the rendezvous to expose what Rudin is and always will be, she has also, less consciously, insinuated a disturbing principle of behavior. By abruptly terminating the conversation and withdrawing to her mother's house, leaving Rudin to shout his justifications to the empty air, she sums up her adherence to a truly radical individualism—a meritorious individualism in her own case, to be sure, but still a principle that makes the gradual growth of community difficult to imagine.

On the contrary, such a principle will more naturally lead to a paroxysm of erratic and carping judgments that will drive men further and further apart; for making the essential self the main criterion of value decreases the availability of solid, stable evidence without in any way decreasing man's desire to comprehend his fellows. Natalia at least has the rendezvous scene, problematical as it is, as confirmation of her opinion. But all of the other characters, none of whom knows what happened at that meeting, share her compulsion to judge Rudin. They fall to the task as if tracking some prey, and their lack of hard evidence seems only to intensify the almost religious certainty with which they make their assessments. In this context, even the rare positive judgments of Rudin—for example, the one Lezhnev offers when the two men meet toward the end of the book—must fail to effect a true rapprochement. The change in Lezhnev's opinion comes from no discernible reason; it is like grace, and as such may be requited with gratitude but not genuine affection. Not surprisingly, when Lezhnev offers Rudin a "refuge" in his house, Rudin thanks him for the gesture but declines.

In all, the condescension, petty malice, and abrupt anger that prevail in *Rudin* make for a noisome brew, and this is not a pleasant book. It is however, for the same reason, immensely informative about the state of obshchestvo in the mid-1850's. It begins to explain why, beyond the obvious disagreements over philosophy and politics, this grouping was so highly unstable—for the salient point about obshchestvo is precisely that all such disagreements were continually aggravated by the petulant and erratic personal judgments of the members composing it. The most striking accounts of this period describe social gatherings where men were time and time again called upon to assert their convictions (*ubezhdenie*, a word that gained considerable currency in this period), and then had the sincerity of these convictions discounted.[6] An unwillingness to accept others at face value prevailed, even though this ran counter to the acknowledged need for political unity. The significance of *Rudin* is that it shows this rampant suspicion to follow logically from the nature of obshchestvo itself, from its commitment to a part-whole view of the world and to the related concept of "man as such."

Turgenev, of course, had an especially intimate view of this state of affairs, since he was one of those most widely suspected of lacking the courage of his asserted principles. Significantly, there was no particular act that was called into question; up to this point in his career, Turgenev's political credentials were in good order and even included a period of forced confinement for writing an illegal eulogy of Gogol. Instead, some quality perceived as underlying all Turgenev's actions troubled his contemporaries. This negative view of his character may have been correct, but it can be argued that the mode of judgment was itself more detrimental to the progressive cause than the flaws in Turgenev's spiritual condition.

Some concrete sense of daily life in obshchestvo in the mid-1850's is given in the following story told by Chernyshevsky: "Dobroliubov said to Turgenev, who was boring him with his alternately amiable and witty remarks, 'Ivan Sergeevich, it bores me to talk with you, so let us stop this conversation,' and he got up and crossed over to the other side of the room," cutting off all subsequent efforts at discussion by the exasperated Turgenev.[7] The particular piquancy of the anecdote derives from the way it shows life mirroring art: Dobroliubov is no more willing than Natalia to countenance explanations from a man judged wanting in some essential way. The anecdote also dramatically expresses the dynamic conditioning obshchestvo in general, a convergence of ideas and interests that moved men to meet and talk, but in the end offered them no means of bridging their disagreements.

IV

The fact that Chernyshevsky was the approving narrator of this anecdote and Dobroliubov its main actor is also to the point, since the final collapse of obshchestvo took the form of a split between the *raznochintsy*, whom these two radical critics represented, and various elements of the liberal dvorianstvo. The felt need for an entity to oppose the prevailing order, which for a while kept in check, if it did not resolve, the outstanding differences, dissipated as emancipation neared and class and personal interests asserted themselves more urgently.

The course of the relationship between Turgenev and the radical critics describes in fine obshchestvo's collapse. At first, even at occasions of considerable rancor, the discussion proceeded with a sense of a common goal; each party at bottom believed that the other, like the deviant of a sect, could be brought back to see the evident truth he was perversely ignoring. Thus the radical critics consistently acknowledged Turgenev's talent, arguing only that he failed to develop his own correct insights. For his part, though he thought the radical position was in many ways misguided, Turgenev remained cordial on a personal level, admired Chernyshevsky's intellectual energy, and, perhaps most revealingly, created in *Fathers and Sons* what is surely the most powerful and sympathetic image of the *raznochinets* personality. But *Fathers and Sons* may also be said to symbolize the definitive end of obshchestvo.

The conclusion of the novel expresses a new level of conflict, a lack of sympathy with the radical position so great that it is now difficult to imagine Turgenev and Dobroliubov meeting socially, even if only to turn their backs on each other. The life of the raznochinets hero is shown to have been absolutely fruitless, his death an apathetic acceptance of this fact. The famous description of Bazarov's grave in the book's final lines is telling:

> However passionate, sinful, and rebellious the heart hidden away in that grave, the flowers that blossom there glance out at us with innocent eyes: they speak to us not only of all-embracing peace, of that vast repose of "indifferent" nature; they tell us also of everlasting reconciliation and life without end.

This ending, with its confused meanings and its sentimentality, seems to confirm the very worst opinion the radical critics came to hold about Turgenev—that beyond being politically cautious (which was natural enough for the era), he eventually succumbed to an urge to discount politics altogether, to abstain from critical thought in the face of increasing odds. This is less than fair to Turgenev in general and to *Fathers and Sons* in particular, for the final note of the book is not solely one of despair and wishful thinking. The chapter that ends with the description of Bazarov's grave begins with one of the most positive visions in all of Turgenev, the double wedding of the Kirsanovs, father and son. It appears that the problem of radical individualism has been surmounted sufficiently to permit a picture of real harmony among a group of men and women, and that is no small imaginative achievement for the times. What remains troubling is just how this harmony might be extended to the world at large, for the Kirsanovs, though they occasionally worry about and tinker with social problems, do not finally seem very concerned with anything but their own happiness. In other words, the part of the world they inhabit stands in uncertain relation to the whole.

Turgenev was not explicit in *Fathers and Sons* about how this issue could be resolved, but his essay "Hamlet and Don Quixote," published two years before the novel, suggests what he had in mind. In it he says:

> This whole life is nothing but the eternal accommodation and eternal warring of two ever dividing and ever uniting principles. If we were not afraid of troubling your ears with philosophical terminology, we would bring

ourselves to say that Hamlet is the expression of the radical centrifugal force, according to which all that lives considers itself the center of creation.... Without this centrifugal force (egoism), nature could not exist, just as it could not exist without the opposite, a centripetal force according to which all that lives lives only for another.[8]

The passage, like the essay in general, is pervasively influenced by an assumption that the universe is composed of inalterable units in flux. Men, whether they tend toward Hamlet's example or Don Quixote's, have fixed natures, and this ensures the random quality of life. Turgenev's vision thus has a prominent pessimistic component, for there is no way to escape the "centrifugal" force entirely. But the vision has a tremendous potential for success as well, since Turgenev claims that an impulse toward harmony, a universal "centripetal" force, also exists. It is only necessary to recognize this—to comprehend the possibility concretely—for man to find real, sustaining hope. The significance of the Kirsanov family lies precisely in its ability to focus such hope. It is not an instrument to effect change in the world, but it can point in what direction change should go; it provides a visible moral alternative, which in fact was always one position inherent in the idea of obshchestvo.* By taking this approach Turgenev has given his politics a quiescent tone, but it remains politics nonetheless.

The limitations of Turgenev's position are obvious enough. It is worth noting, however, that contemporaries, including the radical critics, were no more persuasive in the arguments they put forward, and in fact often seemed only to be repeating this position with a different emphasis. It is interesting, for example, that Chernyshevsky's novel *What Is to Be Done?*, which in many ways is a programmatic statement of the radical critics' views, as well as an implicit rebuttal to *Fathers and Sons*, similarly attributes great importance and potential to the family. To be sure, Chernyshevsky's family is

---

* It may clarify matters to put this in rhetorical terms, since rhetoric has tried to systematize various kinds of part-whole relationships. Metonymy substitutes the part for the whole, and tends to suggest that the present term conditions the absent one. A classic textbook example is "sail" for "ship." Synecdoche uses the part to symbolize the whole. To interpret as metonymy the phrase "that man is all heart" is an error, for the point here is not that the heart is the crucial part animating the whole (as a sail is said to do for a ship); rather this is a synecdoche because the symbolic connection of the heart with courage suggests a judgment about the man's essential character. In synecdoche one of the terms *recapitulates* the other. Kenneth Burke suggests that metonymy *reduces* whereas synecdoche *represents*; according to these definitions Turgenev is writing in a synecdochic mode. See Kenneth Burke, *A Grammar of Motives* (Berkeley, Calif., 1969), especially the chapter "Four Master Tropes," pp. 33–51. I have also been influenced by Hayden White, *Metahistory* (Baltimore, 1973).

composed of raznochintsy, not members of the dvorianstvo; but the more basic point is that in both novels the family is viewed as the best means of avoiding the fullness of a corrupt society. Indeed *What Is to Be Done?*, for all its revolutionary ardor, restricts itself almost exclusively to questions of domestic arrangements. Who sleeps where, the protocol of entering another person's room, meal and work schedules—these are the main issues of the book. *What Is to Be Done?* is in many ways the family novel par excellence.

Such a narrow focus is not surprising. The radical critics, even more than Turgenev (though from a totally different ideological perspective), were convinced of the awesome evil of the world, and as certain that direct confrontation with the status quo was doomed. Their writings are often built around images that suggest the dilemma in its most paralyzing form: thus society is like a virulent disease that infects all who come into contact with it, including those trying to eradicate it;[9] or it is like a box enclosing all who live in Russia, so that anyone of a mind to overturn it is defeated by his own physical situation.[10] Given this extreme view, it becomes critical to find some entity, like the family, that is relatively removed from prevailing values and hence amenable to reform.

It is true that beyond the common realization of the potential of the family, there are significant distinguishing features in the views of Turgenev and the radical critics. The following comment by Dobroliubov, which sums up the radicals' position, neatly indicates some of the differences:

The question of so-called *family morality* is one of the most important social questions of our time. We will even say that it is significantly more important than all other questions because it enters all others and has a meaning more internal, whereas the remaining ones are generally limited by external circumstances. Our literature, recently preoccupied with these external social questions, has almost forgotten about family relations, about the meaning of women in society. Some have even wanted to find some kind of natural opposition between family and social relations, but this opposition is purely artificial and extremely absurd. No matter what is said about different means of improving life in society, these always have their beginnings and ends in the relations within the family, understood not only in the sense of marital bliss but in a much broader sense. In the family the most complete natural blending of personal egoism with the egoism of others is achieved, and there is set up the foundation and basis of that brotherhood, that solidarity, whose creation alone can serve as the lasting bond of a correctly organized society.[11]

In stressing the family's "internal meaning," its privileged status relative to those social questions that are "limited by external circumstances," Dobroliubov is recapitulating the topographical vision I discussed above. Indeed the passage is informed throughout by a belief that action in a circumscribed sphere will prove more efficacious than action in the world at large. It is in the family, Dobroliubov tells us, that "the most complete natural blending of personal egoism with the egoism of others is achieved." The elements he has included in his analysis are familiar: man as a radically individualistic creature (an ego); the need, nevertheless, for harmony among men; and a part-whole vision of the world where this drama is played out. The conclusions he arrives at, however, diverge considerably from Turgenev's. The intellectual furniture is the same, but it has been rearranged to alter the final effect.

To Dobroliubov success within the family leads directly to an even greater success. The vision that separates the family from society also brings them together in a new relationship; in some basic way that overrides the apparent "natural opposition," the family acts as the crucial determinant of society's condition. As Dobroliubov says, the "means of improving life in society . . . always have their beginnings and ends in the relations within the family." In other words, change in the smaller unit will necessarily mean change in the whole. And in fact this sense of systematic alteration is if anything even stronger in *What Is to Be Done?* Reform at the level of the family means to subvert society's awesome corrupting power step by small step.

There is nothing of this sense of progressive change in *Fathers and Sons.* Whereas the radical critics suggest that the family can directly serve to move Russia toward social harmony and equality, Turgenev believes the family can only bring into focus an ideal condition that may provide men with hope. This is an important distinction; still the two positions grow out of common assumptions, and, what is more important, they end in visions that are similarly limited, lacking any coherent conception of broad-scale political change. If Turgenev produces only a representation of the ideal, the radical critics do no more than offer a reduction of political life to domestic arrangements. The times militated against any truly transforming political vision. In this context it became most urgent to show—to picture powerfully and dramatically—the constraints under which men labored. This Turgenev did, and the skill with which he did it certifies his importance as a social novelist.

HUGH MCLEAN

Eugene Rudin

The topic of literature and society, well worn as it is, continues to fascinate us, both in its broad theoretical aspects and in its specific Russian manifestations. Reviving the old Renaissance metaphor that literature holds a mirror up to nature, the Russian civic critics of the last century told us that literature was nothing but a pale reflection of social reality, perhaps dispensable if we could behold the original in all its fullness. As Chernyshevsky put it, those who live by the sea have no use for seascapes. Going to the other extreme, the Formalists of the early decades of this century told us that literature and society have nothing to do with one another, that to connect them is as absurd as, in the famous example of the medieval mystery play, for the audience to assault the actor who played Judas. Suggestive as it is, however, the Judas example begs a fundamental question in the epistemology of art. The unfortunate actor, however innocent in his real person, was *representing* another real person, one who was in fact guilty, and the ambiguities of that word "represent" bring us back into the thick of the tangled circuitry linking literature and life.

In his illuminating paper Professor Todd has demonstrated a whole series of parallels in *Eugene Onegin* between the literary—the narrative and structural—choices made by the author-narrator and the life choices made by his characters. Just as literary choices had to be made among the prescriptions, styles, and preferred genres of competing schools—classicism, sentimentalism, and romanticism —so the characters' life choices were made among various options determined in part by social factors, that is, such things as moral principles, styles, and fashions. Thus both literary choices and life choices are made within a larger frame called "culture"; literary styles and life-styles are not fenced off from one another, but actually occupy different parts of a common territory. Furthermore, the relationship between them is much more than one of analogy or even coexistence: it is an operative one, involving complex interactions in both directions.

Later critics, following Belinsky, have laid the greatest stress on the direction of life to art: the accuracy with which real Russian life is reproduced within the confines of Pushkin's novel. Pushkin himself had pointed the way, for instance by playfully asserting the existence of a real-life model for his Ideal, Tatiana (that the assertion is believed to be at least partly false only complicates the issue with a bit of Sternean confusion). More significantly, Pushkin inserts into his novel the most real of characters, namely himself—that is, an author-narrator who at certain points, at least, is clearly to be identified with Aleksandr Sergeevich Pushkin. Throughout the novel Pushkin manipulates the literature-life relationship as artfully as any conjurer, constantly reminding us that however illusory their appearances and disappearances, the rabbits he pulls from his authorial hat are red-blooded and alive. Or are they?

An even defter feat of Pushkin's sorcery involves what seems, through the power of his illusionism, to be the reverse direction, literature to life. As Professor Todd has discerningly shown, Pushkin's characters themselves have been formed by literature, by their reading. They articulate their emotions and predicaments according to literary models; even their dreams turn out to be culturally determined. In thus asserting the power of literature over human psychology, Pushkin is in fact pushing us yet another step back from "life." Since it is the psychology of fictional characters that is involved, he is actually holding literature's mirror up to literature's mirror. The effect of this mirror trick, however paradoxical, is totally convincing, perhaps precisely because we are all subliminally aware of the pervasive cultural determinism that informs our own thoughts and actions.

In the search for a more comprehensive synthesis of the problem of literature and society in nineteenth-century Russia, it seems potentially rewarding to attempt a cross-pollination of two interesting papers, Professor Todd's and Professor Ripp's, applying Ripp's method to Todd's material and vice versa. The following is a summary outline of such an experiment.

In *Eugene Onegin* Pushkin employs a synecdochic strategy, using Ripp's definition of that term, though his parts are more numerous and more comprehensive than Turgenev's. Taking a broader perspective, he lets his characters escape from their gentlefolks' nests to both Moscow and Petersburg, thus setting up that enormously suggestive triangle of contrasting gentry life-styles identified with these places, a triangle Tolstoy was to use so effectively after him. Turgenev, in contrast, seems to find the urban environment uncongenial, for reasons too complex to be speculated on here. Pushkin also marks the passage of time more fully than Turgenev, by comprehensively detailing the effect of the passing seasons on both nature and men (the individual's adaptations to the seasons, of course, also take place within a system determined by culture). Turgenev, with the exception of the last chapter and the epilogue, limits himself to a single summer. And even in the last chapter the passage of time—several years—is only stated, and its effect on the characters' bodies briefly noted. Still, the freedom with which each author chooses to recount only particular "parts" or scenes from the characters' lives, omitting all others, constitutes a structural similarity between the two novels, perhaps going back to the anticlassical rebellion of the Byronic narrative poem, of which the "free novel" is the heir. Further, the irony in which Pushkin, like Turgenev, bathes his characters, especially his hero, properly qualifies *Eugene Onegin* as a modern novel in Lukács's definition, not an epic (though one wonders whether Turgenev's dream of a Russian epic did not after all come true in his lifetime with *War and Peace*).

Following Pushkin's synecdochic structure to its transcendental limits, one finds a philosophical pessimism actually quite similar to Turgenev's. Neither writer, it seems, had a very high opinion of man's ultimate significance in time and space. To be sure, in each novel the pessimistic implications of the failure and futility of the hero's life are particularly offset by the relative success and satisfaction of the heroine's. At the end of *Rudin* Natalia Lasunskaia is presumably happily married to Volyntsev, although Turgenev assiduously avoids bringing them on stage in their married state. In *Eugene Onegin* Tatiana, although wistfully married to a man she does not love, at least has the satisfactions afforded by her virtue and

fidelity and by the social creativity of her salon. Nevertheless, both
Turgenev and Pushkin reach past their more or less happy heroines
to articulate a humbling sense of the ultimate insignificance—"noth-
ingness," to translate their word literally—of all human things. Turgenev writes of how "swift and insignificant" (*bystra i nichtozhna*)
our life is (the phrase is Rudin's, but Turgenev says the same thing
many times elsewhere in propria persona, for instance in the *Poems
in Prose*). And Pushkin, for all his humor and effervescent vitality,
takes a similarly dim view of life's metaphysical worth, even using
the same word, *nichtozhnost'*, to refer to it: "ee nichtozhnost' razu-
meiu / I malo k nei priviazan ia" ("I understand its insignificance /
And little am I bound to it"). Life is something "light," an intoxicat-
ing beverage to be enjoyed while one can; yet blessed is he who
leaves life's feast early, without drinking its goblet to the dregs or
reading its novel to the end. Youth, at least, possesses grace and
charm and physical beauty; old age's distinguishing features are gout
and cuckoldom—better avoided.

Now applying Professor Todd's method to *Rudin*, we find a much
less complex structure, not only in space and time but also in "realities." The playfulness, the shifting from the narrator's plane to the
characters' plane, is missing: we have entered the age of high realism. But the ambience of culture, and specifically literature, its for-
mative influence on the characters, is still very much present, though
perhaps used less effectively than in *Eugene Onegin*. Twenty-five
real years have passed since the appearance of *Eugene Onegin* and
—if we date the main action of *Rudin* at about 1840—about ten literary ones. In that time Rudin has accompanied his creator to Germany for philosophical studies, and there drunk deep of Kant and
Hegel, as well as Goethe, Novalis, and even Bettina von Arnim. He
later intoxicates Natalia, then still innocent of such heady libations,
with sips from all of them. She in turn is reading a history of the
Crusades and apparently makes the mistake of transposing their ethical imperatives and character models to her own time, thereby creating a disastrous moral yardstick for measuring poor Rudin. Though
Turgenev does not articulate this point further, we are perhaps entitled to view Rudin as an ironically futile crusader for progress, his
various abortive efforts and minor martyrdoms culminating in his
"heroic" but useless self-immolation on behalf of an alien revolution,
and a failed one at that.

There is one work that has been read very carefully indeed by
both the hero and the heroine. Rudin quotes it directly, and Natalia,

who uses it as a fortune-telling book, finds in it a passage that serves as an appropriate epitaph to her romance with Rudin. That book is *Eugene Onegin* itself.

The many parallels of both character and situation between *Eugene Onegin* and *Rudin* have already been explored by generations of Russian *gimnazisty*, not to mention scholars, and surely need no further elaboration here. But it may be worthwhile to recollect how Turgenev's characters use Pushkin's novel. In his farewell letter or "confession," Rudin advises Natalia to follow Pushkin's "beatitude" prescribing that we live in tune with life's seasons ("Blessed is he who in youth was young"), and he is honest enough to recognize that he himself needs the advice more than she. The passage Natalia selects at random from *Onegin* after reading this letter (we cannot help suspecting the author of secretly guiding her fingers) poignantly evokes the unrevisability of life's novel, the painful irrevocability of memories:

> He who has felt is haunted ever
> By days that will not come again;
> No more for him enchantment's semblance,
> On him the serpent of remembrance
> Feeds, and remorse corrodes his heart.
> (I, 46)*

For all their familiarity with *Eugene Onegin*, however, both Natalia and Rudin must be given rather bad marks on their ability to apply its lessons to life. Natalia, who is said to know her Pushkin by heart, surely should have learned from Tatiana's experience that it is not a very good idea to make passionate declarations of love to a young man one hardly knows, especially in a bucolic setting. And Rudin should perhaps have learned from Eugene that such opportunities must be seized when they are offered; life, as Professor Todd observes, gives us few second chances. In fact, Rudin acts more irresponsibly than Onegin, since he is confused about his own feelings and leads Natalia to believe he is more serious about her than he is. Like Eugene, Rudin may have read *Adolphe*. Certainly Turgenev had, for Rudin's earlier life, as Lezhnev recounts it, bears many resemblances to Adolphe's and indeed to Constant's own, with its frequent periods of vassalage to older women. But if the Eugene-Adolphe experience of the ugly aftermath of a faded love is Rudin's reason for turning tail so cravenly at Avdiukhin Pond, he fails to

---

* A. S. Pushkin, *Eugene Onegin*, trans. Walter Arndt, 2d printing, rev. (New York, 1963).

articulate the vision; nor does the author do it for him. In truth, this chilling picture of Adolphe's slavery and ennui probably has little to do with Rudin's behavior. His real motive seems to be an unliterary, if hardly natural, failure of sexual response that Turgenev does not care to explore further, although he gives it a larger symbolic resonance.

Rudin's second failure to respond is also an obvious echo of *Eugene Onegin*: his refusal to challenge Volyntsev to a duel after Volyntsev's dinner-table insult. Instead, he contents himself with a "visit of explanation" to Volyntsev, ostensibly to reveal Natalia's and his mutually declared but otherwise still secret love, and to give Volyntsev an opportunity to step aside magnanimously. This visit only serves to muddy the emotional waters even more. Here too it seems that Rudin's failure to fight is hardly due to any wisdom derived from contemplating the tragic results of Onegin's compliance with convention; rather it seems but another instance of his ineffectuality and lack of spirit.

As a final effort at synthesis I would like to develop, and somewhat modify, Professor Ripp's notion of the "man as such." I would first modify it to read not "man as such," but "gentleman as such." For the characters in *Eugene Onegin* and *Rudin* are members of the gentry class, and both novels—indeed almost all Russian literature up to the middle of the century—are products of that class. It may need to be reiterated that from the accession of Catherine II (or rather of her husband, Peter III) to the emancipation, the gentry class was in a unique situation, a state of what we might call existential freedom. They had a guaranteed living, whether opulent or not, from their lands, a supply of human chattels to serve them, and, with the abolition of obligatory state service, essentially no serious public responsibilities.* "Service," to be sure, remained a possible option, and custom seems to have dictated that most gentlemen put in at least a few years at it. But for most these were perfunctory years of perfunctory service, as our two novels reflect. Pushkin devotes exactly one line to the "exemplary and noble" service of Eugene's father; but since Eugene is the heir of his clan, he apparently never has to serve at all. Turgenev is equally laconic. He sums up Pigasov's official career in two lines and Rudin's in two words: Rudin is *v otstavke*, retired, and that is all we ever learn about it. (This in-

* Perhaps it is as an icon of this liberation that Peter III's portrait hangs on the walls of Gogol's old-world landowners, those paragons of total, if benevolent, idleness.

creasing divorce of the gentry from civil service and the rise of a professional bureaucracy in Nicholas's reign were, of course, important historical phenomena, which had later literary repercussions, for instance in *Anna Karenina*. But neither Pushkin nor Turgenev takes much interest in such problems of political science.)

The other occupation traditionally assigned to the gentry was agriculture, or rather agricultural management, since Konstantin Levin must have been the only Russian gentleman—at least the only literary one—in the whole nineteenth century to do any physical farm work. For most gentlemen the management of their estates was as perfunctory as civil service, the occasional amusement of dilettantes. The real day-to-day business was left to bailiffs. Rudin expounds some theories of estate management to Mme Lasunskaia, to which she listens with apparent rapture; but her rapture has no practical consequences, for in matters of business she relies entirely on her wily bailiff, a one-eyed Ukrainian, who is robbing her. Eugene Onegin benevolently shifts his serfs from *barshchina* to *obrok* (corvée to quitrent), perhaps as a result of reading Adam Smith, but that is the limit of his managerial involvement.

If he did not serve and did not care for agricultural management, what was a Russian gentleman to do? *Chto delat'?* There was no outlet in the church, as in England, or in business. There was no India where one could lose oneself for a profit; Siberia hardly plays a comparable role for Russians. Fedor Tolstoy, called the "American" because he passed through Siberia and got as far as the Aleutian Islands, is alluded to both in *Eugene Onegin* and in *Rudin* (here via a well-known quotation from Griboedov); but this very sobriquet symbolizes his utterly un-Russian—one might say ungentlemanly—example, which was reinforced by his bad moral reputation. And although Rudin has a déclassé friend named Kurbeev, his partner in an abortive canal project who later becomes a gold-mine operator in Siberia, neither Turgenev nor Rudin has any inclination to follow him there. It is noteworthy, however, that Rudin's poverty is forcing him into such unconventional, nongentry roles as schoolteacher and hydraulic engineer—doubtless an augury of the opening up of a wider range of careers for gentlemen, at least impoverished ones.

But for the present Rudin is an atypical example; Eugene is closer to the norm. In Professor Ripp's quotation from Pirogov, the Russian man, *homo russicus*, seems to be offered the choice of being a businessman, soldier, mechanic, sailor, doctor, or jurist (lawyer); but for a gentleman all these options except soldier were barred by culture, that is, by class prejudice. It just wasn't done. A gifted few could become writers, perhaps even great ones like Pushkin and Turgenev. But what if the talent were absent, to say nothing of the drive? Rudin could not even finish his article on the tragic in life and art, and perhaps it was just as well. In general, the gentry estate, the nobleman's nest, was a difficult locus for intellectual life. That life requires discipline, the stimulation of contacts, and often institutional structures. (Of course there are exceptions, like Tolstoy, but they are rare.) Without work or vital intellectual life, the Russian gentleman was left with only the recurrent needs of the body: the alimentary ones celebrated by Gogol, and the sexual ones not celebrated by Gogol. In Rudin's case there is a symbolic fusion of social and sexual ineffectiveness.

Thus the Russian gentleman of that period represents an ultimate paradox: in a land of unfreedom he is maximally free, although he must bear the burden of guilt for the unfreedom of others on which his freedom depends. He is free, like a prisoner, from the anodyne of work and the pressure of economic necessity. He becomes indeed the "man as such," stimulated by his very idleness to contemplate not only the social disarray but also the existential void, to wonder not only what is to be done but also what does it all mean. Perhaps the absolute nature of his condition as the "man as such" is one reason why these confrontations are so meaningful for us, so universal.

Notes

Notes

Introduction

1. V. Kantorovich, "O nekotorykh aspektakh sotsiologii literatury," *Voprosy literatury*, no. 11, 1969, p. 33.

2. Accounts of the debate and its resolution in the doctrine of Socialist Realism may be found in Edward J. Brown, *The Proletarian Episode in Russian Literature, 1928–32* (New York, 1953); Herman Ermolaev, *Soviet Literary Theories, 1917–1934: The Genesis of Socialist Realism* (Berkeley, Calif., 1963); Robert A. Maguire, *Red Virgin Soil: Soviet Literature in the 1920's* (Princeton, N.J., 1968); and Rufus W. Mathewson, Jr., *The Positive Hero in Russian Literature*, 2d ed., rev. (Stanford, Calif., 1975). Echoes of this controversy could be heard in the literary polemics surrounding Turgenev's *Fathers and Sons* in the late 1950's; see Zbigniew Folejewski, "The Recent Storm Around Turgenev as a Point in Soviet Aesthetics," *Slavic and East European Journal*, 6 (1962): 21–27.

3. For examples, see B. M. Eikhenbaum, "Literatura i literaturnyi byt," *Na literaturnom postu*, 1927; and T. Grits, V. Trenin, and M. Nikitin, in V. B. Shklovskii and B. M. Eikhenbaum, eds., *Slovesnost' i kommertsiia (knizhnaia lavka A. F. Smirdina)* (Moscow, 1929). A translation of Eikhenbaum's article may be found in L. Matejka and K. Pomorska, eds., *Readings in Russian Poetics: Formalist and Structuralist Views* (Cambridge, Mass., 1971). In a chapter appropriately entitled "Crisis and Rout," *Russian Formalism: History—Doctrine*, 2d ed. (The Hague, 1965), Victor Erlich discusses this development in Russian Formalism.

4. Iu. Tynianov and Roman Jakobson, "Problemy izucheniia literatury

i iazyka," *Novyi lef*, no. 12, 1928, pp. 36–37. A translation appears in Matejka and Pomorska, eds.

5. On the several areas of sociological inquiry that Elizabeth Anne Weinberg describes in her survey *The Development of Sociology in the Soviet Union* (London, 1974), only studies of leisure time touch on problems of direct concern to literary scholarship. For a study of Soviet theater audiences based on such research, see Mikhail Deza and Mervyn Matthews, "Soviet Theater Audiences," *Slavic Review*, 34 (1975): 716–30.

6. See especially the work of V. D. Stel'makh, the head of the Sector of Books and Reading at the Lenin Library: *Sovetskii chitatel'* (Moscow, 1968) and "Kakaia kniga u vas v rukakh: sotsiologicheskie zametki o chtenii," *Literaturnoe obozrenie*, no. 5, May 1973. The Lenin Library has also published *Chtenie i kniga v zhizni nebol'shikh gorodov: po materialam issledovaniia chteniia i chitatel'skikh interesov* (Moscow, 1973), and *Kniga i chtenii v zhizni sovetskogo sela* (Moscow, 1974).

7. B. S. Meilakh, ed., *Khudozhestvennoe vospriiatie: sbornik I* (Leningrad, 1971). The proceedings of the conference were gathered in *Problemy khudozhestvennogo vospriiatiia* (Leningrad, 1968).

8. G. N. Ishchuk, *Problema chitatelia v tvorcheskom soznanii L. N. Tolstogo: posobie po spetskursu dlia studentov-filologov* (Kalinin, 1975). This study, published in an edition of only 500 copies, includes an extensive survey of Soviet studies of reading. Ishchuk's analyses tend to degenerate into lists of what Tolstoy said about his readers. Still, the book remains a valuable source of references and could well stimulate other critical studies of Tolstoy's interaction with his imagined reader.

9. Among the exceptions are the monographs listed in note 2 above; Maurice Friedberg, *Russian Classics in Soviet Jackets* (New York, 1959); Vera S. Dunham, *In Stalin's Time: Middle-Class Values in Soviet Fiction* (Cambridge, Eng., 1976); and two monographs by André Meynieux, *La Littérature et le métier d'écrivain en Russie avant Pouchkine* (Paris, 1966) and *Pouchkine homme de lettres et la littérature professionnelle en Russie* (Paris, 1966).

10. Milton Ehre, review of *Ivan Goncharov: His Life and His Works*, by Vsevolod Setchkarev, *Russian Review*, 34 (1975): 229.

11. Elizabeth Burns and Tom Burns, eds., *Sociology of Literature and Drama* (Baltimore, 1973), provide bibliographies and a wide selection of articles.

12. Georg Lukács, *The Historical Novel*, trans. Hannah Mitchell and Stanley Mitchell (London, 1962), esp. pp. 43, 86–87; and *The Theory of the Novel: A Historico-Philosophical Essay on the Forms of Great Epic Literature*, trans. Anna Bostock (Cambridge, Mass., 1971), pp. 144ff.

13. For a critique of Goldmann's method and suppositions, see Jean Franco's essay below. Goldmann's concept of "vision du monde" has recently been used to good advantage in Andrzei Walicki, *The Slavophile*

Controversy: History of a Conservative Utopia in Nineteenth Century Russian Thought, trans. Hilda Andrews-Rusiecka (Oxford, 1975).

14. Harry Levin, "Literature as an Institution," *Accent,* 6 (1945–46): 159–68. A revised version appears in Harry Levin, *The Gates of Horn: A Study of Five French Realists* (Oxford, 1963), pp. 16–23.

15. Ian Watt, *The Rise of the Novel* (Berkeley, Calif., 1957).

16. Hans-Robert Jauss, "La Douceur du Foyer: The Lyric of the Year 1857 as a Pattern for the Communication of Social Norms," *Romanic Review,* 65 (1974): 205–6.

17. Wolfgang Iser, "The Reality of Fiction: A Functionalist Approach to Literature," *New Literary History,* 7, no. 1 (Autumn 1975): 26. The original German versions of this article and the one by Jauss cited above appear in Reiner Warning, ed., *Rezeptionsästhetik: Theorie und Praxis* (Munich, 1975). Other examples of this approach may be found in the following anthologies: Peter Uwe Hohendahl, ed., *Sozialgeschichte und Wirkungsästhetik: Dokumente zur empirischen und marxistischen Rezeptionsforschung* (Frankfurt am Main, 1974); and Jürgen Kolbe, ed., *Neue Ansichten einer künftigen Germanistik* (Munich, 1973). In his article "Marxist Literary Criticism Today," *Survey,* 18, no. 1 (Winter 1972), Peter Demetz describes the challenge that a new generation of East European critics interested in literary reception is posing to traditional "reflective" theories (including Lukács's). For a comprehensive East German treatment of literary reception, see Manfred Naumann et al., *Gesellschaft, Literatur, Lesen: Literaturrezeption in theoretischer Sicht* (Berlin, 1973), which is in the process of being translated into Russian.

18. In the Soviet Union Iu. M. Lotman's exciting and valuable "culturological" studies have analyzed the interplay of social and aesthetic codes in semiotic terms. Based on a wealth of concrete material from Russian culture, these investigations parallel the work Roland Barthes has done with French culture in *Mythologies* (1957), although Barthes pays greater attention to the conventional silences of culture and to the signifying function of all human artifacts and social patterns. "Culture" in Lotman's studies seems at times to have a more narrowly aesthetic meaning than in Western studies, and hence his work tends to focus on the aestheticization of everyday life, of which there are many interesting cases in post-Petrine Russia. See, for example, his excellent article "Teatr i teatral'nost' v stroe kul'tury nachala XIX veka," in *Stat'i po tipologii kul'tury: Materialy k kursu teorii literatury,* vyp. II (Tartu, 1973). Lotman's most recent work, however, has moved toward a broader definition of culture and a more inclusive description of the behavioral styles, roles, and patterns of the Russian gentry: "Poetika bytovogo povedeniia v russkoi kul'ture XVIII veka," in *Trudy po znakovym sistemam,* VIII (Tartu, 1977).

19. It is worth noting that the serial publication of Russian novels during the nineteenth century provided ample opportunity for feedback from

readers and critics to reach the novelist while he was still in the process of writing.

History and Literature: Remapping the Boundaries

1. Roland Barthes, "To Write: An Intransitive Verb?," in Richard Macksey and Eugenio Donato, eds., *The Structuralist Controversy: The Languages of Criticism and the Sciences of Man* (Baltimore, 1970), pp. 150–51.

2. *Ibid.*, pp. 149–50. Michel Foucault, *L'Archéologie du savoir* (Paris, 1969), pp. 14–20.

3. Roland Barthes, "Réflexions sur un manuel [d'histoire de la littérature française]," in S. Doubrovsky and T. Todorov, eds., *L'Enseignement de la littérature* (Paris, 1971), pp. 14–20.

4. I refer not only to Sartre's *Qu'est-ce que la littérature?* but also to his monumental unfinished work on Flaubert.

5. See *Le Dieu caché* (Paris, 1955) and *Pour une sociologie du roman* (Paris, 1964). One of the best short introductions to Goldman's theory is his own early article "Dialectical Materialism and Literary History," *New Left Review*, 92 (July–August 1975): 19–51. Genetic structuralism was a late formulation. For a critique of both Goldmann's and Barthes's theories, see Robert Weimann, "French Structuralism and Literary History," *New Literary History*, 4 (1973): 437–69.

6. Foucault, *L'Archéologie*, p. 14.

7. René Wellek, *Concepts of Criticism* (New Haven, Conn., 1963).

8. Michel Foucault, *The Order of Things: An Archaeology of the Human Sciences* (New York, 1971), p. 387; Louis Althusser, *Résponse à John Lewis* (Paris, 1973), p. 31; Barthes, "To Write," p. 135.

9. F. R. Leavis, *The Great Tradition* (Harmondsworth, Eng., 1962), p. 10; Wellek, pp. 18–19; Georg Lukács, *Studies in European Realism* (New York, 1964), p. 5; Christopher Caudwell, *Illusion and Reality* (New York, 1937).

10. Foucault, *Order*, p. 44.

11. Maurice Merleau-Ponty, *Signs*, trans. Richard C. McCleary (Evanston, Ill., 1964), p. 39.

12. Emile Benveniste, *Problems of General Linguistics*, trans. Mary E. Meek (Coral Gables, Fla., 1971), p. 19. For the use of the term "structure" in other sciences, see Michael Lane, "Structure and Structuralism," in Lane, ed., *Structuralism: A Reader* (London, 1970), esp. pp. 19–39.

13. Notably by Julia Kristeva in *La Révolution du langage poétique* (Paris, 1974). Semiotics should be distinguished from semiology or the science of signs, a term used by Barthes and Kristeva to cover "the large signifying units of discourse."

14. Stefan Zolkiewski, "Deux structuralismes," in A. J. Greimas et al., *Sign, Language, Culture* (The Hague, 1970), p. 11.

15. Tzvetan Todorov, *Grammaire du Décaméron* (The Hague, 1969). For a criticism of his categories, see Jonathan Culler, *Structuralist Poetics* (London, 1975), pp. 76–85, and Robert Scholes, *Structuralism in Literature* (New Haven, Conn., 1974), pp. 102–11. Scholes's book is an important comprehensive study that includes writers such as Todorov, Gérard Genette, and Claude Brémond.

16. Claude Brémond, "La Logique des possibles narratifs," *Communications* (Paris), 8 (1966): 60–76. See also his *Logique du récit* (Paris, 1973), and Vladimir Propp, *Morphology of the Folktale*, ed. Louis A. Wagner and trans. Laurence Scott, 2d ed., rev. (Austin, Tex., 1968).

17. Roland Barthes, in *Communications*, 8 (1966): 4.

18. Boris Tomachevski, "Thématique," in Tzvetan Todorov, ed., *Théorie de la littérature* (Paris, 1965), pp. 263–92.

19. Ju. Tynjanov, "On Literary Evolution," in Ladislav Matejka and Krystyna Pomorska, eds., *Readings in Russian Poetics: Formalist and Structuralist Views* (Cambridge, Mass., 1971), pp. 66–78.

20. R. Jakobson, "The Dominant," *ibid.*, pp. 82–87.

21. Benveniste, pp. 101–11.

22. For Formalism see Matejka and Pomorska, eds., *Readings in Russian Poetics*. For the Prague school see the essays by Jan Mukarovsky in Paul L. Garvin, ed., *A Prague School Reader on Esthetics, Literary Structure, and Style* (Washington, D.C., 1964). For the Soviet Structuralist position see Yury Lotman, *Analysis of the Poetic Text*, trans. D. Barton Johnson (Ann Arbor, Mich., 1976).

23. Umberto Eco, *La struttura assente: introduzione alla ricerca semiologica* (Milan, 1968); Tzvetan Todorov, *The Fantastic: A Structural Approach to a Literary Genre*, trans. Richard Howard (Ithaca, N.Y., 1975).

24. Julia Kristeva, *Le Texte du roman: approche sémiologique d'une structure discursive transformationnelle* (The Hague, 1970), p. 72.

25. *Ibid.*, p. 123.

26. Roland Barthes, S/Z, trans. Richard Miller (New York, 1974). This edition is hereafter cited in parentheses in the text.

27. Jacques Derrida, *Marges de la philosophie* (Paris, 1972), p. 376, quoted in Culler, p. 152.

28. Jacques Derrida, "Structure, Sign, and Play in the Discourse of the Human Sciences," in Macksey and Donato, eds., p. 245.

29. *Ibid.*, pp. 250–51.

30. Derrida has expressed disagreements with the politics of *Tel quel*. For a discussion of in-group relationships, see Mary Ann Caws, "*Tel Quel*: Text and Revolution," *Diacritics*, 3, no. 1 (Spring 1973): 2–8.

31. Philippe Sollers, *L'Ecriture et l'expérience des limites* (Paris, 1968), p. 13.

32. Tzvetan Todorov, Introduction to issue on "Le Vraisemblable," *Communications*, 11 (1968): 139.

33. Roland Barthes, *The Pleasure of the Text*, trans. Richard Miller (New York, 1975), pp. 34–35.

34. Jean-Louis Baudry, "Writing, Fiction, Ideology," *Afterimage* (London), 5 (Spring 1974): 23.

35. Sollers, p. 10.

36. Barthes, *Pleasure*, p. 53.

37. Edward Said, *Beginnings* (New York, 1975), p. xiii.

38. Baudry, p. 24.

39. Barthes, *Pleasure*, p. 14.

40. Jacques Lacan, *Ecrits* (Paris, 1966). For a translation and a commentary, see Anthony Wilden, trans., *The Language of the Self* (Baltimore, 1968).

41. Kristeva, *Révolution*, p. 14.

42. Julia Kristeva, "Le Sujet en procès," *Tel quel*, 52 (1972): 16. See also Philip E. Lewis's review of *La Révolution du langage poétique* in *Diacritics*, 4, no. 3 (Fall 1974): 31.

43. Gilles Deleuze and Félix Guattari, *L'Anti-Oedipe: capitalisme et schizophrénie* (Paris, 1972).

44. Philippe Sollers, quoted in Stephen Heath, "Towards Textual Semiotics," *Signs of the Times* (Cambridge, Eng.), 1971, p. 28.

45. Kristeva, *Révolution*, p. 533.

46. Jacques Derrida, "Positions," *Diacritics*, 3, no. 1 (Spring 1973): 46. For a comment on Derrida's phenomenological use of the term "regional," see Henri Meschonnic, *Le Signe et le poème* (Paris, 1975), p. 407.

47. Renée Balibar and Dominique Laporte, *Le Français national* (Paris, 1974).

48. Louis Althusser, *For Marx*, trans. B. R. Brewster (New York, 1970), pp. 129–51. See also Pierre Macherey, *Pour une théorie de la production littéraire* (Paris, 1966).

The Sociological Method of V. F. Pereverzev

1. *Literaturnaya gazeta*, no. 43, Oct. 25, 1967, p. 6. For an extensive study in English of Pereverzev's sociological method and of the polemics surrounding it in the late 1920's, see my master's thesis, "The Sociological Method of V. F. Pereverzev" (Columbia University, 1949), 212 pp. For a concise discussion of Pereverzev's method against the background of the literary theories of the 1920's, see Herman Ermolaev's *Soviet Literary Theories: 1917–1934* (Berkeley, Calif., 1963), pp. 93–99. Vladimir Seduro summarizes some aspects of Pereverzev's approach to Dostoevsky in his study *Dostoyevski in Russian Literary Criticism: 1846–1956* (New York, 1957), pp. 143–60. Pereverzev's sociological method was widely discussed in Soviet literary journals in the late 1920's. For a bibliography of this criticism (both for and against), as well as a list of Pereverzev's works to 1930, see *Literaturnye diskussii. Bibliografcheskii vypusk*, 1 (Moscow, 1931): 1–10. A bibliography, in English, of works by and about Pereverzev

can be found at the end of my master's thesis. There has been no extensive or intensive discussion of Pereverzev's theories in the Soviet Union since the late 1920's, apart from the critical discussion of his work in *Literaturnaia entsiklopediia,* VIII (Moscow, 1934), 501–12. For a short discussion, see S. Mashinskii, *Nasledie i nasledniki. Stat'i* (Moscow, 1967), pp. 54–66.

2. "O literaturovedcheskoi kontseptsii V. F. Pereverzev. Rezoliutsiia prezidiuma kommunisticheskoi akademii," *Pechat' i revoliutsiia,* no. 4, 1930, p. 3.

3. Pereverzev, "Problemy marksistskogo literaturovedeniia," *Literatura i marksizm,* no. 2, 1929, p. 20.

4. S. Dinamov, "Diskussiia o Pereverzeve i zadachi marksistskogo literaturovedeniia," *Krasnaia nov',* no. 2, 1930, pp. 218–19.

5. P. Butenko, "Gorbachevsko-Pereverzevskaia kontseptsiia problemy kolkhoznoi literatury," *Na literaturnom postu,* 34–36 (1931): 63.

6. V. Pertsov, "Protiv Pereverzeva," *Novyi lef,* no. 2, 1928, p. 47.

7. "O literaturovedcheskoi kontseptsii V. F. Pereverzeva," pp. 4–5.

8. Pereverzev, "Literaturnye diskussii (problemy teorii romana)," *Literaturnyi kritik,* no. 3, 1935, pp. 236–37.

9. Pereverzev, "Voprosy marksistskogo literaturovedeniia," *Rodnoi jazyk i literatura v trudovoi shkole,* no. 1, 1928, p. 86.

10. Pereverzev, *Tvorchestvo Gogolia* (Moscow, 1914), p. 66.

11. Pereverzev, "Problemy marksistskogo literaturovedeniia," pp. 20–21.

12. Pereverzev, "Voprosy," p. 86.

13. The question here is broadly posed. For a contemporary Marxist's view of the "fecundity manifested by the complex history of Marxist aesthetics," see Stefan Morawski's *Inquiries into the Fundamentals of Aesthetics* (Cambridge, Mass., 1974), in particular the chapter "Art and Society," pp. 295–305.

14. Karl Marx, Preface to "A Contribution to the Critique of Political Economy," in Karl Marx and Frederick Engels, *Selected Works* (New York: International Publishers, n.d.), I, 356.

15. Marx, "Theses on Feuerbach," *ibid.,* I, 472.

16. F. Engels, letter to Heinz Starkenburg, Jan. 25, 1894, *ibid.,* I, 392.

17. For a recent study on Caudwell, see David N. Margolies's *The Function of Literature: A Study of Christopher Caudwell's Aesthetics* (New York, 1969).

18. G. V. Plekhanov, Preface to the 3d edition of *Za dvadtsat' let,* in his *Sochineniia* (Moscow, 1923–26), XIV, 183.

19. *Ibid.,* pp. 183–84, 189.   20. *Ibid.,* p. 184.

21. *Ibid.,* p. 123.   22. *Tvorchestvo Gogolia,* p. 66.

23. *Ibid.,* p. 5.   24. *Ibid.,* p. 11.

25. *Ibid.,* p. 12.   26. *Ibid.,* p. 15.

27. Roman Jakobson, *Noveishaia russkaia poeziia* (Prague, 1921), p. 11.

28. Pereverzev, "Sotsiologicheskii metod formalistov," *Literatura i marksizm*, no. 1, 1929, p. 17. For a consideration of Formalist positions on the question of the image in art, see Victor Erlich, *Russian Formalism* (The Hague, 1955), esp. pp. 147–50, 199–201.

29. *Tvorchestvo Gogolia*, pp. 16–17.

30. *Ibid.*, p. 17.

31. A. Veselovskii, *Istoricheskaia poetika* (Leningrad, 1940), p. 317.

32. Bernard, quoted in Matthew Josephson, *Zola and His Time* (New York, 1928), p. 118; S. Freud, "A Note on the Prehistory of the Technique of Analysis" (1920), in his *Therapy and Technique* (New York, 1963), p. 193; Zola, quoted in Josephson, p. 534.

33. For an excellent discussion of Taine's literary views, see René Wellek's *A History of Modern Criticism: 1750–1950* (New Haven, Conn., 1965), IV, 27–57.

34. V. V. Vorovskii, "Maksim Gor'kii," in his *Sochineniia* (Moscow, 1931), II, 202–3.

35. Pereverzev, "Neobkhodimye predposylki marksistskogo literaturovedeniia," in V. F. Pereverzev, ed., *Literaturovedenie* (Moscow, 1928), p. 10.

36. *Ibid.*, pp. 10–11.   37. *Ibid.*, p. 12.
38. *Tvorchestvo Gogolia*, p. 59.   39. *Ibid.*, p. 13.
40. *Ibid.*, pp. 44, 47.

41. Pereverzev, "O teorii sotsial'nogo zakaza," *Pechat' i revoliutsiia*, no. 1, 1929, p. 63.

42. *Ibid.*

43. C. G. Jung, "Psychology and Literature," in *The Spirit in Man, Art, and Literature*, vol. 15 of *The Collected Works of Carl G. Jung*, trans. R. F. C. Hull (Princeton, N.J., 1971), pp. 97, 101, 103.

44. Plekhanov, *Sochineniia*, XVIII, 146.

45. *Ibid.*, X, 13.

46. *Ibid.*, XIV, 192.

47. Plekhanov, *Pis'ma bez adresa, ibid.*, XIV, 54–62; see also V, 316–17.

48. *Ibid.*, XIV, 54.

49. Pereverzev, "Problemy," pp. 8–9.

50. *Ibid.*, p. 8.

51. *Ibid.*, p. 13.

52. A. A. Potebnia, *Mysl' i iazyk*, 4th ed. (Odessa, 1922; first published in 1862), p. 146.

53. *Ibid.*, p. 152.

54. *Ibid.*, p. 146.

55. *Tvorchestvo Dostoevskogo*, 2d ed. (Moscow, 1922), pp. 231–33.

56. Pereverzev, "Sotsial'nyi genesis Oblomovshchiny," *Pechat' i revoliutsiia*, no. 2, 1925, p. 61.

57. Pereverzev, "Neobkhodimye predposylki marksistskogo literaturo-vedeniia," pp. 14–15.
58. Pereverzev, "Teoreticheskiie predposylki pisarevskoi kritiki," *Vestnik kommunisticheskoi akademii*, 31 (1929): 38.
59. Pereverzev, "Problemy," p. 8.
60. *Ibid.*, pp. 27–28.
61. Pereverzev, "Voprosy," p. 86.
62. Pereverzev, "Sotsiologicheskii metod formalistov," pp. 7–8.
63. Pereverzev, "Voprosy," p. 91.
64. *Ibid.*
65. *Ibid.*, p. 99.
66. V. Ral'tsevich, "O metodologii Pereverzeva" *Pechat' i revoliutsiia*, no. 1, 1930, p. 16.
67. Pereverzev, "Voprosy," p. 90.
68. Quoted in I. Anisimov, "Problema Pereverzeva," *Krasnaia nov'*, no. 2, 1930, p. 277.
69. *Tvorchestvo Dostoevskogo*, p. 56.
70. "Dostoevskii i revoliutsiia" (1922), *ibid.*, p. 11.
71. Quoted in I. Anisimov, pp. 277–78.
72. A. Mikhailov, "K kritike metodologii Pereverzeva," *Na literaturnom postu*, 5–6 (1930): 40–41.
73. Pereverzev, "Zakliuchitel'noe slovo Pereverzeva na torzhestvennom zasedanii posviashchennom 35-letiiu literaturnoi deiatel'nosti Gor'kogo," *Vestnik kommunisticheskoi akademii*, 24 (1927): 268.
74. Arnold Hauser, *The Philosophy of Art History* (Cleveland, 1963), pp. 12–13.
75. "Zakliuchitel'noe slovo Pereverzeva," p. 268.
76. *Tvorchestvo Dostoevskogo*, p. 214.
77. "Dostoevskii i revoliutsiia" (1922), *ibid.*, p. 4.
78. *Ibid.*
79. *Ibid.*
80. *Ibid.*, p. 12.
81. *Ibid.*, p. 14.
82. *Ibid.*, pp. 7–9.
83. "O literaturovedcheskoi kontseptsii V. F. Pereverzev," p. 5.
84. Pereverzev, "Na frontakh tekushchei belletristiki," *Pechat' i revoliutsiia*, no. 4, 1923, p. 130.
85. Pereverzev, "O teorii sotsial'nogo zakaza," pp. 62–63.
86. "Na frontakh tekushchei belletristiki," pp. 130–31.
87. L. Trotskii, *K voprosu o politike RKP (b) v khudozhestvennoi literature* (Moscow, 1924), pp. 65–66.
88. Ral'tsevich, p. 34.
89. A. V. Lunacharskii, "O zadachakh marksistskoi kritiki," *Izvestiia*, no. 105, May 8, 1928.
90. Emerson, "Fate," in *Selections from Ralph Waldo Emerson*, ed. Stephen E. Wicher (Boston, 1960), p. 304.

91. Taine, *Histoire de la littérature anglaise*, 12th ed. (Paris, 1905), I, xxxi.

92. P. N. Sakulin, Preface to the 1st edition of *Tvorchestvo Dostoevskogo* (Moscow, 1912), p. xi.

93. *Ibid.*, p. xiv.

94. *Tvorchestvo Dostoevskogo* (Moscow, 1922), pp. 230, 252–53.

95. See my study *Dostoevsky's Quest for Form: A Study of His Philosophy of Art*, 2d ed. (Bloomington, Ind., 1977).

96. Pereverzev, *Literatura drevnei rusi* (Moscow, 1971), pp. 5–6. Among Pereverzev's other works written and published after 1930, one may mention his scholarly editions of the works of V. T. Narezhny (1780–1825) and Aleksandr F. Veltman (1800–1870), published in 1933, and his study of the sources of the Russian realistic novel, *U istokov russkogo real'nogo romana* (1937; 2d ed., 1965). Pereverzev's unpublished works include five full-length manuscripts prepared in the eighteen years of his imprisonment and exile, 1938–56: studies on Pushkin's narrative poems and on Belinsky and the theater (1947); a critique of L. Timofeev's book *Theory of Literature*, entitled "Unfounded Foundations of the Science of Literature" (1950); a study of the Soviet writer A. Makarenko (1951–53); and a theoretical work entitled "On the Foundations of Eidological Poetics" (1949–55). Ms. Helen Scott of the University of Chicago is preparing a dissertation on these works. Pereverzev's studies of Dostoevsky and Gogol have not been republished in the Soviet Union since the 1920's. His theoretical contributions to Marxist aesthetics in the 1920's, like those of many other important Marxist literary critics of that period, also have not appeared in print since then.

Gogol and His Reader

1. See Donald Fanger, "The Gogol Problem: Perspectives from Absence," in Michael S. Flier, ed., *Slavic Forum: Essays in Linguistics and Literature* (The Hague, 1974), pp. 103–29.

2. Thus Gogol speaks in a letter of 1840 of "living and breathing through my works" (XI, 325). In 1843 he writes his friend Danilevsky: "You ask why I don't write you about my life, about all the trifles. . . . But my whole life, for a long time now, has been proceeding within me, and internal life . . . is not easy to convey. Volumes are needed for it. Moreover, its result will appear later, all in printed form." (XII, 139.) As for the notion of his life as a riddle, that runs through his letters from first to last; e.g., describing (at age eighteen) to his mother the varying impressions people have of him in the school at Nezhin, he concludes: "Consider me what you will, but only once I have embarked on my real career will you come to know my true character" (X, 123). Fourteen years later, already famous as the author of *Dead Souls* and all the other artistic work he was to publish in his lifetime, he wrote that only the completion of the epic work "taking form in me . . . will finally solve the riddle

of my existence" (XII, 58). To Zhukovsky, in June 1842, he makes the same point but stresses the amount of time required: "Purer than the mountain snows and brighter than the heavens must be my soul, and then only will I find the strength to commence my heroic deeds and my great calling [*poprishche*]—only then will the riddle of my existence be solved" (XII, 69).

Note: Here and wherever Gogol's writings are cited, reference is to N. V. Gogol', *Polnoe sobranie sochinenii*, 14 vols. (Leningrad: Akademiia nauk SSSR, 1937–52); roman numerals in the parenthetic references are to volume, arabic numerals to page number.

3. Viazemsky, quoted in N. Barsukov, *Zhizn' i trudy M. P. Pogodina*, 22 vols. (St. Petersburg, 1888–1910), VIII, 521. Andrei Belyi, "Gogol'," in his *Lug zelenyi* (Moscow, 1910), p. 95.

4. Roland Barthes, "The Death of the Author," in Sallie Sears and Georgianna W. Lord, eds., *The Discontinuous Universe: Selected Writings in Contemporary Consciousness* (New York, 1972), pp. 7–8.

5. Jorge Luis Borges, "For Bernard Shaw," in his *Other Inquisitions, 1937–1952* (New York, 1968), p. 163.

6. Osip Mandel'shtam, "Vypad," in his *Sobranie sochinenii v dvukh tomakh*, ed. G. P. Struve and B. A. Filippov (New York, 1964–66), II, 272.

7. Walter J. Ong, S.J., "The Writer's Audience Is Always a Fiction," *PMLA*, 90 (1975): 10–12.

8. A. I. Beletskii, "Ob odnoi iz ocherdenykh zadach istoriko-literaturnoi nauki (Izuchenie istorii chitatelia)," in his *Izbrannye trudy po teorii literatury* (Moscow, 1964), p. 27. N. A. Rubakin may be fairly represented in this connection by his *Etiudy o russkoi chitaiushchei publike: Fakty, tsifry, i nabiudeniia* (Studies of the Russian Reading Public: Facts, Figures, and Observations; St. Petersburg, 1895).

9. Victor Lange, "The Reader in the Strategy of Fiction," in Ronald G. Popperwell, ed., *Expression, Communication and Experience in Literature and Language: Proceedings of the XII Congress of the International Federation for Modern Languages and Literatures* (London, 1973), pp. 88–89; my italics. Cf. Wayne C. Booth, *The Rhetoric of Fiction* (Chicago, 1961); Michael Riffaterre, *Essais de stylistique structurale* (Paris, 1971); Wolfgang Iser, *The Implied Reader: Patterns of Communication in Prose Fiction from Bunyan to Beckett* (Baltimore, 1974).

10. Liane Norman, "Risk and Redundancy," *PMLA*, 90 (1975): 285.

11. See Harry Levin, "Notes on Convention," in his *Refractions* (New York, 1966), pp. 32–61.

12. Quoted and discussed by A. Nisin in his very useful book *La Littérature et le lecteur* (Paris, 1959), p. 63.

13. Stephen Gilman, "The Novelist and His Readers: Meditations on a Stendhalian Metaphor," in Charles S. Singleton, ed., *Interpretation: Theory and Practice* (Baltimore, 1969), pp. 157, 160.

14. Booth, p. 138.

15. Viktor Shklovskii defines a writer's relation to a tradition as "his dependence on a certain common store of literary norms, which, like the inventor's tradition, consists of the sum of the technical possibilities of his time." *O teorii prozy* (Moscow-Leningrad, 1925), p. 63. The Russian Formalists argued this point eloquently, but tended to leave it in the realm of theory. For some ventures in practical application, see Shklovskii's book and Boris Eikhenbaum, *Lermentov* (Leningrad, 1924).

16. See M. N. Kufaev, *Istoriia russkoi knigi v XIX veke* (Leningrad, 1927); M. V. Muratov, *Knizhnoe delo v Rossii* (Moscow-Leningrad, 1931); I. I. Zamotin, *Romantizm dvadtsatykh godov XIX stoletiia v russkoi literature* (St. Petersburg–Moscow, 1913), II, esp. 82–95; André Meynieux, *Pouchkine homme de lettres et la littérature professionnelle en Russie* (Paris, 1966).

17. A. S. Pushkin, "Ob al'manakh 'Severnaia Lira'," in his *Polnoe sobranie sochinenii v desiati tomakh* (Moscow-Leningrad, 1956–58), VII, 49.

18. Viazemsky, quoted in S. Balukhatyi, ed., *Russkie pisateli o literature* (Leningrad, 1939), I, 201.

19. Odoevsky, from an unfinished novel, quoted in P. N. Sakulin, *Iz istorii russkogo idealizma. Knjaz' V. F. Odoevskii* (Moscow, 1913), I, 250.

20. The phrase is Viazemsky's; quoted in Barsukov, III, 10.

21. Pogodin, letter of Jan. 20, 1832, quoted in Barsukov, IV, 6.

22. From a draft of "O dvizhenii zhurnal'noi literatury . . . ," VIII, 526.

23. See in Russian the voluminous but incomplete anthology of contemporary reviews compiled by V. Zelinskii, *Russkaia kriticheskaia literatura o proizvedeniiakh N. V. Gogolia*, 3 vols. (Moscow, 1900). In English see Paul Debreczeny, *Nikolai Gogol and His Contemporary Critics, Transactions of The American Philosophical Society*, vol. 56 (n.s.), part 3 (Philadelphia, 1966); and Robert A. Maguire, ed., *Gogol from the Twentieth Century* (Princeton, N.J., 1974).

24. The influence of Schelling is invoked by Annenkov; because of it, he says, Belinsky could find Hoffman's work comparable to that of Shakespeare and Goethe. At the heart of Belinsky's Schellingism he finds a belief that "the external world is a participant in the great evolutions of the Absolute Idea, expressing in each of its phenomena the particular moment and stage of [the Idea's] development. Hence the fantastic element of Hoffmann's stories seemed to Belinsky a particle of the revelation or exposure of this all-creating Absolute Idea, and had for him the same reality as, for example, a true depiction of character or the conveying of any incident from life." P. V. Annenkov, "Zamechatel'noe desiatiletie," in his *Literaturnye vospominaniia* (Leningrad, 1928), p. 189. This work is available in English as *The Extraordinary Decade*, ed. Arthur P. Mendel (Ann Arbor, Mich., 1968); see chap. 3.

25. V. G. Belinskii, "O russkoi povesti i povestiakh g. Gogolia," in his

Estetika i literaturnaia kritika v dvukh tomakh (Moscow, 1959), I, 155.

26. Annenkov, pp. 368–69. See, for more detail, chap. 22 of "Zamechatel'noe desiatiletie" (*The Extraordinary Decade*).

27. V. I. Shenrok, *Materialy dlia biografii N. V. Gogolia*, vols. 1–4 (Moscow, 1892–98); L. Lanskii, ed., "Gogol' v neizdannoi perepiske sovremennikov (1833–1853)," in *Literaturnoe nasledstvo*, vol. 58 (Moscow, 1952), pp. 533–772.

28. D. N. Ovsianiko-Kulikovskii, " 'Liudi 40-x godov' i Gogol,' " in his *Istoriia russkoi intelligentsii* (Moscow, 1908), I, 205–33.

29. Quoted in Kufaev, p. 103.

30. M. I. Sukhomlinov, "Poiavlenie v pechati sochinenii Gogolia," in his *Issledovaniia i stat'i po russkoi literature i prosveshcheniiu* (St. Petersburg, 1889), II, 305–6. A similar argument is made in the opening pages of Nikolai V. Drizen, *Dramaticheskaia tsenzura dvukh epokh* (Petrograd, [1917]). For a useful bibliography of works on the prerevolutionary censorship, see Martin Dewhirst and Robert Farrell, eds., *The Soviet Censorship* (Metuchen, N.J., 1973), pp. ii–iii.

31. Quoted in Barsukov, VI, 44–45.

32. *Ibid.*, p. 47.

33. A. S. Nikolaev and Iu. G. Oksman, eds., *Literaturnyi muzeum* (Petersburg, 1922), I, 96.

34. *Ibid.*

35. Pletnev, journal entry of Nov. 2, 1842, in *Perepiska Ia. K. Grota s P. A. Pletnevym* (St. Petersburg, 1896), I, 634. Nikitenko's letter to Gogol is published in *Russkaia starina*, no. 8, 1889, pp. 384–85.

36. A. V. Nikitenko, *Dnevnik v trekh tomakh* (Leningrad, 1955–56), I, 95.

37. George Steiner, "Under Eastern Eyes," *The New Yorker*, Oct. 11, 1976, p. 159.

38. Vicomte E.-M. de Vogüé, *Le Roman russe*, 4th ed. (Paris, 1897), p. xi.

39. Annenkov, letter to Stasiulevich, 1874, quoted by Eikhenbaum in his prefatory article to Annenkov, *Literaturnye vospominaniia*, p. xx.

40. The best discussions of the derivative and fashionable elements in these stories are by Vasilii Gippius: "*Vechera na khutore bliz Dikan'ki* Gogolia," in Akademiia nauk SSSR, Institut literatury (Pushkinskii dom), *Trudy Otdela novoi russkoi literatury*, I (Moscow-Leningrad, 1948), 9–38; and chap. 2 of his *Gogol'* (Leningrad, 1924).

41. As such it has proved particularly inviting to psychoanalytic interpretation. See, in this regard, Hugh McLean, "Gogol's Retreat from Love: Towards an Interpretation of *Mirgorod*," in *American Contributions to the Fourth International Congress of Slavists* (The Hague, 1958), pp. 225–45; and F. C. Driessen, *Gogol as a Short-Story Writer* (The Hague, 1965). Cf. Simon Karlinsky, *The Sexual Labyrinth of Nikolai Gogol* (Cambridge, Mass., 1976), pp. 59ff.

42. P. M——skii [Iurkevich], *Severnaia pchela*, no. 115, 1835, reprinted in Zelinskii, I, 58.

43. K. Mochul'skii, *Dukhovnyi put' Gogolia* (Paris, 1934), p. 43. Cf. Viacheslav Ivanov, "Gogol's *Inspector General* and the Comedy of Aristophanes," in Maguire, p. 201.

44. Eikhenbaum, "How Gogol's 'Overcoat' Is Made," in Maguire, pp. 267–92.

45. Annenkov, p. 380.

46. L. N. Tolstoi, *Polnoe sobranie sochinenii*, Iubileinoe izdanie (Moscow, 1935–58), XXVI, 874.

47. Mandel'shtam, "O sobesednike," in his *Sobranie sochinenii*, II, 282.

48. "Boris Pasternak o sebe i o chitateliakh," *Grani*, 53 (1963): 79.

49. Norman N. Holland, "Unity, Identity, Text, Self," *PMLA*, 90 (1975): 821.

Readers and Reading at the End of the Tsarist Era

1. *Russkie vedomosti*, nos. 122, 130, and 133, 1887, reprinted in *Sbornik materialov k izucheniiu istorii russkoi zhurnalistiki*, vyp. III (Moscow, 1956), pp. 119–33.

2. *Obshchii svod po imperii rezul'tatov razrabotki dannykh pervoi vseobshchei perepisi naseleniia, proizvedennoi 28 Ianvaria 1897 goda*, I (St. Petersburg, 1905), 188–89, 190–95, 198.

3. L. K. Erman, *Intelligentsiia v pervoi russkoi revoliutsii* (Moscow, 1966), pp. 9–14. Using his figures, I have included the following in the nearly 370,000: rail and post employees; elected representatives and employees of zemstvo, city, and gentry institutions; and those engaged in education, medicine, and the arts.

4. See P. Sakulin, "V poiskakh nauchnoi metodologii," *Golos minuvshago*, nos. 1–4, 1919, pp. 5–37, for a discussion of early histories of Russian literature.

5. Victor Terras, *Belinskij and Russian Literary Criticism: The Heritage of Organic Aesthetics* (Madison, Wis., 1974).

6. P. Miliukov, *Ocherki po istorii russkoi kultury*, part I (St. Petersburg, 1896), p. 3.

7. Iu. Martov, *Obshchestvennye i umstvennye techeniia v. Rossii, 1870–1905 godakh* (Moscow-Leningrad, 1924), p. 17.

8. N. K. Mikhailovskii, *Literaturnyia vospominaniia i sovremennaia smuta* (St. Petersburg, 1900), I, 159; reprinted from *Russkoe bogatstvo*. For a discussion of Mikhailovsky's ideas and subjective sociology, see Alexander Vucinich, *Social Thought in Tsarist Russia: The Quest for a General Science of Society, 1861–1917* (Chicago, 1976).

9. V.V. [V. P. Vorontsov], *Nashi napravleniia* (St. Petersburg, 1893), p. 63.

10. A. N. Pypin, *Istoriia russkoi literatury*, IV (St. Petersburg, 1903), 588; reprinted from *Vestnik Evropy*. For a critique of narodnik views of

culture, see Pypin, "Narodnaia gramotnost'," *Vestnik Evropy*, no. 1, 1891.

11. *Literaturnyi arkhiv materialy po istorii literatury i obshchestvennogo dvizheniia*, no. 5 (Moscow-Leningrad, 1960), p. 67.

12. *Niva*, no. 53, 1894, pp. 22–23.

13. *Ezhemesiachye literaturnye i populiarno-nauchnye prilozheniia*, no. 2, 1897, p. 178.

14. *Ibid.*, no. 1, 1899, p. 639.

15. *Knizhnyi vestnik*, no. 6, 1903, p. 180.

16. M. M. Lederle, *Mneniia russkikh liudei o luchshikh knigakh dlia chteniia* (St. Petersburg, 1895), pp. 41, 119, 104, 109.

17. Archive N. A. Rubakin, Manuscript Section of GBL f 358, k. 12, ed. kh. 17. Rubakin's calculations.

18. *Ibid.*

19. These and all subsequent figures for the size of book editions, unless otherwise noted, are calculated from figures published by Glavnoe Upravlenie po delam Pechati; before 1907 these appear in the yearly *Spisok knig, vyshedshikh v Rossii* (1884–1907), and starting in June 1907 in *Knizhnaia letopis'*.

20. See, for example, Nestor Kotliarevskii, *Mirovaia skorb' v kontse XVIII i v nachale XIX veka* (St. Petersburg, 1914); V. D. Spasivich, "D. S. Merezhkovskii i ego 'vechnye sputniki,'" *Vestnik Evropy*, no. 6, 1897; Vl. Solov'ev, "Pervyi shag k polozhitel'noi estetike," *Vestnik Evropy*, no. 1, 1894.

21. See *Vestnik Partii Narodnoi Svobody*, no. 31–32, Aug. 16, 1907, pp. 1507–8, and no. 19, May 17, 1907, pp. 1170–73.

22. *Rech'*, Dec. 3, 1906.

23. *Ibid.*, Jan. 27, 1907; Dec. 16, 1907; Aug. 30, 1907.

24. *Ibid.*, Dec. 16, 1907.

25. *Ibid.*, July 1, 1907. For Chukovsky's response to modernism see Jeffrey Brooks, "The Young Kornei Chukovskii (1905–14): A Liberal Critic in Search of Cultural Unity," *Russian Review*, Jan. 1974, pp. 50–62.

26. Gredeskul, "Obshchestvo, reaktsiia i narod," *Zarnitsy*, no. 2 (St. Petersburg, 1909), pp. 6–7.

27. *Rech'*, Jan. 20, 1908.

28. *Ibid.*, Nov. 17, 1908; see also Blok's essay, *ibid.*, Oct. 27, 1908.

29. V. Briusov, *Dnevniki* (Moscow, 1927), p. 141.

30. See the symposiums *Kuda my idem?* (Moscow, 1910) and *Intelligentsiia v Rossii* (St. Petersburg, 1910).

31. See Jeffrey Brooks, "*Vekhi* and the *Vekhi* Dispute," *Survey*, 86, no. 1 (1973): 21–50.

32. *Kuda my idem?*, pp. 155–56.

33. *Literaturnyi arkhiv*, p. 277, in a letter to Struve dated Sept. 8, 1910; *ibid.*, p. 285, in a letter dated Sept. 21, 1910.

34. *Russkaia mysl'*, no. 9, 1907, p. 172. See Aikhenval'd's *Etiudy o*

zapadnykh pisateliakh (Moscow, 1910), pp. 217–23, and *Slovo o slovakh* (Petrograd, 1916), pp. 5–24, for a statement of his aesthetic views.

35. *Russkaia mysl'*, no. 9, 1907, p. 172, and no. 1, 1907, p. 226; *Siluety russkikh pisatelei*, vyp. I (Moscow, 1908), p. 256.

36. Aikhenval'd, *Pushkin* (Moscow, 1908), p. 142.

37. *Ibid.*

38. Aikhenval'd, *V sporakh o teatre* (Moscow, 1913), p. 36, and *Etiudy o zapadnykh pisateliakh*, p. 221. See also his *Spor o Belinskom* (Moscow, 1914).

39. *Russkaia mysl'*, no. 1, 1908, p. 184.

40. See Vengerov's *Ocherki po istorii russkoi literatury* (St. Petersburg, 1907).

41. *Rech'*, Oct. 4, 1910.

42. *Intelligentsiia v Rossii*, p. 197. See also Ovsianiko-Kulikovskii's articles in *Rech'*, April 1, 1910; March 28, May 30, Oct. 16, 1911; April 28, 1912.

43. S. A. Vengerov, *Russkaia literatura XX veka: 1890–1910*, I (Moscow, 1914), 12.

44. *Ibid.*, II, part 1 (Moscow, 1915), 215.

45. *Ibid.*, I, 32–33.

46. Printed in *Osnovnyia cherty istorii noveishei russkoi literatury* (St. Petersburg, 1909), pp. 46–47, 55.

47. *Kuda my idem?*, pp. 22–24.

48. *Literaturnyi arkhiv*, p. 277.

49. *Vesy*, Dec. 1909, pp. 185–92.

50. V. Briusov, *Sobranie sochinenii*, IV (Moscow, 1974), 7–10.

51. *Letopis' zhizni i tvorchestva A. M. Gor'kogo*, vyp. I, 1868–1907 (Moscow, 1958), p. 461.

52. *Izvestiia knizhnykh magazinov t-va M. O. Vol'f*, no. 4, 1912, p. 92, and no. 9, 1912, pp. 138–39.

53. *Intelligentsiia v Rossii*, p. 191.

54. *Russkie vedomosti*, Jan. 1, 1910.

55. *Rech'*, Nov. 8, 1910; Korolenko, *ibid.*; Merezhkovskii, *ibid.*, Nov. 9, 1910.

56. *Izvestiia . . . t-va M. O. Vol'f*, no. 7, 1915, p. 105; see also no. 3, 1916, pp. 94–97. For a discussion of their Western European counterparts, see Edward R. Tannenbaum, *1900: The Generation Before the Great War* (Garden City, N.Y., 1976).

57. Verbitskaia describes her first success in the preface to *Kryl'ia vzmakhnuli!* (Moscow, 1918) and her publishing venture in her preface to Leona Frap'e, *Ogon'ki* (Moscow, 1911). For a description of her audience, see V. Dadonov, *A. Verbitskaia i eia romany Kliuchi schast'ia i Dukh vremeni* (Moscow, 1911), pp. 47–49.

58. *Russkie vedomosti 1863–1913 sbornik statei* (Moscow, 1913), pp. 113–27.

59. *Rech'*, March 11, 1909; Miliukov was replying to an article by P. B. Struve in *Slovo*, March 10, 1909.

60. *Rech'*, Dec. 22, 1913; the story being reviewed was by Iv. Shmelev.

61. L. N. Tolstoy, "Predislovie k istorii Matveia," in *Polnoe sobranie sochinenii*, VIII (Moscow, 1936), 362–64.

62. I. M. Bogdanov, *Gramotnost' i obrazovanie v dorevoliutsionnoi Rossii i v SSSR* (Moscow, 1964), p. 9.

63. These and the following statistics are computed from *Obshchii svod po imperii*, I, 38–39, 56–66, 190–95; *Pervaia vseobshchaia perepis' naseleniia rossiiskoi imperii, 1897, g.*, vol. 37, 1903, p. 61, and vol. 24, 1905, p. 67.

64. D. Rovinskii, *Russkiia narodnyia kartinki*, I (St. Petersburg, 1881), pp. ii–iii.

65. I. M. Snegirov, *Lubochnyia kartinki russkago naroda v moskovskom mire* (Moscow, 1861), p. 19.

66. Iv. Ivin, "O narodno-lubochnoi literature. K voprosu o tom, chto chitaet narod (Iz nabliudenii krest'ianina nad chteniem v derevne)," *Russkoe obozrenie*, Sept. 1893, p. 258.

67. For Gubanov and Morozov see A. S. Prugavin, *Zaprosy naroda i obiazannosti intelligentsii v oblasti prosveshcheniia i vospitaniia* (St. Petersburg, 1895), pp. 284–88. For Sytin see A. Z. Okorokov, ed., *Zhizn' dlia knigi* (Moscow, 1962), pp. 17–33; and *Polveka dlia knigi, 1866–1916, literaturno-khudozhestvennyi sbornik posviashchennyi piatidesiatiletiiu izdatel'skoi deiatel'nosti I. D. Sytina* (Moscow, 1916), pp. 11–28.

68. I. A. Golyshev, "Kartinnoe i knizhnoe narodnoe proizvodstvo i torgovlia," *Russkaia starina*, March 1886, pp. 679–726. N. A. Rubakin, "Kakimi sposobami rasprostraniat knigi na Rusi," *Obrazovanie*, 1901, no. 1, pp. 86–99; no. 2, pp. 82–99; no. 3, pp. 20–31. Prugavin, *Zaprosy naroda*, pp. 302–47.

69. Rubakin, in *Obrazovanie*, no. 3, 1901, p. 21.

70. *Polveka dlia knigi*, p. 17.

71. See N. Bunakov, *O domashnikh shkolakh gramotnosti v narode* (St. Petersburg, 1885); N .V. Chekhov, *Tipy russkoi shkoly v ikh istoricheskom razvitii* (Moscow, 1923), p. 35; and Prugavin, *Zaprosy naroda*, pp 1–85.

72. N. P. Malinovskii, "Nekotorye vyvody po dannym shkol'noi perepisi 1911 g.," *Russkaia shkola*, no. 5–6, 1911, pp. 78–79; *Ezhegodnik Rossii 1908 g.*, Tsentral'nyi statisticheskii komitet, M.V.D. (St. Petersburg, 1909), p. cxii.

73. I. P. Bogolepov, *Gramotnost' sredi detei shkol'nago vozrasta v moskovskom i mozhaiskom uezdakh moskovskoi gubernii* (Moscow, 1894), pp. 44–45, 77.

74. Malinovskii, pp. 90–91.

75. The figures on primary schools in the empire in 1911 are from

Odnodnevnaia perepis' nachal'nykh shkol v imperii, vyp. XVI, chast' 2 (Petrograd, 1915), pp. 2–3.

76. *Ibid.,* vyp. XVI (Petrograd, 1916), p. 95.

77. *Pervyi obshchezemskii s'ezd po nachalnomu obrazovaniiu 1911 goda — materialy k s'ezdu* (Moscow, 1911), pp. 164–65.

78. *Odnodnevnaia perepis',* vyp. XVI, chast' 2, p. iv.

79. E. N. Medynskii, *Vneshkol'noe obrazovanie, ego znachenie, organizatsiia i tekhnika* (Moscow, 1916), p. 69.

80. *Ibid.,* pp. 178–87.

81. *Ibid.,* pp. 215–17.

82. The complete list is reprinted in Prugavin, *Zaprosy naroda,* pp. 523–32.

83. Archive N. A. Rubakin, GBL f 358, k. 5, ed. kh. 26, 27. Hereafter cited as Rubakin archive.

84. *Odnodnevnaia perepis',* vyp. XVI, chast' 2, pp. 2–3.

85. See V. G. Bazanov, *Russkie revoliutsionnye demokraty i narodoznanie* (Leningrad, 1974), for a full discussion of narodnik propaganda (p. 500 refers to the cigar wrappers). Evgeniia Taratuta, *S. M. Stepniak-Kravchinskii revoliutsioner i pisatel'* (Moscow, 1973), p. 107. See also V. G. Bazanov, ed., *Agitatsionnaia literatura russkikh revoliutsionnykh narodnikov* (Leningrad, 1970), for a collection of narodnik writings.

86. Rubakin, "Knizhnyi potok," *Russkaia mysl',* no. 3, 1903, p. 20.

87. *Knizhnyi vestnik,* no. 33, 1909, p. 386.

88. *Ibid.,* nos. 25–26, 1915, pp. 5–6; Bobylev, "Kniga i eia kul'turnaia rol' v derevne," *Sbornik permskago zemstva,* nos. 5–6, 1895 (Perm, 1896), p. 121.

89. B. Aref'ev, "Chitatel' narodnoi gazety," *Russkoe bogatstvo,* no. 12, 1898, pp. 26–33, compares the success of *Sel'skii vestnik* among peasants with the failure of a paper published by the Viatka zemstvo.

90. Rubakin, "Knizhnyi potok," *Russkaia mysl',* no. 12, 1903, p. 177.

91. D. D. Protopopov, *Istoriia S. Petersburgskaia komiteta gramotnosti* (St. Petersburg, 1898), pp. 229, 245.

92. Rubakin archive, k. 6, ed. kh. 15, 16; k. 5, ed. kh. 23.

93. *Polveka dlia knigi,* p. 115.

94. E. Nekrasova, *Narodnyia knigi dlia chteniia v ikh 25-letnei bor'be s lubochnymi izdaniiami* (Viatka, 1902), pp. 60–61.

95. G. Iakovlev, "Kakoiu dolzhna byt' krest'ianskaia kniga?," *Nabliudatel',* no. 7, July 1892, p. 53.

96. *Zadachi redaktsii posrednika* (Moscow, 1894), pp. 5–6.

97. V. N. Marakuev, *Chto chital i chitaet russkii narod* (Moscow, 1886), p. 3.

98. Protopopov, p. 226.

99. *Knizhnyi vestnik,* no. 38, 1904.

100. *Ibid.,* no. 42, 1906, p. 1014.

101. *Ibid.,* no. 26, 1909, pp. 316–17.

102. *Vystavka proizvedenii pechati za 1909 god ustroennaia glavnym upravleniem po delam pechati 1910 g.* (St. Petersburg, 1911), p. 16.

103. D. I. Shakhovskoi, "K voprosu o knigakh dlia naroda," *Russkii nachaľnyi uchiteľ*, no. 3, 1885, pp. 163–70; A. S. Prugavin, *Programma dlia sobiraniia svedenii o tom, chto chitaet narod?* (Moscow, 1888), and *Programma dlia sobiraniia svedenii o tom, chto chitaet narod i kak on otnositsia k shkole i knige* (Moscow, 1891); N. A. Rubakin, *Opyt programmy izledovaniia literatury dlia naroda* (St. Petersburg, 1889). Shakhovskoi's survey is discussed in B. V. Bank, *Izuchenie chitatelei v Rossii (XIX v.)* (Moscow, 1969), which includes an account of other similar activities and a bibliography on this subject.

104. S. A. An-skii [Rappoport], *Narod i kniga*, 2d ed. (Moscow, 1913), pp. 67–68.

105. N. A. Rubakin, *Etiudy o russkoi chitaiushchei publike* (St. Petersburg, 1895), p. 152.

106. The peasants' comments are from, respectively, Rubakin archive, k. 5, ed. kh. 1; k. 6, ed. kh. 3; k. 6, ed. kh. 18; and N. Etrinskii, "Pushkin i chitateľ iz naroda," *Obrazovanie*, no. 1, 1900, p. 82.

107. *Trudy s'ezda russkikh deiatelei po tekhnicheskomu i professionaľnomu obrazovaniiu v Rossii, 5 otdeleniia* (St. Petersburg, 1890), p. 3.

108. Rubakin, *Etiudy*, p. 157.

109. Aref'ev, p. 20.

110. Etrinskii, p. 81.

111. An-skii, *Narod i kniga* (Moscow, 1894), p. 137; A. Smirnov, "Chto chitaiut v derevne," *Russkaia mysľ*, no. 7, 1903, pp. 108–12; *Statisticheskii ezhegodnik poltavskago gubernskago zemstva na 1903 god* (Poltava, 1904), p. 143.

112. Rubakin archive, k. 6, ed. kh. 16.

113. V. P. Vakhterov, *Vneshkoľnoe obrazovanie naroda* (Moscow, 1896), pp. 39–42.

114. *Sbornik statisticheskikh svedenii po moskovskoi gubernii*, IX (Moscow, 1884), 144–45.

115. Vladislov Evgen'ev-Maksimov, *Ocherki po istorii obshchestvennykh rabot v Rossii* (St. Petersburg, 1905), pp. 180–81.

116. Nekrasova, p. 77.

117. Rubakin, *Etiudy*, p. 162.

118. Rubakin archive, k. 6, ed. kh. 18.

119. *Ibid.*, k. 5, ed. kh. 26.

120. *Ibid.*, ed. kh. 27.

121. *Ibid.*, k. 13, ed. kh. 6.

122. K. D. Alchevskaia, ed., *Chto chitať narodu*, vol. I (St. Petersburg, 1884), otdel 2, pp. 50–51.

123. *Ibid.*, pp. 28–29.

124. An-skii, 1913, pp. 136–37.

125. Alchevskaia, III (Moscow, 1906), 189–90.

126. V. V. Petrov, ed., *Voprosy narodnogo obrazovaniia v moskovskoi gubernii*, vyp. I (Moscow, 1897), p. 119.

127. An-skii, 1913, pp. 78–79.

128. Alchevskaia, vol. I, otdel 2, pp. 55, 57.

129. *Ibid.*, p. 23.

130. An-skii, 1913, p. 80.

131. A. Meromskii and P. Putnik, *Derevnia za knigoi* (Moscow, 1931), p. 168.

132. Rubakin archive, k. 20, ed. kh. 4.

133. Quoted in L. Kleinbort, "K kharakteristike chitatelia iz naroda," *Vestnik znaniia*, no. 1, 1903, p. 143.

134. *Knizhnyi vestnik*, no. 35, 1904, p. 995.

135. An-skii, 1913, pp. 151–52.

136. Etrinskii, p. 89.

137. An-skii, 1913, pp. 154–55.

138. Rubakin archive, k. 6, ed. kh. 19.

139. *Ibid.*, k. 274, ed. kh. 41.

140. *Ibid.*, k. 7, ed. kh. 13.

141. Kh. Podborovskii, "Voprosy russko-iaponskoi voiny v sovremennoi derevne," *Vestnik znaniia*, no. 11, 1904, p. 107.

142. Rubakin archive, k. 7, ed. kh. 12.

143. N. A. Rubakin, "Knizhnyi priliv i knizhnyi otliv," *Sovremennyi mir*, no. 12, 1909, pp. 13–14.

144. M. I. Slukhovskii, *Kniga i derevnia* (Moscow-Leningrad, 1928), pp. 38–41.

145. See Ivin's article in *Russkoe obozrenie*, 1893, no. 9, pp. 242–60, and no. 10, pp. 768–85.

146. N. Kin, "Krest'iane bibliotekari," *Obrazovanie*, no. 1, 1900, p. 72.

147. *Ibid.*, p. 77.

148. For a recent discussion of the structure of Russian cities, see L. M. Ivanov, "O soslovno-klassovoi strukture gorodov kapitalisticheskoi Rossii," in *Problemy sotsial'no-ekonomicheskoi istorii Rossii* (Moscow, 1971).

149. A. G. Rashin, *Formirovanie rabochego klassa Rossii* (Moscow, 1958), p. 584.

150. An-skii, 1913, p. 69.

151. S. Gorianskaia, "Pervyia bezplatnyia gorodskiia chital'ni v S. Peterburge," *Russkaia mysl'*, no. 10, 1889, pp. 90, 93.

152. Rubakin, *Etiudy*, p. 193.

153. An-skii, 1913, p. 69.

154. Rubakin archive, k. 14, ed. kh. 4.

155. *Ibid.*, k. 258, ed. kh. 45, pp. 2–3.

156. Alchevskaia, II (Moscow, 1889), 70–71, 79–80.

157. An-skii, 1913, p. 85.

158. Rubakin archive, k. 12, ed. kh. 4.

159. *Ibid.*, k. 14, ed. kh. 6.

160. An-skii, 1913, pp. 89–90.

161. Alchevskaia, III (Moscow, 1906), 192.

162. I. V. Babushkin, *Vospominaniia 1893–1900* (Leningrad, 1925), pp. 172–75.

163. *Ezhegodnik vneshkol'nago obrazovaniia* (St. Petersburg, 1910), pp. 281–82.

164. *Obshchii svod po imperii*, I, 39, 56–58. See also G. Guroff and S. F. Starr, "A Note on Urban Literacy in Russia, 1890–1914," *Jahrbücher für Geschichte Osteuropas*, Dec. 1971, pp. 520–31.

165. *Pervaia vseobshchaia perepis'*, vol. 37, 1903, p. 61, and vol. 24, 1905, p. 67.

166. *S. Petersburg po perepisi 15 Dekabria 1900 goda — naselenie*, vyp. I (St. Petersburg, 1903), pp. 60–69. *Petrograd po perepisi 15 Dekabria 1910 goda — naselenie*, chast' 1 (Petrograd, n.d.), pp. 36–51.

167. S. Grigor'ev, "Narodnoe obrazovanie i gramotnost' v Petrograde i Moskve," *Izvestiia petrogradskoi gorodskoi dumy*, Jan.–Feb. 1917, p. 10. See also Robert Eugene Johnson, "Peasant Migration and the Russian Working Class: Moscow at the End of the Nineteenth Century," *Slavic Review*, Dec. 1976. He explains the youthfulness of Moscow's peasant population by the return of older peasant workers to their villages.

168. *Petrograd po perepisi . . . 1910*, chast' 1, pp. 36–51. The census lists the population in five-year age groups, which are further broken down into those native and those nonnative to the city. The immigrants are also divided by date of arrival into five-year groups. My estimate is approximate and probably biased downward. One can identify those who arrived between 1906 and 1909 and gave their ages as sixteen to twenty at the time of the 1910 census as being twelve or older when they arrived. I have included this group in my calculation. However, there were also some twelve-year-olds among those who gave their age as eleven to fifteen at the time of the census and their year of arrival as 1906 to 1909. I have excluded this group from my calculation since their ages at the time of arrival ranged from seven to fourteen, and some of them could have learned to read at a city school. The high rate of literacy among new arrivals seems to suggest that literate peasants were more likely to leave their villages and settle in the city than were the nonliterate.

169. *Obshchii svod po imperii*, I, 188–89.

170. *Pervaia vseobshchaia perepis'*, vol. 37, 1903, p. 61, and vol. 24, 1905, p. 67.

171. "Nat Pinkerton o sebe," *Sinii zhurnal*, no. 42, Oct. 18, 1913.

172. *Knizhnaia letopis'*, no. 14, Oct. 13, 1907, p. 5.

173. *Vystavka proizvedenii pechati za 1909 god*, p. 18. In the *Ukazatel'* to *Knizhnaia letopis'*, detective adventures published in the year are listed by hero. See the volume for 1909, pp. 205–6.

174. *Moskovskaia kopeika*, no. 1, 1909.

175. *Ibid.*, no. 59, 1909.

176. A. Z. Okorokov, *Oktiabr' i krakh russkoi burzhuaznoi pressy* (Moscow, 1970), p. 55.

177. Moscow city council, quoted in P. Zhulev, "Sovremennyi chitatel' iz naroda," *Russkaia shkola*, no. 9, 1912, p. 6; V. I. Lenin, *Sochineniia*, XVIII (Moscow, 1953), 180; Dem'ian Bednyi, *Sobranie sochinenii*, I (Moscow, 1963), 82, 224; L. M. Kleinbort, *Ocherki rabochei intelligentsii*, I (Petrograd, 1923), 13.

178. All figures on the size of editions are derived from respective listings in *Knizhnaia letopis'*, unless otherwise noted.

Pisarev and the Transformation of Two Russian Novels

1. Oscar Wilde, "The Decay of Lying," in *The Artist as Critic: Critical Writings of Oscar Wilde* (New York, 1969), p. 79.

2. See his *Esteticheskie otnosheniia iskusstva k deistvitel'nosti* (Moscow, 1955), pp. 108–20.

3. See, for instance, Ralph Matlaw, "Turgenev's Novels: Civic Responsibility and Literary Predilection," *Harvard Slavic Studies*, 4 (1957): 249–62.

4. Leonid Grossman, *Portret Manon Lescaut* (Moscow, 1922); V. Gippius, in *Venok Turgenevu: 1818–1918* (Odessa, 1918); Richard Freeborn, *Turgenev, the Novelist's Novelist: A Study* (Oxford, 1960); Virginia Burns, "The Structure of the Plot in *Otsy i Deti*," *Russian Literature*, no. 6, 1974, pp. 33–55.

5. A good selection of Turgenev's statements is to be found in *Fathers and Sons*, ed. Ralph E. Matlaw (New York: Norton, 1966).

6. M. Bakhtin, *Problemy poetiki Dostoevskogo* (Moscow, 1963), pp. 5–62.

7. Jan M. Meijer, "Dostoevsky and Russian Realism," *Russian Literature*, no. 4, 1973, p. 11.

8. A. Solzhenitsyn, *Bodalsia telenok s dubom* (Paris, 1975), p. 336.

9. D. I. Pisarev, *Sochineniia v chetyrekh tomakh* (Moscow, 1955–56), I, 192–93. This edition will hereafter be cited in parentheses in the text; roman numerals refer to volume, arabic numerals to page number.

10. For a discussion of this phenomenon, see Isaiah Berlin, *Fathers and Children: The Romanes Lecture* (Oxford, 1972), pp. 31–32.

11. Henry James, "The Art of Fiction," in *The Portable Henry James* (New York, 1968), p. 397.

12. Rufus W. Mathewson, Jr., *The Positive Hero in Russian Literature*, 2d ed., rev. (Stanford, Calif., 1975), p. 90.

13. *Sovremennik*, no. 3, 1862.

14. V. Zelinskii, ed., *Kriticheskie razbory romana I. S. Turgeneva Otsy i deti*, 2d ed. (Moscow: I. I. Pashkov, 1907), p. 20.

15. Aleksandr Herzen, *Sobranie sochinenii v tridtsati tomakh* (Moscow: Akademiia nauk SSSR, 1954–66), XX, 336.

16. *Ibid.*, p. 337.

17. Turgenev, *Polnoe sobranie sochinenii i pisem* (Moscow-Leningrad, 1960–68), VIII, 325.

18. See A. Coquart, *Dmitri Pisarev et le nihilisme russe* (Paris, 1946), pp. 360–61.

19. The paragraph is given in D. I. Pisarev, *Izbrannye sochineniia*, ed. V. Ja. Kirpotin (Moscow, 1934–35), II, 613.

20. *Sochineniia D. I. Pisareva*, ed. F. F. Pavlenkov (St. Petersburg, 1866–69).

21. Evidence on the background of Pisarev's article is given in A. Volodin, "Raskolnikov i Karakozov (k tvorcheskoi istorii stat'i D. Pisareva 'Bor'ba za zhizn')," *Novyi mir*, no. 11, 1969, pp. 212–32.

22. Jan Mukařovsky, *Aesthetic Function, Norm and Value as Social Facts* (Prague, 1936; reprint, Ann Arbor, 1970), p. 75.

The Rhetoric of an Ideological Novel

1. *The Grand Inquisitor*, trans. S. S. Koteliansky, with an introduction by D. H. Lawrence (London, 1930), p. iv.

2. See, e.g., Lawrence's study of Thomas Hardy in his *Selected Literary Criticism*, ed. Anthony Beal (London, 1956), p. 189.

3. F. M. Dostoevskii, *Pis'ma*, vol. IV, *1878–1881*, ed. A. S. Dolinin (Moscow, 1951), p. 53.

4. V. V. Rozanov, *Legenda o velikom inkvizitore F. M. Dostoevskogo, opyt kriticheskogo kommentariia* (St. Petersburg, 1906), p. 69.

5. A. Rammelmeyer, "Dostejevskijs Begegnung mit Belinskij (Zur Deutung der Gedankenwelt Ivan Karamazovs)," *Zeitschrift für slavische Philologie*, band XXI (Heidelberg, 1952), pp. 1–22, 273–92.

6. Nikolai Fedorovich Bel'chikov, *Dostoevskii v processe petrashevtsev* (Moscow, 1936).

7. A. A. Golenishchev-Kutuzov, "Rasskaz A. N. Maikova o F. M. Dostoevskom i petrashevtsakh," *Istoricheskii Arkhiv*, no. 3, 1956, pp. 222–26.

8. V. E. Vetlovskaia, "Ritorika i poetika," in *Issledovaniia po poezii i stilistike* (Leningrad, 1972), pp. 163–84.

9. Maximilian Rudwin, *The Devil in Legend and Literature* (La Salle, Ill., 1973), pp. 15ff.

10. F. M. Dostoevskii, *Sobranie sochinenii* (Moscow, 1956–58), IX, 34. This edition will hereafter be cited in parentheses in the text; roman numerals refer to volume, arabic numerals to page number.

11. D. V. Averkiev, "Likho," *Ogonek*, no. 5, 1880, p. 97.

12. E. Drougard, "La Legende du Grand Inquisiteur et le Christ au Vatican," *Revue des études slaves*, 14 (1934): 224–27.

13. L. M. Rozenblium, "Tvorcheskaia laboritoriia Dostoevskogo-romanista," in *F. M. Dostoevskii v rabote nad romanom Podrostok, Literaturnoe nasledstvo*, vol. 77 (1965), pp. 39ff.

14. *F. M. Dostoevskii, materialy i issledovaniia*, ed. A. S. Dolinin (Leningrad, 1935), p. 84.

15. Robert Belknap, "The Origins of Aleša Karamazov," in *American Contributions to the Sixth International Congress of Slavists, Prague, 1963, August 7–13*, vol. II, *Literary Contributions*, ed. William E. Harkins (The Hague, 1968).

16. Solomon Samoilovich Borshchevskii, *Shchedrin i Dostoevskii: istoriia ikh ideinoi bor'by* (Moscow, 1956).

17. V. S. Dorovatovskaia-Liubimova, "Dostoevskii i shestidesiatniki," in *Dostoevskii: sbornik statei*, Trudy Gosudarstvennoi Akademii nauk, Literaturnaia sektsiia, vyp. 3 (Moscow, 1928), pp. 5–61.

18. Nikolai Leskov, *Polnoe sobranie sochinenii* (Moscow, 1957), III, 363.

19. Dorovatovskaia-Liubimova.

20. Ballin to Dostoevsky, Dec. 19, 1876, IRLI (Pushkinskii Dom) Fond 100, 29643, CCXI b 2.

21. Dostoevskii, *Pis'ma*, IV, 26.

22. Stanley Fish, *Surprised by Sin: The Reader in "Paradise Lost"* (New York, 1967).

Eugene Onegin: "Life's Novel"

Chapter epigraph. Elizabeth Burns, *Theatricality: A Study of Convention in the Theatre and in Social Life* (New York, 1972), p. 126.

1. Information on these developments may be found in S. Ia. Gessen, *Knigoizdatel' A. S. Pushkin* (Leningrad, 1930); T. Grits, V. Trenin, and M. Nikitin, in V. B. Shklovskii and B. M. Eikhenbaum, eds., *Slovesnost' i kommertsiia (knizhnaia lavka A. F. Smirdina)* (Moscow, 1929); A. Meynieux, *La Littérature et le métier d'écrivain en Russie avant Pouchkine* (Paris, 1966) and *Pouchkine homme de lettres et la littérature professionnelle en Russie* (Paris, 1966).

2. A. S. Pushkin, *Polnoe sobranie sochinenii*, 17 vols. (Moscow-Leningrad: Akademiia nauk SSSR, 1937–59), XIII, 93, 95, 179. Subsequent references to this edition will appear in parentheses in the text; roman numerals refer to volume, arabic numerals to page number.

3. In developing an approach to Pushkin's use of conventions, I have found many useful insights in E. H. Gombrich, *Art and Illusion: A Study in the Psychology of Pictorial Representation* (Princeton, N.J., 1960); Erving Goffman, *The Presentation of Self in Everyday Life* (New York, 1959); D. K. Lewis, *Convention: A Philosophical Study* (Cambridge, Mass., 1969); L. Ia. Ginzburg, *O psikhologicheskoi proze* (Leningrad, 1971); and Burns, *Theatricality*.

4. Leon Stilman, "Problemy literaturnykh zhanrov i traditsii v 'Evgenii Onegine' Pushkina," in *American Contributions to the Fourth International Congress of Slavists, Moscow, September 1958* (The Hague, 1958), p. 329.

5. Gombrich, p. 236.

6. Of these the most forthright remains D. Blagoi, *Sotsiologiia tvorchestva Pushkina: etiudy*, 2d ed. (Moscow, 1931), chap. 4. As Blagoi himself admits, he uses drafts when the final version will not substantiate his contentions, and uses the Pushkin of the 1830's when the one who wrote *Eugene Onegin* lacks sufficient historical and class consciousness. Blagoi does, however, avoid what he calls "sociological Calvinism" (p. 39) in discovering cases in which Pushkin's consciousness and social being ran in opposite directions (pp. 42, 121, 155). G. A. Gukovskii, *Pushkin i problemy realisticheskogo stilia* (Moscow, 1957), excludes the author-narrator from the plot (p. 167) although finding him the most attractive character in the novel (p. 241). Gukovsky considers Pushkin a precursor of Chernyshevsky in societal determinism (p. 172). Reading the novel as a bitter commentary on society's perversion of Russian culture and its crippling of Eugene, Gukovsky combs *Eugene Onegin* for evidence of Pushkin's national consciousness and use of national culture as a positive moral norm.

7. Among essays that deal with the entire novel and do not limit themselves to specific formal problems (such as meter or style), the purest Formalist reading is Viktor Shklovskii, "'Evgenii Onegin' (Pushkin i Stern)," in his *Ocherki po poetike Pushkina* (Berlin, 1923), pp. 199–220. It treats the plot of Pushkin's novel as a mere pretext for the deconstruction, à la Sterne, of novelistic conventions. Providing a useful illustration of Gombrich's point that we cannot simultaneously perceive illusionist art as representation and organized form, D. Blagoi followed his sociological reading with an equally unadulterated architectonic one, *Masterstvo Pushkina* (Moscow, 1955), pp. 178–98.

8. Iu. M. Lotman has faced the problem of the novel's complexity by calling attention to its narrator's many points of view and standards for evaluating the characters, which allow many readings of the novel; *Eugene Onegin* takes on its illusory freedom and "lack of structure" by creating a wealth of structural relationships: "Khudozhestvennaia struktura 'Evgeniia Onegina,'" *Uchenye zapiski Tartuskogo gosudarstvennogo universiteta*, Vol. 184, *Trudy po russkoi i slavianskoi filologii*, IX (1966), 5–32. Hugh McLean finds the novel's complexity in its modulation of ironic and lyrical tones: "The Tone(s) of Evgenii Onegin," *California Slavic Studies*, 6 (1971): 3–15. John Fennell concentrates on the novel's contrast of "poetic" and "prosaic" styles: "Evgeny Onegin," in J. L. I. Fennell, ed., *Nineteenth-Century Russian Literature* (Berkeley, Calif., 1973), pp. 36–55. In different ways all three call attention to structural features of the text that a social reading would be unwise to ignore.

9. Raymond Williams, *Culture and Society, 1780–1950* (New York, 1966), pp. 320–25.

10. Georg Lukács, "Pushkin's Place in World Literature," in his *Writer and Critic and Other Essays* (New York, 1971), p. 233.

11. E.g., Stilman, p. 357, and Stanley Mitchell, "Tatiana's Reading," *Forum for Modern Language Studies*, 6 (1968): 20.

12. *Don Juan*, canto 15, stanza 85.

13. *Childe Harold*, canto 3, stanza 13.

14. A. S. Pushkin, *Eugene Onegin*, trans. Walter Arndt, 2d printing, rev. (New York, 1963), p. 37. Unless otherwise noted, I shall use Professor Arndt's verse translation for my longer quotations.

15. See, for example, the poet Baratynsky's comments, quoted in McLean, p. 3.

16. Cf. "Mistress into Maid" ("Baryshnia-Krest'ianka," 1830). Here the heroine with excellent connections and the wealthy hero are doomed to marry each other for economic reasons; however, her games and disguises and his Byronic posing make the marriage ultimately desirable in personal terms as well.

17. Gukovskii, *Pushkin i problemy*, p. 215, holds that the dream is mostly folkloric; A. L. Slonimskii, *Masterstvo Pushkina*, 2d ed. (Moscow, 1963), p. 356, that it is entirely so. Blagoi, *Sotsiologiia tvorchestva Pushkina*, p. 145, states the folkloric thesis most emphatically: "The inner, unconscious world of Pushkin's heroine is entirely woven from the motifs and images of Russian folk tales."

18. Vladimir Nabokov, trans. and comm., *Eugene Onegin*, by A. S. Pushkin, rev. ed., 4 vols. (Princeton, N.J., 1975), II, 506–11; N. L. Brodskii, *"Evgenii Onegin": Roman A. S. Pushkina*, 5th ed. (Moscow, 1964), pp. 235–36.

19. Slonimskii, pp. 356–57, offers many examples of prophetic dreams (replete with rapid streams, dark forests, deserted houses, and wild beasts) in the ritual laments of the Russian folk wedding.

20. In *Eugene Onegin* Pushkin uses *son* both for "sleep" (15 times) and for "dream" (29 times). V. V. Vinogradov, ed., *Slovar' iazyka Pushkina*, 4 vols. (Moscow, 1956–61). However, the ambiguity of the word leaves this distribution open to question.

21. Samuel Richardson, *Clarissa*, 4 vols. (London: Everyman's Library, 1962), I, 433.

22. *Ibid.*, I, 79. Combing the pages of Richardson's novel, one discovers an entire bestiary for Tatiana's imagination; for example, Miss Howe tells Clarissa that men have horns for butting (I, 88), and Clarissa later imagines Lovelace as a lion cub, bear, or tiger (III, 206). Clarissa's description of Lovelace focuses on the repulsive: "His face is a fiery red, somewhat bloated and pimply. . . . He has a great scar in his forehead with a dent, as if his skull had been beat in there. . . . The turn of his fiery eye . . ." (II, 226–27). Apropos of fiery eyes, readers who sometimes find that Nabokov's invaluable commentaries roast Pushkin over a pale fire will be amused to learn that in this instance Pushkin's country miss is a more attentive reader than her distinguished commentator. Ignoring the epistolary novel as a source, Nabokov unjustly faults Pushkin for lending

Tatiana a convention of the "Gothic novel or Byronic romance" before he let her read them in Chapter 7 (Nabokov, II, 410–11). In fact, here, as elsewhere, Tatiana's perceptions are guided by her reading of books that Pushkin names for us.

23. J. W. von Goethe, *Gesammelte Werke in sieben Bänden* (Bielefeld: Sigbert Mohn Verlag, n.d.), IV, 52.

24. This special relationship between a writer and his historical sources has been suggested to me by Herbert Lindenberger, *Historical Drama: The Relation of Literature and Reality* (Chicago, 1975), chap. 1.

25. Lukács, p. 250.

26. See Nabokov, II, 181ff.

27. I have borrowed this description of the functions of language from Roman Jakobson, "Closing Statement: Linguistics and Poetics," in Thomas A. Sebeok, ed., *Style in Language* (New York, 1960), pp. 353–58. He observes that the language of literature not merely calls attention to its aesthetic function but, in diverse genres, evokes other functions as well (p. 357).

28. Nabokov, I, 17, calls our attention to the location of these lines at the very center of the text.

29. For a detailed account of the salon culture in Italy, France, and England, see C. B. Tinker, *The Salon and English Letters: Chapters on the Interrelations of Literature and Society in the Age of Johnson* (New York, 1915).

30. Slonimskii, p. 344, has called my attention to this confluence of sources for Tatiana's famous refusal. On examining them I find that she is closer to V. L. Pushkin's French version than to the original Russian song, which has no profession of love and is darkened by the shadow of death. The passage in *Eugene Onegin* reads "Ia vas liubliu (k chemu lukavit'?) / No ia drugomu otdana / I budu vek emu verna" (8:47). The folk song as published in Chulkov's collection reads "Ia dostanus' inomu drug / I verna budu po smert' moiu." V. L. Pushkin's translation is "Je t'aimerai toujours, ô mon ami, mais je serai fidelle à mon époux." This translation can be found in N. Trubitsyn, "Iz poezdki Vasiliia L'vovicha Pushkina zagranitsu (1803–1804 gg.)," in *Pushkin i ego sovremenniki,* XIX–XX (Petrograd, 1914), 168–69.

31. The most detailed analysis of Eugene as a dandy remains L. Grossman, "Pushkin i dendizm," in his *Etiudy o Pushkine* (Moscow-Petrograd, 1923), pp. 3–36. A. A. Bestuzhev's letter to Pushkin demonstrates the conventionality of Eugene's pose: "I see a fop who is soul and body devoted to fashion, I see a man of whom I meet thousands in real life; for coldness, misanthropy, and strangeness have now become toilet accessories." A. S. Pushkin, *Polnoe sobranie sochinenii,* XIII, 149.

32. Nabokov, III, 16–17.

33. "No chtob prodlilas' zhizn' moia" ("But so that my life could be

prolonged"): "Sans cette amitié je ne puis vivre." B. Constant, *Adolphe* (Paris, 1966), p. 47.

Turgenev as a Social Novelist

1. Turgenev to Pavel Annenkov, in I. S. Turgenev, *Polnoe sobranie sochinenii i pisem* (Moscow-Leningrad, 1960–68), *Pis'ma*, II, 129.

2. *Ibid.*, *Sochineniia*, V, 372–73.

3. B. P. Koz'min, "Vystuplenie Gertsena protiv *Sovremennika* v 1859 godu," in his *Iz istorii revoliutsionnoi mysli v Rossii* (Moscow, 1961), relates an incident that is particularly revealing in this respect, since it involves the journal that was viewed as the most independent.

4. Turgenev, *Sochineniia*, VIII, 189–90.

5. N. I. Pirogov, *Izbrannye pedagogicheskie sochineniia* (Moscow, 1959), p. 55.

6. See B. M. Eikhenbaum, *Lev Tolstoi, Kniga pervaia, 50-ie godi* (Leningrad, 1928), pp. 216ff.

7. *I. S. Turgenev v vospominaniiakh sovremennikov*, ed. V. V. Grigorenko (Moscow, 1969), I, 356.

8. Turgenev, *Sochineniia*, VIII, 184.

9. N. G. Chernyshevskii, "Russkii chelovek na rendez-vous," in his *Polnoe sobranie sochinenii* (Moscow, 1950), V, 156–74.

10. N. A. Dobroliubov, "Kogda zhe pridet' nastoiashchii den'?," in his *Sobranie sochinenii* (Moscow-Leningrad, 1961), VI, 28–60.

11. "Povesti i rasskazy Voskresenskogo," *ibid.*, III, 223.

Index